A.P.J. Abdul Kalam

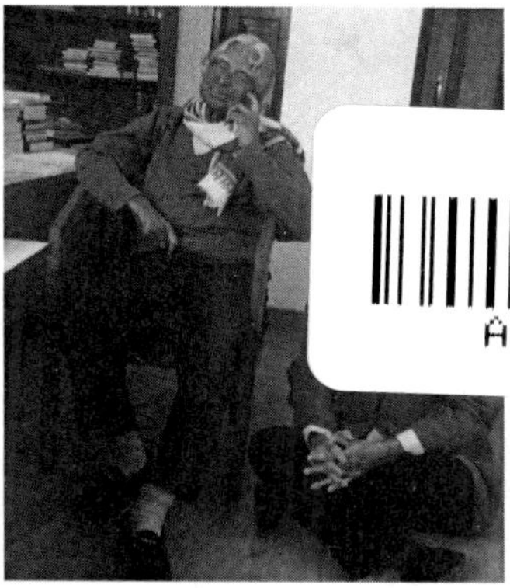

Guru-shishya: the author with Dr A.P. J. Abdul Kalam

Arun Tiwari did his master's in mechanical engineering from G.B. Pant university and joined the Defence Research & Development Laboratory (DRDL) at Hyderabad as a missile scientist in 1982. He was airframe designer and project manager (system integration) in the first three AKASH missile developmental flights. In 1992, Prof. Tiwari was appointed by Dr Kalam as the programme director at the DRDC, developing civilian spin-offs of defence technology. As a member of Dr Kalam's team, he set up the first link of the Pan-Africa e-Network of Telecommunications Consultants India Ltd (TCIL). The network now connects universities and hospitals across the African continent with their Indian counterparts.

In 1999, Arun Tiwari co-wrote *Wings of Fire*, the autobiography of Dr A.P.J. Abdul Kalam. He has written twelve books since.

Arun Tiwari is currently consulting to evolve the blueprint for FDI in the defence sector and towards the creation of a strong Defence Technological Industrial Base (DTIB) in India. He is an adjunct professor in the School of Management Sciences, University of Hyderabad.

Books co-authored by
Arun Tiwari with Dr A.P.J. Abdul Kalam

Wings of Fire: An Autobiography (1999)
Guiding Souls: Dialogues on the Purpose of Life (2004)
You Are Born to Blossom (2006)
Squaring the Circle: Seven Steps to Indian Renaissance (2013)
Transcendence: My Spiritual Experiences with Pramukh Swamiji (2015)

A.P.J. Abdul Kalam
A Life

ARUN TIWARI

HarperCollins *Publishers* India

First published in paperback in 2017 by
HarperCollins *Publishers* India

HarperCollins Publishers India, Cyber City, Building 10-A, Gurugram,
Haryana-122002, India
www.harpercollins.co.in

P-ISBN: 978-93-5264-318-9
E-ISBN: 978-93-5177-692-5

2 4 6 8 10 9 7 5 3 1

Typeset in 11/14 Adobe Jenson Pro
by Jojy Philip, New Delhi 110 015

Printed and bound at
MicroPrints India, New Delhi

FSC MIX Paper FSC® C218906

This product is made of FSC®-certified and other controlled material.

HarperCollins Publishers, Macken House, 39/40 Mayor Street
Upper, Dublin 1, D01 C9W8, Ireland

To

The Youth of India

India must stand up to the world and act like the country of a billion people living together for over two millennia. Countries of a few million assembled in the last few hundred years can't decide the destiny of a great civilization.

– A.P.J. Abdul Kalam

Contents

Part VI: Emancipation

Foreword

There's nothing new to be said about Dr A.P.J. Abdul Kalam, just as there's nothing new to be said about the mountains, the oceans, the earth, the skies, the stars, the sun and the moon. They never cease to amaze and mesmerize mankind, and continue to inspire dreams and visions, from time before time to a timeless eternity.

As in life, even in death, Dr Kalam remained an inspiration. Perhaps the most ideal Indian of our nation, he breathed his last serving the country he loved most, fulfilling a mission he cherished most – speaking before students, igniting a generation of young minds.

On 27 July 2015, the day he passed away, we witnessed the beginning of his lifelong dream – the unity of India. The whole nation united across parties and politics, states and statutes, castes and communities, regions and religions to pay homage to a person we all loved. The next day, huge lines snaked till midnight in New Delhi to see him lying in state at 10 Rajaji Marg. A million or more swarmed to Rameswaram for his burial. Many were simple, poor villagers who walked for days with no means of transport. Charities volunteered free food, free transport and free accommodation. A billion hearts pulsed with prayers. Words no longer mattered. Not since Mahatma Gandhi has any one leader captivated and motivated the minds and hearts of our people like Dr Kalam. From naming roads and islands, universities and institutions, to naming children and awards after him; his name has entered the conscience and conversations of daily life.

Everyone has something to say for Dr Kalam. This is proof of his popularity. However, his singularity as a student, a scientist, a thinker, a writer, a visionary and a leader will be studied and scrutinized by every new generation to come. Why? Because, his life is all about inspiration. He is the rare example of a leader who created his own world, his own reality, his own language – effective to the point where its emulation is not only impossible, but simply too daunting for most leaders to even consider. He created a benchmark for other presidents and prime ministers to aspire to, providing future generations of leaders from all fields a paramount point of reference for self-evaluation.

Dr Kalam's life is a fusion of contradictions – he shunned the ego and materialism that are typical of socio-political prominence, and reconciled austerity with his celebrity status. What intrigues people are not only his humble beginnings, but humble belongings. Everyone was humbled by his finite list of possessions: a wristwatch, six shirts, four trousers, three suits, a pair of shoes and 2,500 books. One cannot help but bow in reverence at his last items. He did not possess even basic household necessities such as a vehicle, television or refrigerator. Beyond that, Dr Kalam did not even write a will for his relatives.

He chose to remain simple and self-effacing in the face of his scientific, societal and political achievements. From a boatman's boy, he went on to become India's eleventh president. Hailed as the 'Missile Man' and the 'People's President', he was conferred twenty prominent national and international awards such as the Von Braun Award, Padma Bhushan, Padma Vibhushan, Bharat Ratna, and forty-eight honorary doctorates from leading universities of the world. Yet none of these accolades left an impression on Dr Kalam's life. His humility and simplicity, despite his overwhelming accomplishments and abilities, reveal a reserve of personal wisdom that matches his gift as a leader.

In addition to being a relentless achiever, Dr Kalam was one of the most gentle and soulful human beings. His words, values and vision are a perfect reflection of the man inside.

He was a teacher who never stopped being a student. He loved problems more than solutions, questions more than answers. To him, every answer was another question, a window to deeper knowledge.

This inner fire for knowledge, fuelled with hard work, honesty, sincerity and purity, helped him grow and evolve. His ability to transform himself from an average student into a successful scientist, then into a popular statesman and finally into a saintly leader is simply phenomenal! Though he has been recognized as a celebrated scientist, he will eventually be remembered as a saint; a man with no personal family who advocated family values as the answer to social evils; one who was single with no child of his own and yet became a father for millions of children; someone who occupied India's highest office from where he reached out to the lowest of the low. But most importantly, he remained a child at eighty-three. Filled with innocence, a childlike curiosity and an unending fascination for life, his energy never seemed to ebb.

My first meeting with Dr Kalam was unexpected and unplanned, completely out of the blue. On 15 March 2001, he had arrived in Bhuj, Gujarat, in an army aircraft, with his entire retinue to review the earthquake rehabilitation operation. He was the principal scientific advisor to the Government of India, while I was just one of the many sadhus serving in the Bochasanwasi Shri Akshar Purushottam Swaminarayan Sanstha (BAPS) camp. We had provided relief supplies to 400 villages, fed almost two million people and constructed temporary tin-tent colonies for 2,500 displaced people. We briefly met at the airport on his way back. Though as a scientist he did not believe in tin shelters in the desert heat of Bhuj, he inquired whether our tin houses remained cool. I proffered, 'As a scientist you should not accept my word, you should see it for yourself.' He spontaneously delayed his flight and visited our tin-tent colony. Not only did he change his opinion when he saw that the houses were cool, he also appreciated our simple science of natural ventilation through crosswinds. He congratulated the sadhus and volunteers and expressed a desire to meet our spiritual leader, Pramukh Swami Maharaj. I was overwhelmed by his humbleness and openness. He was big and well known, I was small and unknown; yet, Dr Kalam had the large-heartedness to call us, change his schedule to accommodate us, and appreciated our little science – which was insignificant compared to his lead role in making India a nuclear power. His ability to accommodate and appreciate others stunned me. This was the beginning of a fourteen-year-long friendship that involved many meetings and many more conversations.

When we once asked him how he managed to remain so young and happy, he replied, 'I only ask: "What can I give?" If everyone asked just this one question to themselves and others, the whole world would remain happy and young.'

He lived to the core this principle of giving time and energy to others. Once, Dr Kalam arrived at the Ahmedabad Circuit House well after midnight. He was yet to have his supper. A little girl stopped him to ask, 'How can I become the best scientist in the world?' Even her doting mother would have replied, 'It's getting late, dear, I'll tell you tomorrow morning.' But not Dr Kalam. He patiently explained, 'What did you just do? Asked a question ... So keep asking, asking and asking until you find the right answer. This is the way to become the best scientist in the world.'

I personally witnessed his care and compassion on a hot summer afternoon in Sarangpur, a village in Saurashtra, on 20 June 2015. He had come to present his book, *Transcendence*, to Pramukh Swami Maharaj. It was 2 p.m. Hot and humid. Very tired after addressing a youth conference, Dr Kalam was approached by a child of six. Everyone was in a hurry. The boy waved a loose, torn paper. It was scruffy and crumpled. Dr Kalam allowed him through the security cordon. The boy wanted his autograph, but didn't have a pen. Very lovingly, Dr Kalam borrowed a pen and signed the paper which the boy carelessly crumpled back into his pocket. Dr Kalam smiled. 'Never disappoint a child, for he is living his first years of life.' Just minutes later he was being escorted to his car. A ninety-year-old farmer raised his hand from the crowd. Instantly, Dr Kalam walked up to him. His great-grandson wanted a picture with Dr Kalam. Satisfying him, he said, 'Never disappoint an old man, for he is living his last years of life.' His philosophy of life was this simple. He never wanted to see a sad face on this earth.

Once, at our BAPS Swaminarayan Mandir in Shahibaug, Ahmedabad, he was surrounded by a wall of media persons. They began shouting questions regarding the dangers of nuclear power plants. I was both puzzled and perplexed. Very calmly, like a principal, Dr Kalam said, 'First put down all your pads and pens, mikes and cameras. I want to offer you a free partnership. From tomorrow, all of you are free partners in making our nation smile. Daily, write something, print something that will make our nation smile.' Everyone was stunned into a thought-provoking silence.

Incredible as it may sound, I can never forget how he left the Rashtrapati Bhavan. During his last week as the president in June 2007, I mustered up the courage to visit him. It was more than just courtesy, it was our long-standing friendship. Earlier, I had visited the Rashtrapati Bhavan on many occasions for lively discussions and invitations, but this time it was for his farewell. Unsure of what to say, I chose to remain silent, deeply saddened to see such an exemplary president retire from his post when India and Indians all over were still rooting for him to continue. Sensing my discomfort, he jovially sprang up from his presidential chair and asked buoyantly, 'Brahmavihariji, have you seen the Rashtrapati Bhavan?'

I replied, 'No, just your office.'

With a bright smile, he said, 'Come, let me show you today what I am leaving tomorrow!' Without a shadow of sorrow, he cheerfully gave us a personal tour of the Rashtrapati Bhavan. He left the highest office on a high note, unattached and unaffected by his achievements. A man is idolized by the way he lives, and immortalized by the way he leaves.

And truly, Dr Kalam left the world in the way he always wanted, spontaneously, keeping everyone wondering. I remember vividly, the evening of 11 September 2006. President Kalam had come to meet Pramukh Swami Maharaj, whom he regarded as his ultimate spiritual teacher, at the Swaminarayan Akshardham in New Delhi. After their spiritual exchange, he produced a handwritten note. It was a Sanskrit verse transliterated in Tamil. He read it as a prayer before Swamiji. 'Shatam jivo sharadah' which means 'May you live a hundred years'. Returning his sentiment, Swamiji said, 'You too should live a hundred years.' Then, he gently elaborated, 'God has blessed each one of us with a set number of years on this earth. We should be happy with the lifespan that God gives.'

On leaving the room, President Kalam turned to me and requested, 'Please tell Swamiji, whatever my age, I want to breathe my last in front of students.' Hence, the sudden sad news of his passing away while addressing the IIM students at Shillong on 27 July seemed surreal and supernatural, like a prayer fulfilled. It shocked me, but knowing it was Dr Kalam's own wish, it comforted me. The truth of his faith in his students, in his speeches, in his work, in his country and in humanity – but more so in his Guru and God – still reverberates. He was a man with his mission accomplished.

The way he left, he still lives. Dr A.P.J. Abdul Kalam continues to live in the imaginations of children, in the innovations of youth, in the aspirations of adults, in the inventions of scientists and in the vision of our nation. He has inspired us to dream once again with our hearts and minds; to dream with our eyes open, for world progress, prosperity and peace. I cannot thank Professor Arun Tiwari enough, his close friend and co-author of many books, for authoring this timely biography – a timeless gift for generations!

Sadhu Brahmaviharidas
BAPS Swaminarayan Sanstha, Ahmedabad.
Friday, 11 September 2015

Introduction

Every age has its heroes and every hero has a story. The worldwide attention that the demise of A.P.J. Abdul Kalam attracted and the profound grief expressed by millions of people across the world upon his sudden passing are testimony to his stature as a hero of this age. Dr Kalam's stellar career won him the highest civilian honour of the Indian nation, the Bharat Ratna, and culminated in his term as the eleventh president of India. But he was not born to power. He came from a geographically isolated village, was raised in a poor family, studied in publicly funded schools, worked in the government throughout his life – and made his mark through a simple and pious existence. Kalam was a rare human being who would soften even the hardest hearts of his critics and adversaries by his caring manners, impeccable character and truthful conduct. This book presents in a most accurate manner the details of his long life of eighty-three years, his salient achievements, his ideals, and his legacy.

The first part, 'Simulation', is based on the Aristotelian dictum that man is by nature a social animal. Society is something that precedes the individual. Anyone who either cannot lead the common life or is so self-sufficient as not to need to – and therefore does not partake of society – is either a beast or a god. The eight chapters in this part capture the growth of the child Kalam to adulthood, wherein he did what was told him by the system, got educated, graduated in physics – and then realized that his heart lay elsewhere. The hovering seagulls at the shore of his island birthplace had created a desire in him to fly. Becoming a pilot was his dream, and he sought a way into the air force through the aeronautical engineering route, which was the only way possible at that time. He changed his studies accordingly; but when he failed in his selection, he joined HAL (Hindustan Aircraft Limited, as it was known then) and later the Aeronautical Development Establishment, two of the only choices available in those days. This part of his life, spanning from 1931 to 1962, sees him acquiring an identity of an engineer, with a flair for innovation and the grit to get things done in imperfect situations.

The second part, 'Creation', presents Kalam's years in aerospace. He was among the first batch of young scientists inducted into the new set-up in the country to undertake space research, and his growth coincides with the growth of the Indian Space Research Organization (ISRO), as it came to be known. Kalam had the good fortune of working with the legendary Vikram Sarabhai and Satish Dhawan. He was made project director of India's first Satellite Launch Vehicle (SLV) and anointed for still senior roles in the organization. This phase of his life saw the evolution of his leadership traits, and Brahm Prakash refined his essential ingenuity and tempered his impatience with the status quo by imparting finer management skills to Kalam. The support he received from his seniors after the failure of the first SLV flight – and the envy that he evoked after its success a year later – taught him some great lessons about how the world works and how one must decide to play the game of life.

The third part, 'Realization', gives the details of his leadership of the Indian missile programme, which led to his ascent to the corridors of power in Delhi. His rise in stature was not, however, without a realization that the expenditure on technology projects from taxpayer's funds entails a 'what do you give back to society' element. Here, the well-known facts of Kalam's great success are intentionally kept in the background to highlight the more important aspect of how he made his endeavours happen. It emerges that he was working within the very same political and bureaucratic system that is often cited as a reason for non-performance, tardiness, and even outright failure by all and sundry in the Indian establishment. Leadership is one of social science's most examined phenomena. In industrial, educational, and military settings, and in social movements, leadership plays a critical – if not the most critical – role. This part establishes the great contribution of Kalam in creating a new brand of leadership: one that gets things done without excuses.

The fourth part, 'Expansion', looks at his Delhi years as a scientist bureaucrat. It captures the reasons behind the not-so-successful story of the Indian Light Combat Aircraft project, and offers useful suggestions to free the stagnating mammoth Indian aeronautical industry. Kalam's vision of a developed India by the year 2020 emerged out of his insights into how larger forces that run the world must be handled in the national interest. His involvement with the Pokhran nuclear tests is given perspective, and certain myths are corrected for posterity. This part also captures Kalam's less pleasant experiences in the newly created office of the principal scientific adviser to the Government of India, and the snub he received upon his delayed retirement from the government service.

The concluding two parts of the book, 'Dispersion' and 'Emancipation', present his years as the eleventh president of India and map his emergence as a great leader of the people post-presidency. A current of transformation drives Kalam's evermore spiritual focus through these years. Well-known and discussed issues are not repeated here, and emphasis is placed on how Kalam realized the blending of his scientific mind with his spiritual heart. His pointed observations on the role of families in creating a climate of corruption, and also their capacity to overcome it, are explained. His formula of success for youth is elucidated. Kalam's unfinished agenda of fostering global cooperation in space for developing a sustainable international economic system is given mention. His passion for new medical wisdom based on traditional well-being and cutting-edge technology is outlined, and his vision of Thorium-based nuclear power is recorded for future generations. Underpinning the book is Kalam's spiritual journey, which is exemplified in his profound fellowship with Pramukh Swamiji. He would advocate in his later years a fourfold way of life based on righteousness, knowledge, austerity and devotion.

The meaning of life is a philosophical and spiritual question concerning the significance of living or existence in general. The reader will find it expressed in different forms through the eighty-three-year-long journey of Kalam. By reading about Kalam's life, the reader will find his or her own personal answers for 'What should I do?', 'Why am I here?', 'What is life all about?' and 'What is the purpose of my existence?' The author was privileged to be closely associated with Kalam for thirty-three years, as his subordinate scientist developing missile systems, his technology manager developing civilian spin-offs of defence technology, and finally, his co-author and speechwriter. The author shares with the reader Kalam as a champion of the underdog, a man who would untiringly use his position as a platform to inspire and uplift the less fortunate. Ultimately, the author proffers the reader Kalam the saint, someone free from all the three poisons of mind, namely greed, aversion and lethargy. In this book, he can be seen as a truly pious man with a disciplined mind and in total control of his senses – a man well worthy of emulation.

PART ONE
SIMULATION

Life isn't about finding yourself. Life is about creating yourself.

– George Bernard Shaw
Irish playwright and Nobel laureate

1.1

The Paradise of Hope

> Three grand essentials to happiness in this life are something to do, something to love, and something to hope for.
>
> – Joseph Addison
> Seventeenth-century English essayist

It was on the second day of the sixth month of the year 1350 in the Islamic calendar, corresponding to Thursday, the fifteenth day of October in 1931, that Jainulabdeen and Ashiamma were blessed with the arrival of their fifth child and fourth son. The boy was born, as children mostly were in those times, in their ancestral home: a modest traditional house with a small, tiled verandah facing the street, near the Ramanathaswamy Temple on Pamban Island.

Pamban Island is steeped in religious tradition and history. Located 2 kilometres from the mainland between peninsular India and Sri Lanka, its 30-kilometre-long land mass narrows to a fine point, reaching towards Sri Lanka. It has two main settlements: Pamban and Rameswaram. Pamban, situated at the western edge of Pamban Island, is a fishing village and a harbour; it is the main point of entry to Rameswaram, the larger settlement,which is one of the most sacred Hindu religious sites in the country.

Rameswaram is a pilgrimage destination for countless Hindus every year. The erstwhile town of Dhanushkodi, which was laid waste by a cyclonic storm in 1964, is at the southern opposite tip of the island, closest to Sri Lanka. In the years that Jainulabdeen and his wife

Ashiamma were raising their family, Dhanushkodi was still a thriving town, supported largely by devotees of the Rama temple. It is believed that the god Hanuman with his army of monkeys constructed a bridge here to Lanka for Lord Rama's army.

Rameswara means 'Lord of Rama' in Sanskrit; an epithet of Shiva, the presiding deity of the Ramanathaswamy Temple. According to the Hindu epic Ramayana, Rama, the seventh avatar of the god Vishnu, prayed to Shiva here to absolve any sins that he might have committed during his war against the demon king Ravana in Sri Lanka, about 50 kilometres away. In much later times, Islam arrived on the island through Malik Kafur, the head general of Alauddin Khilji, the ruler of the Delhi Sultanate. Malik Kafur reached Rameswaram during his three military campaigns in the early fourteenth century, in spite of stiff resistance from the Pandyan princes.

The region remained a conflict zone over the following centuries, and was ruled variously by the Nawab of Carnatic, the Nawab of Arcot, and Muhammed Yusuf Khan, a warrior in the Arcot troops. In 1795, Rameswaram came under the direct control of the British East India Company and was annexed to the Madras Presidency. By the time of British rule, Christianity had arrived on the island, and its devoted band of adherents joined the equally devoted Muslims and Hindus on this small but hallowed piece of land in the Palk Strait.

Jainulabdeen was a pious man. He lived with his family in a community whose economy was based on marine products – fish and shells – and the business of providing basic services and provisions to the island's pilgrims. He also owned a small coconut grove, 4 miles from his house. The sixth month in the Hijri calendar is known as Jumada Al-Thani; it is on the twentieth day of this month that Prophet Muhammad was blessed with the birth of his daughter Fatima Zahra. On this day in 1931, Jainulabdeen named his infant son Abdul Kalam – quite aptly, as Kalam's life would unfold – after the great Indian scholar and eminent political leader of the Indian Independence movement, Abul Kalam Azad. Jainulabdeen and Ashiamma's boy was thus called 'Azad' as he grew up in his joint family of ten children.

Azad's mother Ashiamma hailed from an affluent Tamil Muslim family. One of her forebears had been bestowed the title of Bahadur by the British. She had married Jainulabdeen at the age of twenty-five and given birth to five children, Azad being the last. After Azad's arrival in the family, Jainulabdeen became imam of the local mosque. His congenial ways and inscrutable conduct won him respect and social influence across the three religious communities on Pamban Island. He enjoyed close friendships with the chief priest of Rameswaram temple, Pakshi Lakshmana Shastrigal, and Rev. Father Bodal, the priest of the Christian fishing community and builder of St Antony's Church at Oriyur on the eastern shore of the island.

Jainulabdeen and Ashiamma gave Azad quite a comfortable childhood. Life's basic amenities – shelter, food, clothing and education – were provided, and all of life's complications were kindly managed. Of greater significance, though, were the loving environment they fostered at home and the example they set for young Azad in their routine. Of the more formative lessons early in Azad's life was the willing daily toil of his parents to make ends meet. While the family was not especially poor by the standards of the time, scarcity was a constant challenge. Azad would get up early in the morning and watch his parents settling down to work immediately after their Fajr (daybreak) prayer. Even before the sun emerged out of the sea, Azad would see his father heading out to their coconut grove. He would mimic Jainulabdeen, stepping out of the house before daybreak and playing in the fresh air alive with the cacophony of seabirds.

Azad was sent to an Arabic school along with other children in the Muslim community, but he also attended the panchayat elementary school, where Hindu teachers taught him humanities, sciences and English. Azad's innate brilliance and cheerful disposition captured the attention of his teachers. One teacher, Muthu Iyer, took a particularly keen interest in influencing and shaping young Azad's development, such that he became a cherished friend of the family. Azad had three close childhood friends: Ramanadha Sastry, Aravindan and Sivaprakash. The three boys were from orthodox Brahmin families, but they would all play with Azad as children from one family.

Loose communal boundaries and cordial relations between the three religions in Rameswaram were a happy feature of the society in Azad's childhood. During the annual Sita Rama Kalyanam ceremony, Jainulabdeen, his elder son Maracayer and son-in-law Ahmed Jallaluddin would arrange boats with a special platform for carrying idols to the middle of the pond called Rama Tirtha. From time to time, Jainulabdeen would meet with Pundit Pakshi Lakshmana Shastrigal and Father Bodal at the family's home, where they would sit over cups of tea, discussing issues facing the people of Rameswaram. The society that Azad was born to was indeed remarkable for its harmony – religious and social events were celebrated, and problems managed, across community lines.

This remarkable inter-religious experience of Azad's formative years was to have a profound influence on his later life. He enjoyed a society that seemed enriched rather than divided by its different faiths. Undoubtedly, Jainulabdeen was Azad's role model in his penchant for embracing those of all faiths. His piety was balanced not merely by a tolerance for other religions, but a deeply spiritual understanding of the brotherhood of man that is integral to the religion of Islam. And his acknowledgement of those of other faiths as part of his own community was warmly reciprocated.

When Azad was about six years old, Jainulabdeen embarked on a project of building a wooden sailing boat that would ferry pilgrims to Dhanushkodi. He worked at building the boat on the seashore with a relative, Ahmed Jallaluddin, who later married Azad's elder sister Zohara. The two men employed the traditional carvel planking method in their boat building, where planks are affixed edge to edge on to a sturdy underlying framework. Azad would sit, intently watching as wooden planks were prepared and affixed to the frame, and the form of a boat began to appear. He was fascinated by the seasoning of the hull and bulkheads with heat from wood fires. Azad learned that the abrasion resistance of wood varies according to its hardness and density. His father explained that the wood must be protected; it could rapidly deteriorate if permeated with freshwater or marine organisms. With his innate curiosity, Azad took note of such details.

Throughout his life, he was intrigued by the qualities of materials, and how these qualities could be put to use for a greater purpose.

At any rate, the boat business was a great success for the family, and Jainulabdeen employed some men to operate it. There were days when Azad would slip in among the crowd of pilgrims and sit on the boat. He would listen on these trips, captivated by the stories of how Hanuman and his army of monkeys built the bridge from here to Sri Lanka for Rama; how Rama brought back Sita, stopping at Rameswaram again to perform penance for having killed Ravana; how Hanuman was sent to bring a large Shivalingam but when it took longer than expected, Sita made a lingam with her own hands so as not to delay the worship.

These stories and many others floated around Azad in different tongues and forms, as people from all over India converged at the boat service. The bright, engaging youngster naturally found himself welcome. Even at this age, Azad possessed a certain magnetism, and there was always someone willing to talk to him, share a life story, religious perspectives or reasons for making the pilgrimage. It was a blissful time in Azad's life, but as with everything, it would pass, and times would quickly change for the growing boy. Nevertheless, his experience of meeting people and making friends from all walks of life and faiths was to stay with him for the rest of his years. His love of the sea would also remain. Even as an adult – when he was not working – Kalam could sit for hours, looking out to sea, contemplating the rhythm of the waves, and following the poetic motion of flocks of gulls over the water.

Interestingly, Azad's lifelong passion for flight began with his observation of seabirds during primary school. When Azad was studying in the fifth grade, a lesson given by his teacher Siva Subramania Iyer on avian flight made a lasting impression on him. To teach about a bird's flight, Iyer drew a diagram of a bird on the blackboard, depicting the wings, tail, body and head. He carefully explained how birds create lift and fly, how they change direction while flying, and how birds fly in formations of ten, twenty or more. For nearly an hour, he lectured to a quiet and seemingly attentive class. He then asked whether the students now understood how birds fly. Azad, ever the inquiring type, stood up and frankly said that he did not. Iyer then asked the other students whether they understood. Most of the students said they did not either.

Siva Subramania Iyer was not the least perturbed by their response; he simply took the class to the seashore to show birds flying. Azad observed the seabirds and began to understand their flight. He saw the simultaneous flapping wings and twisting tails, which were the physical imperatives for their flying. But more significantly, Azad realized that a bird is powered by its own life and the motivation to fly – its will. The lesson left a deep impression on Azad, and he would develop a fascination with flying far beyond that of its basic mechanics. For him, Siva Subramania Iyer's class was not merely about comprehending the physics of how a bird flies. A bird's flight would become a metaphor for willpower, for striving – and for rising beyond earthly limitations.

Siva Subramania Iyer was not one for limitations himself. An orthodox Brahmin with a conservative spouse, he was something of a rebel. He would do his best to break social barriers so that people from varying backgrounds could mingle easily. Azad emerged as his star pupil, and he would tell him to study hard and develop, so he would become the equal of the highly educated people of the big cities. One day, Iyer took Azad to his house and offered him a meal. Iyer's wife was astonished at the idea of serving food to a Muslim boy in her ritually cleaned kitchen. She refused to serve Azad in her kitchen and offered the food outside. Iyer was quite unruffled and didn't express anger with his wife. He instead served Azad himself and sat down beside him to eat his meal.

Iyer's wife watched Azad and her husband eating from behind the kitchen door. When Azad was leaving the house, Iyer asked him to come again. Reading his perplexed expression, Iyer told him that once you decide to change the system, such problems ought to be confronted: 'You must learn to defeat the problem and not get defeated by it.' When Azad came for a meal the following week, Iyer's wife brought him inside the kitchen and served food to him, just as she would to her own child.

In October 1942, under the darkness of World War II, a cyclone hit the Bay of Bengal, generating destructive gusts of more than 100 miles per hour near Pamban Island and saturating the coastal areas with driving rains. Jainulabdeen's boat was dashed to pieces and his coconut grove razed to the ground. Jainulabdeen kept his poise and did not react to his misfortune beyond saying *'Inna lillahi wa inna ilayhi raji'u'*. When Azad asked the meaning of this phrase, Jainulabdeen replied, 'It often happens in this world that man loses something, or suffers some calamity. On such occasions, Islam teaches us to willingly resign ourselves to our misfortune, taking that to be God's decree. God has made this world for the purpose of putting mankind to the test. Here, receiving and losing are both designed as a trial for man. Therefore, when man receives something, he should prove himself to be a thankful servant of God. And when he loses something, he should adopt the attitude of patience. Only one who can do so will pass God's test.

The phrase *'Inna lillahi wa inna ilayhi raji'u'* translates loosely as 'We are from God and to God we shall return.' It is indeed an acknowledgement of God's guardianship over His creation. Azad learnt from this incidence an attitude of surrendering to God's will instead of complaining against fate. He learnt the secret of converting loss into a new discovery. Jainulabdeen told Azad, who was deeply worried by the family's losses,

وَمَآ أَصَٰبَكُم مِّن مُّصِيبَةٍ فَبِمَا كَسَبَتْ أَيْدِيكُمْ وَيَعْفُوا عَن كَثِيرٍ

> Whatever misfortune happens to you is because of the things your hands have wrought, and for many (of them) He grants forgiveness.[1]

This verse of the Quran tells us that whenever a man is afflicted by some misfortune, it is necessarily the result of one or more of his own actions. Complaining against others in this world is meaningless. When everyone must suffer the consequence of his own actions, protesting and complaining against others is only a waste of time. It will in no way solve the problem.

This is a merciful system devised by nature itself, and its acceptance is a revelation: nature has placed our problems in our own hands, and we are thus not left dependent on the charity and compassion of others. If problems that face us were the result of others' actions, we would be reduced to begging for others' kindness. But God has created the world in such a way that He has made one's concerns one's own personal affair. That is, one can construct his life by dint of his own efforts. Everyone's future is in his own hands.

Jainulabdeen was not a man to need the charity and compassion of others. With singular determination, he set to the task of building a new boat, using whatever he could salvage from the wreck of the old boat. When his father procured teak logs for the purpose, Azad learned that the main reason for teak wood's durability is that it is not eaten by white ants. Wood normally serves as food for white ants, and once they have made inroads, it quickly degenerates. Yet foes as they are of wood in general, they pose no threat to teak. The reason is quite simple. Teak has a bitter taste, which is not to the liking of the white ant. This example of an inherent quality acting as a life preserver set young Azad thinking. He saw in this the way of nature. To preserve teak from the depredations of the white ant, nature did not formulate demands or utter protests, but simply endowed teak with such a property as would keep its insect attackers at bay. Kalam would later say, 'Just as wood has an enemy in the white ant, so do men have their human enemies in this world. Now what should a man do to save himself from them? Taking a leaf out of nature's book, he should strive to produce in himself such qualities as will keep his enemies away from him, and refrain from indulging in any injurious course of action.'

Inspired by the hard work of his father in building the new boat, Azad ventured into his first line of work: selling tamarind seeds. The pressures of World War II on the textile, paper and jute industries created a sudden demand in the market for the seeds. Azad started going door to door, collecting seeds and selling them to the trading shop. A day's work would fetch him a princely sum of one anna (one-sixteenth of a rupee), which was enough for a hearty meal in those times. Azad would proudly present the coin to his mother at the end of the day for safe keeping.

The Pamban area was initially unaffected by World War II. But soon India was forced to join the Allied forces, and troops were deployed to counter any Japanese invasion by sea. The train halt at the Rameswaram railway station was suspended, and the train now passed through, stopping only at the Dhanushkodi terminus. Azad's cousin Samsuddin was a newspaper vendor, and he drafted Azad into catching and then distributing the newspapers thrown in bundles from the moving train. It is during this tumultuous phase of India's modern history that Azad started noticing pictures of national leaders in the newspapers; and he was captivated by the idea of an independent, self-determined Indian nation.

World War II ended, and freedom from British rule was imminent. Gandhiji declared, 'Indians will build their own India', and an unprecedented hope filled the air. Azad asked Jainulabdeen's permission to leave the island and study at the district headquarters in Ramanathapuram. Jainulabdeen told Azad, as if thinking aloud, 'I know you have to go away to grow. Does the seagull not fly across the sun, alone and without a nest? You must forego longing for the land of your memories to move into the dwelling pace of your greater desires; our love will not bind you, nor our needs hold you.'[2]

Ashiamma produced all the coins Azad had earned by selling tamarind seeds and distributing newspapers door to door, now a significant amount towards Azad's school fees. When an emotional Azad resisted, she said, 'Mothers only give.' Azad travelled with his elder cousin Samsuddin and brother-in-law Ahmed Jallaluddin to Schwartz High School at Ramanathapuram. He was enrolled as A.P.J. Abdul Kalam. The letters A, P and J indicate his genetic lineage – his great-grandfather Avul, his grandfather Pakir and his father Jainulabdeen.

1.2

The Beginning

Every new beginning comes from some other beginning's end.

– Seneca
Roman Stoic philosopher

Built in 1785, the Schwartz Higher Secondary School in Ramanathapuram had a characteristic old-world charm. There was not much else, however, that was remarkable about the place. The large grounds, the big trees, the high ceilings and columns had been built along a familiar utilitarian model of colonial-era institutions. The desks and benches were battered by the years. Kalam's first reaction to the school was one of indifference. His enchantment with the rustic and simple life of Rameswaram was strong, and the fusty orderliness of his new school in Ramanathapuram seemed foreign and unwelcoming by comparison.

Within a few days of his arrival, Kalam visited the Sethupathi Raja Palace. It was the first stately building he had seen in his life, and he was awed by its faded grandeur. He learned from his new friends in school that the Raja of Sivaganga and the Sethupathi of Ramanathapuram were great kings who were subdued by the Nawab of Arcot in the eighteenth century. The throne of Arcot itself had two rivals in these times: Chanda Shahib and Muhammed Ali, the former supported by the British, and the latter, the French. This paved the way for a series of military conflicts amongst several nominally independent rulers and their vassals – struggles for succession and territory, and a struggle for supremacy between the French East India Company and the British East India Company.

Eventually, the British East India Company prevailed, establishing its dominance among the European trading companies within India. The French company was thereafter corralled in the several enclaves of Pondicherry, which remained under French control until their ceding to the Indian Union in 1956. In 1910, the British carved out a new district, Ramnad, from portions of Madurai and Tirunelveli districts, with the intention of maintaining tighter governance over this area. Later, the district was renamed Ramanathapuram in conformity with the Tamil name for this region.

The Schwartz Higher Secondary School itself was named in honour of Christian Frederick Schwartz (1726–98), a celebrated German Lutheran Protestant missionary who came to India in 1750. Kalam learned, to his amazement, that all Christians are not the same. He discovered that, apart from the Eastern Churches, there are ostensibly two main categories of Christians: Catholics whose leader is the Pope and Protestants who do not accept the Pope's authority. Protestants advocate a doctrine of justification by grace of faith in God on the basis of scripture, shunning certain practices of the Catholic Church. Lutheran Christians are the followers of Martin Luther, an early sixteenth-century dissident German priest, and the prototype Protestant. Schwarz's success in gathering new adherents for his Lutheran Church exceeded that of any other Protestant missionary in India. Moreover, and perhaps of far greater significance, he managed to win the esteem of Muslims and Hindus in spite of his proselytizing.

At Schwartz, Kalam's first lesson was in dealing with the unknown others. The approach of the school's faculty contrasted with the teachers at Rameswaram, where every student was treated as an extended family member. The town of Ramanathapuram at this time was a thriving but discordant town of some fifty thousand people. The social coherence and harmony of Rameswaram was absent here, as perhaps it would have been in almost any urban centre. Furthermore, while the teachers at Schwartz were refined in their methods and demanding of the students, their manner was, at first, somewhat austere. Kalam felt uncomfortable in this new setting, but he realized he must adapt: 'Despite my homesickness, I was determined to come to terms with the new environment, because I knew my father had invested great hopes in my success.'[1]

A rapport with S.T.R. Manickam, a revolutionary nationalist, was to be a saving grace for the young Kalam. Manickam housed a large library of books in Ramanathapuram and encouraged people to access them; the library was a welcome escape for Kalam – both from his homesickness and the mundaneness of class work. Kalam was first drawn there by his innate curiosity, but quickly found solace in the company of good books. It was in this library that he discovered the seminal 1925 book *The Law of Success*[2] by American author Napoleon Hill, who proclaimed in the introduction that he wrote the book for high-school students. Kalam was transfixed by a sentence in the first few pages of this book: 'Whatever the mind can conceive and believe, it can achieve.'

From these words, a new understanding of the power of thought penetrated the young Kalam's inquiring mind. The idea that man alone has the power to transform his thoughts into physical reality, that man alone can dream and make his dreams come true fascinated him; that a thought energized with willpower is like a seed which, when planted in fertile soil, germinates, grows, and multiplies itself over and over again infused him with a new energy. Iyadurai Solomon, a teacher at Schwartz, was the first to recognize this spark in Kalam's young mind. Kalam, for his part, found reassurance in Solomon's company and positivity: 'He [Solomon] made me feel very comfortable in class with his warm and open-minded attitude. He would encourage me by saying that a good student could learn more from an ordinary teacher than a poor student even from a great teacher.'[3]

Iyadurai Solomon was a patriot by heart. He overstepped his assigned syllabus to give his young students a clear perspective of India's protracted struggle for freedom that was about to succeed. The students themselves felt enthusiastic at the prospect of India gaining Independence, and Solomon's excursions from the regular curriculum were welcomed. This was a few years after Gandhi's Quit

India movement, and the preceding years had seen a marked change in the attitude of the British authorities to Indian Independence. The expectation of a new era of self-determination was exciting for Kalam and his peers.

While the Quit India movement had galvanized unprecedented popular support for self-rule in those years, Kalam learned from Solomon that the term 'Indian Independence movement' encompassed activities and ideas not just from Gandhi and his contemporaries, but from efforts to end British rule as early as the late nineteenth century.

The expectation of freedom had unleashed a darkness, though, that had been long suppressed by colonial force. Kalam read in disbelief the news reports about a slew of atrocities committed by members of the Muslim community against their Hindu compatriots in the districts of Noakhali, in the Chittagong Division of Bengal in October–November 1946. The very notion of communal violence was utterly foreign to Kalam; it was a cruel shock after the idyllic inter-religious society that had sheltered him in childhood. For him, Hindu and Christian neighbours were more than friends and teachers – they were part of his extended family. The very thought that men could wound and kill their neighbours was profoundly disturbing for the teenage Kalam.

The young students at Schwartz sat in regular prayer meetings when Gandhi camped in Noakhali for four months and toured the district in a mission to restore peace and communal harmony. The failure of his peace mission foreshadowed a more drastic breakdown of communal relations. During Gandhi's tour, the Congress leadership accepted Partition of India; the mission and relief camps were abandoned. The greater number of the riot survivors migrated to West Bengal, Tripura and Assam.

On 14 August 1947 Pakistan was declared a separate nation, and at 12.02 a.m., just after midnight, on 15 August 1947, India also became an independent nation. Communal bloodletting involving Hindus, Sikhs and Muslims on an unprecedented scale followed, with horrors that could scarcely be conveyed in words. Some fourteen million people were displaced and as many as one million perished during

Partition. It had given rise to the largest mass migration in human history. The national upheaval had barely abated when Nathuram Godse, a militant Hindu nationalist, assassinated Mahatma Gandhi in New Delhi on 30 January 1948.

Kalam was deeply grieved by this turn of events, news of which reached the calm deep south mostly in stark black-and-white accounts of daily papers. He took some time off from school to stay at Rameswaram with his parents and became withdrawn. Kalam would sit in the mosque for long hours alone, deep in contemplation. One day, Jainulabdeen sat by the side of his son and asked the reason for his sorrow. Kalam said, 'Father, our world is marred by injustice and dishonesty and all kinds of atrocities at both the individual as well as the communal level. Why do people feel free to do as they please, unfettered by moral considerations?'

Jainulabdeen told Kalam, 'The freedom, which people abuse, has been given to them not as their power but an obligation. Our world is a testing place, and on the Day of Judgement all without exception will be called to account for how they have used this freedom. If they have ignored and denied the truth in this world, they shall be obliged to accept it, because their options will have run out, and subterfuge and pleas for mercy will be of no avail; by that time it will be too late either to beg for forgiveness or to attempt to make amends.'

He added, 'Son, do not ever wait to be forced to be good: be good by your own free will, here and now. And do not worry beyond a point about what is not in your control. Man is constantly under trial in this world. To pass all tests, you must learn your limitations along with your intellectual limitlessness. By doing so, you will be saving yourself from all misapprehensions and exercising your free will in the sphere of reality, to the pleasure of Allah.'

In any event, the political turmoil and communal upheaval of Partition had been more than a thousand miles away from tranquil Rameswaram, and its brutality had seemed from another universe. The birth of the Indian nation brought change, though, and Jainulabdeen would play his part in the new, autonomous India. Just after Independence in 1947, panchayat board elections took place at Rameswaram. Jainulabdeen, who had earned respect across the communities of the island, was elected the president of the Rameswaram panchayat board. He was, however, certainly not one to savour the fruits of his new position.

One afternoon, Azad was reading his lessons loudly in his house when a visitor came and asked for Jainulabdeen. Azad told him that his father had gone for namaz. The visitor said, 'I have brought something for him, can I keep it here?' Azad called to his mother for her consent, but she was also praying and did not respond. Azad asked the man to leave the bundle of clothes he had brought on the cot and continued his study. When Jainulabdeen returned and saw the bundle he asked Azad, 'What is this? Who has given that?' Azad told him, 'Somebody came and left this for you.' Jainulabdeen became immediately enraged and gave Azad a thorough beating – one of the very few of his life. Azad was frightened and began weeping. His mother embraced and consoled him.

When his anger subsided, Jainulabdeen touched his son's shoulder lovingly and advised him not to receive any untoward gift from anyone – ever. He quoted the Hadith, 'When the Almighty appoints a person to a position, He takes care of his provision. If a person takes anything beyond that, it is an illegal gain.' He told Azad that such a gift is always accompanied by some purpose and so is dangerous: it is like touching a snake and in turn suffering its poisonous bite. This incident taught Azad a valuable lesson for his later life in public office.

Kalam returned to Schwartz and again became immersed in his studies. His only diversion was to spend time with S.T.R. Manickam. Kalam was curious to know, after such a horrendous start, what kind of country India would become. Manickam would reassure him, telling him that horrific though Partition had been, this too would pass. He also explained the sincere work of Dr B.R. Ambedkar in drafting the Constitution of India. Manickam told Kalam of how this most learned man was adapting and incorporating elements from the constitutions of the world's great democracies: the United States of America, Australia, Canada, Ireland, Germany, France and inevitably, the statutes of Great Britain.

The Constitution of India as the supreme law of the nation came into force on 26 January 1950. The date of 26 January was chosen to commemorate the Purna Swaraj (Absolute Self-rule) declaration of independence of 1930. Manickam would make time to help Kalam, and the young students who would gather around him, understand the great political changes written about in the newspapers. Perhaps more importantly, Manickam shared with Kalam Benjamin Franklin's famous words apropos the Constitution of the United States: 'The Constitution only gives people the right to pursue happiness. You have to catch it yourself.'

By this time, Kalam was well ensconced at Schwartz, and his talents had been noted. The mathematics teacher, Ramakrishna Iyer, developed a special fondness for him. Ramakrishna Iyer believed that true education is not a process of pouring into a student from outside, but of calling forth what is within. He saw it not as a process of memorizing but a process of nurturing, of allowing, of evoking. He felt that it was ultimately a matter of bringing forth the person that is meant to be. For Ramakrishna Iyer, education was manifesting the inner divine potentialities of students, and he saw a great innate potential in young Kalam. He told Kalam, 'Book-based education cannot make a true man. Physical health, mental purity, intellectual acuteness, moral power and a spiritual outlook on life – with the right effort directing its aim – must combine if perfection is to be achieved. Students should be diligent, Brahmachari (observing chastity), adherents to satya (truth) and dharma (righteousness), to countenance their optimum physical and mental abilities and attain a righteous mode of living.'

Ramana Maharshi, the ancient sage of the modern era, died on 14 April 1950. There was a condolence meeting in the school. Students were told that Ramana Maharshi was noted for his belief in the power of silence and his relatively sparse use of speech, as well as for his lack of concern for fame or criticism – and his special love of animals and plants. Ramakrishna Iyer told Kalam that evening, 'Sat-chit-ananda (Existence, Consciousness, Bliss) is a description of the subjective experience of God. This sublimely blissful experience of the boundless, pure consciousness is a glimpse of ultimate reality.' Not understanding much of this, Kalam nonetheless deduced the simple fact that if your inner world is peaceful and without conflict, your outer world will be no different.

Kalam decided to pursue his Bachelor of Science and secured admission at St Joseph's College, Tiruchirappalli. But before leaving Ramanathapuram, he sought a joint session with his three great teachers to comprehend the great upheavals of those times. Some other students also joined. This meeting gave Kalam some deep insights that indeed triggered a long-term transformative process in him.

His teachers told him that India had asserted its sovereignty, and established itself as a state among the world's nations. It had implemented a secular, democratic system of governance based not merely on an inherited British tradition, but also calling on select provisions of other prominent countries' systems. It had instituted the rule of law in its dominions – an imperative for its citizens – and made some efforts to put the law to use as a tool for India's self-transformation. It had thus laid the foundations for relative peace and economic stability on the subcontinent. Moreover, it had expressed its will for self-determination by creating institutions, such as the Council of Scientific and Industrial Research (CSIR), the Atomic Energy Commission (AEC) and the Planning Commission.

But Kalam's teachers lamented that other challenges remained, and there appeared to be scant political will to address these. First and foremost: The government was failing to educate the citizenry. India began its first decade with a mere 18 per cent of its population classed as literate. Further, India's unequal distribution of landownership was a stumbling block for development, and vested interests would naturally resist reform in this area. And on an international level, India appeared to be without a cogent vision for its place in the world; foreign policy was adrift, and India would be blown to and fro by events and moved by the tides of the times, rather than steered according to its national priorities.

This succinct, clear-sighted analysis of the country's predicament lodged itself in Kalam's mind, all the more deeply for the respect he felt for his teachers. He would be reminded of their words, at any rate, by his observations over the coming years that tallied with their thoughts. His native wisdom would also tell him, though, that thoughts and words could not be enough to bring greatness to India.

1.3

Disillusioned Learner

> Your visions will become clear only when you can look into your own heart. Who looks outside, dreams; who looks inside, awakes.
>
> – C.G. Jung
> Swiss psychiatrist and philosopher

Kalam arrived at St Joseph's College at Tiruchirappalli to study for his intermediate cum graduation. He had never travelled out of Ramanathapuram, and this was his first exposure to a large town. The imposing college building with its renaissance-style spires and cloisters captured his imagination, and he felt surprisingly at home with its European ambience. The college had been established in 1844 by the Society of Jesus (the Jesuits) – a male order of the Catholic Church – and affiliated to Madras University since 1869.

Kalam was lodged in a three-storey hostel building, sharing a room with an orthodox Iyengar Brahmin from Srirangam and a Syrian Christian from Kerala. Kalam was not an outstanding student in terms of examination grades, but an insightful proclivity that had awakened under the guidance of his three great teachers at Schwartz would now come to the fore. His engaging intellect helped him gel with his room-mates, and he became the leader of the trio, in and out of college.

The three friends would walk through the town in their free time. Tiruchirappalli was the capital of the early Cholas in the third century BC. With the passage of time, power changed hands between the Pallavas, medieval Cholas, Pandyas, Delhi Sultanate, Madurai Nayaks and finally rested with Chanda Sahib, Nawab of the Carnatic, before British rule. The Nayaks made Tiruchirappalli their capital in the seventeenth century and augmented the magnificent Rock Fort Temple.

The Rock Fort Temple, perched 83 metres high on a massive outcrop, lords over the town with stony majesty. The Pallavas first hewed the ancient rock and the Pandyas cut small cave temples on its south side, but it was the tactically adept Nayaks who later made strategic use of this naturally fortified position. There are more than 400 stone-cut steps to climb to the top, which the three friends vigorously did without even once stopping. Kalam was disappointed to find that the Thayumanaswami Koil, the rock's largest temple, was closed to non-Hindus.

Kalam knew well by now that possibly the most critical factor for success in school is a close and nurturing relationship with at least one teacher. It is a tremendous benefit for a student to feel there is someone within the school whom he knows, to whom he can turn, and who will act as an advocate for him. The hostel warden and English teacher Reverend Father Sequeira was one such teacher for Kalam at St Joseph's.

The Reverend Father saw each student as an individual with hopes, dreams, strengths and vulnerabilities. And he worked to create a classroom atmosphere in which each student could see their fellow students in this light – an atmosphere in which respect for others became the guiding principle. He fostered a learning environment in which all his students felt safe to share their thoughts and feelings; and in which making a mistake would be seen as an opportunity to learn rather than an obligation to feel like a failure. Kalam would later recollect fondly of the Reverend Father's kindness:

> Reverend Father used to visit each boy every night with a Bible in his hand. His energy and patience was amazing. He was a very considerate person, who took care of even the minutest requirements

of his students. On Deepavali, on his instructions, gingelly oil would be given to everyone for the ritual head bath.[1]

Kalam was now twenty years of age. The nation's first general elections, to constitute the Lok Sabha, were held between October 1951 and February 1952. The population of India at this time was 360 million, of which 173 million were registered voters, and 45.7 per cent of these voters turned out to exercise their franchise. The Indian National Congress (INC) won a landslide victory, securing 364 of the 489 seats and 45 per cent of the total votes polled. Jawaharlal Nehru became the first democratically elected prime minister of the country.

Prime Minister Jawaharlal Nehru, as head of the former provisional parliament, had already moved a raft of constitutional changes, which were passed amidst a good deal of public clamour on 18 June 1951. The first amendment of the Constitution of India made several alterations to the fundamental rights provisions of the Constitution that had been finalized barely a year earlier. The amendment provided powers to the government against the abuse of freedom of speech and expression, validated laws pertaining to the abolition of zamindari, and clarified that the right to equality does not bar the enactment of laws that provide 'special consideration' for weaker sections of society.

A debate on the topic was held in the central hall of St Joseph's, with hundreds of students present. Why did the Nehru government pass the first amendment? Critics of Nehru decried his government's alterations to the Constitution as authoritarian, whereas his supporters argued that the loss of some freedoms was a reasonable price to pay for ensuring unity and stability in the first few years of independent India. It was Kalam's first taste of the complexity of national affairs. He did not understand the nuances of the issue, and decided to focus on his immediate studies rather than become engrossed in political concerns.

A few months later, however, when Kalam visited Rameswaram during the Christmas holidays, he made a stop at Ramanathapuram to reconnect with S.T.R. Manickam, and captured the learned revolutionary's take on these developments. Manickam told Kalam that freedom of expression is, frankly, the most Indian and holy of values. From ancient times, India had been largely a tolerant, pluralist land, nurturing a variety of religious faiths and practices. A myriad of versions of the epics like the Ramayana and the Mahabharata were publicly recited, and even the atheistic views openly aired by the Charvak received due consideration by their contemporaries. Manickam explained that India has long exhibited an almost infinite capacity for absorbing divergent views, lifestyles and religious practices. Freedom of expression even has its place in the Rig Veda, with the maxim: *Ekam sat viprah bahudha vadanti* – Truth is one, but the wise men speak it as many.

Kalam departed from S.T.R. Manickam's house with much to ponder. But after arriving at Rameswaram and meeting his parents and family members, he could not help but notice a change within himself. Kalam was feeling a strange disconnect. While physically present there in his family home, Kalam's mind was far removed, and he appeared preoccupied or distracted to his family. His mother was first to detect the malady. She picked up the issue while serving him breakfast. Kalam opened his heart to his mother and shared with her his doubts for the new trajectory of his life: Was he on the right path, studying in a city and preparing himself for a job that would take him further away from his roots? The more he became involved with the world around him, the more he was feeling himself being drawn away.

Ashiamma smiled and said lovingly to her grown-up and yet still innocent child that whenever one is ambivalent or unsure about a decision one has to make, one should surrender to the will of Allah. And the method for doing this is by *Istakhara*. This is a prayer asking Allah to help one make a choice, usually meaning choosing the better of two options. In Istakhara, she explained, you are essentially asking Allah about His will; you are discussing your issue with Allah and seeking His expert advice. Then there is no point in worrying. That night, Kalam assiduously recited the Istakhara prayers. He then slept deeply, waking up the next morning with his mind uncluttered and his resolve clear. He packed his bag and left for Tiruchirappalli the following day. He knew in his heart that his life would take him far from the comfortable seaside village of his childhood.

During his BSc, Kalam encountered a number of great teachers who urged him to pursue further higher education. He found his mathematics teacher Prof. Thothathri Iyengar particularly inspiring, and it is during this time that Kalam felt that his consciousness was shifting to a higher plane. It is important to discuss this shift, for no life can truly be purposeful without a transformation in a person's inner world. Kalam recounted:

> I had an opportunity at St. Joseph's College to witness a unique scene of a divine-looking personality walking through the college campus every morning, and teaching mathematics to various degree courses. Students looked at this personality, who was a symbol of our own culture, with awe and respect. When he walked, knowledge radiated all around. The great personality was Professor Thothathri Iyengar, our teacher.[2]

In his third year at St Joseph's, Kalam was made the secretary of the vegetarian mess. One Sunday, he invited the rector, Reverend Father Kalathil, to lunch. This marked the beginning of a year-long spiritual fellowship of a great Jesuit and a young seeker. His discussion of great men of the ages was particularly inspiring for the young Kalam:

> I uniquely remember the lectures given by the highest authority of the Jesuit institution, Reverend Father Kalathil ... He used to talk about good human beings present and past and what makes a good human being. In this class, he gave lectures on personalities such as Buddha, Confucius, St. Augustine, Caliph Umar, Mahatma Gandhi, Einstein, Abraham Lincoln and moral stories linked to our civilizational heritage.[3]

Kalam learned from Rev. Father Kalathil that everyone has two natures; one is lower and the other higher. The lower nature consists of various defects like anger, impatience and greed, ignorance and sloth. It is very stubborn. It hates to change and release its grip. The lower nature has a very strong will that may not always manifest itself openly, and wants its way without paying the price of hard work or perseverance. It is full of pride and selfishness. It exhibits itself as personal vanity.

Rev. Father Kalathil taught Kalam that purity, humility and austerity are the three most potent weapons to tame and conquer our lower natures. A certain level of development is necessary to interpret which thought forms come from the higher self, and which from the lower. We can also determine which wishes and endeavours of the higher self may be mixed in with tendencies from the lower self; their original shade twisted, coloured or dirtied. When messages from the higher self are tainted with lower-self motives, a disorder is created in the soul that gives rise to emotional illness. Rev. Father Kalathil shared with Kalam his wisdom, cultivated over years of pious conduct and disciplined living, that various tendencies have different colours – and in many cases different tones and scents.

A most common manifestation of the lower self occurs where a person may want something selfishly, and because he does not want to admit his selfishness, he rationalizes his desire and deceives himself about his motives. We can see all this very clearly – especially in others – and indeed, this kind of self-deception is a foundation of much conflict among people. While the forms of the higher self have an entirely different character to those of the lower, and are more subtle, they are ultimately more powerful. And it is inconceivable that the higher self could give rise to human conflict. The treacherous lower self, though, has no limit to its dissembling.

Kalam learnt a crucial skill from Rev. Father Kalathil: seeing through the masks people wear. These masks are indeed a mode of living in the lower nature, in the world of conveniences and comforts. We put on masks when we recognize that we may come into conflict with our surroundings, thereby giving in to our lower selves. This is because we are not ready to pay the price for rising above our lower natures. Subconsciously, we decide to present different images of our selves in order to avoid certain difficulties, unpleasantness, or disadvantages. These images become our masks, other layers of our selves, which have nothing to do with the reality of the higher selves or even the temporary reality of the lower selves. Kalam came to know

now that when a person is emotionally sick, it is always a sign that, in one way or another, a 'mask self' has been created. The person does not realize he is living a lie. He has built a layer of unreality, and is thus not being true to his real personality.

Rev. Father Kalathil taught Kalam to understand himself in the light of this wisdom. He was led by his teacher to comprehend the truth that beyond the layers of his lower self is the realm of his higher self; and the higher self is the ultimate and absolute reality which he must eventually reach. In order to reach it, he must first face his lower self, or his temporary reality, instead of covering it up, because that puts an even greater distance between him and his own higher self. To face the lower self he must, at all costs, tear away the mask self.

Kalam's test arrived soon enough. A relative living in Sivaganga proposed a marriage alliance. The easy way out was to offer an excuse – that he was busy with studies, waiting to settle down, etc. But Kalam refused to wear this mask self. And he resisted the cravings of the lower self for a companion, for his higher self could see he would tread a long path alone. He thus decided he would not marry; and he declared his decision loud and clear to all in the family, and through them to the community. Kalam's teacher Professor K.V.A. Pandalai writes in his reminiscences: 'He [Kalam] slowly began to realize that through science, spiritual enrichment and self-realization were possible.'[4]

Indeed, Kalam's quest for self-realization was becoming paramount for him, and it received no less of his diligence than his academic pursuits. As with the academic sphere of his learning, which he by now saw as intrinsic to his spiritual development, Kalam would gather new understandings from reading, discussion and contemplation. Perhaps the only difference for Kalam in these facets of his learning was the structure dedicated to his academic progress. Revelations of a spiritual nature would come with a higher sense of timing, arising in the manner of fortuitous accidents.

One Thursday evening, Kalam went to the dargah of Nathar Vali, a Sufi saint who came to Tiruchirappalli in the eleventh century and was among the first Sufis to bring Islam to south India and Sri Lanka.

He sat for many hours in contemplation. Then a fakir appeared, as if from nowhere, and sat down by his side.

'What are you seeking, young man?' he asked.

'I am trying to see my real self,' said Kalam.

'So what is the problem?' the fakir asked.

'I am unable to see it,' said Kalam.

'Scrub the *nafs*,' said the fakir.

'What is that?' asked Kalam.

'Nafs is a term for the baser, lower, egotistical and passionate facets of human nature which, along with *tab* (literally, physical nature), comprise the vegetative and animal aspects of human life. Some of the other synonyms for nafs are devil, passion, greed, avarice, egocentricity, etc.,' answered the fakir.

'So nafs is not soul?' asked Kalam.

'No. The soul is *ruh*. The central aim of a good human life is the transformation of nafs from its deplorable state of egocentricity through various psycho-spiritual stages to a state of purity and submission, to the will of God,' said the fakir.

'What are these various psycho-spiritual stages?'asked Kalam.

'The Holy Quran provides a very deep understanding of the psycho-spiritual phenomena that go through a human life. A clear distinction is made between nafs, *qalb, sirr* and ruh,' the fakir said.

'Please explain, I am really ignorant,' said Kalam.

The fakir explained: 'The term qalb stands for the heart which is the cradle of thoughts and emotions. This heart is the seat of beatific vision as well. But for the vast majority, it is the battleground of two warring armies: those of nafs or passion, and ruh or spirit. Cleaning of the qalb is a necessary element in spiritual discipline for travellers on the right path.'

'And what is sirr?' asked Kalam.

'The faculty of sirr is believed to be located in the middle of the chest, where the physiological heart exists. By "emptying of the sirr" we mean diverting one's attention from the mundane aspects of human life and fixing it on the spiritual realm.'

'You have used two different verbs – cleansing of qalb, and emptying of sirr. Why?' inquired Kalam.

The fakir replied, 'I am happy you are getting into the concept. The emptying signifies negation and obliteration of ego-centred human propensities. Ruh is a dormant spiritual faculty that needs to be worked upon by constant vigil and prayer, in order to achieve the illumination of the spirit.'

'It appears so systematic and orderly,' said Kalam.

'Young man, there is a well-defined sequence of actions. The purification of the elementary passionate nature (*tazkiya-e-nafs*), followed by cleansing of the spiritual heart so that it may acquire a mirror-like purity of reflection (*tazkiya-e-qalb*), fortified by emptying of egoistic drives (*taqliyya-e-sirr*) and remembrance of God's attributes (*zikr*), gloriously culminating in illumination of the spirit (*tajjali-e-ruh*) – this is the essential spiritual journey,' said the fakir with a tone of finality, and got up to leave.

Peace entered Kalam's heart. He did not get up to see the fakir off, but sat with his thoughts, unmuddied and calm, for another hour or so. That night, he enjoyed a sound sleep, and when he arose the next morning, he decided to abandon his study of physics. Engineering would now be his calling. In any event, he would have to pursue engineering to realize his dream of flying. He could have made this choice two years earlier, but fortunately even now there was a suitable course available at the Madras Institute of Technology (MIT). He promptly applied for the three-year postgraduate diploma in aeronautical engineering.

Kalam's application was successful; but admission to this prestigious institution was a costly affair. Kalam's sister Zohara came to his aid. She pawned her gold bangles and chain to provide for his admission fees, and in doing so taught Kalam all about real sacrifice: That it should be done from love. That it should be done readily, not after exhausting all other options. That it should be done for people who need your strength because they don't have enough of their own.

1.4

Bootstrapping

Science is about knowing; engineering is about doing.

– Henry Petroski, American engineer

With the dawn of Independence, the need for establishing a sound technological basis for industrial advancement of the country was recognized. A new generation of highly skilled, trained professionals would be needed to propel the new nation forward. Madras Institute of Technology, the first self-financing engineering institute in the country, was established in 1949 to this end. At a time when other engineering institutions were offering conventional courses in civil, mechanical and electrical engineering at the undergraduate level, Mr Chinnaswamy Rajam launched the experiment of introducing, for the first time in the country, new areas of specialization in engineering. The courses he introduced were aeronautical engineering, automobile engineering, electronics engineering and instrument technology. During its early years, the institute offered a diploma in engineering to science graduates, a policy that made possible Kalam's shift from physics to engineering.

The theme of bootstrapping, or lifting oneself up the social and economic ladder through individual effort, hard work and personal responsibility always fascinated Kalam. He found the idea of lifting oneself, pulling oneself up by the bootstraps so inspiring. Could the near impossible be achieved through hard work, tenacity and personal initiative, without the backing of inheritance or someone powerful lending a supporting hand? Kalam joined MIT with a determination to realize his childhood dream of flying.

The decision emerged from his self-realization at the dargah of Nathar Vali in Tiruchirappalli. Kalam had by now understood that no one cared very much about the direction his life would take, the principles he stood for, and his skills and qualifications – apart from himself. Therefore, any fraction of his life lived in the hope of someone else's approval was in fact wasted. People would never notice, and he would be unfulfilled, waiting for something that would not happen. The only one whose opinion ultimately mattered was the person whose face he had to see in the mirror at the end of the day. If he was not satisfied with who he was and what he was doing, then he had failed.

His last year at St Joseph's made Kalam realize that the science of the working of the physical world was not his calling in life. He was far more attracted to making things and doing things. Undoubtedly, he was a knowledge seeker; but more important to him was applying knowledge to creative solutions that would serve some purpose. And he was inexorably drawn to flight. When Kalam arrived at MIT, he was enthralled by two decommissioned aircraft displayed there. The mere sight of these flying machines was an inspiration, much as the seagulls hovering over the water at Rameswaram had been in his primary school years. 'Kalam would later recall: I felt a strange attraction towards them, and would sit near them long after other students had gone back to the hostel, admiring man's will to fly free in the sky, like a bird.'[1]

Kalam found himself at ease with the study of engineering subjects. He discovered his natural talent for *technical drawing*. He found he could easily look at things on different planes and from different perspectives: the plans, elevations and sections came to him without much struggle. Studying subjects like aviation, control techniques and defence systems that are used in airplanes and spacecraft held a great fascination for him. His self-esteem grew with the acquiring of skills to design, construct, develop, test and maintain the parts of any type of aircraft, both theoretically and practically.

His class in MIT was small – there were only eight students – and this allowed Kalam to interact closely not only with his classmates, but also with members of the faculty. Kalam felt a strong affinity with Prof. Sponder, his teacher for technical aerodynamics. Prof. Sponder was an Austrian who had been captured by the Nazis during World War II and imprisoned in a concentration camp. Incidentally, there were two Germans on the academic staff: Prof. Walter Repenthin, who headed the aeronautical engineering department, and Prof. Kurt Tank, who designed the Fockle-Wilf FW 190 single-seat fighter plane, an outstanding combat aircraft of World War II. The tension between these men and Prof. Sponder was palpable.

Aviation had been firmly established during World War II as a critical facet of modern warfare. From the Battle of Britain, waged by the German Luftwaffe against the RAF during the summer and autumn of 1940, to the great aircraft carrier battles between American and Japanese Pacific fleets, dominance in the air shaped the course of the war. And the final blows of the war, the nuclear obliteration of Hiroshima and Nagasaki in August 1945, were delivered from the skies. The major combatants engaged in an aviation war of economic attrition and technology: massive industrial production of aircraft and munitions required huge investment, and the imperatives of war drove technology forward with unprecedented haste.

The streamlined cantilever monoplane quickly proved its worth in almost every role, although a few older biplanes remained in niche roles for much of the war. Engine power and aircraft performance increased exponentially, first with forced induction, then with jet and rocket engines making their appearance by the end of the war. Avionics systems became almost infinitely more sophisticated and widespread, with power-assisted flight controls, blind flying instrumentation, radio communications and radar tracking replacing the naked eye and binoculars used by World War I flight crews. The rapid pace of aviation development in those years was such that a World War I pilot would barely have recognized the aircraft of the latter days of World War II, not much more than a generation later.

The students at MIT, and indeed the whole world of aviation, were the beneficiaries of this war-inspired revolution in their field. Along with new knowledge in medicine – and of course decolonization – it was one of the few truly positive outcomes from the war. And Kalam's new mentors had personally taken part in this revolution. Their approach was thus strict, grounded by practical experience and open-minded; and their abilities engendered the admiration of their students.

Kalam particularly admired the individuality and high professional standards of Prof. Sponder, who was always calm, energetic and in total control of himself. Prof. Sponder kept abreast of the latest technological advancements and expected his students to do likewise. Kalam would spend a good deal of time talking to him. The pair would take a regular stroll in the late evenings through the sprawling MIT campus, its lawns and trees a cool escape from the balmy heat of Madras. He would enjoy their philosophical discussions about the nature of civilization as it applied to the various peoples of the world.

Prof. Sponder told Kalam that he indeed envied the great Indian civilization and the enduring identity of Indian people. In contrast, the history of Austria had seen its domain expand and contract with the rise and then decay of its once great empire. The nadir of its fortunes had seen the country annexed as part of 'greater Germany' by Adolf Hitler's regime, an event which led to considerable personal suffering for the professor. Prof. Sponder said that while Indians never invaded any other country, their great civilization 'digested' the religion and customs of the invaders. The invaders, who came to plunder this bountiful land and expand their existing territories, would for the most part be subsumed themselves. They would become Indian over a generation or two, and never return to the countries of their origin.

Another teacher whose impression on Kalam would last throughout his life was Prof. K.V.A. Pandalai, who taught him aerostructure design and analysis. Prof. Pandalai was a cheerful, friendly and enthusiastic teacher. He would bring a fresh approach to the course every year. Kalam reached a deeper understanding of intellectual integrity through Prof. Pandalai and embraced it as an approach for the rest of his life. Kalam had learned early of the need to be true to one's own thinking and to hold one's self to the same rigorous standards of evidence and proof to which one holds one's antagonists. Kalam trained himself to practise what he advocated for others, and would, like all truly great men, freely admit discrepancies and inconsistencies in his own thought and action.

Prof. Pandalai also instilled in Kalam the importance of intellectual humility. He taught Kalam how to be conscious of the limits of one's knowledge. He drew attention to the need for sensitivity to circumstances in which one's native egocentricity is likely to function self-deceptively, and encouraged mindfulness of bias, prejudice and limitations of one's viewpoint. Kalam had never been one to claim to know more than he actually knew. He realized that humility does not denote spinelessness or submissiveness. It denotes a lack of intellectual pretentiousness, boastfulness or conceit, combined with a clear insight into the logical foundations of one's beliefs. For his part, Prof. Pandalai termed the lack of intellectual integrity, intellectual hypocrisy.

Prof. Narasingha Rao, a mathematician, not only taught Kalam theoretical aerodynamics but initiated him to the higher planes of abstract thinking. Kalam learned from him that in every field of study, you can learn more from studying God's contribution to that field than the contributions of all the world's experts. Prof. Rao would say that God is 'doubly infinite', or just plain 'infinite', because God has no beginning or end. He always existed and always will. On the other hand, we humans are 'semi-infinite' because we have a beginning – conception – but we have no end. How long we live – that is, how long our bodies live – isn't of great import. Of far greater consequence is that our soul will exist forever. Kalam would later remind those close to him that, from an eternal perspective, the time between conception and bodily death is fairly unimportant.

Prof. Rao gave Kalam a very interesting analogy that he would share with all his colleagues in later life. Mathematicians often use the Greek letter epsilon (ε) to refer to a 'small quantity'. Whether one 'lives' for only a few hours, minutes or seconds after conception or for

100 years, that time is always an ε compared to eternity/infinity (∞). In other words, once you are conceived – your soul is created – you are brought into being. You are going to be forever and ever. Conception, fertilization or ensoulment is therefore the most awesome moment of our lives because once we begin/exist, we have a soul that will exist forever in the presence of God, family, saints and angels.

Prof. Rao imparted other, more earthly wisdom to Kalam. Kalam used to have a savings account in the Imperial Bank of India, the oldest and the largest commercial bank of the Indian subcontinent. On 1 July 1955 it became the State Bank of India. When Kalam discussed this change with Prof. Rao, the professor gave him the great insight that the connections between financial institutions and individual people are fundamental for society. Banks are central to activities like the construction of houses, the funding of a hospital, the building of a new university, or the construction of a new road or railway line. Finance provides structure to these and other enterprises and institutions throughout society. If finance succeeds for all of us, it helps to build a good society.

Kalam spent a month in the summer of 1956 in Rameswaram, nursing his ailing father. Jainulabdeen was his first teacher – and always remained the foremost. He never lied to Kalam. If Kalam asked him a question, he always answered it. Kalam knew many things at a young age, because his father encouraged him to know things, express doubts and seek answers. One day, Jainulabdeen lamented that Kalam was not settling down to a family life. He said, 'Look, Azad, until you have a son of your own, you will never know the joy, the love beyond feeling that resonates in the heart of a father as he looks upon his son.' Kalam said nothing; and Jainulabdeen did not extend the conversation.

Before Kalam returned to MIT, Jainulabdeen made all his children sit together and told them a profound observation that he had made in his eighty-two years. He said, 'It is not dirt but the fear of dirt which is the sign of man's degradation. The official families, whose children learn expensive habits of living, prosper only for a generation or two. The merchant families who are industrious and frugal may prosper for three or four generations. The families who till the ground and study books and have simple and careful habits prosper for five or six generations. The families who have the virtues of respect for one's father, elders and ancestors and friendliness, prosper for eight or ten generations. Know this and never be cruel and rude to the poor.'

Back at MIT, Kalam shared his father's reflections with Prof. Sponder. The professor told Kalam that his father's thoughts were indeed profound wisdom for a good life. Prof. Sponder said, 'The kind of knowledge which regards things in their individual capacity alone and takes the part for the whole, mistaking each entity for a complete substantiality and truth and thus giving rise to likes and dislikes in the mind, is the minimum of knowledge, the grossest of perceptions and the crudest type of understanding.'

Prof. Sponder regretted that this was the case in his own life and millions of others in the conflict-ridden Europe of his forefathers. The professor continued: 'A higher knowledge is the mutual relationship among things. I am concerned with you and you are concerned with me. This is a socialistic type of knowledge, to which we have risen today. The jungle type of living follows the law of the fish, as they call it, the larger one swallowing the smaller. Though today we are gradually rising from the law of the jungle where each one flies at the throat of another and swallows the lesser one, and have come to a socialistic kind of understanding of mutual appreciation of individual values, we are still far away from that highest type of knowledge that your father shared with you.'

The professor then shared his own insight on the matter of the urge for higher knowledge, an urge which was to preoccupy Kalam for much of the following six decades: 'Why are we so miserable in our human existence? The simple answer is that human life is incomplete. Human knowledge is not the whole of knowledge, and there are further stages of the evolution of the universe, of which the human level is only one link in the long chain of this process. What pushes us forward and urges us onwards is the existence of a higher principle beyond us. We become restless merely because of the fact that there is something higher above us. The very existence of something higher is enough to push us onwards. The unconscious urge of the lower to realize the higher is indeed evolution, and this is what your father conveyed to you.'

Kalam's third and last year at MIT was a year of transition, and it was to have a great impact on his later life. It would serve to define his approach towards work, and was to have an abiding effect on his formulation of successful management principles. When he had finished his coursework, Kalam was assigned a project to design a low-level attack aircraft, together with four other colleagues. He assumed the responsibility of design and preparing the requisite drawings. The other teammates distributed amongst them the tasks of designing the propulsion, structure, control and instrumentation of the aircraft.

When Prof. K. Srinivasan, the guide and the director of MIT, reviewed their work, he said he found their progress dismal, and bluntly expressed his disappointment. Kalam asked for a month's time to complete the task, since he had to get input from five of his colleagues to complete the system design. Prof. Srinivasan told him, 'Look, young man, today is Friday afternoon. I will give you three days' time. By Monday morning, if I don't get the configuration design, your scholarship will be stopped.'

Kalam was shocked by Prof. Srinivasan's ultimatum, as the scholarship was his lifeline. Without it, he could not continue with his studies. There was no option but to finish the task, and he was galvanized into action. Kalam later recalled:

> My team felt the need for working together around the clock. We didn't sleep that night, working on the drawing board and skipping our dinner. On Saturday, I took just an hour's break. On Sunday morning, I was near completion, when I felt someone's presence in the laboratory. It was Prof. Srinivasan, studying our progress. After looking at my work, he patted and hugged me affectionately. 'I knew I was putting you under stress and asking you to meet a difficult deadline. No stress, no progress!'[2]

Kalam learned an inescapable truth from this incident. He realized that we are all playing the ultimate game of life, whether we want to or not. Those who play the game well win in life, while those who play it poorly suffer. Those who do not know they are playing the game suffer from the crueller fates of existence. Our destiny is to win at the ultimate game of life, for our destination is to sit with God. The fates of life only step in when we play the game poorly or refuse to play it at all.

Kalam identified two mighty opponents in the game of turning ambitions into accomplishments – namely, fear and ignorance. One feeds the other, as they are allies – an axis of negativity, you might say. Kalam also understood that knowledge is the antidote for the poisons of both ignorance and fear. But just as too little knowledge keeps us enslaved to fear and ignorance, too much knowledge gained too quickly can be similarly detrimental. When we increase our awareness of life and its negative factors too quickly, the sudden influx of such knowledge can cause anxiety and feelings of helplessness, and we can suffer a net loss of knowledge. In other words, we can lose more ground than we have won by gaining knowledge too quickly. The tendency is then to shut down our drive for knowledge, as it is hurting us. Becoming fearful or stressed from knowledge gained, however, is nothing to feel ashamed of; in fact, it can be a sign of becoming more aware, more conscious.

Kalam was given a surprise accolade on his last day at MIT. The graduating students and faculty members were posing for a group photograph as part of a farewell ritual. The students were lined up in three rows behind the professors, who were seated in the front. Unexpectedly, Prof. Sponder stood and looked for Kalam, who was standing in the last row. 'Come and sit with me, said the Professor. You are my best student and hard work will help you earn a great name for your teachers in the future … Let God be your hope, your stay, your guide and provide the lantern for your feet in your journey into the future.[3]

In 1957, at the age of twenty-six, Kalam graduated from MIT. He now felt prepared to take his place in the world; and he was ready for his learning to manifest – making things, solving real-life problems. He would now reach for the skies.

1.5

Cog in the Wheel

> As the Wheel of Time turns, places wear many names. Men wear many faces. As the Wheel weaves, we can only watch, and study, and hope.
>
> – Robert Jordan
> *The Eye of the World*

From MIT, Kalam was selected as a graduate trainee at Hindustan Aircraft Limited (HAL) in Bangalore, where his duties would involve the overhauling of both piston and turbine engines. He felt proud to see the HF-24 Marut fighter-bomber, designed by his teacher at MIT, Prof. Kurt Tank. Kalam was told that it was the first fighter aircraft made in India, and HAL had built the first military aircraft in South Asia. He was at HAL for six months.

Actively encouraged by the young Maharaja of Mysore, Jayachamarajendra Wadiyar, and the diwan of Mysore, Mirza Ismail, Walchand Hirachand had established Hindustan Aircraft Limited in Bangalore in 1940 to repair and overhaul foreign aircraft. William Pawley of the Intercontinental Aircraft Corporation of New York set up the organization and equipment for the factory, and a large number of machine tools and equipment were sourced from the United States. To boost British military hardware supplies in Asia to counter the increasing threat posed by imperial Japan during World War II, the British India government bought a one-third stake in the company in 1941.

In 1943, the factory was handed over to the United States Air Force but retained Hindustan Aircraft management. The factory expanded rapidly and became the centre for major overhaul and repairs of American aircraft and was known as the 84th Air Depot. The first aircraft to be overhauled was a Consolidated PBY Catalina, followed by every type of aircraft operated in India and Burma (now Myanmar). When it was returned to Indian control two years later, the factory had become one of the largest overhaul and repair organizations in the East. In the post-war reorganization, the company built railway carriages as an interim activity. After India gained Independence in 1947, the management of the company was passed over to the Government of India.

Kalam worked on the overhaul of engines for Blackburn Cirrus Majors, a British in-line four-cylinder aircraft engine. The term 'engine overhaul' means to strip down an engine and rebuild it as new. This entails the disassembly of the engine, the inspection of its components, the replacement of defective or worn parts, the repair or replacement of these parts and the reassembly of the engine. Further, the engine is tested and subjected to trial run prior to its return to full operating level.

Kalam learned that aircraft engines are only good while flying, the purpose for which they are built. Aircraft must be flown at a minimum interval, and its engine brought to its operating temperature on a regular basis. If an aircraft is used less frequently than this suggested interval, its engine will become prone to moisture build-up, and corrosives will accumulate in the engine oil. These would shorten the service life of the motor. Also, some engines will be exposed to extreme conditions, and this should be taken into account. An engine operating primarily in dusty conditions, near salt water, in varied climates or any combination of these is subject to extra wear.

The imperative for aviation is safety, and in performing his work of overhauling aircraft engines, Kalam had to apply his utmost diligence. Exactitude is crucial; the result of tardiness in this line of work can be catastrophic. Nevertheless, he enjoyed his new job. His disciplined approach and analytical bent stood him in good stead for its challenges, and he found it exhilarating to be involved in sending a machine into the skies. He would notice in the course of his time at HAL that disciplined and rigid though the demands of the tasks were, even its most precise work would call on the intuition – an aspect of the higher nature. He later recounted:

> The demonstration of the delicate art of beta (blade angle control) by HAL technicians still lingers in my memory. They had neither studied in major universities, nor were they merely implementing what their engineer-in-charge was suggesting. They had been working hands on for years, and this had given them something like an intuitive feel for the work.[1]

Two new employment opportunities presented themselves to Kalam, who was now armed with an engineering degree and tested by practical experience. The Indian Air Force was offering positions through short service commission, and the Directorate of Technical Development and Production, DTD&P (Air), under the Department of Defence Production, Ministry of Defence, was recruiting engineers. Kalam applied for both and was called for the interview by the Indian Air Force at Dehradun and DTD&P (Air) at New Delhi in January 1958. Kalam had thus far never travelled beyond the southern regions of the subcontinent, and he was now to venture out into the vastness of his country for the first time. He boarded the Grand Trunk Express at Madras Central station and managed to secure a window seat.

Ever a student of India's cultural tradition, Kalam bought *Discovery of India* by Jawaharlal Nehru to utilize the forty hours' journey time. Nehru wrote it during his imprisonment during 1942–46 at Ahmednagar Fort in the Deccan. Between reading Nehru's fine historical discourse and viewing for the first time the length of this verdant, abundant land, Kalam garnered a new understanding of his nation and its history. He understood the allure of the rich and fertile plains of the Ganga and its numerous tributaries that invited invasion from the people of hostile desert and mountain lands.

Moreover, Kalam could see for himself the geographical features that had ensured that the land of his Tamil forefathers was mostly undisturbed by invaders from the north. The part of India south of the Tropic of Cancer had been shielded throughout the millennia by the Vindhya and the Satpura mountain ranges. The Dravidian people thus had suffered invasions only by the most determined of adversaries, until the time of British colonial rule.

After appearing for the interview at DTD&P (Air), Kalam had some free time in Delhi, as the interview at Dehradun was still a week away. He visited the dargah of Hazrat Sheikh Khwaja Syed Muhammad Nizamuddin Auliya. Hazrat Nizamuddin was a famous Sufi saint of the Chishti order. Kalam found much peace through his contemplation in mosques and dargahs. He found himself drawn towards the Islamic Sufi tradition, with its emphasis on self-realization through devotion and prayer. For him, the mystical facets of his religion were becoming equally important as its everyday practices.

Kalam recalled his experience years earlier at the dargah of Nathar Vali in Tiruchirappalli. That evening at the dargah of Nathar Vali initiated Kalam on his destined path, and he could feel the divine energy once again while he sat through the qawwali. In Sufi practice, music is a way of reaching the soul, entrancing the listener by prayers wrought with the power of soaring vocals and rhythmic accompaniments. Its purpose is to awaken a sense of devotion that our mundane lives have buried deep within. While Kalam felt the power of qawwali, he was unsure about the exact meaning of the lyrics; but the invocation of love for Allah, Prophet Muhammad, Hazrat Ali, or the Khwaja was as plain to him as it was heart-rending.

Kalam took a train to reach Dehradun for his much anticipated appointment with the Air Force Selection Board. It passed through the historic city of Meerut, where India's First War of Independence began in 1857, and then Piran Kaliyar near Roorkee, sanctified by the dargah of the thirteenth-century Sufi saint of the Chishti order, Alauddin Ali Ahmed Sabir Kalyari. Kalam felt imbued with a calm spiritual energy by the time he reported at 1 AFSB, or the Air Force Selection Board, located in Clement Town of Dehradun.

Kalam easily cleared the stage one test of the selection process, consisting of an IQ test and several other examinations conducted on the first day. Twenty-five candidates were selected for the stage two test, which involved a psychological evaluation and numerous group trials spread over five days. Kalam cleared all of them. Finally, an interview was conducted on the last day. Kalam finished ninth in the batch of twenty-five candidates examined through stage two, to select eight officers. Kalam could barely contain his dejection: 'I was deeply disappointed. It took me some time to comprehend that the opportunity to join the Air Force had just slipped through my fingers.'[2]

A despondent Kalam decided to spend sometime in Rishikesh. He bathed in the Ganga and walked into the Sivananda Ashram situated a little way up the hill. There, he met Swami Sivananda. His Muslim name aroused no reaction in Swamiji, who inquired about the source of his sorrow, even before Kalam had uttered a word. Kalam told him about his unsuccessful attempt to join the Indian Air Force and his long-cherished desire to fly. Swamiji told him to take life in his stride as it unfolds: 'Accept your destiny and go ahead with your life. You are not destined to become an air force pilot. What you are destined to become is not clear to you now but it will be at the right time. Forget this failure, for it had its own purpose to lead you to your destined path. Become one with yourself; that is all you have to do, the rest is done to you.'

Kalam returned to Delhi and visited the DTD&P (Air) office to inquire about the result of his interview. They handed him his appointment letter, and he joined the very next day as a senior scientific assistant (SSA), with a basic salary of Rs 250 per month. He was posted at the Technical Centre (Civil Aviation), where he would certify and inspect aircraft for airworthiness. If Kalam was not flying aeroplanes, he would at least be helping to make them fit to fly.

Kalam attended to his work with the discipline of a soldier and equanimity of a saint. But he would feel pangs of creative energy and wondered at times if quality assurance was the correct line of work for him. After a few months, Kalam was sent to the Aircraft and Armament Testing Unit (A&ATU) at Kanpur to participate in the tropical evaluation of the British Folland Gnat. The Gnat was a single-seat lightweight ground attack and interceptor fighter aircraft that was to be inducted into the Indian Air Force. The first flight of an Indian Air Force Gnat was in the United Kingdom on 11 January 1958. The craft was delivered to India in the hold of an American military transport aircraft C-119, and accepted by the Indian Air Force on 30 January 1958.

Even in those days, Kanpur was a crowded city. It was Kalam's first exposure to the north Indian winter, and for a young man accustomed to the year-round warmth of the deep tropics, its chill was a rude shock. He was also troubled by the ubiquitous potato dishes, served from breakfast to dinner. He felt overwhelmed by the loneliness that pervaded the city. The people on the streets had all come from their villages in search of jobs in factories in the city, leaving behind the scent of their soil and the protection of their families.

Kalam befriended an elderly technician, Rajnath Pandey from Allahabad. Their relationship started with Kalam enlisting Pandey's help in buying a quilt to survive the freezing December nights in Kanpur. Then one day, Pandey invited Kalam to visit the dargah of Hazrat Sayed Badiuddin Zinda Shah Madar, at nearby Makanpur. Pandey told Kalam that his family had been visiting the dargah for more than a hundred years. Kalam was surprised at the devotion of a Brahmin to a Muslim saint and gladly accepted the invitation. Pandey told Kalam that Hazrat Madar was the descendant of Prophet Muhammad (peace be upon him). Kalam was amazed to see thousands of people, particularly non-Muslims, at the dargah.

Pandey told Kalam that whatever is wished at the dargah would manifest at the right time. Clearly, people had faith in its power, given the sight of multitudes of them offering ornate coverings (chadar) to drape the grave. Others would tie red strings on the trellis around the tomb as wishes (mannat), with the promise of giving in charity – the most popular kind of beneficence being provisions for the community kitchen (langar), where the hungry were fed free of charge and without any discrimination.

Pandey shared with Kalam the horrendous tales of the First War of Independence. The siege of Cawnpore was a key episode in the war. The besieged East India Company forces and civilians in

Cawnpore surrendered to rebel forces with assurances of safe passage to Allahabad. Under circumstances that till now remain unclear and controversial, however, their evacuation from Cawnpore turned into a brutal massacre in which most of the Company's men were killed. And there was further unnecessary carnage. As an East India Company rescue force from Allahabad approached Cawnpore, 120 British women and children who had survived the initial onslaught by the revolutionary forces were killed in what came to be known as the Bibighar massacre. Following the recapture of Cawnpore and the discovery of the massacre, the outraged Company forces engaged in widespread retaliatory atrocities against captured rebel soldiers and local civilians.

Kalam was more than sympathetic with the aims of the Independence movement. But Pandey's recounting this ghastly incident from the country's freedom struggles reaffirmed his views on war – it only engendered misery, and there were surely more enlightened ways to solve grievances between peoples. A domestic war was also brewing in the time that Kalam was in Kanpur. Having long developed the habit of reading newspapers, particularly the editorial pages, Kalam was thus aware of the simmering trouble between India and China. Persecuted by the Chinese military, the Dalai Lama reached the Indian border on 30 March 1959. Indian guards escorted him to the town of Bomdila in the present-day Arunachal Pradesh.

The Indian government had already agreed to provide asylum to the Dalai Lama and his followers. Soon after his arrival in Mussoorie on 20 April 1959, the Dalai Lama met with Prime Minister Nehru, and the two talked about the Tibetan government in exile, which was to be headquartered at Dharamshala in Himachal Pradesh. The Dalai Lama's travails led Kalam to ponder the state of the world. Why must people of peace and worship face brute military force? Had evolution made humans more peaceful, or was mankind innately prone to violence?

Kalam went to Sankisa in nearby Farrukhabad district when the Dalai Lama visited there, some nine months after his exile to India. Historically known as Sankasya, Sankisa is one of the four unchanging sacred Buddhist sites, the others being Bodhgaya, where all Buddhas attain enlightenment; Sarnath, where they begin their teachings; and Shravasti, where they extend the teaching and defeat doctrinal opponents. At Sankisa, all Buddhas descend to earth after spending the rainy season retreat in heaven. During his visit to Sankisa, the Dalai Lama spoke about the kalachakra.

Kalam later read about the kalachakra tradition, which deals with cycles of time. His avid reading of Western philosophy and Eastern wisdom was leading him inevitably to an understanding that science is intrinsic to spirituality, and vice versa. Moreover, the laws that govern the universe are not merely in consonance with spiritual principles; they pertain as much to atoms as they do to our experience of life.

Around this time, man was experimenting with science and the atom with the reckless ignorance of a teenager. On 13 February 1960, France conducted its first nuclear test, code named *Gerboise Bleue* (Blue Desert Rat) in the Sahara Desert of Algeria. With an explosive yield of seventy kilotons, it was around four times as powerful as the Hiroshima bomb; and it was exploded above ground, where it would lay waste the surrounds. Army personnel were deployed at the site, human guinea pigs for the scientists to gather a better understanding of the effects of radiation on the human body. Lives were ruined here, not to mention the massive environmental degradation and the eradication of numerous species at the site. This was a sinister perversion of science, and a misuse of the powers in the universe. How could man wreak such havoc on his own species and his own planet?

Kalam spent many lonely nights pondering such existential questions. He was not grown enough to know the answers; but the questions were agitating his mind nonetheless. He could see that violence, reconciliation and cooperation are all part of human nature. He felt that evolution didn't just shape man to be violent or peaceful: it shaped man to respond flexibly and adaptively to different circumstances – and to risk violence only when it made adaptive sense to do so. Kalam was pained that instead of competing for food, which had become relatively easy to attain in most parts of the world, mankind was now competing for material resources like oil and minerals.

1.6

Noah's Ark

> No institution can possibly survive if it needs geniuses or supermen to manage it. It must be organized in such a way as to be able to get along under a leadership composed of average human beings.
>
> – Peter Drucker
> Management consultant, educator and author

The story of Noah's ark fascinated Kalam right from his days at Schwartz, where it was taught to him. A question that niggled as he grew was how Noah, living as he did more than a thousand years before the Iron Age, could possibly have constructed a vessel of the size of the ark as described in the Bible. He would have had to accomplish this task without iron hammers, axes or saws with which to fell trees or cut to equal size those which nature had uprooted. To hold them together without nails is another seemingly unimaginable task. The history of shipbuilding tells of no vessel even remotely this size in the epoch in which Noah lived. Nor does the biblical text intimate that Noah found a vessel which had been constructed by heavenly sources; on the contrary, it says specifically that he was to build it.

Equally hard for Kalam to imagine was how Noah could have harvested, transported and stored enough food to keep himself, his family and a very large assortment of animals – some of considerable size – alive for as long a period as the ark was occupied. The question of the carnivorous species appeared to him particularly problematic.

Furthermore, archaeology had so far discovered no evidence of a flood of this magnitude having occurred at the time when Noah lived. What could be a reasonable way to understand the narrative of Noah but as a metaphor? More importantly, what could be the lesson of this metaphor?

Kalam reasoned Noah as representing the link between two contrasting worlds. He was born during the days of *hamas* (dishonesty), lived through the recreation, and entered a world in which man recognized the need for law. It was here that Kalam found the essence of this metaphorical tale. The Creator of the world was the one who first brought about a man whose distinction was his superiority over the animals, but who was still not fully aware that without law he could not survive. Kalam interpreted Noah's ark as the idea of living by institutions, families, communities, schools, hospitals, courts, nations and so forth.

Kalam's whole world and achievements had been founded on living with institutions – and his family. The scale of investment and manpower required for the aeronautical industry mandated institutional support, which could only come either from governmental or corporate sponsors. Kalam's skills, honed by the very best educational institutions of the era, had first been fostered by his family. Now, his abilities were in demand, and were utilized for evermore important projects for the nation. Kalam was prospering in a world in which man recognized the need for law. But in his mind, he was reaching for a place beyond this in evolution – his urge for a higher understanding that Prof. Sponder spoke of had been awakened; and it could not be ignored.

In any event, Kalam's career would continue to take him to new places, and broaden his worldly horizons. A large number of aeronautical projects were undertaken in the 1950s and 1960s, the most important of which were the hovercraft, the Vertical Take-off and Landing (VTOL) Platform and the DART target, a pilotless flying system using autonomous rendezvous technology. The Aeronautical Development Establishment (ADE) was created in 1959 to provide research and development support to HAL. Aeronautical engineers working in various organizations dealing with military aviation were pooled to form the core team of this new organization. Based in Bangalore, ADE was tasked with the acquisition of aeronautical equipment for the Indian Air Force, and it was here that Kalam would work, at least for the time being.

As Kalam was entering the ADE, Air India International was entering the jet age. On 21 February 1960, Air India International acquired a Boeing 707–420 aircraft and became the first Asian airline to induct a jet aircraft in its fleet. Jet services to New York International Airport, Anderson Field (later J.F.K. International Airport) via London were inaugurated that same year on 14 May. On 8 June 1962, the airline's name was officially truncated to Air India, as it remains to this day. On 11 June 1962, Air India became the world's first all-jet airline. India was now finding its feet as a technological nation, and the five Indian Institutes of Technology (IITs) were grooming young engineers and scientists such as Kalam to help propel the country forward into the final decades of the century.

Kalam was charmed by Bangalore, the garden city of India. It was a contrast to the crowded, polluted roughness of Kanpur and the high-born, overbearing ambience of Delhi. Kalam had by now internalized the pluralism of Indian society. He had long observed India's uncanny inclination for bringing out extremes in her people. He guessed that this was because Indians had been both afflicted and enriched by centuries of invasion and migration. Loyalty to different rulers and regional and caste sentiments had dulled the will of the Indian people for a single national identity. As a survival strategy, Indian people evolved an extraordinary ability to be alternately compassionate and cruel, sensitive and callous, deep and fickle.

Already an inveterate student of human nature and behaviour, Kalam was bemused by the affectations of the people he saw in the country's cities. He felt that city life had severed an essential attachment to the land, the soil. To the untrained eye, Indian cities may appear colourful and picturesque; to the critical eye, Indian city dwellers seemed but shoddy imitations of their various masters. In Kanpur, Kalam saw paan-chewing imitations of Awadh kings, in

Delhi there were so many facsimiles of stiff-necked British rulers, and in Bangalore he could see dog-walking sahibs. In none of India's cities, though, did Kalam find the depth and authenticity of Rameswaram. He concluded that the divided sensibilities and existential pressures of city life seemed to have mutated the relationship between the heart and the head of otherwise earthy Indians. The transition from an almost composite system of values of pre-colonial India to a modern unified system remained a pathetically slow work in progress.

By this time, Kalam had developed an even more voracious reading habit. He tapered his visits to dargahs and started spending more time in libraries. At work, the vagaries of bureaucratic organization meant that Kalam would have to rely on his own initiative. Never one to sit idle, he decided to become proactive in making a personal contribution to the aeronautics of the military. Kalam recalled years later: 'The workload at Aeronautical Development in its initial years was not much. In fact, I had to generate work for myself at first, until the tempo gradually built up.'[1]

Convinced of the versatile role a hovercraft could play in India's defence forces, Kalam advocated the idea to higher officials in ADE. Based on his preliminary submissions, a project team was formed to design and develop an indigenous hovercraft prototype. Dr O.P. Mediratta, director of ADE, asked Kalam to lead a four-member team. They were given three years to realize the working model.

On 3 November 1961, Prime Minister Jawaharlal Nehru received the 20,000-tonne Majestic-class aircraft carrier HMS *Hercules* from Britain at Bombay's Ballard Pier. The ship, named INS *Vikrant*, under Captain Pritam Singh Mahindroo, contained one squadron each of Sea Hawk fighters and French Breguet Alize Anti-Submarine Warfare (ASW) planes. Kalam was called back to Delhi to assist in the work on a Vertical Take-off and Landing Platform.

On 21 September 1962, a border dispute between China and India erupted into full-scale war. It started in earnest with a major Chinese offensive across the McMahon Line. The McMahon Line was a line on the map that had been agreed by the British and Tibetan governments in 1914 as the territorial border. With the annexation of

Tibet by China, the McMahon Line was the effective border between India and China. The Sino-Indian war was a national humiliation for India, with China quickly advancing from the McMahon Line into Indian territory. The Soviet Union, the United States and Great Britain pledged military aid to India. China then withdrew its forces, and the war ended on 19 November 1962.

Prime Minister Nehru later told parliament:

> I remember many a time when our senior generals came to us, and wrote to the defence ministry saying that they wanted certain things ... If we had had foresight, known exactly what would happen, we would have done something else ... what India has learnt from the Chinese invasion is that in the world of today there is no place for weak nations ... We have been living in an unreal world of our own creation.[2]

Many Indians like Kalam viewed the war, though, as a conflict waged by parties of wildly disparate effectiveness; and little of this related to the combat abilities of the military personnel at the front line. India's forces were led by argumentative politicians and clashing generals under a philosopher prime minister – who spouted fancy doctrines like Panchsheel ('five virtues', an abortive 1954 treaty with China) – and a defence minister who delighted in inflicting his acid tongue and rapier intelligence on those around him. Their adversaries were a rugged revolutionary and a victorious military genius: Mao Zedong and the prime minister, Zhou Enlai, the latter perhaps the finest strategist of his generation. And the Chinese leadership had no parliamentary or media pressure to divert their attention from their goals. It was a textbook war of the prepared overwhelming the unprepared.

The Sino-Indian war coincided with the Cuban Missile Crisis. A direct and dangerous confrontation between the United States and the Soviet Union occurred in October 1962, in which the world's two nuclear superpowers came dangerously close to conflict. In July 1962, Soviet premier Nikita Khrushchev reached a secret agreement with Cuban premier Fidel Castro to place Soviet nuclear missiles in Cuba to deter any future invasion attempt by the US. Upon receiving intelligence of the missiles' deployment, the United States retaliated with a navy embargo, effectively blocking Cuba by sea. The ensuing stand-off led the world perilously close to a nuclear holocaust.

Around midnight Moscow time on 26 October 1962, Prime Minister Khrushchev sent President Kennedy a long, emotional message that raised the spectre of nuclear annihilation. 'If there is no intention,' he said, 'to doom the world to the catastrophe of thermonuclear war, then let us not only relax the forces pulling on the ends of the rope, let us take measures to untie that knot. We are ready for this.'[3] With subsequent negotiation and concessions from both sides, the crisis was over.

In an effort to avert a recurrence of this dangerous nuclear brinksmanship, a direct telephone link between the White House and the Kremlin was established; it became known as the 'Hotline' or 'Molink'. Also, having approached the brink of nuclear conflict, both superpowers began to reconsider the nuclear arms race and took the first steps in agreeing to a nuclear test ban treaty.

Kalam's take from this was the supremacy of morality. During this crisis, military action was viable as a first response, but thankfully, the morality of using weapons to reach a resolution was considered. The weighing of the likely greater conflict and subsequent massive loss of human life against the efficacy of military action led to a decision that proved correct. Kalam concluded that leaders must consider the morality of the situation carefully before choosing military action as a first response. This ensures that empathy remains. The empathy preserved through the Cuban Missile Crisis by the parties' restraint allowed the moral questions to be examined. Leaders such as Kennedy and Khrushchev knew that violent actions would receive violent reactions.

The hovercraft development project proved a tough nut to crack for Kalam and his small team. None of the team members had any experience in designing and building a machine from scratch, let alone a complex aeronautical craft sturdy and reliable enough for military applications. Moreover, the practical problems they faced were manifold, the most obvious being that there were no designs or standard components available. Kalam tried to read as much literature as he could find on hovercraft, but there was not much available. He tried to consult people knowledgeable in that area, but could find none. He now understood, through this disillusioning experience, the difference between a developed country and a developing one. Only consistent work over years and decades – even across generations – makes a country great. Meanwhile, Kalam understood that he had no option but to proceed with whatever he knew and whatever was at hand. He was also under no illusion that he would have to rely on his own will and determination:

> There is always the danger that a person with my kind of background – rural or small-town, middle-class, whose parents had limited education – will retreat into a corner and remain there struggling for bare existence ... I knew I had to create my own opportunities. After all, the Wright brothers made the first aeroplane after fixing bicycles for seven years! [4]

After spending a few months at the drawing board, Kalam proceeded straight to hardware development. Part by part, subsystem by subsystem, stage by stage, his vision began to materialize. Defence Minister V.K. Krishna Menon took a special interest in the small project. He was very passionate about building a capacity for developing indigenous weapon systems. Whenever he was in Bangalore, he called Dr Mediratta and Kalam to apprise himself of their progress and ask if they needed any help.

The project was completed to schedule. The hovercraft moved on a 40 mm cushion of air, bearing a load of 550 kilograms, including the tare weight of the vehicle. It was named *Nandi* after the vahana (wagon) of Lord Shiva. But by that time, Krishna Menon was out of office in the wake of the Sino-Indian war debacle, and in the new order not many people shared his enthusiasm for the military applications of an indigenous hovercraft. The project was shelved, and indigenous hovercraft were never manufactured – though thousands were required and imported regularly. Kalam was heartbroken.

> So far, I had believed that the sky was the limit, but now it appeared that the limits were much closer. There are boundaries that dictate

> life: you can only lift so much weight; you can learn only so fast; you can work only so hard; you can only go so far![5]

One evening, Kalam saw the book *The Pushcart War* in a bookshop window while he was wandering on Brigade Road. It was an illustrated children's novel written by Jean Merrill. He was struck by the first sentence, 'The Pushcart War started on the afternoon of 15 March 1976 when a truck ran down a pushcart belonging to a flower peddler.' How could a flower peddler wage a war? Why was the story set in the future? He decided to purchase the book.

The book narrated the story of a group of New York City pushcart peddlers, led by Morris the Florist, who battled the tyrannical trucking companies. The pushcart peddlers were armed only with pea-shooters – good for flattening tires – and their wits. The theme of the book was the disadvantaged, the weak and the outcasts rising up against their oppressors and, of course, winning the day. Kalam started identifying himself as an underdog. He decided to change his style and become more competitive. To come from behind and win is indeed a great feeling, he concluded.

Many months had passed by when Dr Mediratta called Kalam, asking if *Nandi* was functional. A few days later, he brought Prof. M.G.K. Menon, director of the Tata Institute of Fundamental Research (TIFR), to meet Kalam. Prof. Menon asked Kalam several questions about the machine and even took a ten-minute ride. Finally, Kalam could see someone, at least, appreciating his toil of many years. Prof. Menon gave Kalam a gentle hug and said that he would see him soon.

A week later, Kalam received a letter asking him to come to Bombay for an interview at TIFR, for the position of rocket engineer at the newly formed Indian Committee for Space Research (INCOSPAR). Kalam took the next train with a strange, calm feeling of certainty. Kalam reminded himself that the best way to win was to not need to win. The best performances are accomplished when you are relaxed and free of doubt. What if he is a pushcart peddler? What if he meets the mightiest truckers in Bombay? After all, he did not apply for any post – and yet he was called.

1.7

No Free Lunch

> Between stimulus and response there is a space. In that space is our power to choose our response. In our response lies our growth and our freedom.
>
> – Viktor E. Frankl
> Neurologist and Holocaust survivor

Space research activities were initiated in India during the early 1960s, when applications using satellites were in the experimental stages, even in the United States. With the live transmission of the Tokyo Olympic Games across the Pacific by the American Satellite 'Syncom-3' demonstrating the power of communication satellites, Prime Minister Nehru quickly recognized the benefits of space technology for India. The space programme, although originally the private vision of a few scientists, was quickly elevated to one of the highest-priority programmes of the Indian state.

A new organization, INCOSPAR, was set up in 1962 under the Department of Atomic Energy with Dr Vikram Sarabhai, director of the Physical Research Laboratory (PRL) in Ahmedabad, at the helm. The organization was tasked with formulating the Indian space programme. Dr Vikram Sarabhai was a playful, Shri Krishna-like successor to the solemn and remote Dr Homi Bhabha. Like Shri Krishna, Dr Sarabhai was versatile, playing several roles in his efforts to nurture the inchoate space programme in its early years. He was a roving diplomat, teacher, strategist, friend, counsellor, leader and system builder. Within India, the unusual combination of his scientific eminence, aristocratic background and disarming simplicity created a loving loyalty – often amounting to devotion – among those who knew him.

The sheer force of Sarabhai's personality subdued cluttering dissent, a typical malady in Indian organizations. His reputation enabled him to slice through the bureaucratic jungle; he was assured of loyal support at all levels – from the peon to the prime minister. As his predecessor did before him, Dr Sarabhai set out to secure cooperation from the spacefaring powers. He first turned to the United States.

Dr Sarabhai initially made overtures to NASA (National Aeronautics and Space Administration) in 1961, during his stint as a visiting Professor at the Massachusetts Institute of Technology (MIT), Massachusetts. He told NASA of India's plans to start a space science research programme at select facilities, namely, the Physical Research Laboratory, Ahmedabad; the Tata Institute of Fundamental Research, Bombay; and the Tata Institute of Nuclear Physics (TINP), Calcutta. He also described his plans to recruit trained Indian physicists for European countries and the United States.

During his meetings with NASA officials, Dr Sarabhai explored possible cooperative endeavours that could be mutually beneficial to both NASA and India, including magnetic fields, solar radio astronomy, geomagnetism, atmospheric studies from 30 to 150 kilometres, trapped particles in radiation belts and electrojet studies. With the intention of furthering these fields of research, Dr Sarabhai discussed the possibility of a cooperative sounding rocket programme between India and NASA and also a telemetry receiving facility at PRL in Ahmedabad.

Sounding rockets are one- or two-stage solid propellant rockets used for probing the upper atmospheric regions and for space research. They also serve as easily affordable platforms to test or prove prototypes of new components or subsystems, intended for use in launch vehicles and satellites. NASA had developed sounding rockets that played an important role in the International Geophysical Year (IGY), an eighteen-month period (1 July 1957 to 31 December 1958) coinciding with high solar activity. The IGY entailed an intensive investigation of the natural environment – the earth, the oceans and the atmosphere – by some 30,000 participants representing sixty-six nations. More than 300 instrumented sounding rockets launched from sites around the world made significant discoveries regarding the atmosphere, the ionosphere, cosmic radiation, auroras and geomagnetism.

While INCOSPAR was being constituted, the United Nations Committee on the Peaceful Uses of Outer Space (COPUOS) passed a resolution recommending and sponsoring the creation and use of sounding rocket launching facilities, especially in the equatorial regions in the southern hemisphere. Taking the cue from the United Nations, Indian scientists proposed a site in southern India to NASA. To help choose the most appropriate location, NASA shared volumes of their Wallops Island handbooks.

The coastal village of Thumba, (8°33'N, 76°56'E), in the state of Kerala, was judged a suitable location. Its proximity to the magnetic equator (0°24'S) was ideal for launching sounding rockets to undertake geographical investigations, particularly those dealing with the interaction of neutral and charged particles in the earth's magnetic field.

INCOSPAR commenced its work as part of the Tata Institute of Fundamental Research, led by Prof. M.G.K. Menon. Its first task was to recruit the cream of India's young scientists with expertise in this sphere and groom them with the necessary skills and competencies to fulfil their new roles. It was this that had brought Prof. Menon to the Aeronautical Development Establishment, Bangalore, where he had identified Kalam as one of his new young charges for the organization. Kalam was awed by Dr Vikram Sarabhai, the head of INCOSPAR, not the least for his graciousness in their first meeting; but also for his almost clairvoyant manner of appraising Kalam in his interview in Mumbai:

> There was none of the arrogance or the patronising attitudes, which interviewers usually display when talking to a young and vulnerable candidate. Dr Sarabhai's questions did not probe my existing knowledge or skills; rather they were an exploration of the

> possibilities I was filled with. He was looking at me as if in reference to a larger whole. [1]

The primary objective for the new team of scientists was fairly straightforward. They were to establish a modest rocket-launching facility at Thumba and provide facilities to the international scientific community to gather data. Although Dr Sarabhai must have had this in mind, there was initially no mention of developing satellites or launching vehicles.

Although Trivandrum was the state capital of Kerala, it was a somnolent and unhurried town with nineteenth-century tiled houses lost amidst coconut palms. The roads were narrow and curvy, with sharp turns and fast-changing slopes. Kalam knew no cooking, and there were hardly any eating places there at that time. He boarded with his other colleagues in a lodging house that provided the most basic amenities. Many of the scientists would visit the railway canteen for meals. As there was no canteen even at the workplace, each of them would buy his snacks and lunch after eating breakfast and go to the bus stand, to catch a mofussil bus to Kazhakkutam. After alighting from the bus they would walk for about a kilometre. The trip would take around an hour.

Thumba was a small village known only for fishing. The site at Thumba lay between the railway line and the seacoast, and covered an area of approximately 600 acres. Within this area stood an ancient church of St Mary Magdalene at Pallithura and the bishop's residence. Prof. Vikram Sarabhai met many politicians and bureaucrats to procure the site, but to no avail. Resolute to succeed, and with almost evangelical zeal for the purity of his mission, Prof. Sarabhai decided to meet the bishop and plead his case personally. At that time, Reverend Father Peter Bernard Pereira was the bishop. Prof. Sarabhai met him on a Saturday. The bishop heard him patiently and asked him to come to the Sunday morning mass where he would present the matter before the community. Kalam would later recall the vision and high-mindedness with which the bishop requested his congregation's support for the Thumba facility:

> The bishop said, 'My children, I have a famous scientist with me who wants our church and the place I live for the work of space science research. It is true that science enriches human life. What he is doing and what I am doing are the same. Within six months, our abode and church will be newly built and given to us. Children, can we give them God's abode, my abode and your abode for a scientific mission?' There was a pin-drop silence for a moment, ruptured by a loud 'Amen' from the congregation.[2]

The newly built rocket launching pad was set amidst coconut groves, and the church building served as the main office for the scientists. The bishop's house was converted into a workshop. A cattle shed became the laboratory for the sounding rockets. There were no strict working hours, and it was common practice for the scientists to time their departure to the last bus of the evening. Soon, a jeep was acquired for transporting the scientists home after late-night shifts. While the facility creation work was in progress, it was decided to send seven rocket engineers for training with NASA. Kalam was one of these seven.

Kalam landed at the Langley Research Center (LaRC) in Hampton, Virginia, United States, in March 1963. The Center conducted basic research in a variety of fields for aeronautical and space flight and had management responsibility for the Lunar Orbiter and Viking projects and the Scout launch vehicles. Kalam found the presence here of his colleague Ramabhadran Aravamudan a great blessing. Aravamudan had arrived six months earlier to learn radar tracking, radio telemetry and other ground instrumentation systems. They lived in the hostel attached to the centre and would eat at the self-service cafeteria. One of their challenges was trying to pick vegetarian fare from the typically American carnivorous offerings at the cafeteria. Mashed potatoes, boiled beans or peas, bread and lots of milk became their staple diet during their time at LaRC.

After completing their training at LaRC, Kalam and Aravamudan went to Goddard Space Flight Center (GSFC) at Greenbelt, Maryland. This facility was named after Dr Robert H. Goddard, a rocket theorist as well as practical inventor who first launched a liquid-propellant rocket in March 1926. Goddard Space Flight Center was responsible for unmanned spacecraft and sounding rocket experiments. It operated the worldwide Space Tracking and Data Acquisition Network (STADAN), which later became Spaceflight Tracking and Data Network (STDN). It also managed development of the Thor-Delta launch vehicle, which was to be used for the first ballistic missile deployed by the United States Air Force.

In the third and final phase of their training, Kalam and Aravamudan were posted at the Wallops Flight Center (WFC) at Wallops Island in Virginia, which was the only rocket flight-test range owned and operated by NASA. Wallops launched Scout boosters and sounding rocket experiments, with instrumentation developed by scientists and engineers throughout the United States and the world.

On weekends, Kalam and Aravamudan would go to Washington DC in an old Dakota plane, which NASA used to fly free of cost for its employees. Hotels in Washington would offer discounted room rates for NASA personnel but the rate was still around $6 per night, which was an exorbitant amount for them. The pair would stay up, roaming around the nation's capital in the quiet hours of the night, before catching the early-morning shuttle flight back to Wallops.

Immediately upon Kalam's return to Thumba, the Nike Apache rocket was successfully launched with the Vapour Cloud payload on 21 November 1963. This marked the beginning of the Indian space programme. It was followed by the launch of Russian M-100 and French Centaure sounding rockets. While the M-100 could carry a payload of 70 kg to an altitude of 85 km, the Centaure was capable of reaching altitudes of 150 km with a payload of approximately 30 km.

The launch pads were still being built. The only covered buildings were the church, the bishop's house and a small school building – and all of them had been vacated because they came within the safety zone. These served as offices, storage houses and laboratories. Since the only vehicle was always busy, the scientists had to either walk or use a bicycle to move within the range. Kalam, who was not a cyclist, would hitch a ride with Aravamudan. Even rocket parts and payloads were transported on bicycles. Decades later, Aravamudan fondly recalled their time at Thumba, which was characterized by plenty of hard work interspersed with light-hearted entertainment:

> During launch campaigns we had no weekends or holidays. But at other times, we would either go to the beaches at Kovalam or Shankumukham or catch an old Hollywood movie at Srikumar Theatre. Kalam, being from Rameswaram, loved to swim; he would spend hours on the beach at Kovalam. Though Kalam was a vegetarian, he loved the egg masala with parantha at Xavier's College on the Main Road near the Secretariat.[3]

In 1965, TERLS (Thumba Equatorial Rocket Launching Station) rented a beautiful old building called 'Ingledine' opposite the Trivandrum Raj Bhavan and converted it into a club with two badminton courts, a table tennis table and a room for card games. Kalam was an enthusiastic badminton player. He took great interest in setting up the club, buying furniture, getting a canteen going and so forth. Every evening there would be friendly badminton matches, with the losers having to shout the winners a bonji each, which is how a glass of lime juice was referred to in Trivandrum. Kalam would doggedly fight a match to earn a free bonji.

While his leisure time was filled with the standard diversions of young bachelors, Kalam's work was anything but mundane: 'At TERLS, I was involved with building payload housing and jettisonable nose cones. Working with the nose cones led me, as a natural consequence, into the field of composite materials.'[4]

The exigency in aerospace for light, strong and temperature-resistant materials has always made developing high performance composites a primary research activity of aerospace organizations worldwide. In a related initiative in the ongoing quest to lighten its rockets, NASA had achieved weight savings of 25 to 30 per cent with filament-wound motors over comparable all-metallic vessels. Kalam was tasked with formulating advanced composite materials and setting up India's first filament-winding machine, to build non-magnetic payload housings for the two-stage sounding rockets and rocket motor casings.

Kalam approached his new assignments with hallmark enthusiasm. He was by now utilizing his interpersonal skills at work almost as much as his analytical and scientific talents. Kalam relied not merely on tapping the inspiration and expertise within his team. He would engage with select industry scientists and engineers, who would readily proffer their knowledge and support to help achieve these pioneering indigenous efforts in aerospace. Kalam's trademark charismatic personality was just beginning to play its part in matters of national significance.

Rockets had first made their impression on the world in south India, under Hyder Ali and Tipu Sultan late in the eighteenth century. These Mysorean rulers had successfully deployed thousands of Mysorean rockets against British East India Company forces, who had been awed by their glare and terrifying destruction. Now, Kalam and his team brought rockets back to the subcontinent with the first Indian-designed and Indian-built space rocket, the RH-75. This sounding rocket, designated for its 75 mm diameter, was an outstanding success – due in no small part to Kalam's pivotal work. The RH-75 made its maiden flight on 20 November 1967. This was the fifty-second launch of a sounding rocket from TERLS. The RH-75 was flown twice again in 1967 and another twelve times in 1968, making a total of fifteen RH-75 flights.

Prime Minister Indira Gandhi formally dedicated TERLS to the United Nations on 2 February 1968. After the ceremony, Dr Sarabhai invited the prime minister to the Rocket Engineering Division. Pointing his fingers towards Kalam and his younger colleague C.R. Sathya, Dr Sarabhai said to the prime minister, 'They are waiting for you to switch on the machine.' A smiling Indira Gandhi quipped, 'Is it so? What does this machine do?' Kalam suggested Sathya should answer. Nervous to the core in the presence of this august personage, Sathya briefly explained the machine's working and its importance. 'Glad to know about it, where is the switch?' asked the jubilant prime minister. The event brought smiles to the faces of Dr Vikram Sarabhai, Kalam and, of course, Sathya.

Dr Sarabhai argued that technology in space was practically worthless without a vast array of other technological systems on the ground. It was therefore imperative that an Indian National Satellite System was developed. This would ensure that the practical benefits of advanced technologies, particularly telecommunications, broadcasting, meteorology and search and rescue operations could be deployed for the service of the Indian people. Dr Sarabhai told Kalam it is important for everyone working in the organization to be mindful that the plans for space technology were driven by real needs on land.

During the early 1960s, NASA was planning a series of advanced technology satellites known by the acronym ATS. There was a need to field-test an ATS configuration which involved the direct broadcast of television to receivers from a satellite. At the time, this technology was untested. The commercial and political advantages of a satellite system that could beam programmes directly to television sets attracted NASA policymakers, though.

The three countries that were large enough and close enough to the equator for testing a direct-broadcast satellite were Brazil, China and India. Brazil proved uninterested; the population was concentrated in a few cities, and conventional television broadcast technology was clearly more feasible. The People's Republic of China was out of the picture for political reasons. India was the logical choice. It was densely populated, yet only Delhi had a television transmitter – a small one, left behind by a Dutch electronics company after a trade show.

Dr Sarabhai prudently seized this opportunity. He requested NASA to allow the use of an ATS satellite for a year to conduct a satellite instructional television experiment in India's villages. He saw this as a great opportunity to convince India of the need to invest heavily in space technology and a unique chance to learn the ground segment of a satellite system from the Americans. Moreover, he saw it as a chance to baptize a whole generation of Indian scientists and engineers in this avant-garde technology, so that they could make their own satellite in the future. The Indian Department of Atomic

Energy and NASA signed an agreement for the Satellite Instructional Television Experiment (SITE) in 1966.

Dr Vikram Sarabhai was a visionary. His brilliance in his field was coupled with a revolutionary desire to use technology for the betterment of his country and its people, and was perhaps only surpassed by his enlightened management and diplomacy. Kalam venerated Sarabhai, and his unconscious was filled with a desire to emulate his achievements. He later marvelled at Dr Sarabhai's inherent gift for reaching out and securing international cooperation: 'Vikram Sarabhai enjoyed global stature. While he secured cooperation of NASA in the Satellite Instructional Television Experiment (SITE) programme, the first Indian satellite, Aryabhata, was put into orbit in 1975 from a Russian cosmodrome.'[5]

The Indian government soon enough recognized the imminent role of space communications in nation building, and an Experimental Satellite Communication Earth Station (ESCES) was established in 1967 at Ahmedabad. On 15 August 1969, INCOSPAR, under the Department of Atomic Energy, was made independent as the Indian Space Research Organization, and the Department of Space was created by the prime minster of India, institutionalizing space activities in India.

Kalam had been instrumental in the birth of India's aerospace programme, and as Dr Sarabhai had anticipated, it led to a thriving technological sector in the country. India, which had languished in the nineteenth century in many respects, was now propelled towards the twenty-first century by this visionary scientist and his team. Kalam was determined to build on the work of Dr Sarabhai, and like this brilliant, noble man, Kalam had his own vision for the country. And he knew from the challenges he had faced in developing indigenous technology, his vision would entail plenty of hard work. It is impossible to get something for nothing. But most significantly, the RH-75 project had demonstrated to him the freedom that comes with strength and self-reliance.

1.8

Unreasonable Men

> Human progress is neither automatic nor inevitable. It requires sacrifice, suffering, and struggle; the tireless exertions and passionate concern of dedicated individuals.
>
> – Martin Luther King Jr
> African-American Civil Rights movement leader

In January 1968, Kalam received a message that Dr Sarabhai wanted to urgently see him in Delhi. Travelling to Delhi from Trivandrum was no simple matter in the late 1960s. After changing many flights, Kalam reached Delhi and contacted Dr Sarabhai's office for an appointment. He was asked to meet Dr Sarabhai at 3.30 a.m. at the Hotel Ashok. Why 3.30 a.m.? The secretary offered no explanation. Unsure about how to reach there at that ungodly hour, Kalam decided to wait in the lobby of the hotel overnight. A dinner at the hotel was beyond his means, so he ate in a roadside eatery and came to the lobby by 11 p.m. He identified himself at reception as a guest of Dr Sarabhai and was escorted to an elegant lounge. He had never seen such opulent surroundings.

After some moments of astonishment, Kalam noticed a book kept on a nearby sofa; its owner must have absent-mindedly left it there, he thought. To fill the long hours of waiting constructively, Kalam picked up the book and started browsing through it. It was a popular self-help book, the kind that tells the reader he is born to win, born to be rich, born to succeed. Kalam observed, during his training in the United States, that self-help books were very popular in America. It was not that such books couldn't be found in India; they were just less prevalent. But their popularity in America was too powerful a phenomenon to overlook. These books, dispensing advice to millions on matters physical, psychological and spiritual, must be making a difference in the lives of their readers.

He was skimming over paragraphs and turning pages rather nonchalantly when a passage captured his attention. It was a quotation from George Bernard Shaw. The gist of the quote was that all reasonable men adapt themselves to the world. Only a few unreasonable ones try to change the world. All progress in the world comes from these unreasonable men. Waiting in the lobby in the middle of the night for an appointment a few hours later was certainly not a reasonable proposition for Kalam. Nor was a 3.30 a.m. appointment reasonable for Dr Sarabhai, who had, nevertheless, set its time.

The whole scenario was at best unorthodox. But Dr Vikram Sarabhai was, by most measures, an unorthodox man. An egalitarian scientist of patrician lineage, he was successfully running an understaffed, overworked enterprise pioneering space research in India, a country that seemed indifferent to technology. For his part, Kalam appeared somewhat eccentric in manner. He looked careless, casual and sloppy – but he had a hawk's eye on his interests, consistency in his purpose and an appetite for hard work only rivalled by his tenacity. Moreover, his scientific acumen was balanced with a firm belief in God, from which he derived inspiration:

> I have been always a religious person in the sense that I maintain a working partnership with God. I was aware that the best work required more ability than I would ever possess and therefore I needed help that only God could give me. So I must make a true estimate of my own ability, then raise it by 50 per cent by putting myself in God's hand and then get down to work with no doubts and fears in my mind.[1]

While Kalam sat and read, whiling away the time in the early hours of the morning, another man entered the lobby and seated himself opposite Kalam. Neither man bothered to interact, leave alone make pleasantries. From his mannerisms, gait and taut appearance, he was perhaps a service officer. He was well built; his hair was neatly trimmed and combed; he was wearing a suit with a striped tie; his shoes were shining – and notwithstanding the odd hours he sat erect, looking alert and animated. He seemed, in contrast to Kalam, to be quite at ease in the hotel's luxurious surroundings. And quite disconcertingly, he appeared to almost look straight through Kalam, as if he were not there at all.

Despite his aloofness, there was some magnetism in this man, and it distracted Kalam from his reading. He was saved from his distraction soon enough, however, by Dr Sarabhai's secretary, who stepped into the lobby and announced that Dr Sarabhai was ready to meet 'them'. Who was this man? In whichever way he was connected to Dr Sarabhai, why should Dr Sarabhai meet them together, wondered Kalam. Dr Sarabhai received them with his characteristic charm and introduced them to each other. 'Good morning, gentlemen. Kalam is my colleague in Space; Kalam, he is Group Captain Narayanan from Air Headquarters.'

Dr Sarabhai ordered coffee and outlined his plan of developing a rocket-assisted take-off (RATO) system for military aircraft. This would help our warplanes to take off from short runways in the Himalayas, he informed his contrasting guests. Hot coffee arrived, and Dr Sarabhai most graciously engaged his young guests in light conversation. As soon as the coffee and discussion concluded, Dr Sarabhai rose to his feet and asked them to accompany him to the Tilpat Range, near Faridabad, south of Delhi.

It was about an hour's drive to the range, which was functioning at the time as an Air Force Depot. Dr Sarabhai showed them a Russian RATO plane parked there. It was not covered, and Kalam felt that it had only just arrived, perhaps as recently as a day earlier. 'Rockets have been used simply to assist the main propulsion in the form of rocket-assisted take-off. Because of the heavy propellant use and the various practical difficulties of operating rockets, the majority of rocket planes have been built for experimental use, as interceptor fighters and space aircraft.'

Dr Sarabhai spoke to the two younger men with the ease and fluency of a master teacher. 'If I get you guys the rockets for study, would you be able to make indigenous equivalents and mount them on our HF-24 aircraft in eighteen months' time?' 'Yes, we can,' both men affirmed simultaneously. Dr Sarabhai's face beamed, reflecting their enthusiasm. He dropped them back outside the Ashok Hotel and proceeded for his breakfast meeting with the prime minister. In an instant, Kalam understood the reasonableness behind the unreasonable meeting time of 3.30 a.m.

The next day's newspapers carried a story on India taking up the indigenous development of rocket-assisted take-off aircraft. Kalam realized that for the first time in his life, he was working not for a project, his organization or even an enlightened boss like Dr Sarabhai. He was working for his country. He was working for India. It was a thrilling feeling, one that Kalam had never had before. He understood now that patriotism is much more than a conviction that your country is superior to all others because you were born in it. He trembled when he heard of the confidence that had been expressed in him.

The next day he went to the library of the National Defence College on Tees January Marg and sat for a few hours to learn about RATO aeroplanes. Rocket-powered flight was pioneered in Germany. The first aircraft to fly under rocket power was the Lippisch Ente ('Duck' in German), in 1928. The first rocket plane ever to be mass-produced was the Messerschmitt Me163 interceptor in 1944, one of several German World War II attempts at rocket-powered aircraft. Russians flew the Bereznyak-Isayev BI-1 in 1942. The Japanese also produced approximately 850 Yokosuka MXY-7 Ohka rocket-powered suicide-attack aircraft in World War II.

In 1947, the rocket-powered Bell X-1 was the first aircraft to break the speed of sound in level flight and the first of a series of National Advisory Committee for Aeronautics (NACA)/NASA rocket-powered aircraft. The North American X-15 and X-15A-2 designs were used for around a decade and eventually reached Mach 6.7 and over 100 kilometres in altitude. In the 1950s, the British developed mixed-power designs to augment the performance of the then current turbojet designs. The rocket was employed in short bursts to deliver the speed and height required for high-speed interception of high-level bombers, and the more efficient turbojet engine was otherwise used. Increased turbojet engine output, the advent of missiles and advances in radar had rendered this configuration obsolete by the time of Kalam's meeting at the Ashok Hotel. But in order to defend the high altitude of its territory, from short runways in the Himalayas, India needed its own RATO planes.

The Russian RATO system shown to Kalam and Narayanan at the Tilpat Range was capable of generating a 3000 kgf thrust with a total impulse of 24,500 kilogram seconds. It weighed 220 kilograms, and had a double-based propellant encased in steel. The development work was to be carried out at the Space Science and Technology Centre (SSTC) where Kalam was working with the Defence Research and Development Organization (DRDO), HAL, DTD&P (Air), and Air Headquarters where Narayanan was posted. The project relied on cooperation between organizations and people, and it suited Kalam admirably. Kalam always believed in the sanctity of institutions. India's ancient civilization, he felt, had survived invasion, colonial rule and all manner of setbacks because its people lived as members of institutions – of families and communities – rather than as individuals. Indian people derived meaning in their lives not from their individual strength, but from living in harmonious social relationships.

By this time, Kalam knew that technology is only purposeful with reference to people, who must use it for their benefit. He knew full well that any promising early-stage technologies developed in the laboratories require 'maturation', in the form of additional development, testing, prototyping, and eventually their intended application. He therefore opted for a composite structure for the RATO motor, using filament fibreglass and epoxy. The filament winding machine facility was fully operational, and he needed a good 'product' to make it mature. He decided to use another two nascent technologies in the project, namely composite propellant with event-based ignition and a real-time jettisoning system.

The first static test of the RATO motor was conducted in

February 1969. Another sixty-four tests followed in the next four months. All this was accomplished with only twenty engineers working on the project – and some astute management. The marriage of technology and human skills holds infinite promise, but it is hard to properly realize. Through the RATO project, Kalam learned the secret of managing technology-intensive projects. Failure of these most often lies in the execution, specifically the mishandling of the technology. Lack of knowledge and inadequacy of skills lead to this mishandling. Knowledge and skills must therefore be fostered for success: knowledge comes from learning; skills come by doing. And there are no short cuts here.

RATO brought forth a more profound understanding of leadership in Kalam. Dr Sarabhai fascinated him, and Kalam's admiration for his boss bordered on idolization; but he felt no wish to emulate his inimitable style. Working on the RATO helped Kalam realize that leadership was something that could be learned and developed over time. Leadership was a function of specific internal processes and interpersonal skills that are accessible to everyone, not only a select few. The perceptions, behaviours and skills that individuals integrate to motivate others to action play a critical role in the success or failure of new ventures, projects and goals. In order to master these skills, individuals must view them as competencies – behaviours that require careful reflection, evaluation and practice.

Kalam shared with me four internally oriented and four externally oriented competencies. 'It is useless to go for externally oriented competencies without working on internally oriented ones,' he would say. The internal work includes gaining self-awareness, asking powerful questions, communicating with a purpose and developing an entrepreneurial mindset. The externally oriented competencies that follow the internal mastery are how to manage and mobilize change, how to collaborate with others, leverage differences to maximize performance and become more resilient and adaptable.

Two significant developments occurred during the RATO project. The first was the release of a ten-year profile for space research in the country by Dr Sarabhai. This document made it clear that the long-term priorities of the ISRO would be linked to national development. Telecommunications, remote sensing for resource surveys and meteorology were the areas identified where ISRO would best serve the nation's progress. Furthermore, the active international cooperation dominant in the early years of the Indian space programme was to be dispensed with. The organization would now become largely self-reliant; its work would revolve around the development and deployment of more indigenous technology.

Kalam was a pioneer of this swadeshi space programme, and the new regime was especially favourable for his resourceful, self-motivated approach. He had proved his mettle with the RH-75 rocket project, which had indeed inspired confidence in the halls of power to take the ISRO in this bold new direction. From now, the ISRO's objectives would have to be realized by the designing, fabricating and launching of Indian satellites, including geosynchronous ones, with Indian launch vehicles.

The second development was the formation of a Missile Panel in the Ministry of Defence. Kalam was invited as a member of the panel with Narayanan. The bitter lessons of the 1962 war had been duly noted. The national leadership felt there was now little choice but to pursue a similar swadeshi approach to developing military hardware and weapon systems. To cater for immediate demands of national defence until indigenous systems could be deployed, a large number of Surface-to-Air Missiles (SAMs) were obtained from Soviet Russia. Narayanan was appointed director of Defence Research and Development Laboratory (DRDL), Hyderabad, to fast-track the development of indigenous missile systems.

While working together on RATO motors and on the Missile Panel, Kalam and Narayanan alternately played the roles of student and teacher, as demanded by the situation. Narayanan was very eager to learn about rocketry, and Kalam was very curious to know about airborne weapon systems. Opposites in many ways, they had much to learn from each other, even in terms of their approaches to tasks, though they were equally focused on their work. Kalam would later write admiringly of Narayanan's commitment to the duties before him:

> The depth of Narayanan's conviction and his force of application were inspiring. Right from the day of our pre-dawn visit to the Tilpat Range with Dr Sarabhai, Narayanan was always busy with the RATO motor. He had arranged everything that was required before being asked. 'You name the thing and I will get it for you, but do not ask for time,' he said. At times, I laughed at his impatience.[2]

When Kalam compiled the Bill of Material for the RATO motor, he realized that virtually nothing indigenous was available. He felt despondent. Was there no remedy or alternative? Would the Indian nation be doomed forever to the farce of 'screwdriver science' – importing and assembling other countries' creations? Could a developing country afford to produce this kind of technology?

Kalam identified procurement procedures as the root of indigenous development woes. He enumerated seven points, or seven liberties he proposed be granted him. These were: single-point financial approval and no up-and-down movement of paper in the bureaucratic hierarchy; air travel for all people on work irrespective of their rank-based entitlement; accountability to only one person; lifting of goods by air cargo; involvement of the private sector wherever possible; placement of orders based on technical competence and not on the lowest price; and expeditious accounting procedures. None of the seven points were scientific, but the lack of such proactive approaches was hampering science's progress in the country.

Such demands were unheard of in government establishments. But if the RATO project was an entirely new game, what was wrong with a new set of rules? How could procedures laid down by colonial officers – and premised on a fundamental mistrust of Indian people – continue to be employed in the vain hope that projects of national importance would be accomplished? When Dr Sarabhai stipulated an eighteen-month deadline for delivering an indigenous RATO system, could he give the freedom to work efficiently? And Dr Sarabhai did. Upon hearing Kalam's plea for administrative liberalization – and seeing the inherent sense of his proposals – Dr Sarabhai approved the seven-point plan without a second thought.

That day, Kalam learned from Dr Sarabhai that trust is the basis of all business. If trust is lacking, the parties involved must take the necessary steps to allow it to improve. The foundation of trust should permeate every aspect of your organization. Work on RATO progressed without glitches thereafter, and it indeed became a glowing success story of indigenization.

RATO taught Kalam the power of integrity and the importance of truthful communication. Its success was largely due to its treating people in the organization as deserving to know the facts. Dr Sarabhai knew that you cannot give your staff half the story. You cannot hide the story. You must treat them as true equals. And as you communicate honestly and you communicate truthfully and you communicate with respect, your people will work for you to the best of their ability; they will work for you whenever you need them, and they will work harder than you have requested. With this lesson, it was time for Kalam to now move on to another plane.

Part Two
CREATION

Life is a series of natural and spontaneous changes. Don't resist them – that only creates sorrow. Let reality be reality. Let things flow naturally forward in whatever way they like.

– Lao-tzu
Philosopher and poet of ancient China

2.1

Indra's Net

> We live in a cosmos of infinite realms upon realms, mutually containing one another. Different people have different journeys for different reasons. You can't judge, but you can celebrate that there are connections everywhere.
>
> – The Ayatamsaka Sutra
> Chinese Buddhism

Kalam was handpicked by Dr Sarabhai as the project director for the Satellite Launch Vehicle (SLV). This would be the first indigenous rocket development endeavour to put a satellite in a low-earth orbit, which means at an altitude of between 100 miles (160 kilometres) and 1,200 miles (2,000 kilometres), with an orbital period of between approximately eighty-eight minutes and 127 minutes. Objects below 100 miles of altitude will experience very rapid orbital decay and altitude loss under the gravitational pull of earth. A target of putting a 40 kg satellite load into a 400 km orbit was set.

SLV was conceived as a four-stage rocket with all solid-propellant motors along the lines of the American Scout launch vehicle first used in the 1960s. The Scout (an acronym for Solid Controlled Orbital Utility Test system) was designed in 1957 at the NACA Langley Center. It was the first – and for a long time, the only – orbital launch vehicle to be entirely composed of solid fuel stages. The standard Scout launch vehicle was approximately 75 ft (23 m) in length, with a launch weight of 47,398 pounds (21,500 kg).

The Scout design persisted, as it was the most proven and reliable of the satellite launchers of the times. Indian scientists had no prior experience of designing a launch vehicle, and a four-stage, all solid-propulsion design was easier than the complex liquid equivalent and seemed to be the most likely route for success. By 1971, the design phase of the launcher was completed, and of the six designs Dr Sarabhai chose the third – hence the name SLV-3. It was a vehicle measuring 22 m in length and weighing 17,000 kg, and it could place a 30 kg satellite into near-earth orbit. Though SLV-3 resembled Scout in its morphology, the sub-assembly and fuel assemble were designed afresh by Indian scientists and engineers.

Besides Kalam, the core SLV-3 project team consisted of Dr S. Srinivasan, Ved Prakash Sandlas, D. Narayana Moorthi, G. Madhavan Nair, M.S.R. Dev, M.K. Abdul Majeed, D. Sasikumar, P.S. Veeraraghavan and A. Sivathanu Pillai. Dr V.R. Gowariker, M.R. Kurup and A.E. Muthunayagam were tasked with developing the first, second and third stages. Kalam was given the additional responsibility of developing the fourth stage, which would be a composite motor.

The world of technology is deeply interconnected and marked by fierce competition. In 1960, President Charles de Gaulle proclaimed the French aspiration to reach space. The Centre National d'Etudes Spatiales (CNES), was formed on 1 March 1962, with the task of planning and executing the French space programme. Diamant (French for Diamond) was the first French space launcher. Diamant was the first satellite launcher and the only one at that point of time not built by either the USA or USSR.

In early 1969, Kalam received a call from Dr Sarabhai stating that he would be visiting Trivandrum along with Prof Curien, president of the French space organization, CNES. Kalam was asked to give a presentation about the fourth stage to the CNES team. After the presentation was made, Kalam was told that SLV-3 fourth stage was also being considered as the upper stage for the French four-stage launch vehicle Diamant BC. A decision was taken in the same meeting that the SLV-3 fourth stage should be reconfigured to match and suit both French and Indian satellite launch vehicles. Kalam recalled his enthusiasm:

> We were just in the design stage, and here was a visionary whose dream was that Indian scientists could build an upper-stage rocket system compatible with both Indian and French satellite launch vehicle systems ... this resulted in an interesting partnership when the European Space Agency's Ariane launched the Indian APPLE satellite, that would use the SLV-3 fourth stage as an apogee boost motor later in the future.[1]

This experience gave Kalam two important messages. First, whatever your position in the organizational hierarchy, a leader with an open mind locates the right person and encourages him to succeed. The second was that a great leader imbues his team members with confidence and makes them feel that 'we can do it'.

As a matter of fact, the Diamant and SLV airframes were incompatible. Kalam had to modify the SLV-3 fourth-stage design to suit the Diamant airframe. The 400 mm diameter was changed to 650 mm and the propellant mass went up from 250 kg to 600 kg. It took the team two years to develop the new design that would be the Diamant rocket's third and upper stage. Then France abruptly abandoned its national launcher programme in favour of the European Ariane launcher in 1975. Kalam was very upset, but Dr Sarabhai enlightened him about the complexities of international collaborations in aerospace. There is give and take in so many forms and spread over long periods of time, sometimes across generations of people. International technology exchange is like Indrajaal. No good work done ever goes waste; it gets reflected somewhere else and utilized.

The satellite launching station at Sriharikota Island on the east coast of the Indian peninsula in Andhra Pradesh, chosen in 1969 for launching bigger rockets, became operational in 1971. It was named Sriharikota Range (SHAR). On 9 October 1971, the Rohini RH-1 satellite, a two-stage rocket using a solid propellant, was launched from SHAR. It carried a 7 kg payload to an altitude of 19 km.

In 1970, Kalam attended the Bombay National Electronics Conference, where Vikram Sarabhai announced plans for an Indian National Satellite (INSAT). The INSAT was primarily a direct-broadcast satellite, to be placed into orbit with the intention of educating Indian villagers through television. Attending the conference was an eminent array of academics, industrialists, politicians, bureaucrats, researchers, scientists and engineers, as well as a substantial crew of Indian journalists. It was a perfect place to build consensus for a national satellite. Sarabhai's presentation of the INSAT plans thrilled the crowd. 'Dissenters' with prepared questions were planted in the audience by the well-connected 'Sarabhai boys', to help allay any genuine doubts about the project.

Kalam had started seeing the greater context wherein his work was placed. He realized that SLVs and missiles were indeed two fruits of the same tree of rocketry. Almost parallel to his work on SLV, the DRDO was gearing itself for developing an indigenous surface-to-air missile. Narayanan, who worked with Kalam on RATO – and was now promoted to the rank of air commodore – was given the reins of DRDL, Hyderabad. With his hallmark impatience, he chose the quicker route of one-to-one substitution by reverse engineering, rather than following ISRO's policy of new design and indigenous technology development.

Indigenous replication of the Russian missile SA-2 was taken up at DRDL with the code name Devil. SA-2 was a simple two-stage missile design with three sets of four cruciform fins. Guidance control and initial roll stabilization was provided by electronics in two of the rear fins. Once launched, its main booster burned for four to five seconds before the primary sustainer motor ignited and burned for another twenty-two seconds. The warhead of the missile was filled with 130 kg of high explosives. Its nose section was equipped to hold a variety of fuses – proximity, impact and command.

The SA-2 was indeed a potent air-defence weapon in its time. It was perhaps best known for downing a United States U-2 spy plane over Cuba on 27 October 1962, but it was successfully deployed elsewhere. The North Vietnamese shot down a United States F-4C fighter aircraft in 1965, and in the same year a United States RB-47 was shot down over the Black Sea – both using SA-2s. As the pace of the Devil project picked up, the frequency of the Missile Panel meetings increased.

It was Kalam's practice to brief Dr Sarabhai over the telephone immediately after every Missile Panel meeting. After attending one such meeting on 30 December 1971, Kalam spoke to Dr Sarabhai by phone from Delhi airport, before boarding his flight for Trivandrum. Dr Sarabhai was in Trivandrum and was to return to Bombay in the night. He instructed Kalam to meet him at Trivandrum in the airport immediately after alighting from the aeroplane.

When Kalam reached Trivandrum, a pall of gloom hung in the air. The aircraft ladder operator Kutty told him with tears running down his cheeks that Dr Sarabhai was no more. He had passed away an hour earlier following a cardiac arrest. Kalam was flabbergasted. He had just spoken to Dr Sarabhai and expected to see him. He stayed back at the airport till Dr Sarabhai's mortal remains were airlifted to Ahmedabad for the last rites. Kalam told me once, 'Let no man in the world live in delusion. Without a guru none can cross over to the other shore.' When I asked him 'How does one find the guru?', he replied, 'Let each man take the path according to his capacity, understanding and temperament. His true guru will meet him along that path. I was doing my work to the best of my ability and respecting my situation, and Dr Sarabhai came into my life.'

Prof. M.G.K. Menon was given interim charge of the Indian space programme. He convened a large national seminar of scientists, engineers, technocrats and administrators to discuss and define the ten-year profile prepared by Dr Sarabhai, who was declared the father of the Indian space programme. The Thumba Equatorial Rocket Launching Station was renamed in his honour.

Recognizing the growing demands and importance of space activities, the government in June 1972 constituted an independent Space Commission and a Department of Space. It invited Prof. Satish Dhawan, the director of Indian Institute of Science (IISc), Bangalore since 1962, to head both organizations. Prof. Dhawan also took over as chairman of the ISRO, which functions under the Department of Space.

In May 1972, Dr Brahm Prakash joined as the first director of the Vikram Sarabhai Space Centre (VSSC). Dr Prakash was the creator of the Nuclear Fuel Complex (NFC) in Hyderabad, the former chief of the Department of Metallurgy at the Indian Institute of Science (IISc) and one of the scientific secretaries for the first United Nations conference on the peaceful uses of atomic energy that was held in Geneva in 1955.

The RATO system was tested on 8 October 1972 at Bareilly Air Force Station in Uttar Pradesh, where a high-performance Sukhoi-16 Jet aircraft became airborne after a short run of 1,200 metres, as against the usual length of 2 kilometres. The sixty-sixth RATO motor was used for the test. The test was adjudged an unqualified success, and the effort was said to have saved some five million dollars. Kalam and Narayanan's partnership, under the stewardship of the visionary Dr Vikram Sarabhai, had now paid its dividends, and the benefits of swadeshi aerospace were abundantly clear: 'Including trial expenses, we spent less than Rs twenty-five lakhs on the entire project. The Indian RATO could be purchased at Rs. 17,000 per piece, and it replaced the imported RATO, which cost 4000 dollars.'[2]

After assuming the leadership of the SLV-3 project, Kalam faced conflicting demands on his time. He had to attend to committee work and correspondence, make material procurement decisions, preside over reviews and briefings; and he needed to stay abreast of a wide range of developments. But his change in status did not alter the way he lived in any respect. Kalam came to Trivandrum in 1968 and stayed at Indira Bhavan Lodge in a humble corner room on the ground floor. In all his time in Trivandrum, he stayed in this same room. The room did not have an attached bathroom then, but only a common one on the same floor. With a single bed, a table and a chair, the small room was meant only for basic single accommodation – it was intended for use by bachelors on a meagre salary, who could afford nothing better. His landlady later recalled Kalam's spartan lifestyle: 'Kalam did not have visitors at the lodge. Once he was back from the office, he would sit for reading. At the lodge, he communicated with only a watchman (security guard) upon whom he depended for getting provisions and food from nearby hotels.'[3]

Kalam started his day with a stroll of about 2 km around the lodge. He would prepare a mental schedule for the day during his walk and decide two or three things that he would like to accomplish that day. At least one of these important tasks must further a long-term goal. 'Without a long-term definite chief aim, a life is like a rudderless ship – it goes nowhere,' he would remind me.

Once in the office, Kalam would first clean his desk. Within ten minutes he would segregate the papers there into three categories: matters that required immediate action, matters of low priority which could be kept pending and general reading material. He would then put the high-priority papers in front of him on the desk, walk to his secretary's desk and place the rest of the papers there, out of his sight.

On New Year's Day 1975, Kalam accompanied Dr Brahm Prakash to DRDL for a review of the Devil missile project. The review noted excellent progress, but Kalam observed that a one-on-one philosophy had taken precedence over the generation of design data. Consequently, the design engineers had not been able to pay adequate attention to the necessary analysis, which was the practice at ISRO. Kalam learned that a successful reverse engineering process in itself was not merely concerned with creating a copy or changing a prototype in some way. It was more an analysis in order to deduce design features from the prototype, with little or no knowledge about the procedures involved in its original production.

Narayanan told Kalam that reverse engineering was an accepted and well-developed practice in the development of military systems. The Western Allies at the end of the war captured technical documents for the V-2 Rockets and related technologies from the German military. The Americans then focused their reverse engineering efforts via Operation Paperclip, which led to the development of the PGM-11 Redstone rocket. The Soviets captured German engineers to reproduce technical documents and plans, and worked from captured hardware, in order to make their clone of the V-2: the SA-11/R-1 rocket.

In contrast to the galloping progress at DRDL, the SLV-3 was taking shape slowly. Instead of following a straightforward process of replicating a prototype, the SLV-3 was trekking along many developmental paths. The project had been formulated in such a way that the major technological work centres could handle propellant production, rocket motor testing and launch of any large diameter rocket. Prof. Dhawan introduced a sponsorship programme for research in space science and technology (RESPOND) in universities and national laboratories, to assist in the project's development.

At any rate, the assiduous technological development of the SLV-3 would eventually bear its fruit. For a year, from 1 August 1975 to 31 July 1976, hundreds and sometimes thousands of villagers gathered daily in front of each of 5,000 television sets – installed outside like a processional deity of a temple – to watch educational television. Indian engineers had placed the television sets in remote and especially backward villages spread in six clusters across the subcontinent. It was an experiment in social engineering and rural upliftment as much as it was in technology. The television programmes had been carefully formulated to educate the villagers on how to lead better lives and grow more food. Most villages were beyond the electricity grid and required solar electrical installations to power the sets.

The triumph of SITE ensured the organization's ongoing support and prestige, both within India and internationally. For Kalam, the success of the project was an especially personal accomplishment. Rameswaram Panchayat School, where he had been first inspired by a class on flight nearly four decades earlier, now had a satellite television. Kalam's father was beaming with pride. He died in 1976 at the ripe old age of 102 years, immensely proud of his son's achievements.

It was during the tumultuous period of the mid-1970s, with the Emergency of Prime Minister Indira Gandhi and the resulting suspension of democratic rights, that Kalam began to deeply ponder the country's social and political landscape. He could see a widening gulf between the interests of the political class and the aspirations of India's poor millions. A nascent idea, 'Strength respects strength', would crystallize over time in Kalam's vision for the country's future. He could see the potential for the country and its people to become empowered, just as he had been – by education, hard work and the nurturing of technology.

In his immediate duties, he could see that his hard work and pioneering efforts in indigenous aerospace – fostered by his late boss and mentor Dr Vikram Sarabhai – had now raised the country's international status in the field. ISRO's enhanced status facilitated an increase in recruitment for the first time after Sarabhai's death. Thousands of young professionals from elite engineering institutions now clamoured to join its ranks. SITE opened critical paths in the rapidly emerging European space programmes. ISRO was accepted as an equal partner in several critical cooperative programmes managed by the European, French and German space programmes. India may not have joined the 'space race', but it was a force to be reckoned with in aerospace.

Moreover, there were evermore practical applications for the aerospace industry, and pressing concerns for the nation's people that the new technologies of ISRO needed to address. One of the worst cyclonic storms to hit the Indian shores struck Andhra Pradesh on 19 November 1977. The most affected areas were in the delta region of the River Krishna, where a storm surge of up to 6 m in height from the Bay of Bengal wreaked havoc on its coastal populations. Landslides severed the railway lines on the Waltair-Kirandal route. Fields of paddy and cash crops were submerged by the waves. Thirteen sailing vessels went missing in the storm, and at least 50,000 people were killed. Hundreds of bodies were later found floating in the waters, and those bloated beyond recognition were consigned to mass funeral pyres.

The horrific scale of the casualties highlighted a need for early warning systems for tropical cyclones. Beginning with the launching of TIROS-I in April 1960, satellites were used to detect tropical cyclones. Techniques were developed to determine in real time a tropical cyclone's strength from characteristics seen on satellite imagery.

Wind speed could be ascertained from the data, and differences in temperature between the surrounding storm clouds and the eye of the cyclone could determine the strength of the weather pattern: the larger the temperature difference, the stronger the tropical cyclone. ISRO's satellites could now be deployed to help save lives, giving early warning to millions living in low-lying coastal areas in the cyclone-prone regions of the subcontinent.

The SLV-3 Apogee rocket, developed as a common upper stage with Diamant, was scheduled to be flight-tested in France. Some problems surfaced during the system integration, and Kalam was needed in France to attend to them. Two days before Kalam's scheduled departure to France, his mother passed away. He took the first available bus to Nagercoil, and boarded the night train to Rameswaram. He performed her last rites and returned to the railway station from the burial ground. Years later, he remembered that there was little time for grief: 'The next morning I was back at Thumba, physically exhausted, emotionally shattered, but determined to fulfil our ambition of flying an Indian rocket motor on foreign soil.'[4]

With his parents gone, Kalam threw his entire being into the SLV project. He withdrew from every other activity. He stopped playing badminton in the evenings and stayed back at work, even on weekends and holidays. A stoic calm enveloped him. Kalam immersed himself in his duties and quiet contemplation, exercising much self-control, as some men are apt to do, in overcoming his grief.

2.2

Vasudhaiva Kutumbakam

The sole meaning of life is to serve humanity.

– Leo Tolstoy
Russian novelist

Preoccupied with his work with the SLV-3 project, Kalam felt comfortable, and enjoyed a great sense of purpose. He would never tire of meeting with people, discussing, arguing, explaining and understanding – at least so far as it applied to his work. On a personal level, he started to feel a strange aversion for the usual social interactions, and had no patience for idle gossip and small talk. When he was not working, he would mostly seek solitude, reading some good book or listening to Carnatic music. He was convinced that living according to reason and virtue is to be in harmony with the universe's divine order. He hypothesized that this order was coded in one's talents and the situations of one's life at any point of time. These talents must be identified, nurtured and refined, and the situations in one's life must be understood and attended to. For this, he needed to be at peace within.

Nevertheless, Kalam found that interacting with people and coordinating their efforts was his special talent. The development of the SLV-3 was his latest medium to manifest this talent. These were indeed the transformative years for Kalam. He was realizing the importance of living a purposeful life; and he had freed himself from the prison of sensory pleasures and miseries hidden behind merrymaking. He was past his forties, and the diversions of youth no longer held any allure for him. While he had settled into a confirmed bachelorhood, his lifestyle was more that of a monk or a sadhu; he was now happily engrossed simply in work and contemplative pursuits.

This is not to say that Kalam was aloof or cold; he continued to enjoy, throughout his life, lasting, meaningful friendships. And at this time, he developed a particularly strong emotional bond with Dr Brahm Prakash. Dr Prakash was an outstanding scientist, an inspiring leader and a self-effacing man who had been the first Indian to head the Indian Institute of Science's Department of Metallurgy. Under his leadership, the Atomic Energy Establishment's Metallurgy Group developed techniques for the extraction and fabrication of a variety of nuclear-grade metals. The 'closed nuclear fuel cycle', which was the goal of the Indian nuclear programme, was essentially about materials of high purity, and Dr Brahm Prakash was at the centre of this effort. Kalam found in him his mentor teacher. Dr Sarabhai was like an angel to Kalam – inspiring and guiding – but almost not from this world. Brahm Prakash, however, was like Naranarayan, the embodiment of divine grace right in front of him. Kalam saw in Brahm Prakash his departed father.

Dr Brahm Prakash recognized in Kalam his own self, from his youthful days in Lahore. Dr Brahm Prakash was one of millions who lived through the trauma of Partition. He lamented to Kalam one day that there were many books written on the Nazi holocaust, but no one had really ever written of the callousness of the British colonial rulers with their Partition of India. They had arbitrarily drawn a line on the map, deciding the nationality of millions of people, with a total disregard of the consequences. He told Kalam once, 'Hitler has been established as a monster of human history, and rightly so. But the devils in the garb of suave politicians on the Indian subcontinent who created the colossal human tragedy of Indian Partition got away with their sins, after Mahatma Gandhi settled their account with his sacrifice.'

Dr Brahm Prakash and Kalam would often take long strolls. Dr Brahm Prakash was a heavy smoker but when walking with

Kalam, he would not light a single cigarette. They both shared a sense of concern for the suffering of others and an aspiration to see that suffering relieved. Dr Brahm Prakash treated Kalam as his son, and Kalam garnered from him the education of the finer aspects of life that he had missed with his father.

Dr Brahm Prakash taught Kalam the essence of the virtue of respect. Respect is about the worth you put in people around you and in your own self. One must have regard for the worth of others. Likewise, one must have regard for the worth of oneself. But the most important lesson Kalam learned from Dr Brahm Prakash was that of humility, which he explained to Kalam as the respect for one's own limitations. Dr Brahm Prakash told Kalam, 'Humility is not the act or posture of lowering oneself in relation to others. Humility is about having a clear perspective and respect for one's place in context.' In a religious setting, this can mean recognition of the self in relation to God, acceptance of one's defects, and submission to the divine grace as a member of any great religion of the world.

Kalam also learned from Dr Brahm Prakash his first lesson in the transformation from 'I' to 'We.' He explained to Kalam:

> This is the most important process leaders go through in becoming authentic. How else can they unleash the power of their organizations unless they motivate people to reach their full potential? If our supporters are merely following our lead, their efforts are limited to our vision and our directions ... Only when leaders stop focusing on their personal ego needs are they able to develop other leaders.

In May 1973, Dr Brahma Prakash informed Kalam of the visit of Werner (Freiherr) von Braun, the legendary inventor of the V-2 and the Saturn-V rockets. He chose Kalam to receive von Braun at Madras and escort him to Trivandrum. Kalam took this assignment as a great gift. Werner von Braun was almost universally revered in the field of rocketry as one of the greatest rocket scientists and champions of space exploration of his era. His V-2 rocket was the world's first long-range guided ballistic missile. It was also the first man-made object to cross the boundary of space.

Kalam and von Braun boarded an Avro aircraft in Madras for the ninety-minute flight to Trivandrum. Kalam was pleased to sit beside his hero of rocketry, and was even more gratified by this great man's down-to-earth politeness. Kalam broke the ice by mentioning to von Braun his visit to NASA's Wallops Island. In turn, von Braun asked about Kalam's work and intently listened to his brief dissertation, as if he were just another practitioner of rocketry. Kalam later wrote: 'I never expected the father of modern rocketry to be so humble, receptive, and encouraging. He made me feel comfortable right through the flight. It was hard to imagine that I was talking to a giant of missile systems, as he was so self-effacing.'[1]

Those unforgettable ninety minutes also allowed Kalam to hear von Braun's great story of human courage, of how he had prevailed in the most adverse situations. He understood from von Braun, in this short time, how the anchor of the intellect could save a person from the most trying of life's challenges. In March 1945, when Allied forces defeated Germany, von Braun used his research and access to technical documents to broker a new life in the United States. He knew that regardless of the Nazi atrocities, no major world power would refuse the Nazi regime's technological advances. The post-World War II geopolitical jockeying between the major world powers would manifest in a race for technological superiority, which would be inextricably linked to rocketry and aerospace technology.

Von Braun told Kalam that he and his entire rocketry team were brought to the United States and immediately given employment with the military, as the Americans had no technological capacity of the sort he had developed with his team in Germany. American rocket scientists would take another five years to reach the level of V-2 technology. Befitting his scientific stature, the US government appointed von Braun as technical director of the US Army Ordnance Guided Missile Project in Alabama. During the 1950s, von Braun also became one of the most prominent advocates of space exploration in the United States. Americans accepted him as their own hero. Strength respects only strength.

In 1960, von Braun's rocket development centre was transferred from the army to the newly established NASA and received a mandate to build the giant Saturn rockets. Accordingly, von Braun became director of NASA's Marshall Space Flight Center and the chief architect of the Saturn V launch vehicle, the superbooster that would propel Americans to the moon. Von Braun impressed upon scientists and engineers the importance of recording their work accurately and diligently on paper and seeking collective review before publishing it. He said, 'Had I not created dossiers of my work, I would have been killed and buried in an unmarked grave. The records of my work not only saved my life, it saved years of hard work and scientific data of immense value for future research.'

While Kalam was in France at CERN for the SLV-3 Apogee rocket project, he witnessed the genesis of a fascinating and successful Franco-German aerospace collaboration. French work with geosynchronous orbit telecommunications began in 1967. France joined hands with Germany to develop two experimental Symphonie satellites. The small (230 kg) spacecraft, with three-axis stabilization and two 6/4 GHz transponders, were launched by the US in 1974 and 1975. The Symphonie system was highly successful in providing telecommunications links throughout Europe and to other continents. Both spacecraft far exceeded their design life of five years.

Kalam wondered: What if India and China, instead of fighting over concocted issues, joined hands like France and Germany? Why are Asians caught in a perpetual cycle of self-degradation and petty conflicts? When France and Germany – who were adversaries in the bitterest wars of the last century – can join hands, what stops India and China, who had enjoyed 2,000 years of peace!

On 19 April 1975, India entered the space age by launching its first-ever satellite, the Aryabhata, from Kapustin Yar, Astrakhan Oblast, in Russia. A Kosmos-3M launch vehicle was used to put the satellite into a near-circular orbit at an altitude of 600 km. The satellite was constructed as a twenty-six-sided polyhedron with a diameter of 1.4 m. All of its faces, except the top and bottom, were covered with solar cells. Named after the fifth-century astronomer and mathematician Aryabhata, the 360-kg spin-stabilized satellite enabled ISRO scientists and engineers to learn the basics of satellite technology in designing, building and operating the satellite. Kalam admired the diligence of his Russian counterparts:

> Our first satellite was launched by a Soviet Rocket, Cosmos-3M, on 19 April 1975 from Kapustin Yar Test Range. Although language is a huge barrier while working with Russians, they are very thorough in their schematic and mathematical expression. I witnessed the development of Indo-Russian collaboration from the traditional importer model to a more symbiotic relationship through joint defence research and development and manufacturing.[2]

The year 1975 also saw the creation of The European Space Agency (ESA), an intergovernmental organization comprising twenty-two member states' representatives. It was headquartered in Paris. The science missions were based at European Space Research and Technology Centre (ESTEC) in Noordwijk, the Netherlands, the earth observation missions at ESRIN in Frascati, Italy, ESA Mission Control (ESOC) in Darmstadt, Germany, and the European Space Astronomy Centre (ESAC) located in Villanueva de la Canada, Madrid, Spain. The European Astronaut Centre (EAC), that would train astronauts for future missions, was set up in Cologne, Germany. After World War II, many European scientists left western Europe in order to work in the United States. They realized that by returning to their countries and working solely on national projects, they would not be able to compete with the two main superpowers; and this had brought them all together.

The Aryabhata was followed by Bhaskara-1, launched on 7 June 1979 from Kapustin Yar aboard the Intercosmos C-1 launch vehicle. The 444-kg satellite made by ISRO was fitted with two television cameras operating with invisible (600 nanometre) and near-infrared (800 nanometre) frequencies that collected data related to hydrology, forestry and geology. It also boasted a satellite microwave radiometer (SAMIR) operating at 19 and 22 GHz for study of the ocean and such phenomena as water vapour, liquid water content in the atmosphere, etc. ISRO used the Franco-German Symphonie satellite for the Satellite Telecommunication Experiments Project (STEP)to establish satellite-based post and telegraph services during 1977–79.

Not all of the memorable happenings of these years were positive. One tragic aeronautical event, which unfolded right in front of Kalam, led him to deeply contemplate the profound issue of mortality. He was sitting in Bombay's Sahar Airport passenger lounge, waiting to take the evening flight to Trivandrum on New Year's Day in 1978, when the deadliest aviation accident India had seen occurred nearby. Air India passenger flight AI 855, bound for Dubai from Sahar Airport, crashed just off the coast of Bandra, almost immediately after taking off from the airport. All 213 passengers and crew on board were killed. The aircraft involved was a Boeing 747 named *Emperor Ashok*. A sad Kalam reflected, while flying back to Trivandrum later in the night, that no one wants to die. Even people who want to go to heaven don't want to die to get there. And yet death is the destination we all share. No one has ever escaped it. And that is as it should be, because death is very likely the single best invention of life. It is life's change agent. It clears out the old to make way for the new.

At least in rocketry of the kind that Kalam was now engaged in, mechanical failure or human error rarely had any opportunity to cause the loss of life. It could, however, cause great distress. The first experimental flight trial for the SLV-3 was scheduled for 10 August 1979. The primary goals of the mission were to realize a fully integrated satellite launch vehicle to evaluate on-board systems like stage motors, guidance and control systems and electronic subsystems – and to evaluate ground systems, like checkout, tracking, telemetry and real-time data facilities in launch operations built at SHAR. The rocket took off at 7.58 a.m. Stage I performed perfectly; but the second stage went out of control. The flight was terminated after 317 seconds, and the rocket's shattered wreck splashed into the sea, 540 kilometres off the Sriharikota coast. Kalam was mortified by this dramatic failure, as he would later recount:

> I felt a strange mix of anger and frustration. Suddenly I felt my legs become so stiff that they ached. The problem was not with my body;

> something was happening in my mind ... The premature death of my hovercraft Nandi, the abandoning of the RATO, the shelving of the Diamant; all came alive in a flash, like a long-buried Phoenix resurrecting.[3]

'What do you suppose could have gone wrong?' somebody asked Kalam. He walked away without answering. He was too tired to think. The launch had been preceded by a night-long countdown. Moreover, Kalam had had hardly any sleep in the week prior to the launch. Completely drained, mentally as well as physically, he went straight to his room and collapsed in his bed. It was inevitable that those who want to reap the benefits of this great nation must bear the fatigue of supporting it.

Dr Brahm Prakash came to Kalam's room but left without disturbing his sleep. He returned after about an hour, but Kalam was still sleeping. Dr Brahm Prakash quietly sat outside his room. When Kalam finally woke up late in the afternoon, Dr Brahm Prakash took him to the canteen for lunch. He made light conversation during the meal, carefully avoiding any mention of the SLV-3. Dr Brahm Prakash was a godsend with his kindness and helped Kalam through this ordeal.

In the evening there was a press conference. A large contingent of Indian and international press – and of course the entire ISRO top brass – were present. Kalam was ready to be skinned alive. Prof. Satish Dhawan took charge of the situation. First, he surprised everybody with his opening statement, congratulating the SLV-3 team for achieving a flawless launch and their successful development of the first-stage booster motor. He mentioned Kalam by name, saying that he had shown exemplary leadership; that he had put in a mammoth effort involving thousands of people over seven years – and had never allowed personal likes and dislikes to come in the way of his duties.

One correspondent asked, 'Twenty crores of taxpayers' money has been drowned in the Bay of Bengal.' Prof. Dhawan kept his cool and answered,

> What is being attempted in the space programme in India has far-reaching consequences. You will not be able to count the amount of money that would go out of the country in the future if India does not have its own communication and remote-sensing satellites. Please understand the billions of dollars' worth of work done by low-paid and frugally living employees of our government organizations.

There was a pin-drop silence. He then added that he was confident that in exactly a year's time, SLV-3 would successfully place a satellite in orbit. Prof. Brahm Prakash retired in November 1979, and Dr Vasant Gowariker assumed his former position.

The SLV-3 was launched on 18 July 1980, successfully placing the Rohini satellite RS-1 into orbit, thereby making India the sixth member of an exclusive club of spacefaring nations. The successful culmination of the SLV-3 project showed the way to advanced launch vehicle projects such as the Augmented Satellite Launch Vehicle (ASLV), Polar Satellite Launch Vehicle (PSLV) and the Geosynchronous Satellite Launch Vehicle (GSLV). Prof. Dhawan asked Kalam to take up the Space Launch Vehicle Directorate at ISRO headquarters. His mission would be to preside over the space programme for remote sensing and communication satellites, linking the corresponding launch vehicle systems, including the launch complex. Sivathanu Pillai took over as Kalam's lieutenant.

This was a time for change. Kalam's old comrade Narayanan, who had reached the rank of air vice marshal, had by now retired. In his absence, the entire programme of military rocketry was languishing under a persistent apathy. There was a leadership vacuum at the DRDO and Dr Raja Ramanna, the scientific adviser to the defence minister of India, invited Kalam to give his input to the missile programme:

> The DRDO needed somebody to take command of their missile programmes, which had been stuck at the drawing board and static test bed stages for quite a while. Prof. Ramanna asked me if I would like to join DRDO and shoulder the responsibility of shaping the Indian Guided Missile Development Programme.[4]

On 26 January 1981, Republic Day of India, Kalam was awarded the Padma Bhushan, the third-highest civilian honour of the country. On the same day, Prof. Satish Dhawan received the Padma Vibhushan, the second-highest civilian honour in India. Dr Brahm Prakash called Kalam and said that he felt as if his son had received the Padma Bhushan. The Anna University, Madras, conferred on Kalam the honorary degree of Doctor of Science. He received the degree in the convocation from Dr Raja Ramanna. Dr Kalam joined DRDO as director on 1 June 1982.

2.3

Smiling Buddha

> It is better to rise from life as from a banquet – neither thirsty nor drunken.
>
> – Aristotle
> Greek philosopher and scientist

Dr Kalam was fully aware of the burden he was taking on his shoulders. He was being interpolated into an organization with a radically different culture to that of ISRO; and it was, at that time, functioning poorly. He had worked at ADE earlier but those were the formative years of the DRDO, when it was created more or less in mimicry of the Advanced Research Projects Agency (ARPA) in the United States. Its purpose had always been to expand the frontiers of technology and science for military applications, with the aim of reaching beyond the forces' immediate requirements. In this, it was now lagging behind. Kalam's quest would be to help the organization shed its stultifying low morale and reliance on foreign technology, and inspire a new culture of self-empowerment to lead it towards the twenty-first century.

Dr Kalam had studied the evolution of DRDO from close quarters since its inception. Its beginnings were more emotional than strategic. Veneration for science was obvious in the choice of Dr Kothari as the first Chief of DRDO. Dr Kothari had worked under the legendary Meghnad Saha during his master's at Allahabad University, and had done his PhD under the father of nuclear physics Ernest Rutherford at the University of Cambridge. Special Weapon Development Team (SWDT) did the initial work. This team was later expanded into DRDL, a full-fledged laboratory at the campus of Defence Science Centre, Delhi, in June 1961. The laboratory was moved to Hyderabad in February 1962 on land in the Chandrayanagutta area provided by the state government that had once housed the barracks of the erstwhile Nizam's army. The debacle in the 1962 Sino-Indian war had provoked serious discussion of missile technology development in India, raising the profile of the DRDO in the halls of power.

The top brass of the organization decided first to develop a wire-guided anti-tank missile. The anti-tank missile was a totally indigenous product – its propulsion, control, guidance, power supply and materials were all Indian. There were no computers, and electronic circuits were used to make calculations. The missile was test-fired near Imarat, a village on the outskirts of Hyderabad. Dr Kalam had visited this place earlier during his time as a member of the Missile Advisory Committee. The tests proved the anti-tank missile reliable.

This project had laid the foundation of India's missile programme and helped to train many technologists, including A.V. Ranga Rao, S. Krishnan, K. Rama Rao, Z.P. Marshal, H.S. Rama Rao and J.C. Bhattacharya. Dr Kalam had met each one of these learned gentlemen during the course of the SLV-3's development, and some of them even came to Trivandrum to participate in technical reviews. Many from the group of more than fifty scientists who were involved in the development of India's anti-tank missile, went on to set up Bharat Dynamics Limited (BDL), Hyderabad. BDL became the production agency of missiles. And in the late 1960s, the Government of India embarked on the licensed production of French-developed SS-11B anti-tank missiles at BDL.

India conducted its first successful nuclear bomb test on 18 May 1974 at the army base, Pokhran Test Range (PTR), in Rajasthan. It was the first confirmed nuclear weapons test by a nation outside the five permanent members of the United Nations Security Council – the victors of World War II – namely, the USSR, the United Kingdom, France, China and the United States. The country's entry to the 'nuclear club' put an immediate focus on the missile technology for delivering nuclear warheads. The nation's politicians, of all political hues, would henceforth look towards the DRDO for long-range missiles that could take the country's nuclear capability beyond static tests in the desert.

The rocketry demands in the forces were both immediate and long-term. In the years leading up to the Pokhran nuclear test of 1974, the Indian Air Force was suffering from lack of spare parts for the Soviet Union's SAM-2 missiles for their high-altitude air defence needs. The Government of India decided in 1972 to solve this problem by re-engineering the parts. In parallel, a programme called Valiant was launched under Squadron Leader R. Gopalaswamy to build a rocket engine powered by liquid propellants. Gopalaswamy started a project to pioneer the development of a semi-cryogenic liquid rocket engine. He set up a test facility at the Jamnagar Air Force Station and joined DRDL in 1964. The engine was tested on 10 June 1974 in the presence of Dr Kalam.

DRDO simultaneously turned its attention to building a guidance package, because the inertial navigation system formed an essential part of a long-range missile. A team headed by D. Burman and comprising P. Banerjee and Avinash Chander built a platform-based inertial navigation system (INS). It was tested on board an Avro aircraft during 1974–75. By now, DRDL had built substantial infrastructure in the fields of propulsion, navigation and manufacture of materials. As it did not have its own range, the Indian Space Research Organization's Sriharikota base and the Indian Air Force's Suryalanka Base, Andhra Pradesh, were used for flight testing the SAM-2. Dr Kalam was present for two of these flight trials.

Dr Kalam had a series of discussions with Dr Arunachalam, the chief of DRDO and his boss. Dr Arunachalam had considerable experience in technology development. He had received his PhD degree in materials science and engineering from the University of Wales in 1965. He had then worked at the Bhabha Atomic Research Centre for more than a decade and the National Aeronautical Laboratory at Bangalore, before joining the Defence Metallurgical

Research Laboratory, Hyderabad, as its director in 1975. Dr Kalam and Dr Arunachalam could clearly envisage the demands for missile technology multiplying in the following decades. Equally, both were convinced that only a dynamic, cohesive organization had any chance of meeting the nation's requirements.

They moreover concurred that there was a need for a cultural renaissance in the system. Dr Arunachalam was aware that almost all senior scientists at DRDL were living with the pain of frustration and repressed anger. The sudden shelving of the Devil missile programme without consultation had hurt them. There was also a perception that senior officials in the Ministry of Defence had cheated scientists of this laboratory. It was clear to Kalam that the burial of the Devil was essential for a revival of hope and vision. Dr Arunachalam gave Dr Kalam a free hand and promised his complete backing for the change. He was good to his word.

Dr Kalam immediately did two things. He created a Directorate of Management Services and invited Colonel R. Swaminathan, the head of Missile Control Laboratory and a DRDO veteran, to head the new group. In doing so, he aimed to address the career issues of the scientists and facilitate the smooth functioning of the organization. He also recruited his former lieutenant at ISRO, Sivathanu Pillai, to DRDO and helped him to organize the programme management. These two able officers and trusted friends of Dr Kalam indeed acted as his two hands in managing the DRDL, drawing the threads of its damaged morale together to form a strong fabric of cooperation.

The new team was to adopt a more informal, consultative management style, which was unfamiliar to the bureaucratically orthodox DRDO. Dr Kalam evoked the concept of management by participation and made earnest efforts to involve middle-level scientists and engineers in the management of the laboratory. Kalam saw it was imperative that decisions on vital scientific and technological problems were taken quickly and collectively:

> Throughout my career I had zealously pursued openness in scientific matters. I had seen from very close quarters the decay and disintegration

> that go with management through closed-door consultations and secret manipulations. I always despised and resisted such efforts.[1]

At any rate, one of the challenges of these years, and it ran counter to his dynamic and flexible nature, was organizational rigidity. Dr Kalam took some time to change the underlying organizational culture of DRDL. The prevalent mindset of reverse engineering had served the institution in previous decades, when there was an exigency for armaments. Rocketry for the forces had to be cobbled together to meet immediate defence needs in the wake of the Sino-Indian war of 1962. The new culture of innovation and technological development was the only way to serve the country's future as a military and technological power.

With this objective in mind, Dr Kalam undertook some measured organizational changes. He first inducted 280 young engineers in 1984, which was perhaps the biggest-ever induction in an Indian scientific organization. Dr Kalam evolved a matrix organization in which, by retaining the traditional hierarchical structure of the laboratory, he introduced a task-driven work system. The scientists working in technology divisions were made system managers and given exclusive responsibility for one project. An external fabrication wing was created under P.K. Biswas, who had formidable experience of working with public sector undertakings (PSUs) like HAL, and private sector industry such as L&T, Godrej and Tata. Just as he had done early in his career in developing the RH-75 rocket, Dr Kalam would rely on the best technical and scientific minds he could muster – in and outside the government service.

Dr Kalam also formed a high-level decision-making body called the Missile Technology Committee to map the way forward. According to Dr Kalam's and the committee's reckoning, the existing Prithvi missile could not be converted into a long-range missile, so he created a pitch for a ballistic missile involving re-entry technology. On Dr Kalam's insistence, a development project on re-entry technology was included. Days of debate and weeks of thinking finally culminated in a long-term Guided Missile Development Programme.

Dr Kalam invited Z.P. Marshall, the chairman and managing director of BDL, N.R. Iyer, A.K. Kapoor and K.S. Venkataraman to synthesize all debates and decisions into a clear and well-defined scheme for missile development for the following ten years. The scheme was outlined in a paper that was sent for approval by the Cabinet Committee for Political Affairs (CCPA). The paper was given its final shape after consulting the representatives of the three defence services. The final document estimated a budget of fifty million dollars over a period of twelve years.

Dr Kalam, accompanied by Dr Arunachalam, made a presentation to Defence Minister R. Venkataraman. The three service chiefs and the nation's top-level bureaucrats were present. The discussion went on for more than an hour. India needed missiles; but was it possible? Did the track record of DRDO support its claim? Fifty million dollars were a significant sum of money, and who would take a twelve-year-long shot? What would be the political fallout? Would the services wait for the outcome? Were there other options? The meeting ended without a decision or even any indication of the department's intentions. The defence minister, however, asked Dr Kalam and Dr Arunachalam to meet him later in the evening.

Both the scientists were unsure of what exactly was in store for them. Dr Arunachalam was anxious and verbalized his doubts: What if only ten million are sanctioned? Or, if they get only twenty million, which missile would they take in that case, and which others should they discard? Dr Kalam had by now, though, developed a strong sense of intuition, bordering on the prescient. He had no such thoughts. He had a vision of a SLV-sized rocket soaring into the sky and re-entering thousands of miles away with its payload. His vision gave him a calm assurance.

When evening arrived, a relaxed defence minister communicated to them the government's decision to approve an integrated guided missile programme, and not just fund one or two projects that were being asked. The DRDO, however, would have to shoulder the responsibility for the programme till user trials were completed and production was launched, and not just confine itself to research and development. The defence minister asked Dr Arunachalam and Dr Kalam to rework their figures, incorporating the additional scope of work, and to meet him the following morning. Dr Arunachalam knew full well that Dr Kalam was taking the night flight to Madras on his way to Rameswaram to attend the wedding of his niece Zameela (his brother's daughter) the following evening. But Dr Kalam did not say a word about it. He handed over his ticket for cancellation to Dr Arunachalam's secretary.

Dr Kalam and Dr Arunachalam huddled together in the latter's office and worked till midnight. They decided to extrapolate the dots from the minister's words by themselves and give a clear, rational plan to him. Dr Arunachalam arranged dinner from his house, and even as they ate they were busy working. While much detail was uncertain, both the scientists were convinced of one thing: never before in India was such a plan attempted, but now that it had been decided, it must succeed. The Integrated Guided Missile Development Programme (IGMDP) was conceptually born in the wee hours of 14 May 1983. It included Dr Kalam's dream of a SLV-3-sized rocket taking off and the payload returning through the atmosphere. They named the idea REX or re-entry experiment launch vehicle and asked for it the modest budget of ten million dollars. Defence Minister Venkataraman was visibly pleased with the plans shown to him the next morning, and said that it would now be his task to get the plan sanctioned by the cabinet. Kalam later happily recalled the minister's supportive approach: 'Turning to me, he (R. Venkataraman) said, "Since I brought you here (to DRDO), I was expecting you to come with something like this. I am happy to see your work."'[2]

Dr Kalam had thankfully bowed before the minister and turned towards the door, when he heard Dr Arunachalam telling the defence minister how 'Dr Kalam had to sacrifice going to Rameswaram today for his niece's wedding and competed this work even without saying as much as a word about his predicament'. It amazed Dr Kalam that a person of Dr Arunachalam's stature was concerned about a wedding taking place on a far-flung island, in a small house of ordinary people. And what the defence minister of India did next amazed him even more.

The office of the defence minister put Dr Kalam on an Indian Airline flight leaving for Madras an hour later, and tied up with an Indian Air Force (IAF) helicopter that was running a shuttle to Madurai in the late afternoon. The helicopter was ready for take-off when the flight landed at Madras airport, and Dr Kalam was airborne again in less than ten minutes. At Madurai, the air force commandant even gave Dr Kalam a lift to the railway station and a ticket to Rameswaram. Dr Kalam boarded the train when it was about to leave the platform. Dr Kalam reached his ancestral home in time for the wedding. There were no mobile phones then, and Dr Kalam was expected to attend the wedding. Unmindful that the machinery of government had moved virtual heaven and earth for Dr Kalam to be there in time, they were simply delighted with his arrival, and went about the business of the marriage. Dr Kalam was overwhelmed, though, by the noble, kind efforts of the minister and the defence personnel.

The defence minister was likewise accommodating to the missile programme: he stood by his word and got the IGMDP plan approved by the cabinet. An unprecedented budget of Rs 388 crore (fifty million dollars in those days) was sanctioned. The five indigenous missiles of the programme were given appropriately and unmistakably Indian names, in keeping with the spirit of the nation's tryst with indigenous missile technology. The surface-to-surface missile was called Prithvi (the earth), the tactical core vehicle for short-range air defence was named Trishul (the trident of Lord Shiva), the medium-range surface-to-air defence missile was given the title Akash (the sky) and the anti-tank missile project was called Nag (the serpent). Dr Kalam dubbed the missile of his vision Agni, as the payload would re-enter the atmosphere as a ball of fire.

Following the vision of Defence Minister Venkataraman in right earnest, these projects were aimed towards the realization of indigenous state-of-the-art technology. Dr Kalam's team was not merely confining itself to re-engineering missiles available elsewhere in the world. The development of Nag would entail innovative thermal-seeker technology. The inertial navigation system of Prithvi, the phased array radars and capability to handle multiple targets through Trishul, the ram-rocket propulsion motor in Akash and the re-entry technology through Agni, were indeed aimed to achieve a genuine self-reliance in missile technology.

Kalam took his own good time to identify the right leaders to handle the five missile projects. There was no dearth of talent and experience in the good mix of services officers with operational experience, hard-core technology experts and young blood with grit and determination. Kalam was looking for men who could clearly visualize the goal of developing a missile system, seeing it through field trials and taking it right up to the stage of production. Dr Kalam was conscious that a wrong choice of leader would undo the whole achievement of getting the programme sanctioned. He was looking for not only five project directors but a leadership brigade that would sustain missile development through the next twenty-five years. He felt that he should be circumspect in this new situation:

> Many of my senior colleagues – naming them would be unfair, because it could be only my imagination – tried to befriend me during this period. I respected their concern for a lonely man, but avoided any close contact. Through loyalty to a friend, one can be easily led into doing something that is not in the best interests of the organization.[3]

Dr Kalam by now had developed astute insights into the working styles of people, but he wanted to follow a scientific approach. He asked Col R. Swaminathan to study the managerial grid model, a style of leadership model developed by Robert R. Blake and Jane Mouton doing the rounds in those days. Col Swaminathan came up with a report defining the basic aspect of a person's working style as to how he plans and organizes tasks. At one extreme was the cautious planner, who would carefully spell out each step before making any move. With a sharp eye for what could possibly go wrong, he would try to cover all contingencies. At the end of the spectrum was a fast-tracker, who would weave and dodge without a plan. Inspired by ideas, he would always be ready for action.

Another aspect of a person's style Swaminathan brought out in his report was control – the energy and attention devoted to ensuring that things happened in certain ways. At one extreme was the tight controller, a strict administrator with frequent checkpoints. Rules and policies were to be followed with religious fervour. At the opposite end were those who move with freedom and flexibility. They had little patience for bureaucracy. They delegated easily and gave their subordinates wide latitude for movement.

Dr Kalam wanted his leaders to be men who had the capability to grow with possibilities, with the patience to explore all possible options and with the wisdom to apply old principles to new situations; people with the skill to negotiate their way forward. He wanted his men to be accommodating – to be willing to share their power with others and work in teams, delegating good jobs, assimilating fresh opinions, respecting intelligent people and listening to wise counsel. They would have to be able to resolve conflict amicably and take responsibility for slip-ups. Above all, his men must be able to take failure in their stride and share both their successes and failures. Kalam told Swaminathan that he wanted leaders who would tread the middle path: those who could control without stifling dissent or being rigid and those who could make swift progress without breaking rules. 'Find me people who neither indulge in excess nor suffer with deficiency,' he told Col Swaminathan.

2.4

Strength Respects Strength

If your actions inspire others to dream more, learn more, do more and become more, you are a leader.

– John Quincy Adams
The sixth president of the United States

Dr Kalam had now assumed the role of Missile Man of India. The political and bureaucratic establishment was easily convinced that missiles could perform certain military and strategic roles better than other types of weapons. This was due in no small part to Dr Kalam, who successfully conveyed their virtues: Ballistic missiles can be launched in poor weather or at night. They travel at supersonic speeds and can thus reach strategic targets – enemy installations that are far from the missile's point of deployment – in a very short time. They can also be directed at enemy ground forces, aircraft or naval targets. And they are more difficult to detect and intercept than aircraft, not to mention their being more economical. Moreover, they can act as a serious deterrent to belligerent states by virtue of their ability to carry warheads.

Dr Kalam selected Col V.J. Sundaram to lead the Prithvi surface-to-surface missile project. Col Sundaram had belonged to the Indian Army Corps of Electronics and Mechanical Engineers (EME) and held a master's in aeronautical engineering. DRDL had produced several components for the Devil missile, including a solid rocket booster with high-strength steel casings and a specific impulse of 200 seconds, and a second-stage three-tonne liquid-propellant engine, fuelled by a combination of xylidiene and tri-ethylamine, oxidized by inhibited red-fuming nitric acid and di-nitrogen tetroxide. Could it be used for powering a ballistic missile that could reach its target 150 to 250 kilometres away within five to ten minutes, fitted with a warhead weighing somewhere in the order of 500 to 1000 kilograms?

The work on the Devil missile was revived to test a strap down inertial navigation system (SDINS), supported by a computer that would implement control, guidance and navigation. Its computer was built in the Special Purpose Computer Division (SPCD) and was powered by an off-the-shelf LSI-V03 (PDP, programmed data processor, equivalent) processor module. Other interfaces for gyros, accelerometers, telemetry, launch control, etc., were developed in various in-house PCB (Printed Circuit Board) facilities. Dr Kalam was determined to make use of whatever components that were available; yet the team would have to go beyond the evolutionary ancestry of surface-to-surface V-2 and Scud missiles. These missiles could never deliver a warhead within a CEP (circular error probable) measured even in kilometres – the CEP being the radius of a circle, whose boundary is expected to encompass the landing points of 50 per cent of the missiles fired. Kalam was talking about a CEP of less than 100 metres.

The Trishul was conceived as a quick-reaction surface-to-air missile that could also be used as an anti-sea skimmer from a ship against low-flying attacking missiles. To lead Trishul's development, Dr Kalam was seeking a man who not only had a sound knowledge of electronics and missile warfare, but who could also communicate technical complexities to his team in order to promote understanding and earn his team's support. He found Commodore S.R. Mohan – an electronics engineer, who came to DRDL from the Indian Navy – the most suitable candidate to lead the project.

Commodore Mohan would oversee the development of the missile's intended scheme of dual command guidance: the missile would initially rely on ka-band gathering and then transfer to the tracking radar for its guidance. The missile would have electronic counter-countermeasures against all known aircraft jammers. As the missile would employ a dual-thrust propulsion stage using high-energy solid propellant, propulsion expert A.K. Kapoor was made Commodore Mohan's deputy. Trishul had to be capable of a rapid reaction time, high-frequency operation, high manoeuvrability, high lethal capability and multiple roles for the three services.

For Agni, Dr Kalam wanted an old-timer who would share deep insights into developing strategic systems. His two juniors at Madras Institute of Technology, K. Rama Rao and R.N. Agarwal, were available, and he decided to give Agarwal the command. Agarwal had been head of the aeronautical test facility and would therefore best understand the design needs of the re-entry payload. Dr Kalam appointed Rama Rao as chief of composites. Rama Rao's team would focus on the design of the re-entry stage module, wherein the fiercely guarded carbon-carbon composite technology would be utilized.

Dr Kalam took some time to ponder the management needs of Akash, which involved ramjet propulsion technology, and Nag, the guidance of which was based on an imaging infrared (IIR) passive-seeker technology to ensure high-hit accuracy in both top- and front-attack modes. These were futuristic undertakings, and he selected the relatively youthful pair Prahalada and N.R. Iyer to head the Akash and Nag projects respectively.

Dr Kalam emphasized to all the men he selected that to be effective project leaders, they must be empathetic to a diverse array of needs. He always said that there are two facets of leadership in an organization in which a leader must be especially adept. One is in comprehending the broad needs of the overall mission requirements, and the other is being aware of the needs of each department to effectively leverage their work. A project director must understand the mission requirements and the needs of each department and effectively prioritize and deliver material requirements, mostly in the form of funds.

In those days, there was no forum in DRDL where issues of general importance could be openly discussed and debated. Dr Kalam knew from his first-hand experience at SLV-3 that scientist engineers were indeed very vulnerable people. They performed their own specialized tasks for high-stakes projects – which are inevitably subject to their numerous colleagues' input and the vagaries of a myriad of factors – over which they have little control. They thus work under great anxiety and insecurity. Once they stumble – they lose confidence and focus – it becomes difficult for them to regain their footing. Dr Kalam was more than aware of the challenges they faced, and knew that their morale must be sustained within the workplace itself: 'I did not want any of my scientists to face disappointments alone. I also wanted to ensure that none of them set their goals when they were at low ebb.'[1]

Dr Kalam thus created a forum and named it the 'Science Council'. All scientists in the laboratory – juniors and seniors, veterans and freshers – would sit together once every three months and let off steam. In the very first meeting of the Science Council, a senior scientist, M.N. Rao, stood and asked Dr Kalam, 'On what basis did you select these five Pandavas?' He meant the five project directors whom Dr Kalam had personally selected.

Dr Kalam gave a very patient answer. He said that as the project director of SLV-3, he had acquired certain experiences. Based on these experiences, he recognized that the directors of the missile projects must control the three key parameters of scope, schedule and budget, and understand the nuances of team dynamics. Dr Kalam explained that he spoke to at least fifty people in the course of his deliberations. Some said that they were fanatical about driving productivity and meeting schedule commitments. Others said they had the ability to spot red flags; they were zealous communicators, and were well respected by their peers and bosses. Dr Kalam said that the five project directors he had selected had an ability to balance what needs to be done, as driven from the plan, with what should be done to meet the mission's requirements – even if this is counter-intuitive and not exactly in accordance with the project's road map. These project managers would not only manage – they would lead.

A young scientist wanted to know how Dr Kalam would stop these projects going the way of the Devil missile project. Dr Kalam explained to him, and through him to all the doubting Thomases, 'The participation of the production centres and user agencies right from the design stage has been ensured, the budget is in place, and there is no question of going back till the missile systems are successfully deployed in the battlefield.' His answer received a thunderous ovation from the audience. He had won his team's confidence. In September 1983, Defence Minister R. Venkataraman visited DRDL. There was no doubt in anyone's mind about the credibility of the IGMDP.

Dr Brahm Prakash passed away on 3 January 1984 at the age of seventy-two, in Bombay. Dr Kalam keenly felt his loss. In the memorial service organized for Dr Brahm Prakash, Dr Kalam spoke at length about his mentor teacher. Dr Kalam shared with the congregation that when Brahm Prakash returned to India in 1948, he was given a position in the then nascent Atomic Energy Commission in Bombay. Towards the end of 1950, when the Indian Institute of Science was seeking a suitable person to head the Department of Metallurgy – and the setting up of the Atomic Energy Commission's metallurgy laboratory was in its early stages – he was deemed the logical choice for the job. Dr Homi Bhabha, who was also a member of the court of the IISc, proposed that Dr Brahm Prakash would assume leadership of the Department of Metallurgy in Bangalore, on the firm understanding that he would return to Bombay as soon as the programme of work gained momentum there.

Side by side with his academic responsibilities in Bangalore, Brahm Prakash maintained a continuous link with the atomic energy programme, attending discussion meetings in Bombay and also undertaking tours abroad during the summer vacations. To maintain one of these positions was a serious endeavour for any scientist. To maintain both without sacrificing attention to the duties of either, is a herculean task; and Dr Brahm Prakash did it with aplomb. By early 1957, Dr Bhabha decided that it was time to allow Dr Brahm Prakash to return to Bombay. Dr Brahm Prakash was the first project director for the Nuclear Fuel Complex (NFC) that was set up in Hyderabad in 1971. Dr Kalam said, 'By the detailed portrait of a *sthitaprajna* given in the Bhagavadgita – an individual of steadfast mind with clarity in action, who remains unperturbed under any circumstance – Brahm Prakash was the real-life model.'

Around this time, Dr Kalam was playing a key role in developing Pinaka rockets for the artillery at the Armament Research and Development Establishment (ARDE) in Pune. These would replace the Russian BM-21 'Grad' Launchers the Indian Army was operating. The Pinaka rockets would generally be deployed in a battery of seventy-two rockets. Aptly named after the divine bow of Lord Shiva, all the seventy-two rockets could be fired within forty-four seconds, laying waste an area of around 1 sq. km. Like his guru Brahm Prakash, Dr Kalam managed to juggle multiple workloads and work across boundaries of organizations, with relative ease. This was a skill that would serve him throughout the following decades.

Another of Dr Kalam's myriad skills that was increasingly exercised in these years was his adroit diplomacy, which he had learned from his mentor Dr Vikram Sarabhai. Nevertheless, international politics could at times stymie even Dr Kalam's best efforts. In 1985, he visited the United States as part of a team to buy a supercomputer from Cray Inc., in Seattle, US, that was ostensibly required for weather forecasting. Dr Kalam needed it for computational fluid dynamics analysis of the Agni re-entry payload. India did not have a hypersonic wind tunnel, and the only way to simulate its re-entry stage was to model it and test it using computation. Only the United States and Japan had the supercomputing technology. The Americans snubbed Dr Kalam's delegation, bluntly conveying their decision not to sell the machine to India.

Indian scientists were again compelled to follow a swadeshi approach to technological development; but it would be for the greater good. Indian computer experts rose to the challenge of creating an indigenous supercomputer of the Cray computer's capability, then in the gigaflops range. The Centre for Development of Advanced Computing (C-DAC) was created in Pune in 1988, as India's national initiative in supercomputing, under the leadership of Dr Vijay Bhatkar. *The Wall Street Journal* took notice of the development with a front-page headline: 'Angry India Does IT' when the C-DAC delivered the supercomputer PARAM, three years later.[2] Like many properly focused indigenous endeavours, this swadeshi computing effort was the seed of a new field of opportunity for the nation, which would continue to be harvested well into the new century.

While Dr Kalam valued the friendship of many people from other countries, and would remain throughout his life relaxed with people of any race or creed, he was uncomfortable with the geopolitical approach of the Western world. He saw the West as the geopolitical aggressor. In Dr Kalam's view, which he shared with me in various discussions on the topic, the age of blocs came to an end in 1991 with the collapse of the USSR. From this time, the group of seven or eight industrialized Western nations became the hub of the world, transforming all of Africa, Asia and Latin America into markets. How the entire humanity can be made to follow only one path, one opinion and one ideal, he wondered.

India needed to remain cognizant not merely of geopolitical developments in the West, but also significant events close to its own borders. China conducted its first nuclear test on 16 October 1964, almost a decade ahead of India, and its missile programme was centred on how to carry the bomb. China's first missile was Dongfeng (DF, 'East Wind' in Chinese). The DF1 was developed with active participation by the Russians. The liquid-propelled, 590-km-range R-2 missile was the starting point. As this missile would not even reach American military bases in Japan from the Chinese mainland, China upgraded it to DF2 with a range of 1,200 km. The DF-2 missile was deployed along the Sino–North Korean border, in striking range of the whole *Japanese archipelago*. Over several years, China developed the DF-3 to be capable of reaching American bases in the Philippines, the DF-4 to reach the US territory of Guam Island in the western Pacific and the DF-5 for its capability of striking continental United States in 1981 – all using liquid propellant.

Large liquid-propellant missiles were intrinsically long and had thin skins. They could not be filled with propellants in a horizontal position without causing serious body damage. An unfuelled missile would first be erected on the launching pad and receive preliminary targeting alignment and on-board equipment checks. It would then be filled with oxidizer and fuel – operations which must be performed separately, because combined, oxidizer and fuel would spontaneously ignite. The missile, somewhat deformed by the loaded propellants, would then undergo final alignment and checks, and data corresponding to the assigned range would be fed into the missile's instruments.

All these preparations would consume, on average, no less than four hours. This made them vulnerable to detection by reconnaissance satellites (orbiting the earth every ninety minutes) and subsequent preventive strikes. The Chinese thus developed silos and rail-race systems until they succeeded in their first solid-propellant, 1,700-km-range rocket JL-1 in 1982. Thereafter, China regularly sold missile technology to Pakistan, Iran, Syria, Iraq, Libya, Saudi Arabia and North Korea.

In April 1987, Canada, France, Germany, Italy, Japan, Great Britain and the United States jointed hands and created the Missile Technology Control Regime (MTCR), in order to curb the spread of unmanned delivery systems for nuclear weapons. The MTCR specifically targeted delivery systems that could carry a minimum payload of 500 kg a minimum of 300 km. The MTCR was not a treaty, but a voluntary understanding among member countries sharing a common interest in controlling missile proliferation. The partner countries committed to applying an export embargo pertaining to a common list of controlled items. This list included virtually all key equipment and technology needed for missile development, production and operation.

In June 1987, the visionary behind the IGMDP, R. Venkataraman, was elected the eighth president of India. By this time, work on Prithvi was nearing completion. The MTCR embargo could have given rise to insurmountable obstacles, had it not been for Dr Kalam's astuteness and championing of indigenous technological production. He guided the development of clustered liquid-propellant rocket engines with programmable total impulse, with the foresight of attaining different payload-range combinations. With the help of the ordnance factory at Khadaki (near Pune), Dr Kalam had also completely eliminated the import of the propellant for Prithvi engines.

Dr Kalam took a keen interest in modernizing and expanding

the ordnance factories organization and secured massive funding for development of propellants and high-energy materials for the warheads. The ordnance factories had been the largest and oldest departmentally run defence production enterprise in India. The history of the organization dated back to British rule in India when the first factory, the Gun Carriage Agency, was established in 1801 at Cossipore in Calcutta. Over the years, the number of factories had grown, with a rapid expansion taking place post-1962. The war with China, and the subsequent desire for self-reliance in defence production, led to the establishment of sixteen new factories, which saw a surge of expansion compared to the five that were set up between 1949 and 1962.

The Prithvi was successfully flight-tested on 25 February 1988 at SHAR. It was a watershed event in India's military development, as this test established India's capability to develop the basic modules for future guided missiles. The Prithvi had the provision for modification from a long-range surface missile to an air missile; it could also be deployed from a ship. A CEP of less than 100 metres was achieved. The successful launch sent political shock waves across the region, particularly in unfriendly neighbouring countries.

The response of the Western bloc was initially one of surprise – and then of indignation. The MTCR, with the United States at its head, imposed a coordinated technological boycott on India. The supply to India of computer processor chips, radio-frequency devices, electro-hydraulic components, maraging steel, magnesium alloy, gyroscopes, accelerometers, carbon fibre, glass fibre – almost any product or material that could have an application in India's missile programme – was banned. President Venkataraman – the former defence minister – spoke to Dr Kalam over the telephone and expressed his satisfaction for having handed him the reins of the missile programme. He told him not to be deterred by the technology sanctions, reminding him of the aphorism, 'When the going gets tough, the toughs get going.'

Inspired by the words of the president, Dr Kalam collaborated with public and private sector industries and academic institutions, in a bid to assert the complete independence and self-reliance of India's missile technology. The nation's missile programme must continue, despite the best efforts of foreign powers to scuttle it. Led by Dr Kalam, the truly swadeshi partnerships developed maraging steel for rocket motors, carbon-carbon composites and resins for the re-entry vehicle of the Agni missiles, magnesium alloy, phase shifters for passive electronically scanned array radar, winding machines and so forth. The Mishra Dhatu Nigam Limited (MIDHANI), the Defence Metallurgical Research Laboratory (DMRL), and private industries together developed a crucial magnesium alloy, which was denied to India by Germany. The international campaign to thwart India's missile programme had merely slowed its progress.

On New Year's Day 1989, Dr Kalam declared at the Science Council meeting, 'As a country located in one of the world's most unstable regions, India can hardly afford to be dependent on imported weaponry if it wants to be taken seriously in the emerging world order.'

2.5

Crystal Cathedral

> Never cut a tree down in the wintertime. Never make a negative decision in the low time. Never make your most important decisions when you are in your worst moods. Wait. Be patient. The storm will pass. The spring will come.
>
> – Robert H. Schuller
> Christian evangelist and author

The DRDO had acquired approximately 2,100 acres of land in the 1970s for the purpose of developing a range for anti-tank missile testing. The land was in the Pahadi Shareef area near Hyderabad, famous for the dargah of Hazrat Syedna Baba Sharfuddin of the Chisti lineage of saints. But for a dilapidated building in that area called Imarat, the entire landscape is dominated by ancient rock formations, which are around 2,500 million years old and considered amongst the oldest and hardest rocks in the world. Kalam later recalled his impressions of the place:

> The terrain was barren – there were hardly any trees – and dotted with large boulders typical of the Deccan plateau. I felt as if there was some tremendous energy trapped in these stones. I decided to establish a model high-technology research centre here ... this became my mission.[1]

Dr Kalam was mindful that his primary challenge in the IGMDP was the development of requisite basic technologies. Missile development without an adequate technological foundation would be doomed to failure. It was indeed imperative that front-line research was conducted in areas such as special materials, embedded electronics and software. These would comprise the bedrock upon which an ambitious missile programme could be successfully constructed. Moreover, facilities for testing and evaluating missile systems would be required. Dr Kalam invited Prime Minister Rajiv Gandhi to lay the foundation stone for the new facility in August 1985. It was named Research Centre Imarat (RCI).

The RCI would test and evaluate missile components, modules, sub-assemblies, major sub-assemblies and completely integrated missiles in order to weed out design, fabrication and integration deficiencies. For these purposes, the centre would have an inertial instrumentation laboratory, full-scale environmental and electronic warfare test facilities, a composites production centre, a high enthalpy facility and a state-of-the-art missile integration and checkout centre. This was going to be a Herculean task. Dr Kalam invited M.V. Suryakantha Rao to lead this effort, with a younger Krishna Mohan to assist him.

In accordance with the established procedure, Dr Kalam approached the Military Engineering Services (MES) to perform the construction work for the RCI. The MES informed him that they would require five years to complete the necessary building infrastructure. Dr Kalam immediately took the matter to the highest levels in the defence ministry, knowing that years of delay would hamper the RCI's progress beyond redemption. He secured a landmark decision to give the contract for the works to MECON Limited, a public sector company under the Ministry of Steel, Government of India. MECON, based at Ranchi, was India's front-line engineering, consultancy and contracting organization. Dr Kalam sought their full range of services, from concept to commissioning, including turnkey execution.

As the next logical step, Dr Kalam looked for a suitable site for missile flight trials. The search concluded near Balasore, a town in northern Orissa. Here, Proof and Experimental Establishment

(PXE), Chandipur, had been set up in 1895, and it was decided to create the new test range around its campus. The PXE range had unique characteristics. The water receded at low tide to a distance of about 3 km from the shore, which provided a temporary stretch of hard seabed suitable for various firing operations. The seawater and the underlying seabed would provide a soft cushion for the fired projectiles and make the launch vehicle's recovery easy, both of which were required to examine the missiles' strength of design. At low tide, the seabed would become sufficiently hard to allow movement of loaded vehicles, and even tanks, during range operations. Dr Kalam felt that the site fitted the requirements of a proof range admirably.

Dr Kalam visited the site for a personal inspection. He stood at the seashore. The tide had receded. He saw many children, barefoot and running on the hard, warm sand, searching for brass parts of the shells that had been fired by PXE the previous day. His childhood years flooded his mind, when he would go door to door collecting tamarind seeds and delivering newspapers. He reflected that almost half of the world's population lives in rural regions – and mostly in a state of poverty. Inequalities in human development have been one of the primary reasons for unrest and, in some parts of the world, even violence. But then poverty is not only being hungry, naked and homeless. The poverty of being unwanted, unloved and uncared for is the greatest poverty – and is even crueller. He resolved in his heart that someday he would work for making children cared for.

It was not easy to travel to Balasore. Dr Kalam would reach Calcutta by air and from there travel by car to the town. The parlous condition of the road would make the 250-km journey an odyssey of eight bone-jarring hours, or even more at times. Once, there was complete road block near Kharagpur, and Dr Kalam had to take a diversion into the forest area at night. He was dozing with his eyes half closed, somewhere between Bhagabanpur and Patashpur, when the driver braked suddenly. Dr Kalam immediately awoke, startled. A barasingha (swamp deer) was standing in the middle of the road, unmoving, its fiery red-orange eyes staring at the car through the darkness. Its unbroken gaze, which seemed to aim right through to him in the car, haunted Dr Kalam for the rest of his visit.

Prime Minister Indira Gandhi visited DRDL on 19 July 1984. Dr Kalam had met the prime minster on several prior occasions, but this time he would be receiving her on behalf of his laboratory. Dr Kalam noticed the friendship between Dr Sarabhai and Prime Minister Nehru, and how it helped Dr Sarabhai progress with his vision for aerospace in India. The prime minister asked pointed questions. She appeared determined to see more practical results from the state's investment; she obviously viewed science as much more than a lofty pastime of academics and schoolchildren. But she was also quite prepared to redesign institutions to achieve more synergy between science and technology, and took a direct interest in key scientific appointments.

What Dr Kalam realized was that although she retained her father's respect for science and scientists, she had also learned much after his death and now linked 'science' more strongly to 'technology'. She congratulated Dr Kalam for taking a decision to not import high-tech facilities and taking the hard but ultimately more rewarding route of achieving his goals with Indian industry and people. Dr Kalam told her, 'Madam, even we want to purchase materials from overseas; but no one will sell them to us. The Western countries are jealously guarding their technology.' Prime Minister Indira Gandhi told Kalam, 'Put them in their place.'

Dr Kalam's flair for bringing people from different walks of life together and inspiring them for a common purpose, would again come into play. Dr V.S. Arunachalam organized a conference on IGMDP on 27 September 1984. Dr Kalam invited around 100 academicians and industry captains and solicited their partnership in the missile development programme. Dr Kalam said,

> Technology development, its further adaptation and application has never been a very straightforward process. A successful technological innovation requires a strong interactive mechanism, complete with the feedback loop for various stakeholders, for example – industry, extraneous knowledge sources, inspection and certification agencies

> and most importantly, the users or the market. However, the problems become acute in a rapidly changing technological and economic environment. The Space and Atomic Energy programme has elevated India to a stage where the country has demonstrated some remarkable strengths in modern technologies for achieving development goals. There exists a chain of national laboratories, specialized research and development agencies, Indian Institutes of Technology (IITs), universities and other academic institutions of higher learning, which are capable of providing world-class expertise, technically trained manpower and technological support to the industry. Let us join our hands in developing world class missiles together.

Until this time, there had been a great chasm between government laboratories and academicians. On one side was the status consciousness of the government scientists turned officials, and as a counterforce there was the intellectual arrogance of the academicians. On that day, Dr Kalam indeed bridged that divide, and in the process won many hearts.

By the summer of 1985, all the groundwork had been completed for building RCI. Prime Minister Rajiv Gandhi laid the foundation stone of the RCI on 3 August 1985. The prime minister told the DRDL family that he understood the hardships faced by Indian scientists and expressed his gratitude towards those who persevered, staying in their own country to work. He said that nobody could concentrate on the demands of scientific work, unless he is free from the trivialities of daily life. Further, he promised his wholehearted support to make RCI a truly world-class centre in terms of working environment and amenities. Kalam noted some differences between the new prime minister and his mother:

> There was a childlike curiosity in him (Rajiv Gandhi) ... The grit and determination displayed by his mother was also present in him, although with a small difference. Madam Gandhi was a taskmaster, whereas Prime Minister Rajiv Gandhi used his charisma.[2]

MECON acquitted themselves well in their construction of the magnificent RCI campus, finishing the work without any time delay or financial overruns. President R. Venkataraman inaugurated the laboratory on 27 August 1988. It was indeed the vision to develop technologies and systems rather than particular missiles that had made the organization's accomplishments possible. President Venkataraman held Dr Kalam's hand for a long time and told him that he was indeed proud of his achievements. He advised Dr Kalam to focus on small and medium enterprises and encourage them to carry out innovations at the developmental level.

Invited by the US Air Force, Dr Kalam visited the United States in September 1988 with Dr Arunachalam, Dr Roddam Narasimha of National Laboratory and K.K. Ganapathy of HAL. The Aeronautical Development Agency (ADA) was established to manage the LCA (Light Combat Aircraft) programme, and it was seeking the supply of the General Electric F-404 engines for the future Light Combat Aircraft project of India. The four veteran scientist engineers used the long-haul flight to the USA to reflect on the self-reliance of Indian strategic sectors. While the better part of the forces' low-technology military equipment was provided by the ordnance factories, India was still critically dependent on Western sources to meet its growing requirement for high-technology armaments. Only concerted efforts – partnerships between government, industry and educational sectors – could hope to address this glaring strategic vulnerability.

After finishing work at the Pentagon in Washington DC, the team flew to San Francisco on their way to Los Angeles for a meeting with Northrop Corporation, the United States' leading aircraft manufacturer. Dr Kalam utilized this opportunity to visit Crystal Cathedral, built by his favourite author, Robert Schuller. Crystal Cathedral is a stunning modern church of titanic proportions, constructed in 1980 in Orange County, Los Angeles. Dr Kalam saw the Research Centre Imarat as his own Crystal Cathedral, and he prayed to God in gratitude for its completion.

Dr Kalam held the religious places of all faiths in the highest esteem. He realized early in his life that visiting places of spiritual importance brings people in contact with others following a spiritual path, and this creates a sort of resonance. Dr Kalam told me once that saints and sages can indeed help us by giving their association and sharing their spiritual knowledge and realizations. Thus, it is of prime importance to align our lives with their revelations, so that we can also make spiritual progress.

By this time, Dr Kalam had started spending most of his time at RCI. A villa was constructed for him in the guest house complex. Dr Kalam had a childlike fascination with the full moon. He used to tell me that the full moon was a time when mysterious things happen and wishes come true. There was a large tree in the compound, and Dr Kalam loved to sit under the tree alone late on full moon nights. On one such moonlit night, perhaps Dr Kalam visualized RCI as a world-class avionics centre.

Dr Kalam ensured that, like the Crystal Cathedral, everything about the RCI was outsized: its campus, its deer population, the density of its trees, the buildings that house its laboratories and its arched main entrance. He was convinced that the proportions of the campus would inspire expansive dreams for its scientists, to lead the country forward into the new millennium.

And he knew that a scientist, of all people, must have a dream or vision. Dr Kalam was not sure when he conceived his idea of the re-entry test vehicle REX, exactly how it would be achieved. But like any good scientist, he was well versed in the physics of re-entry and knew the principles that would allow a missile re-entering the atmosphere to endure its searing trajectory.

Dr Kalam learned, at the Goddard Centre in 1963, the concept of the ablative heat shield described first in 1920 by Robert Goddard, based on his study of meteors. Goddard understood that although meteors entering the atmosphere at the 'Karman Line' (around 100 km above sea level) usually meet a fiery end and disintegrate, this is not due only to the heat factor. While a meteor would enter the atmosphere at a typical speed as high as 30 miles per second, and massive heat of friction is thus generated, the interior of the meteor would remain cold. The erosion and destruction of the meteor is due largely to chipping and cracking of the suddenly heated surface. The ramifications of Goddard's discovery were enormous for aerospace development.

The Agni missile payload would be delivered at hypersonic speed, but considerably slower than a falling meteor. This nevertheless called for the design and development of a re-entry vehicle structure that could cope with the scorching heat of the atmospheric drag and aerodynamic heating of atmospheric re-entry. In this way, the missile would not meet the fate of the regular meteor as it falls towards earth. Ablative thermal protection systems were thus required for the re-entry vehicles, wherein thermal energy would be expended by way of sacrificing the material. It would protect the payload by keeping the inside temperature below a limit of 40° Celsius, when the temperature of the outside skin would be greater than 2,500°C. An inertial navigation system with the on-board computer could then guide the payload to the target location.

Dr Kalam needed a team to develop the carbon-carbon composite material for the nose and carbon-phenolic material for the after body. Dr Kalam also needed an especially skilled team for the development of finite-element-based software to model the surface recession (ablation) with time. Two models were required to study the chemical and mechanical aspects of ablation. First, for the material removal by oxidation of carbon at high temperatures (chemical ablation) using analytical expressions and second, erosion of carbon-phenolic layered material by aerodynamic surface shear (mechanical ablation). With all the relevant testing, a consortium of four DRDO and the CSIR laboratories accomplished the task of building the Agni missile re-entry structure, in the short span of eighteen months.

Another challenge involved in the Agni payload design related to the tremendous speed with which it would re-enter the atmosphere. This was estimated at twelve times the speed of sound. At this speed, there was no knowing how to keep the vehicle under control. And to carry out a test to ascertain its behaviour, there was no wind tunnel capable of generating speeds of that order. Dr Kalam again found himself having to circumvent the limitations of indigenous technology and scientific infrastructure:

> If we sought American help, we would have been seen as aspiring to something they considered their exclusive privilege. Even if they consented to cooperate, they would be certain to quote a price for their wind tunnel test greater than our entire project cost.[3]

He found the solution with Prof. S.M. Deshpande at the IISc. With four young scientists working in the field of computational fluid dynamics, Prof. S.M. Deshpande developed a unique software that simulated hypersonic conditions, not available anywhere in the world. This creative approach to negotiating the countless barriers imposed by the Western bloc was the hallmark of the Agni missile project's success, and the ingenious efforts of Dr Kalam and his team effectively nullified the embargo of the Missile Technology Control Regime. While the Western world was guarding every facet of its technology, Dr Kalam was creating his own technology to achieve India's national defence imperatives.

Dr Kalam never allowed problems to defeat him. He faced problems head-on and defeated them with his innovative methods – and by seeking appropriate help from appropriate people. As a manager, Dr Kalam explored the potential of the non-cognitive factors – attributes, dispositions, social skills, attitudes, and intrapersonal resources – of the people around him. He was particularly interested in employing those factors that high-achieving individuals draw upon to accomplish success. Within his discipline, Dr Kalam presented a role model to hundreds of scientists of his time in grit, tenacity and perseverance.

2.6

Chariot of Fire

The most powerful weapon on earth is the human soul on fire.
– Ferdinand Foch
Supreme commander of the Allied forces in World War I

The first flight trial of the Agni missile was scheduled for 20 April 1989, at Chandipur. It would be an unprecedented exercise. A missile launch involves a wide array of safety hazards, far greater than those of space launch vehicles. This calls for the location of a launch site over a remote area of land or water. The Bay of Bengal provides an ideal stretch of sea over which missiles can be safely fired; it is, in a sense, a protected sea. On the western side, it can be monitored from peninsular India and in the east, there is the Andaman and Nicobar Islands chain. This means that telemetry stations can easily be set up to cover most of the bay area.

All preparatory activities for the launch went as scheduled. The people living in nearby villages were moved away at the time of the launch, which attracted media attention and led to much controversy. When the launch day arrived, though, the whole nation was watching the DRDO. Foreign pressure had been exerted through diplomatic channels not to go ahead with the flight trial. But the Government of India took a firm stand for its national defence prerogatives. Defence Minister K.C. Pant stationed himself at Balasore for the duration of the launch.

At T-14 seconds, the computer signalled 'hold', indicating that one of the instruments was functioning erratically. It was promptly rectified. Now, the down-range station asked for a 'hold'. The Car Nicobar tracking station, which was networked with other tracking stations and naval ships via satellite to chart Agni's flight path, reported a problem. In another few seconds, multiple 'holds' were necessitated. This resulted in an unintended internal power consumption, and the launch had to be aborted. The missile had to be opened up to replace on-board batteries. The anticlimax caused widespread disappointment. Defence Minister Pant left for Delhi with a promise to return soon. Dr Kalam had to lift his team out of their despondency, and he did so with characteristic realism: 'I lost my launch vehicle in the sea and had to rebuild the whole thing. Your missile is in front of you. In fact, you have lost nothing but a few weeks of rework.[1]

The media predictably went up in arms, circulating various interpretations of the postponement of the flight to suit the fancy of a wide spectrum of readership. At any rate, the missile was made ready for the launch on 1 May 1989. The defence minister arrived as per his promise. But again at T-10 seconds a 'hold' appeared, and one control component was found malfunctioning. A control valve had burst, and nitrogen gas had leaked in one of the motors. The launch was aborted once again. Such things are very common in rocketry – and happen quite often elsewhere. But the expectant nation was in no mood to appreciate the difficulties of test missile deployment.

Dr Kalam did not like a cartoon published in *The Hindu*, his favourite newspaper, which showed a villager counting some currency notes and commenting to another, 'Yes, it's the compensation for moving away from my hut near the test site – a few more postponements and I can build a house of my own.' 'People just do not understand the complexities involved in our work,' Dr Kalam explained. Nonetheless, the humour of Amul's cartoon recommending their butter as a propellant and the missile being called IDBM for Intermittently Delayed Ballistic Missile, was well received.

In an exemplary show of wholesome leadership, an undistracted and resolute Dr Kalam remained with his team, monitoring all its activity. Though a change in weather conditions at Chandipur was predicted, Dr Kalam prepared for a third attempt to launch before the onset of the monsoon season. The launch was slated for 22 May 1989. Defence Minister K.C. Pant arrived on the day prior to the launch. It was a full moon night. He invited Dr Kalam and General K.N. Singh for a walk after their dinner. The waves of the Bay of Bengal were crashing and roaring at high tide. Mr Pant asked Dr Kalam, 'What would you like me to do to celebrate the success tomorrow? What gift would you like for yourself?' Dr Kalam recalled his reaction to the defence minister's offer:'What did I want? What was it that I did not have? What could make me happier? And then I found an answer. We need 100,000 saplings to plant at RCI.'[2]

The defence minister's face lit up with a friendly glow. 'You have brought the blessings of mother earth, Kalam. We will succeed tomorrow,' he said. Finally, on 22 May 1989 at exactly 7.17 a.m., the Agni missile blossomed into a chariot of fire that propelled India into an exclusive club dominated by the world's technological and military giants. The 300-odd scientists at the control centre watching the pencil-thin missile arc across the sky on television monitors thumped each other on the back. Dr Kalam was bodily lifted on the shoulders of the jubilant scientists.

Meanwhile, Agni was igniting nervous reactions in many of the world's capitals, stretching from Washington to Beijing. Only five countries – the US, the Soviet Union, France, China and Israel – had developed IRBM (missiles with a range of 500 kilometres to 5,500 kilometres) technology. For India, Agni represented a quantum leap in strategic capability. At 7.20 a.m., three minutes after Agni blasted off, Defence Minister K.C. Pant picked up the hotline that had been specially set up between the Chandipur Control Centre and the prime minister's office on Race Course Road and said just one word to the prime minister: 'Congratulations.' Rajiv Gandhi immediately understood what Pant meant. On the previous two occasions that Pant had called on the hotline, he was the bearer of bad news. This time, the prime minister was delighted. He stayed on the line, asking a number of technical questions, which showed how keenly he had followed the project. He had a very deep understanding of the technology.

The prime minister's subsequent speech in parliament later that day was cautious, in that it did not trumpet Agni's strategic importance. But Rajiv added a line: 'We must remember that technological backwardness also leads to subjugation.' While he stressed that Agni was only a 'technology demonstration' and 'not a weapon system', no one could be in any doubt that Agni had broadened India's strategic defence options more than at any time since the 1974 Pokharan nuclear test. Dr Kalam declared, 'The launch is a boost to the confidence of Indian scientists and is a symbol of their cooperation, wherever they are.' Pant aptly pointed out, 'The fact that twice the mission was aborted seconds before the launch only proved that our testing and tracking systems were perfect. The two aborted launches were, in that sense, a tribute to our technology.'

Despite the triumph of the Agni launch, the defence establishment was well aware of rival nations' progress in missile capability. While the Agni missile had been under development, Pakistan too had made advances. It had tested two surface-to-surface missiles, Hatf-1 and Hatf-2, built with the help of China. Pakistan claimed that Hatf-1 had a range of 80 km and its successor, a range of 300 km. This immediately spurred India into the full-scale development of Agni and its four smaller sisters. Once the services decided on their precise role and deployment – and the government gave the go-ahead – the missiles would be put into production and be ready for operational use within five years.

In terms of cost-effectiveness, it made perfect sense for New Delhi to give the green light for production. Agni could deliver – without any chance of being countered – a payload equivalent to four deep-penetration Jaguars with considerable accuracy, but with no danger to pilots or aircraft. Agni was developed at a meagre budget of three million dollars; and it had established India in the league of ballistic missiles nations.

After the rigmarole and unpleasantness of having to relocate people every time a launch was planned – and to avoid the media attention it attracted – Dr Kalam proposed to move the launch site to Wheeler Island, a land mass of about 2 sq. km in area, approximately

20 km off Chandipur coast. But for that, the Government of Orissa would first have to hand the island over to the DRDO. Recollecting how Dr Vikram Sarabhai secured the church grounds at Thumba to set up TERLS, Dr Kalam sought an appointment with the chief minister of Orissa, Biju Patnaik.

Biju Patnaik was a tall man with a regal personality. Dr Kalam had heard accounts of his daredevil piloting acts. On 24 July 1947, he had flown a Dakota aircraft into Java, defying the Dutch siege and flying Indonesian Prime Minister Sultan Sjahrir to Singapore. This act had enabled newly independent Indonesia's participation in the first Inter-Asia Conference in New Delhi. In another heroic act, he had piloted the first plane that left Palam Airport at Delhi at dawn on 27 October 1947. He landed at Srinagar Airport, taking soldiers of 1 Sikh Regiment to save Kashmir.

Biju Patnaik gave Dr Kalam a warm hug. He said, 'Kalam, you are a good person. I have been following your work since Sarabhai's days. Whatever you ask, I will give. Your mission – the missile programme – is very important to the country. Anything needed from Orissa will be yours ... give me a promise (that you will make an ICBM). The day India makes its own ICBM, I shall be stronger as an Indian.'[3]

Wheeler Island later became the missile test facility for most Indian missiles, but Biju Patnaik's promise could not be fulfilled before his death on 17 April 1997.

The successful Agni missile test raised international hackles. Perhaps unsurprisingly, India's pronouncement that the Agni was a 'technology demonstrator project' to establish re-entry vehicle technologies did little to assuage its controversy. India had used a SLV-3 booster motor, a component of its civilian space research programme, for what were transparently military purposes. As with the Prithvi, the United States had opposed the programme as another potential proliferation affront to the MTCR. What seemed to have eluded Western critics, though, was the laudable self-reliance India had achieved in missile technology. The SLV-3 booster motor was a bona fide Indian effort. No external support was ever solicited or received for its development. Dr Kalam said, 'The point is not who will allow India hereafter from asserting our role in the world, the point is who will stop India?'

On Republic Day 1990, the Indian nation celebrated the success of its missile programme. The Padma Vibhushan, the second highest civil award of the Republic of India, was conferred on Dr Kalam and Dr Arunachalam. Two other missile scientists, R.N. Agarwal and J.C. Bhattacharya, were decorated with Padma Shri awards. It was the first time in the history of India that so many scientists working with one organization were selected for the national awards in a single year.

Dr Kalam was invited by the Madurai Kamaraj University to deliver their convocation address. Upon reaching Madurai, Dr Kalam looked for his teacher Iyadurai Solomon, who was by now a Reverend Father and eighty years old. He hired a taxi and looked for his house for more than an hour. He brought him to the convocation and made him sit in the front row. Dr P.C. Alexander, the governor of Tamil Nadu, and chancellor of the University, then invited Reverend Father Iyadurai Solomon to the dais. Dr Kalam said in his lecture, 'Every convocation day of every university is like opening the floodgates of energy which – once harnessed by institutions, organizations and industry – aids in nation building.' He later recounted his former teacher's touching words: 'After my lecture, I bowed down to my teacher. "You have not only reached my goals, Kalam! You have eclipsed them," he told me in a voice choked with emotion.'[4]

A fortnight later, on 7 February 1990, N.R. Iyer and his team celebrated the awards for the missile programme with the maiden flight of the Nag missile. They repeated the feat again the next day. The missile featured a high-strength composite airframe with foldable wings and fins, an Imaging Infra-Red (IIR) seeker with high immunity to countermeasures, an on-board real-time processor, a compact sensor package, an electric actuation system and a digital autopilot. Once launched, the Nag would not need to be guided, allowing the launcher to seek cover. The missile could use its autonomous on-board guidance to hit even a fast-moving tank.

Prahlada and his team launched Akash missile on 14 August 1990, proving the Ram-rocket technology, which had been developed for the first time in India. The medium-range surface-to-air missile (MR-SAM) with a range of 25 km and an altitude of 18 km, Akash would be completely guided by radar. It was fitted with a digital proximity fuse, to detonate its warhead after coming close to a moving target; a direct hit was not necessary. This marked the successful completion of the first phase of the IGMDP.

Towards the end of 1990, Jadavpur University conferred on Dr Kalam an honorary degree of Doctor of Science (DSc) at a special convocation, along with an honorary Doctor of Letters (DLitt) to Prof. Amartya Sen. In the same convocation, an honorary degree was conferred on Nelson Mandela in absentia. Dr Kalam became emotional upon hearing his name clubbed with this great nation builder and academician. The meeting between Dr Kalam and Dr Amartya Sen at the convocation laid a foundation for the future, when they would work together to revive the ancient Nalanda University. Dr Amartya Sen recalled his interaction with Dr Kalam later in his book *Argumentative Indian*:

> Dr Kalam, who comes from a Muslim family and is a researcher of great achievement, has a very strong commitment to Indian nationalism. He is also an extremely amiable person (as I had discovered when I had the privilege of his company at an honorary degree ceremony at Jadavpur University in Calcutta in 1990). Kalam's philanthropic concerns are very strong, and he has a record of helping in welfare-related causes.[5]

The year 1991 began on an ominous note. The Iraqi army had invaded Kuwait. On 15 January 1991, a powerful coalition led by the United States launched Operation Desert Storm, one of the most rapid and decisive military actions of all time. In just over four days of one-sided combat, the coalition would liberate Kuwait, demolish the Iraqi army and take hordes of Iraqi prisoners – all at a minimal cost in casualties. A narrative soon coalesced that focused on the role of new military technologies in the victory, particularly those that exploited the microchip and the digital revolution. Kalam was now regularly questioned about the indigenous military technology's capabilities:

> The nation was quick to draw parallels between the missiles operational in the Gulf War and our own warhead carriers. A common query I encountered was whether Prithvi was superior to a Scud, whether Akash could perform like a Patriot, and so on. Hearing a 'Yes' or a 'Why not!' from me, people's faces would light up with pride and satisfaction.[6]

After the Gulf War concluded on 28 February 1991, in the month of March, over 500 scientists of DRDL and RCI assembled to discuss issues that had emerged in this missile warfare. Dr Kalam posed a question: Was technology or weapon symmetry with other nations feasible, and if so, should it be attempted? A young scientist asked why India is apologetic about calling Agni a missile. Dr Kalam said, 'It is a missile. A rose is a rose is a rose is a rose,' eliciting thunderous applause. The meeting ended after a lively discussion spread over three hours described Desert Storm a testimony of 'revolution in military affairs' by the rapid advances in electronics, information and communication technology.

In the same year, Dr Kalam received an honorary degree of Doctor of Science from IIT, Bombay. The citation described him as 'an inspiration behind the creation of a solid technological base from which India's future aerospace programmes can be launched to meet the challenges of the twenty-first century'. The identity of Dr Kalam as India's Missile Man had been well established by this time.

In July 1992, Dr Kalam took over as the scientific adviser to the defence minister and director general of DRDO. He succeeded Dr V.S. Arunachalam. He would report to Sharad Pawar, the defence minister, in the cabinet of Prime Minister P.V. Narasimha Rao.

2.7

Prophet of Self-reliance

> There is a time in every man's education when he arrives at the conviction that envy is ignorance; that imitation is suicide; that he must take himself for better, for worse, as his portion; that though the wide universe is full of good, no kernel of nourishing corn can come to him but through his toil bestowed on that plot of ground which is given to him to till.
>
> –Ralph Waldo Emerson
> American essayist and poet

Lt Gen. Dr V.J. Sundaram took over the reins of DRDL from Dr Kalam on 10 July 1992. He was heading the Prithvi missile project with Dr V.K. Saraswat as his deputy. Before leaving for Delhi, Dr Kalam initiated the limited series production of the Prithvi and Agni missiles. As a result of the armed services' firm commitment to these two missile systems, the DRDO had been able to shift its focus from technology demonstration, to modifying missile systems to meet the field requirements of the user, in terms of deployment and operability. Programmes were initiated to develop shorter- and longer-range versions of the Agni missile, a supersonic cruise missile and a naval variant of the Prithvi.

The government of India constituted a committee under Dr Kalam, with representation from the three services and defence production units, to create a road map on how to indigenously develop critical key technology as a safeguard against denials by developed countries.

Prime Minister P.V. Narasimha Rao had dismantled the licence raj, the elaborate system of licences, regulations and accompanying red tape that were required to set up and run businesses in India between 1947 and 1990. He was convinced that technological power would raise the nation to a position of greater strength – militarily and economically.

Having developed the SLV-3 and the five missile systems, Dr Kalam had a good grasp of the strategic industrial system in India at this time. Specific to the defence sector, there were thirty-nine ordnance factories geographically spread across twenty-four different Indian locations, eight public sector defence undertakings and consistently expanding large, medium, small and micro undertakings from the private sector. The DRDO laboratories had developed a symbiotic relationship with industry and were considered part of the defence industrial base.

Two decades had elapsed since the departure of Dr Homi Bhabha and Dr Sarabhai, the two great men who had envisioned the atomic energy and space programmes. It was time that someone of that stature captured the big picture for the defence sector. Dr Kalam was now deemed to be in the same league as his former idols, and with his innate facility for visualizing many disparate parts as an integrated, functioning whole, he was eminently suited for this job. How does the nation regulate the phenomenal growth of its public sector factories and ensure that they do not turn into behemoths? What would India need from the industry in the next ten to fifteen years to convert the ongoing research and development efforts into useful and viable products? This was the brief he received from R. Venkataraman when he sanctioned the IGMDP in 1983.

Dr Kalam was fully aware that the manner in which he had overseen missile development would not work at the time of limited series production. The Indian defence industry was conditioned to undertake licensed production. The drawings done by the development agency – which left some details to the inference of the scientist/engineers building the unit – would not meet the ordnance factory's requirements. He was also aware that making a small number of systems for experiential flight trial was a radically different process to making them in a factory setting in large quantities. Standardization, process optimization, quality assurance and reliability were tough disciplines that needed to be evolved for the unprecedented systems and unfamiliar technology.

Dr Kalam had been associated with the Technology Information, Forecasting and Assessment Council (TIFAC), an autonomous organization set up in 1988 under the Department of Science and Technology. It had a mandate to prognosticate with technologies, assess the technologies' trajectories, and support technological innovation by network actions in select technological areas of national importance. Dr Kalam was clear about the path ahead. His close friend from ISRO, Y.S. Rajan – who worked as scientific secretary to Prof. Satish Dhawan, at the ISRO headquarters – was appointed as the first executive director of the new organization.

Dr Kalam studied the findings of the Subramanian Committee, which had included the formidable J.R.D. Tata as a member, published in 1963. The committee pointed out that the knowledge base in design was inadequate for the requirements in the fast-changing aerospace sector. The committee had accordingly suggested that joint design and development of aircraft engines should be pursued with reputed engine manufacturers like G.E., Rolls Royce and Snecma.

India's Missile Man would not merely be confined to aerospace technology. Ever versatile, and with a mind that inquired far beyond the bounds of his own field, Dr Kalam would be instrumental in pioneering various technologies for the less fortunate in society. During 1992, Dr Kalam became acquainted with two doctors at the Hyderabad-based Nizam's Institute of Medical Sciences (NIMS): cardiologist Dr B. Soma Raju and orthopaedic surgeon Dr B.N. Prasad. They inspired him to develop civilian spin-offs of defence technologies in order to assist poor patients with affordable solutions for their treatments. This led to the development of a Floor Reaction Orthosis (FRO) to help polio-affected children walk using advanced composite material developed by DRDL. It also gave rise to a coronary stent made from developing delta-ferrite-free austenitic steel wires with a surface free from wire-drawing-induced micro-channels.

Both Dr B. Soma Raju and Dr B.N. Prasad provided medical input to DRDO scientists in an interdisciplinary biomedical collaboration that was unprecedented in India. Dr Sivathanu Pillai later brought the FRO into production, and with the help of orthopaedic surgeon Dr Narendra Nath, had thousands of patients fitted with the device. The stent, developed by a team under Dr A. Venugopal Reddy and Koneru Bose, was patented as the 'Kalam-Raju Stent'. The introduction of the Kalam-Raju Stent caused a price crash in the market for imported stents, and even today stents are available to Indian patients at the lowest rates in the world. The Technology Institutions (TI) programme of the newly founded ICICI Bank provided one million dollars' funding to set up a Cardiovascular Technology Institute at Hyderabad. This led to the creation of the Care Hospital under Dr B. Soma Raju.[1]

When Dr Kalam was approaching the age of sixty-two years in October 1993, a momentum was created at the DRDO headquarters for his exit. He also received an offer to join Madras University as vice chancellor, perhaps orchestrated as an easy exit route. The news was made public and the newspapers carried stories of 'decks cleared for Dr Kalam's exit'. Dr Kalam's personal file was sent to Prime Minister P.V. Narasimha Rao for approval of his relieving order.

Prime Minister Rao did not sign the relieving order, but called Dr Kalam to meet him with Dr V.S. Arunachalam, who was now working as his adviser in the Prime Minister's Office (PMO). The prime minister asked why Dr Kalam wanted to go to Madras. Dr V.S. Arunachalam remained silent. When the prime minister gave Dr Kalam a querying look, Dr Kalam said that he had reached sixty-two years of age, and it was time for him to retire from government service. The prime minister retorted that he was seventy-two, and should also retire in that case. He wrote on Dr Kalam's file 'service tenure extended till further orders'.

In 1994, The Indian Science Congress invited Dr Kalam to speak at its eighty-first congress held in Jaipur. There, he gave a clarion call for developing technology spin-offs so that health-care imports could be minimized. He stressed that the pain of sickness was being compounded by high costs for treatment, and this must be alleviated by indigenous technology and biomedical ventures. 'Let my brain remove your pain,' he said. Dr Kalam announced the creation of a Society for Biomedical Technology (SBMT) as an inter-ministerial working group to bring doctors, engineers and public service administrators together for this purpose. He assigned its management to his trusted friends Y.S. Rajan, Dr B. Soma Raju and Sivathanu Pillai.

I was appointed as the programme manager to converge the medical, defence, scientific and government social streams. He presented to each member a copy of *Man the Unknown* written by the Nobel laureate and cardiothoracic surgeon Dr Alexis Carrel in 1935. He read aloud to all members a paragraph from the book in the first meeting of the SBMT governing board: 'To progress again, man must remake himself. And he cannot remake himself without suffering. For he is both the marble and the sculptor. In order to uncover his true visage he must shatter his own substance with heavy blows of his hammer.'[2]

When the stent was ready, the question of statutory approval came up. The office of the Drug Controller General of India (DCGI) said that they only regulated pharmaceuticals, and stents did not come under their purview. Indeed, even after the passage of two decades, little has changed.[3] Dr Kalam called up Dr P. Dasgupta, the DCGI, and requested him to provide a no-objection certificate after examining the documents, even if the stent did not strictly fall under his jurisdiction. Dr Dasgupta consented, facilitating the production of the stent. Dr Dasgupta visited the stent manufacturing unit at the Care Foundation, Hyderabad, and told Dr Soma Raju that he was deeply touched by the zeal shown by Dr Kalam in his push for affordable indigenous products. He said that only if those at the helm of the Indian Council of Medical Research (ICMR) and other such bodies showed care for the interests of poor patients and supported innovation, would world-class drugs and treatments become affordable.

The SBMT developed Cytoscan, a PC-based interactive image analysis system for objective assessment of cells for diagnosis/prognosis of carcinomas. Software for classifying cancerous/normal cells on a cervical smear brought together scientists at the Bangalore-based Defence Bioengineering and Electromedical Laboratory (DEBEL) and oncologists and pathologists at the NIMS, Hyderabad. The SBMT developed a social welfare project named Tulasi, after the plant revered as an elixir of life in India, to screen women in rural areas for the early detection of cervical cancer. Dr Kalam requested his friend Mata Prasad, secretary Department of Welfare, to provide financial support for conducting Tulasi's field trials.

I received a call from Dr Kalam to immediately come to Delhi with a request proposal from the SBMT for the funding. There was no Internet for information searches in those days, and word processing had just arrived. All that I could manage at such short notice was a five-page write-up, cobbling together whatever information I could muster on the medical, technical and social aspects of the project. When Dr Kalam saw my meagre effort, he did not like it and scolded me, saying, 'Funny guy, I am seeking fifty-lakh funding for you, and you can't even write a fifty-page proposal! In Delhi, unless you write big, no one gets impressed, no one gives you money. People judge your quality by how much you can write and how well you can speak.'

Fortunately for me, Mata Prasad, the officer with whom the proposal rested, was kind with my write-up. He graciously sanctioned the project and noted that screening poor women in time for fatal cervix cancer is the best form of welfare he had come across and asked me convey his respect for the compassion Dr Kalam had demonstrated for the underprivileged. It is important that people occupying high positions critically examine their capabilities, which are indeed enormous, and use them for the good of faceless poor citizens and solve their problems. He however asked me to modify the title a bit to fit to a scheme and 'spare me from any post-retirement headache for doing this good task given to me by the noble soul Kalam'.

SBMT also attempted to make a cardiac pacemaker, and an external pacemaker was successfully developed. But there was no semiconductor foundry in India – and even at the time of writing, India does not have this vital technological infrastructure – to take this work forward. In another project, the development of a Nd-YAG laser for ophthalmic applications was attempted between L.V. Prasad Eye Institute and the Defence Science Centre, New Delhi. But it did not progress far. DMRL and MIDHANI developed titanium dental implants under the guidance of Brig. T. Ranindranath at the Institute of Nuclear Medicine and Allied Sciences (INMAS), New Delhi. However, the work undertaken to develop a bileaflet heart valve with pyrolytic carbon between DRDL and the Sree Chitra Tirunal Institute for Medical Sciences and Technology (SCTIMST), Trivandrum, also came to nothing.

India clearly had a long way to go to meet its technology needs. Doubtlessly, there would need to be some compromise between the ambition for the indigenous production of all the nation's military and civilian technology needs and what was feasible. For this, the Self-Reliance Committee made a distinction between the concepts of 'self-sufficiency' and 'self-reliance', though both terms had been alternately used in the Indian context. It was settled that self-sufficiency meant indigenously producing everything that the armed forces needed, whereas self-reliance meant equipping the armed forces with a whole range of equipment that might derive from an assortment of foreign and domestic sources. Dr Kalam recognized that an inflexible adherence to 'self-sufficiency' was not an ideal path for a country like India, because India's industrial and research and development bases were not yet sufficiently developed. Thus, self-reliance would be the order of the day, at least for some time to come.

Furthermore, Dr Kalam did not sugar-coat the fact that India's defence production sector and research and development laboratories also suffered from a capability differential with their international counterparts. He felt that joint ventures with countries like Russia and France for co-production and development of defence equipment could be one way of addressing this. Dr Kalam famously said, 'It is not the quantum of investment but the quality of synergy that we build with academia, the private sector and the DRDO that would be the key to improving our design capability in key technologies.' This, along with improved production organization and collaboration with globally respected original equipment manufacturers and design houses, was indeed essential.

The key to self-reliance and eventual self-sufficiency was India's nine Defence Public Sector Undertakings (DPSUs). Unlike the ordnance factories, which were departmentally run organizations, the DPSUs were corporate entities with relatively more financial and operational freedom. DPSUs were also larger and operated in the high-end technology spectrums such as aerospace, electronics and warships. The Hindustan Aeronautics Limited was the largest and accounted for over half of all DPSU production and sales. Bharat Electronics Ltd was the premier defence electronics company, with nine production units and thirty-one manufacturing divisions spread across seven states. Bharat Earth Movers Limited (BEML) catered to the core needs of defence services such as trucks, diesel engines, earthmovers and railways. Bharat Dynamics Ltd (BDL) built strategic and tactical missiles, and underwater and aerial weapons. MIDHANI produced special steels, super alloys and titanium alloys that were the core requirements not only of defence production but also of the space and atomic energy programmes. Mazagon Dock Limited (MDL), Bombay; Garden Reach Shipbuilders and Engineers (GRSE), Calcutta; Goa Shipyard Ltd (GSL), Goa; and Hindustan Shipyard Ltd (HSL), Visakhapatnam, were engaged in shipbuilding and other naval engineering services.

Dr Kalam realized that by and large, the practice of licensed production had had its day. HAL was by this time an industry giant, assembling aircraft; this organization, and others of its type, should now be striving to become international technological leaders in their respective fields. Starting at Bangalore, HAL now had several facilities throughout India including Nasik, Korba, Kanpur, Koraput, Lucknow, Bangalore and Hyderabad. Dr Kalam spent a good deal of effort understanding the growth of HAL. HAL had initially been started for the overhauling of aircraft operating in the region under the British and their companies. HAL's first big order came in 1946, for the repair and overhaul of 100 Tiger Moth Aircraft. These were a 1930s biplane designed by Geoffrey de Havilland and operated by the Royal Air Force (RAF) and others as a primary trainer.

When India gained Independence, HAL was recognized as the authorized service centre for the American aerospace manufacturer, the Douglas Aircraft Company in India. HAL manufactured Percival Prentice Trainer Aircraft. In 1950, HAL was admitted as a member of the Society of British Aircraft Constructors, and was contracted to manufacture Vampire aircraft under licence from the British company De Havilland Aviation Ltd.

After becoming a public sector company under the Ministry of Defence in 1951, HAL had successfully built and flown, within the following ten years, the Marut HF-24 at Bangalore and HS-748 aircraft at Kanpur. The manufacture of Gnat aircraft under licence from the British firm Folland Ltd was commenced in 1956. In 1962, HAL ventured into building helicopters under licence from the French aircraft manufacturer Sud Aviation. Russian cooperation was sought for the manufacture of MiG-21 FL aircraft, including its engines and avionics. In 1964, the first Orpheus 703 aircraft engine manufactured from raw materials by HAL was test-accepted. The engines powered the intermediate jet trainer Kiran aircraft.

By 1973, HAL had delivered MiG-21 M aircraft of the CTS series, produced under licence in 1973, and 'Fly Away' Cheetah helicopters. And by 1977, the helicopters were being produced from the raw material stage. In 1979, HAL entered into a licence agreement with British Aerospace for the manufacture of Jaguar aircraft. The first Jaguar Aircraft built indigenously from the raw material stage was handed over to the Indian Air Force in 1988. Around this time, the Indian Air Force purchased and installed the facilities for the overhaul of Mirage-2000 aircraft of the French aircraft manufacturer Dassault Aviation.

Dr Kalam was deeply involved with the aerospace division of HAL right from the SLV-3 days, and saw through its expansion for the fabrication of missile structures under IGMDP. The Prithvi missile wing bays, aerofoil wings, propellant tanks and aluminium warhead casings were made at HAL's aerospace division. I was involved with

C.S. Maheshwari in getting Trishul airframe sections fabricated there. We worked together in the development of the magnesium casting of the Akash missile section at the Foundry and Forge Division with P.K. Sengupta.

Starting with the manufacture of communications equipment in 1956, Bharat Electronics Ltd (BEL) set up a radar manufacturing facility for the army and an in-house research and development installation in 1966 at Bangalore. In the 1970s, BEL established manufacturing facilities for television transmitters for Doordarshan and began manufacturing frigate radars for the navy. A second unit of BEL was set up at Ghaziabad in 1974 to manufacture radars and troposcatter communication equipment for the Indian Air Force. The Space Electronic Division was instituted at Bangalore to support the nation's satellite programmes in 1982. Dr Kalam brought BEL on board as the principal integrator of the Akash missile system and facilitated the creation of the BEL unit at Hyderabad to manufacture electronic warfare equipment.

The Self-Reliance Committee had underscored the need to improve our self-reliance quotient from 30 per cent in 1992 to 70 per cent by 2005. The committee also identified the critical technologies required – gallium arsenide devices, fibre optics, smart weapon subsystems, heavy particle beams, focal plane array and hypersonic propulsion. It recommended the creation of a Defence Technology Fund of Rs 100 crore to focus on 'core' and 'mother' technology that are necessary for building state-of-the-art defence systems.[4] These would include multimode radars, aero engines, carbon fibres and the stealth capability for Light Combat Aircraft (LCA), for example.

The committee's report underscored the need to create a Self-reliance Implementation Council (SRIC) as the 'mastermind' of the self-reliance endeavour. The SRIC would bring together the heads of DRDO, the army, navy, air force and the Department of Defence Production to ensure that the goals of self-reliance are monitored regularly and effectively. Dr Kalam opted for the tested model of design, development and production of Sukhoi fighter planes in Russia. There, the Sukhoi Design Bureau effectively steered the aeronautical programmes in sync with the production houses.

Dr Kalam felt that in a turbulent world where the status quo and technology are fiercely guarded by established powers, India must make concerted and judiciously formulated plans for its technological progress. It must improve its knowledge base with the active participation of academic institutions in the national programmes. Moreover, all stakeholders must pool their efforts in the programme: they must not be allowed by the political leadership to develop fiefdoms and fight turf wars. Accepting failure is indeed the springboard of success. This is how Dr Kalam envisioned India's tomorrow. With sagacious understanding, Dr Kalam said, 'The whole universe conspires to give the best to those who dream and work. We need to seize them with both hands.'

2.8

The Razor's Edge

> It's a toss-up when you decide to leave the beaten track. Many are called, few are chosen.
>
> – W. Somerset Maugham
> British novelist

Until 1992, Indian passport holders were prohibited from entering Israel. Prime Minister Narasimha Rao brought into the open India's relations with Israel, which had been kept covertly active for a few years during his tenure as foreign minister, and invited Israel to open an embassy in New Delhi. India and Israel share some common ground, in that they are both isolated democracies threatened by neighbours that train, finance and encourage terrorists. It was a strategic imperative that both countries cooperate on defence matters. Dr Kalam was tasked with establishing technological partnerships with many of the world's leading high-tech companies in Israel.

It would not be an easy task. There had been a good deal of negative conditioning that needed to be overcome for a rapprochement. Although both countries gained their independence from the United Kingdom within months of each other, they found themselves headed in markedly different directions for nearly four decades. India became a leader in the Non-Aligned Movement that maintained close relations with the Arab world and the Soviet Union. Israel linked its future to strong ties with the United States and western Europe.

On 6 March 1993, when Sharad Pawar became the chief

minister of Maharashtra, Prime Minister Rao took over the defence portfolio himself. Dr Kalam now had direct access to Prime Minister Narasimha Rao, who shared with him and other nuclear scientists his desire to develop a nuclear bomb. He said that after the cold war had ended in 1991 and with that the 1971 treaty with the Soviet Union, India no longer had any superpower ally. With a menacing China and an openly hostile Pakistan, there was little choice but to become a nuclear-capable nation.

At any rate, the threats to India's security were not only of a tangible military form. On Friday, 12 March 1993, a series of thirteen bomb explosions rocked Bombay. The coordinated attacks were the most destructive bomb explosions in Indian history. This was the first terrorist strike of its kind – planned, coordinated serial bomb blasts – in the world. The attacks resulted in more than 350 fatalities and 1,200 injuries. Dr Kalam told me that the threat that India faced from its enemies was changing its form. He wondered: How does a civilized nation fight hidden groups? How does a pluralistic society cope with the terrorists' modus operandi of continuing random violence?

Years later, Dr Kalam told me that the post-1991 years were perhaps the most threatening for India. We were left with no superpower backer, surrounded by inveterate enemies. Economically weak, we were in no position to build nuclear weapons and bear the burden of nuclear sanctions. In spite of these adverse conditions, Prime Minister Rao was determined to carry out a nuclear test. But when, in 1995, the tests were imminent, the United States got wind of the preparations and put tremendous pressure on Prime Minister Rao to abandon them – and he did so.

In 1996, the navy expressed its urgent need for a quick-reaction air defence system to protect its warships at sea from aircraft and anti-ship missiles. The Pakistani navy had acquired Harpoon missiles from America and Exocet sea-skimming missiles from France. Without any warning, these missiles could – by day or by night and regardless of weather conditions – approach our ships at near-sonic speed and inflict terrible damage. Not only must the warship fire its missile at the earliest, the anti-missile has to 'see' the incoming missile through the visual disturbance of the waves. The deployment of Trishul, the missile that had been intended for this purpose, had been delayed.

Trishul had not yet finished its static trials from a fixed launcher, leave alone the second and far more difficult stage of mounting it and firing it from a sailing warship. The navy had no option but to commission two ships devoid of any missile armaments. Dr Kalam acknowledged the navy's predicament. He did not retreat into denial and offered no excuses. He said, 'The services must be served.' The navy evaluated several systems and settled on the Israeli Barak missile. Thus was born a great partnership. Not only were the Barak missiles installed on Indian Navy ships, but this initial order also blossomed into a 350-million-dollar joint project between the Israeli military technology sector and the DRDO. This collaboration would develop the Barak Extended Range SAM, which could be deployed against targets at distances of over 100 km from a launch site, ten years later. It would be another decade before Dr Kalam would visit Israel.

The theatre of war was changing. The idea to develop an Indian cruise missile crystallized after the 1991 Gulf War, when the American Tomahawk cruise missiles proved their usefulness, crippling Iraq's command and communication centres in short order and leaving its armed forces exposed to air attacks. That a few hundred cruise missiles could isolate the 1.2-million-strong Iraqi military in the space of a few hours seemed incredible. Dr Kalam felt that it was necessary to equip India with a cruise missile system.

Dr Kalam enjoyed tremendous goodwill in the Russian scientific establishment. He called on this goodwill to establish a joint venture, ratified by an agreement signed on 12 February 1998, creating an equal partnership between DRDO and Russia's NPO Mashinostroyenia. Mashinostroyenia was the legendary organization that had developed iconic cruise missiles such as Malakhit and Granit, as well as ICBMs and spacecraft. The purpose of the joint venture would be the design, development, manufacture and marketing of the supersonic cruise missile BrahMos, named after the Rivers Brahmaputra and Moscow.

India held a 50.5 per cent share in the joint venture company. The Russian contingent had been keen for the joint venture to be realized as a private sector company. Had the DRDO's share been 51 per cent, it would have become a public sector company, falling under India's defence ministry. Dr Sivathanu Pillai was appointed the CEO of the BrahMos Aerospace Company and Russia invested 126.25 million dollars according to its commitment. Dr Kalam had once again been the architect of a vital technological alliance, and it was due in no small measure to the relationships he had forged over years, and the international esteem he enjoyed:

> The friendship between Kalam and Yefremov and their belief in their respective teams was a key factor. Yefremov's academic stature and his role as a renowned rocket designer helped remove roadblocks and suspicions in the Russian bureaucracy. On the Indian side, when Kalam forwarded a proposal to Prime Minister Rao, the file came back with his approval the same day.[1]

Not content with merely building a missile of the type of the IGMDP, Dr Kalam wanted the BrahMos missile to be a futuristic weapon – it should be the best and most advanced in its class. Dr Kalam laid down his crisp summation of how this must be achieved. He said, 'Increase the speed. Follow the basic rule of war – when the speed of attack increases, it automatically reduces the response time of the enemy. BrahMos must be faster than the Tomahawk.' The Tomahawk was a long-range subsonic cruise missile. The BrahMos was designed as a supersonic missile. It would have two stages: the first, consisting of a solid-fuel rocket, would take the missile to break the sound barrier (Mach 1). The second stage, a liquid-fuelled ramjet, would propel it to Mach 2.8. The missile would cruise as low as 10 metres above the wave tops, making it a 'sea skimmer'. True to Dr Kalam's vision, the BrahMos is still the fastest cruise missile in operation.

With all his success in harnessing technology for missiles and aerospace purposes, Dr Kalam could see the untapped potential for the Indian civilian aeronautical industry. He regretted the fact that India, which was amongst the first in South Asia to manufacture an aircraft, had not developed its own competitive passenger aeroplane. The National Aerospace Laboratories (NAL) had designed the Saras turboprop multi-role light transport plane using two Canadian Pratt and Whitney turboprop engines. But the Saras would only take between nine and fourteen passengers. Dr Kalam was passionate about the development of a passenger plane with between seventy and 100 seats, that would allow India to connect its regional centres to the major metropolitan cities.

At times, Dr Kalam was loud and vocal about his frustration with the stagnancy in the Indian aerospace industry. He said during tea, after a meeting of the Aeronautical Development Agency (ADA),[2] 'When the Embraer company in Brazil, starting with a turboprop passenger aircraft, can make regional airliners with seventy to 110 seats and smaller business jets, why can't we? If a sleepy, state-owned manufacturer of planes for the Brazilian military could become one of the four biggest makers of commercial passenger aircraft in the world, what is stopping HAL?

His concern was, however, not merely for matters involving technology and aeronautics. Dr Kalam's vision for the country in this time would become global in its scope, and comprehensive, such that it would manifest as a blueprint for the nation's progress in the first decades of the twenty-first century. In 1993, Dr Kalam took over as chairman, Technology Information, Forecasting and Assessment Council (TIFAC). Dr Kalam and Y.S. Rajan together oversaw an extensive study by a team of 500 experts to develop a vision of India as a developed nation by the year 2020. The plan was subsequently published in the book form.

The book examined in depth India's weaknesses and strengths and offered a vision of how the country could emerge as one of the world's first four economic powers by 2020. Far from concerning themselves merely with dry economic data and the technical aspects of the nation's advancement, Dr Kalam and Y.S. Rajan's vision was particularly concerned with improvements in the lives of ordinary Indians:

> What makes a country developed? The obvious indicators are the wealth of the nation, the prosperity of its people and its standing in the international forum. There are many indicators regarding

> the wealth of a nation: the gross national product (GNP), the gross domestic product (GDP), the balance of payments, foreign exchange reserves, rate of economic growth, per capita income, etc. ... Economic indicators are important, but they provide only a part of the picture ... The numbers, impressive though they may appear, can veil considerable human misery, especially that of the common people.[3]

India 2020 identified five areas of progress: agriculture and food processing aimed at doubling the present production; infrastructure with reliable electric power providing urban amenities to rural areas and increasing solar power operations; education and health care directed towards illiteracy, social security and overall health for the population; information and communication technology for increased e-governance to promote education in remote areas, telecommunication and telemedicine; and critical technologies and strategic industries, particularly the growth of nuclear technology, space technology and defence technology.

India 2020 systematically outlined the issues facing the Indian nation and its people. It is curiously prescriptive and flexible, in that it discusses the present approaches to these issues, identifies their merits and demerits and then proffers an array of solutions, in the view that the most feasible could be determined and implemented. Prognostication, at least as far as matters involving technological advancements, is like firing at a rapidly moving target from a moving platform. *India 2020* understood the need to remain open to new developments, as much as it understood the nation's rich heritage in traditional indigenous solutions, such as natural herbal remedies and tribal systems of medicine. Furthermore, Dr Kalam and Y.S. Rajan were equally comfortable with adopting the best health-care methods from other civilizations, such as Chinese acupuncture for the management of certain chronic pain conditions.

Unsurprisingly, given its proponent's scientific background, Vision 2020 also championed using the latest innovations for age-old problems. It suggested how technology could be employed to eradicate malaria, by mapping out mosquito-breeding areas with remote sensing satellites. Additionally, it saw a fresh role for the lasers developed by the DRDO to treat glaucoma and cataracts. Dr Kalam and Y.S. Rajan were adamant, though, that India should not simply imitate the ideas of other nations. India should exercise the inherent creativity of its people in formulating the most appropriate solutions for its issues. Some of the suggested ideas were novel but brilliant, such as the use of biodegradable tapioca-lined paper packages as a substitute for the environmentally deleterious plastic variety.

Whatever innovations would be adopted, though, must be 'user-friendly' and enhance the average person's quality of life. Technology should not be alienating for any portion of society. As a man who had dedicated his life to technological advancement yet advocated a simple lifestyle, Dr Kalam was well aware of modernization's drawbacks. He suggested that progress should not make the common person apprehensive, as this could lead to inefficiency and lower levels of customer gratification. One should be able to anticipate changes that are likely to occur as a result of modernization and adapt accordingly.

At any rate, Dr Kalam expressed supreme confidence that by becoming self-reliant, our national self-esteem would rise immeasurably. Our technology would forge ahead, thereby raising the standard of our products and above all, the question of indebtedness to any other nation would be eliminated. Dr Kalam's assertion – that if the nineteenth century belonged to Europe, the twentieth century to the United States, the twenty-first century will definitely belong to India – awakened a long subdued patriotic fervour. Dr Kalam's national profile was elevated from that of the venerable Missile Man to the National Visionary. Through *India 2020: A Vision for the New Millennium*, Dr Kalam shared a dream with millions of Indians.

While Dr Kalam and Y.S. Rajan were applying the finishing touches to their progressive vision of the country's future, the nation's leadership was mired in uncertainty. General elections were held in India in 1996, resulting in the defeat of the Indian National Congress government of Prime Minister Rao. A hung parliament was declared. President Shankar Dayal Sharma invited Atal Bihari Vajpayee, as leader of the Bharatiya Janata Party (BJP), to form a government.

Prime Minister Vajpayee could not muster support from more than 200 of the 545 members of parliament and resigned, ending his thirteen-day government with Pramod Mahajan as the defence minister. During his short tenure, however, Prime Minster Vajpayee was briefed by the outgoing prime minister Rao about the readiness of the nuclear bomb. Prime Minister Vajpayee gave a go-ahead just before his government fell.

H.D. Deve Gowda took over from Vajpayee as the prime minister. Mulayam Singh Yadav – the former chief minister of Uttar Pradesh, the largest state of India, and a leader of the masses – became the defence minister. He developed a strong personal bond with Dr Kalam and even gave him some Hindi-language lessons. Mulayam Singh shared with Dr Kalam his vision at the South Asian Association for Regional Cooperation (SAARC), established on 8 December 1985. He envisaged a Great Indian Union along the lines of the European Union, with intrinsic economic connectivity and complete freedom of movement of people across the Indian subcontinent. Mulayam Singh told Dr Kalam to be ready with the nuclear bomb. Such was the respect Mulayam Singh gave to Dr Kalam that he would walk into Dr Kalam's office in the South Block whenever he needed him, instead of calling him to his chamber.

But Prime Minister Deve Gowda did not share his predecessors' enthusiasm for India's nuclear programme, and he refused to give permission to carry out nuclear tests.

In November 1996, President Jiang Zemin of China came to India. It was the first visit to India of the head of state of the People's Republic of China. Dr Kalam had read extensively about China and was most reverent towards the Chinese civilization. He asked me while I was assisting him with his autobiography, to brief him on the guiding socio-political theory credited to Jiang Zemin. Known as 'The Important Thought of Three Represents', this theory was ratified by the Communist Party of China at the sixteenth party congress in 2002. Dr Kalam wanted to study this theory while he further refined the *India 2020* vision.

President Jiang Zemin, the paramount leader of China, articulated that a nation is powered by three powerful forces. He asserted that the three must be represented in the government, to prevent the implosion and dissipation of creative and productive energy into internal squabbling and even conflict. He defined the 'three represents' as: the advanced social productive forces carrying out economic production, the progressive course of China's advanced culture taking care of the cultural development of its people, and the fundamental interests of the majority leading to a political consensus.

Since the founding of the Communist Party of China in 1921, and communist China in 1949, three major theoretical expressions have been formulated to guide the nation building at different stages. Mao Zedong's 'Thought' combined Marxism with the practical situation of the Chinese revolution. The aim of Deng Xiaoping's 'Theory' was to build socialism with Chinese characteristics. And the 'Three Represents' theory marked another milestone for both party and nation building.

What relevance did these have for India? Dr Kalam said, 'The government must always represent the development trend of India's advanced productive forces. It means that the government's programme, principles, policies and all its work must be in line with the laws governing the development of productive forces; it must embody the requisites for constantly furthering the release and development of productive forces, especially advanced productive forces; and it must steadily raise the people's standard of living by developing the productive forces.'

Dr Kalam also propounded his now familiar mantra on the role of academic and ideological principles in nation building: 'Government's programmes, principles, policies and all its work must embody the requisites for guiding the development of a national, scientific and popular socialist culture geared to the needs of modernization, the world and the future. These must be implemented in order to improve the ideological and ethical standards and scientific and cultural levels of the whole nation and to provide motivation and intellectual support for India's economic development and social progress.'

Dr Kalam added, 'Saying that the government represents the fundamental interests of the overwhelming majority of the people means that in its programme, principles, policies and all its work, it must persevere in taking the fundamental interests of the people as its starting point and objective, give full expression to the people's enthusiasm, initiative and creativity; and enable the people to constantly obtain tangible economic, political and cultural benefits on the basis of social development and progress.'

The situation of the Indian government at that time starkly contrasted with the 'Three Represents' theory. The Gowda government collapsed in April 1997, and the Congress withdrew its support for the coalition. The reason given was that, although Gowda's minority United Front government was dependent upon the Congress, he did not consult the party regarding important matters. Inder Kumar Gujral, widely regarded as a peacenik and minister for external affairs in Gowda's cabinet, was chosen as the new coalition leader. Prime Minister Gujral reappointed every single minister from Gowda's cabinet. He also publicly stated that there would be no change in economic or foreign policies.

Prime Minister Gujral was of the view that 1997 was not the right time for nuclear testing. He preferred to maintain the country's existing nuclear deterrent, and was concerned about the ramifications of India brandishing its nuclear capability. He felt that the country could not afford the economic and diplomatic fallout that would doubtless follow nuclear tests – sanctions and international opprobrium – much less his government maintain its tenuous hold on power. In any event, Prime Minister Gujral was a great admirer of Dr Kalam and his contribution to India's space and missile-building capability.

Both Prime Minister Gujral and Defence Minister Mulayam Singh believed that Dr Kalam symbolized the scientific strength of India. To send a powerful message about the importance the government gave to India's security – not just to the nation but also across the world – they decided that Dr Kalam should be awarded the Bharat Ratna, the nation's highest honour. This award was announced in November 1997. He was the second scientist after Sir C.V. Raman to receive the award.

Part Three

REALIZATION

Life is a dream for the wise, a game for the fool, a comedy for the rich, a tragedy for the poor.

– Sholom Aleichem
Nineteenth-century Yiddish author

3.1

Major General Prithviraj

> The atomic bomb made the prospect of future war unendurable. It has led us up those last few steps to the mountain pass; and beyond there is a different country.
>
> – J. Robert Oppenheimer
> Father of the atomic bomb

Politically, the world is a complex system of competing forces and interests. The world order remains in equilibrium – and peace prevails – when these forces compensate each other, like the two weights pushing down on the arms of a pair of scales. The equilibrium is delicate; any small event may disturb its stillness – and this is especially so with the myriad of opposing forces on the subcontinent. The equilibrium here was disturbed in 1998 when Pakistan tested the nuclear-capable Ghauri missile, a weapon of mass destruction that could threaten India's heartland.

While India had been treading a long path of science and technological development and had been at some pains not to offend international anti-nuclear sentiment, Pakistan had quietly become fully nuclear-capable. Moreover, it had done so with the complicity of a rogue state and forces inimical to India, unmindful of worldwide consequences. This was nuclear proliferation by proxy, and it had delivered weapons of mass destruction into Pakistan's hands; its military could now deploy nuclear missiles capable of striking targets deep inside Indian territory.

In a sinister barter that would deeply trouble observers throughout the world, Pakistan had obtained North Korean No-Dong missiles and in return provided the secretive regime nuclear design and enrichment equipment. India had no option now but to develop its nuclear capability in symmetry with Pakistan's, to regain the delicate balance between the countries. For this, it was imperative that the Agni family of ballistic missiles were nuclear-weaponized without any further delay. Dr Kalam had, at any rate, been advocating this for several years. He had even built some consensus within the establishment on this; but the political leadership was reluctant to move forward in the face of international pressure, and nuclear testing was abandoned. Reluctance would now give way to resolve.

The 1998 general elections gave an exclusive public mandate for the Bharatiya Janata Party (BJP). The BJP election campaign had already voiced the party's intention to further the nation's nuclear weapons programme if it were voted to power. The election victory indeed cleared doubt in anyone's mind on the nuclear question. There was now a broad consensus that India should become an openly nuclear power, if for no other reason, then to be afforded its deserved status on the world stage. The Pakistan missile shock would only add urgency to the nuclear issue.

The bitter experience of 1995, when the plans of testing the nuclear bomb were leaked to the United States, was still fresh in the leaders' minds. International pressure led by the US had been exerted such that testing had to be aborted. This time, India was not simply exercising a defence prerogative; the nation's military capabilities had to be brought in symmetry with its most implacable foe's. Prime Minister Vajpayee therefore decided that every measure should be taken to keep the impending nuclear trials from being exposed. He did not share his intelligence with his cabinet colleagues, including even, of all people, Defence Minister George Fernandes, who remained none the wiser for these developments.

Pokhran had seen the beginnings of nuclear India, and it would now herald its coming of age as a full-fledged nuclear power. Pokhran is a small town in a remote location in the Thar Desert, in the

Jaisalmer district of Rajasthan. The first underground nuclear test was performed here in 1974. It is surrounded by rocks, sand and five salt ranges. The name Pokhran means 'place of five mirages', an apt name for this arid, scorched wasteland. In any event, the semi-desert conditions with uninterrupted clear skies, gently undulating terrain and only shoulder-high thorny bushes didn't provide much cover against spy satellites. World powers, both benign and hostile, had been watching Pokhran from the skies for some time, seeking any clues of a nuclear test.

Within a fortnight of securing a vote of confidence for his coalition government in the parliament, Prime Minister Vajpayee called Dr Kalam and Dr R. Chidambaram and authorized them to conduct the nuclear tests. Brajesh Mishra, principal secretary to the prime minister and his most trusted aide, was nominated as the single authority in the bureaucracy for their liaison. Thirty days' time was thought reasonable notice for those responsible to carry out the tests. President K.R. Narayanan was scheduled to tour Latin America from 26 April to 10 May 1997. Dr Chidambaram's daughter was getting married on 27 April; his absence before this significant family event would betray to all observers that something momentous was afoot. A full-moon-night enthusiast, Dr Kalam suggested the Buddha Purnima Day for the tests, which would be 11 May 1998. With barely any discussion, everyone concurred wholeheartedly on this auspicious date.

The Pokhran range area had been under the charge of the 58 Engineer Regiment of the Indian Army's Corps of Engineers. The regiment had dug three shafts over the preceding several years, working during the night hours to avoid detection of their activities by spy satellites. There were many dry, abandoned wells in the area, and a few of them were deepened and widened into 50-metre-deep shafts. The shafts and facilities were kept in a state of continuous readiness for more than a year so that a test could be done within as little as ten days of a decision.

As part of the strict protocol to maintain secrecy, Dr Kalam and Dr Chidambaram donned army greens whenever they visited Pokhran, and their real identities were never officially revealed to the people working there. Dr Kalam was known as Major General Prithviraj, and Dr Chidambaram was called Major General Natraj. Dr Anil Kakodar, director, Bhabha Atomic Research Centre (BARC), and the 100-odd scientists and technologists from the BARC and DRDO who descended on Pokhran to conduct the tests, were also given army fatigues and false military identities.

A nuclear weapon derives its destructive force from nuclear reactions, either fission (fission bomb) or a combination of fission and fusion (thermonuclear bomb). Both reactions release vast quantities of energy from relatively small amounts of matter. This series of tests would explode six bombs. A thermonuclear device was lowered into a 200-metre-deep shaft codenamed White House and sealed. A fission bomb was set in place at the bottom of a 150-metre-deep shaft codenamed Taj Mahal and sealed. A sub-kiloton bomb was placed in a shaft named Kumbhakaran. The other three 50-metre shafts for the second test series were designated Navatala ('new well' in Hindi), abbreviated as NT 1, 2, and 3.

A thermonuclear weapon is a nuclear weapon that uses the energy from a primary nuclear fission reaction to compress and ignite a secondary nuclear fusion reaction. The result is an explosion of much greater power than that of a single-stage fission weapon. It is colloquially referred to as a hydrogen bomb, because it employs hydrogen fusion. The fission stage in thermonuclear weapons gives rise to their fusion. The concept of the thermonuclear weapon was first developed and used in 1952 and has since been employed in the design of most of the world's nuclear weapons. The fission–fusion combination is favoured for its efficiency: A thermonuclear weapon weighing little more than 1,000 kilograms can produce an explosive force comparable to the detonation of more than 1.2 million tonnes of trinitrotoluene (TNT) explosive material used in general warfare. A nuclear device no larger than traditional bombs can devastate an entire city by blast, fire and radiation.

Sub-kiloton devices are low-yield nuclear devices. They are used as tactical nuclear weapons for battlefield support purposes to replace short-range missiles and bombs. One of the purposes for the Pokhran nuclear tests, which were more of a scientific rather than military nature, was to provide data for computer simulation for designing nuclear weapons and to provide technical inputs for ultra-low-yield experimental blasts. Since the atomic bombings of Hiroshima and Nagasaki, nuclear weapons have been detonated on over two thousand occasions for the purposes of testing and demonstration – sometimes at great cost to the environment and humanity. The early atmospheric or above-ground tests and high-altitude or exoatmospheric nuclear explosions were especially deleterious to the environment and surrounding populations.

Dr Kalam, Dr Chidambaram and Dr Kakodkar were standing together near the test site in the moonlit night of 10–11 May 1998. But for the sound of the wind there was total silence. Suddenly, all three uttered, almost simultaneously, the name of Dr Homi Bhabha. This led to an hour-long discussion between the three great minds of nuclear energy about the dream of Dr Bhabha, to meet the energy needs of India using electricity derived from nuclear fission.

In the 1950s, Dr Homi Bhabha dreamed of securing India's long-term energy independence through the use of uranium and thorium reserves found in the monazite sands of coastal regions of south India. India had only around 1–2 per cent of the global uranium reserves, but about 25 per cent of the world's known thorium reserves – one of the largest national shares of global thorium. Dr Bhabha was of the view that with total reserves of thorium in India amounting to over 500,000 tonnes in the readily extractable form, the country could produce 500 Gigawatt of electrical energy annually for at least four centuries. Kalam was quite familiar with the science involved in Dr Homi Bhabha's vision, and wrote about it in the book I co-authored with him:

> When mixed with natural uranium plutonium-239 undergoes fission to produce energy. Interestingly, in this process, uranium-238 gets transmuted into plutonium-239 and 'breeds' more fuel than it consumes. For this reason, such reactors are called Fast Breeding Reactors (FBR). Thorium itself is not a fissile material, and thus cannot undergo fission to produce energy. It is only on building up

> the inventory of plutonium-239 that thorium can be introduced as a blanket material in the reactor and transmuted to uranium-233 for use in the third stage.[1]

The three scientists paid tribute to the great soul Dr Bhabha. Each one of them felt they had been lucky to meet this science legend. Future generations fed on the propaganda of consumerism would hardly believe that such visionaries had walked on Indian soil, the trio of Dr Kalam, Dr Chidambaram and Dr Kakodkar lamented. Each of these men had dedicated much of his life to fulfilling the dream of nuclear self-reliance, bequeathed them by Dr Bhabha. They knew that without Dr Bhabha, they would not be standing there that night.

The day of 11 May 1998 broke with heavy gusts blowing the powdery desert sands. The wind was likely to take the dust created by the explosion towards the town of Pokhran. They would have to wait. Prime Minister Vajpayee cancelled all his engagements for the day and stayed at home near the secured hotline from the test site. Dr Kalam remembered a very beautiful sentence he read somewhere in his young days: 'You usually have to wait for that which is worth waiting for.'

Dr Kalam called at 3.00 p.m. to tell the prime minister that the winds were dying down and the tests could be conducted during the next hour. At 3:43:44.2 p.m. IST, the first three devices were detonated simultaneously. The combined force of the three blasts lifted an area about the size of a cricket ground to a few metres above the earth, sending billowing clouds of dust and sand into the air. In contrast to the 1974 explosion, there was no thought of claiming that these were 'peaceful tests'. Indeed, government officials quickly emphasized the military nature of the explosions. 'These tests have established that India has a proven capability for a weaponized nuclear programme,' Brajesh Mishra told reporters.

Two days later, on 13 May 1998 the two sub-kiloton devices lowered in NT 1 and 2 were detonated underground. The device in NT 3 was pulled out and taken back under orders from Dr R. Chidambaram, as he felt that the team already had the results they wanted with just five blasts. As he told the team laconically, 'Why waste it?' The Pokhran-II nuclear test had now proved the arrival in India of more powerful and lighter nuclear weapons, small enough to be carried by missiles.

Pakistan was quick to respond to the tests. On 28 May 1998, Pakistan carried out nuclear tests at Ras Koh Hills in the Chagai district of Balochistan province. It was followed by another test on 30 May 1998. Prime Minister Nawaz Sharif famously said, 'If India had not exploded the bomb, Pakistan would not have done so. Once New Delhi did so, we had no choice because of public pressure.'

Nevertheless, Dr Kalam was derisive of the commotion in the Western media following the tests of May 1998. He told me, 'Why should Britain have a nuclear arsenal, but not India? Why did nobody say anything when the French were conducting atmospheric nuclear tests in occupied Algiers? Are these not reasonable questions? The answer does not lie in claiming that Britain and France have a divine right to nuclear weaponry, but a truly ethical example of unilateral nuclear disarmament, which the West was not interested in and neither were the Soviets and the Chinese.'

While we were discussing this, I could not help but think of the unlikely military personality, Major General Prithviraj, wearing his uniform with a very un-military abandon. I wondered if the spy satellites hovering over Pokhran had captured images of Dr Kalam's hair. The flowing silvery locks that protruded incongruously from the military hat of Major General Prithviraj would have been a dead giveaway.

While he would have been quite unconvincing as a military officer, Dr Kalam had a veritable arsenal of other talents. In January 1999, Dr Kalam published his autobiography *Wings of Fire*,[2] which I co-authored. Besides the story of his life and the grateful mention of his parents, teachers and mentors who shaped him to succeed, the book introduced to the world Dr Kalam's penchant for poetry. The book contained many of his poems and his favourite poems of others.

Do not look at Agni
As an entity directed upward
To deter the ominous

Or exhibit your might.
It is fire in the heart of an Indian.

Do not even give it
The form of a missile
As it clings to the
Burning pride of this nation
And thus is bright.

The book was very well received by the public and critically acclaimed. Bhawani Prasad Chattopadhyay in *The Statesman* called it 'a book worth its weight in gold'. Prof. M.S. Mukunda at IISc wrote in *Resonance*, 'There is something that everybody can extract from this book ... The book is worthy of being read by every Indian.' When a reporter asked journalist and broadcasting executive M.V. Kamath – in an interview published in *The Asian Age* – which book would he make compulsory reading, he answered, 'A.P.J. Abdul Kalam's *Wings of Fire*.'

Some months after the book was released, Dr Kalam was going through the hundreds of letters with me that the readers of *Wings of Fire* had sent him. One reader wrote that he felt like a fellow-traveller with Dr Kalam while reading the story of his life. Dr Kalam was deeply touched and explained to me the metaphor of life as a journey that is given form in the Quran. Dr Kalam said, 'The course of the journey metaphor in the Quran explains life as a moral journey. A man is given the gift of free will. There is good moral life and there is bad immoral life. There is a good way, straight path and there is a bad way, a convoluted path. Then there are many fellow-travellers. There are righteous fellow-travellers. There are wicked fellow-travellers. There is God as a guide and the Shaitan as the misleader permitted by God to test man. God is ever ready to support the righteous and obstruct the wicked. He sends fellow-travellers accordingly.'

On 20 February 1999, Prime Ministers Atal Bihari Vajpayee and Nawaz Sharif created history by opening the gates of friendship at the Wagah border, breaching the walls of hatred that had symbolized India–Pakistan relations for the preceding fifty-one years. When

Prime Minister Vajpayee arrived at the border check-post in the Delhi–Lahore bus accompanied by twenty-two eminent Indians, Prime Minister Nawaz Sharif stood there to receive him. As the two leaders shook hands and embraced, hundreds of people lined up on both sides of the border, celebrating the event. It was a defining moment in the history of the subcontinent. Despite the nuclear tests on both sides of the border, the leadership of the countries managed to make inroads towards a peaceful coexistence.

Nevertheless, India would continue to pursue its full nuclear capability. The Agni-II was first tested on 11 April 1999 from a converted rail carriage, with a roof that slid open to allow the missile to be raised to the vertical launch position by two large hydraulic pistons. The launch process was controlled from a separate railcar. The missile was launched from Wheeler Island near Balasore. The missile splashed down in the Bay of Bengal 2,100 kilometres downrange. The liquid propulsion stage of Agni-I was replaced by a solid propellant motor, making Agni-II an all-solid-propellant system. The missile would shortly see a road-mobile configuration, lending flexibility and reducing vulnerability to first strike.

In April 1999, the Pakistani incursion into the area that divided the Indian territory of Ladakh from the northern areas of the state Jammu and Kashmir, took the Indian Army by surprise. It was known that some elements of the Pakistani armed forces were covertly training and sending Pakistani troops and paramilitary forces into territory on the Indian side of the Line of Control (LOC). The latest infiltration, though, was more serious, aimed at severing the link between Kashmir and Ladakh and forcing Indian troops to withdraw from the Siachen Glacier. But that it would happen almost immediately after the historic visit of the Indian prime minister to Pakistan, where he was accorded such a warm reception, only added to India's dismay. The Ladakh incursion made little diplomatic sense.

Before the Partition of India in 1947, Kargil was part of the Baltistan district of Ladakh, a thinly populated region with diverse linguistic, ethnic and religious groups, living in isolated valleys separated by some of the world's highest mountains. The Kashmir war of 1947–48 concluded with the LOC dividing the Baltistan district, with the town and district of Kargil lying on the Indian side. After Pakistan's defeat in the war of 1971, the two nations signed the Simla Agreement promising not to engage in armed conflict with respect to that boundary.

After the incursion in Kargil, Nawaz Sharif, prime minister of Pakistan during the conflict, claimed that he was unaware of the operation, and that he first learned about the situation when he received an urgent telephone call from Prime Minister Vajpayee. He blamed the incursion on his generals.

The fundamental fact is that hawkish tendencies exist in both India and Pakistan, and both nations need to reduce them. Just as jihadis exist in Pakistan, anti-Pakistan hardliners exist in India. The issues and enmity between the countries cannot be solved easily. Processes are complex and opinions are formed over many years. There are, however, so many brilliant people on both sides; and such great natural resources. Combined, or at least cooperative, India and Pakistan could have been far ahead of China, and perhaps among the greatest of developed nations in the world. Dr Kalam's understanding of such conundrums was philosophical, and inspired by ancient scripture:

> In Mahabharata, when Bhishma was lying on his bed of arrows, waiting for the moment of his death and the Pandavas approached him for his advice, he told them, 'Nobody is anybody's friend. Nobody is anybody's enemy. It is the circumstances that make enemies and friends.' The world will not be the same in a few decades from what it is today. The evolving strategic thinking process must be responsive to the new world order.[3]

It was time for Dr Kalam to move out of DRDO. He felt that he had stayed for a little too long. Dr V.K. Aatre, chief controller (R&D) of DRDO and erstwhile director of the Naval Physical and Oceanographic Laboratory (NPOL), Cochin, took over from Dr Kalam. But the Government of India was in no mood to let Dr Kalam settle down to retirement.

In November 1999, The Office of the Principal Scientific Adviser (PSA) to the Government of India was created. Dr Kalam was appointed the first occupant of this exalted position. The PSA would evolve polices, strategies and missions for the generation of innovations and support systems for multiple applications. Moreover, the PSA would generate science and technology tasks in critical infrastructure, economic and social sectors in partnership with government departments, institutions and industry. This office would also function as the secretariat to the Scientific Advisory Committee (SAC) to the cabinet.

Dr Kalam felt that carrying out evidence-based studies for policy and strategy initiatives was particularly important. Development and pilot project efforts were necessary to nucleate and catalyse multi-disciplinary projects or help to network institutions with common goals for enhancing national competitiveness and national-security-related technologies. Dr Kalam invited Y.S. Rajan, his long-time friend who was now retired from TIFAC, to head his new team. If life is a journey, Y.S. Rajan was a fine fellow-traveller for Dr Kalam.

3.2

Aarif

> Your only obligation in any lifetime is to be true to yourself. Being true to anyone else or anything else is not only impossible, but the mark of a fake messiah.
>
> – Richard Bach
> Author of *Jonathan Livingston Seagull*

The PSA office was housed in the Vigyan Bhavan Annexe, the adjacent building to Vigyan Bhavan, a premier convention centre the Government of India had built in 1956 adjacent to the vice-president's house on Maulana Azad Road. Dr Kalam had his personal secretary H. Sheridon transferred to the new office. Dr Rajan took over as Dr Kalam's scientific secretary. For the first few weeks, it was not clear what the new office would do. Memories of the sleepy times of ADE in the early 1950s and the uncertainty of the post SLV-3 days at ISRO returned. But like then, Dr Kalam and his team would make their own work. Drawing from his rich experience at ISRO headquarters and at the Department of Science and Technology (DST), Dr Y.S. Rajan made the PSA a functional entity in the Government of India.

Instead of allowing his office to become another add-on to the great scientific bureaucracy that had evolved over the years in India, Dr Kalam perceived a pressing requirement for new means of achieving his goals. Unquestionably, he was a veteran in handling tortuous bureaucratic matters; his ability here was one of his strong suits. He had secured DGCI approval for the stent, presided over distribution of FRO to the needy and relocated people every time he had launched a missile in Balasore. He had successfully negotiated bureaucratic mazes by a persistent and straightforward approach – and with his trademark charm. But now, he sought an innovative approach to the corridors of power.

Not that one could discount the power of his charm, nor his commitment to seeing a project through to fruition. But not everyone was A.P.J. Abdul Kalam, and even with his abilities and stature, he sometimes felt challenged by the intricacies of the government bureaucracy. Furthermore, he was no longer young by any stretch, and he felt an urgent need to move forward with his plans. There had to be better methods for doing good work within the system; Abraham Lincoln's fundamental principle of a *government of the people, by the people, for the people* became his guiding light. Dr Kalam decided to create a niche for his office, by boldly taking socially relevant issues – which had been lost in the labyrinth of multiple ministries – directly to the Cabinet for approval and implementation. He was determined to make a difference in the lives of everyday Indians, and he would circumvent red tape and vested interests to do so.

Conversely, he would bring his eyes and ears closer to the people. For this, he would need to identify the best minds of the times, which was another of his strong suits. When Dr Kalam moved out of the mighty corridors of the South Block to understand the larger problems of the people of India in his new role, he found resonance in three people: Dr Kakarla Subbarao, professor of radiology at the Albert Einstein Institute of Medicine in New York, who had been called by N.T. Rama Rao, the chief minister of Andhra Pradesh to set up Nizam's Institute of Medical Sciences in Hyderabad; R.M. Lala, the co-founder of the Centre for the Advancement of Philanthropy (CAP) and its chairman since 1993; and Chandru Shahani, the chairman of Klenzaids, an engineering company in Mumbai, working in the field of clean manufacturing settings for the biological and electronics industries.

Dr Kalam drew on Dr Kakarla Subbarao's passion for bringing the best of medical science for the service of his patients, whatever their background. While working at the affiliated hospitals of Albert Einstein College of Medicine in New York at Montefiore, Jacobi and Bronx-Lebanon, Dr Kakarla Subbarao came in contact with thousands of poor African American patients who faced discrimination at every turn. Even after segregation ended, African American people faced all manner of bigotry and racism in the great American cities. They had poorer schools, lesser resources directed to their areas and suffered from prejudice based on the colour of their skin. Their needs were often ignored; they were mostly treated as an afterthought by those in power. Dr Subbarao played a key role in the formation of the Telugu Association of North America (TANA), and brought Telugu-speaking people together in America before he was called back to India. Inspired by Dr Kalam, Dr Subbarao used his life's savings to create a trust for the study of radiology and an international school for children in the Shaikpet area of Hyderabad.

Dr Kalam came to know about R.M. Lala after reading his book *Celebration of the Cells*, written in the form of letters to a friend who had been diagnosed with cancer. Lala chose journalism as his career at the age of nineteen and established the first book-publishing house from India in London in 1959. He founded *Himmat Weekly* with Rajmohan Gandhi, a biographer and grandson of Mahatma Gandhi, which he edited for a decade. In 1974, Lala joined the Tata Group and was working director of the Sir Dorabji Tata Trust when Dr Kalam first met him. He shared with Dr Kalam that he had worked in the Tata trusts for almost twenty years before J.R.D. Tata had invited him to actually join the trusts. But JRD never interfered in his duties, even though he was the chairman and had the power to do so. He possessed, along with Dr Kalam, the same attribute of all truly great leaders: he knew when to use his power and when not to use it.

Chandru Shahani was suffering from a rare type of blood cancer when Dr Kalam met him first in 1999. His indomitable spirit touched Dr Kalam. Their friendship over the years facilitated the indigenous development of biologics. Although the US Food and Drug Administration (FDA) had approved many forms of biological therapy, others remained experimental and were available to cancer patients principally through participation in clinical trials. Dr Kalam used his good offices to take care of the regulatory issues for these therapies. Shahani developed four mobile-level biological facilities to cultivate and contain bacteria to stimulate the body's immune system to act against cancer cells.

In May 2000, Dr Kalam invited fifty medical experts, directors of government laboratories, researchers and industrialists to Vigyan Bhavan. This diverse selection of prominent minds attended this meeting to brainstorm on how life-saving treatments based on modern techniques could be made affordable in India and other developing countries. The magnitude and severity of preventable and treatable non-communicable diseases – diabetes, stroke, cancer and heart disease – had brought the affordability of medicines to the forefront of global public health. Dr Kalam called on these eminent people of the health sector to evolve a blueprint for more timely and affordable access to medicines, not only in India but for the whole world's poor.

There was a general consensus at the meeting that if medicines were priced at the cost of production under an alternative research and development system, they would immediately become more affordable. Moreover, the budgets of government subsidy programmes and charities would be able to provide greater coverage and treatment to those who needed it. Dr Kalam told the members, 'Multinational corporations founded on the wealth amassed during colonialism would never work for the poor of this world. They undertake research as a money-multiplying activity. Indian companies must find solutions for their own people. They would become great multinational corporations eventually, as their products will be used by three billion poor people of the world.'

This meeting proved the beginning of three great developments in Indian health care: the development of a malaria vaccine, indigenous liver transplants, and stem cell research in ophthalmology. Not much, though, could be achieved in the way of bringing down the high cost of patented pharmaceuticals, stents, and cancer treatment using biologics.

Indigenous agricultural development also had long been a keen interest for Dr Kalam, and it featured heavily in his *India 2020*. He now initiated a pilot project involving 3,000 farming families that implemented a systemic approach for the cultivation of rice, wheat and pulses. The constant supply of input materials such as seeds, fertilizers and pesticides had been met through people's participation with the creation of the Agro Service Centre and the Seed Growers Association. Knowledge empowerment of farmers with improved cultivation technology was given a special thrust. This made a significant impact on the productivity of crops, particularly rice and wheat. Productivity of rice in project areas increased from 2 to 5.5 tonnes per hectare and of wheat from 0.9 to 2.6 tonnes per hectare. Most encouraging was the readiness of the farmers to adopt the new technology. Dr Kalam kept a close eye on the project and was gratified with the results: 'I was continuously in contact with Paliganj farmers of Bihar. The TIFAC mission has resulted in doubling the productivity of rice and wheat in areas near RP Channel-5 in Bihar using innovative integrated farming and marketing methods.'[1]

In January 2000, I accompanied Dr Kalam on a visit to Bihar. We stayed at the Government Guest House near the Bihar assembly. It was a British colonial-era building with gloriously high ceilings, large wooden stairs made of massive teak planks, decorative lamps and, of course, vintage furniture. It possessed a kind of stiff-necked, fusty charm; but not all was to Dr Kalam's liking. We sat down to breakfast the first morning after we arrived, and Dr Kalam became immediately agitated. The staff had prepared for him a typically English breakfast of toast and jam. He called me and asked me to go down to the kitchen to see if something 'eatable' could be served: 'Don't tell me that these guys eat this for breakfast here!'

The cook most respectfully explained to me that most of the sahibs who came from Delhi were served this breakfast. I told the cook that Dr Kalam was not a sahib, he was a saint. The cook enthusiastically cooked hot bhaat in about fifteen minutes' time and served it to Dr Kalam, who ate it gleefully.

In the evening, Dr Kalam was taking his usual post-dinner stroll in the sprawling courtyard of the guest house, when he noticed a giant tamarind tree. He became animated and said, 'Look, funny guy, these funny guys have such a big tree full of tamarinds, but did not put even one in my bhaat. Why are we Indians so blind to our own gifts and unsure of the soundness of our traditions that we mimic the eating habits and foods of the foreigners?'

Throughout, Dr Kalam was a curious mix of simplicity of habits and great intellectual complexity; but he was by no means a sahib yearning for the trappings of a glorious past. Everything in his life was forward-looking and progressive. Even his spartan lifestyle served its purpose here; he had no extraneous retinue or pointless attachment to material goods that could impede his progress – physical or spiritual. Even as age advanced on him, he kept up a cracking pace, his sprightly gait matched by a similarly sprightly mind.

And his focus remained on bringing technological progress to his country. On 5 May 2000, Dr Kalam inaugurated the first telemedicine link connecting Care Hospital with Mehboobnagar District Hospital on a V-SAT link provided by the Hughes Escorts Communications Ltd. Dr B. Soma Raju opened a new facility of Care Hospital at Banjara Hills, Hyderabad. Dr Kalam joined the board of directors of Quality Care India Ltd., the holding company that owned the Care Hospitals.

Education, as Dr Kalam knew, is the key to technological development. In October 2000, Dr Kalam met Azim Premji during his visit to the Wipro-GE Centre at Bangalore. This installation built GE's advanced medical equipment in India, significantly reducing its cost. Premji briefed Dr Kalam about the educational initiative that he was planning. Dr Kalam asked Premji how Wipro reached its high stature in the business world. Dr Kalam was quite taken with Premji's reply and later quoted it in several of his speeches:

> Sir, I can say that there are three aspects that come to my mind. First: Sweat for generations and the hard work of teams. Second: We work for customers' delight. Third: A bit of luck. The third point will not be of any consequence if the first two aspects are not achieved. In Wipro, what we have tried to do is wealth generation with social concern.[2]

On 26 January 2001, a massive earthquake measuring 7.9 on the Richter scale struck Gujarat. More than 30,000 people perished in the calamity. The epicentre of the quake was some 300 kilometres west of Ahmedabad near the town of Bhuj, which bore the brunt of the destruction. On 15 March 2001, Dr Kalam and Y.S. Rajan visited Bhuj to review the rehabilitation work in the aftermath of the earthquake that struck Gujarat on 26 January 2001. There, Dr Kalam met Sadhu Brahmaviharidas, a disciple of Pramukh Swamiji, the head and inspirer of BAPS.

Sadhu Brahmaviharidas asked Dr Kalam a startling question: 'After the detonation of the first atomic bomb, Robert Oppenheimer remembered the Gita: "Time I am the shatterer of the world." What came to your mind after you detonated India's first atomic bomb?' Dr Kalam said, 'The energy of God does not shatter, it unifies,' to which Sadhu Brahmaviharidas replied, 'Our spiritual leader, Pramukh Swami Maharaj is a great unifier. He has unified all our energies to regenerate and restore life from the rubble of damage.' Deeply impressed, Dr Kalam expressed his desire to Y.S. Rajan to meet such a swami.

On 30 June 2001, Dr Kalam and Y.S. Rajan met Pramukh Swamiji in New Delhi. Swamiji was sitting on a sofa, and another sofa was kept for Dr Kalam. Humbled by Pramukh Swamiji's gentle and gracious presence, Dr Kalam opted to sit down on the floor along with the other sadhus present in the room. As Dr Kalam did not know a word of Gujarati, Pramukh Swamiji's language, and Pramukh Swamiji would not understand English, Sadhu Brahmaviharidas first became the interpreter, and later a very close friend after many such meetings with Swamiji over the next decade.

Dr Kalam told Pramukh Swamiji that India had had a vision before 1857 to be an independent nation. The struggle persisted for the following ninety long years. During this time the entire Indian society – people from all walks of life, rich and poor, young and old, elite and ordinary, educated and illiterate – all came together in this aim. The goal was singular and focused, and it was well understood that India must be a free country.

Dr Kalam told Pramukh Swamiji that he had worked for forty years in three of the great scientific fields of India – atomic energy, space research and defence research. Dr Kalam said that he was pained to see that despite the passage of fifty years since India attained Independence, there was no new vision. It was still a developing country. It was not strong economically, it was not cohesive socially, not even stable at times, its energy deficiency was unbearable, it had serious security threats, and it had crippling dependency on imports of oil and critical technology.

Dr Kalam further informed Pramukh Swamiji that five hundred experts at TIFAC had pondered for more than a year upon what should be the new vision after Independence. A vision for making India a developed country by the year 2020 had emerged. The experts, after much deliberation, had identified five important areas by which to transform India into a developed country in the next twenty years. These areas were education and health care, agriculture and food processing, information and communication, infrastructure, and critical technology for the strategic sectors of atomic energy, space and defence.

Dr Kalam said that as the principal scientific adviser to the Government of India, he was visiting various organizations and meeting people from all walks of life. His goal was to distil a clear vision that could inspire the nation, but there was not much movement. Dr Kalam very candidly expressed that he felt that it was not enough to secure a mandate from the government or even the finances; the problem lies in having people to carry out this mission of developing the nation.

Pramukh Swamiji heard Dr Kalam patiently, allowing him to finish. Then, spontaneously, Swamiji pointed out, 'Along with the five areas, you need a sixth one – faith in God.' This utterly new dimension which the scientists and thinkers had not yet pondered upon generated a discussion that lasted for more than an hour. Swamiji explained that development in all the proposed five areas was necessary, but a nation is as good as its people. The quality of people is enhanced by cultural and moral values. Both of which are sustained by spiritual values. Hence, with progress and prosperity, the inner spirituality of India should be developed through faith in God. We must enhance life along with lifestyle.

Dr Kalam was riveted by this revelation and very candidly agreed that he felt the problem lies in people; not having the people to carry out this mission. He understood that to realize this great dream (of a developed India), three types of people are needed – *punyatma* (virtuous people), *punyaneta* (virtuous leaders) and *punyadhikari* (virtuous officers) ... how can their numbers be increased?[3]

Dr Kalam informed Pramukh Swamiji that he was contemplating the establishment of a five-member trust to implement the plan evolved in his *India 2020* book and sought Pramukh Swamiji's blessings. Pramukh Swamiji concluded the meeting saying, 'It's good that you've come here today. It has given us much joy. You are like a Vedic rishi. The rishis of the past have done both; given us science and served society. You too are a rishi – serving society through science.' Pramukh Swamiji prophetically blessed him to lead India.

Dr Kalam had been hoping to set up a trust to realize his dream, but now felt something more than a trust was needed to motivate a nation. He was not clear what was needed, but after meeting Pramukh Swamiji, Dr Kalam was deeply satisfied and felt that whatever was needed would come. His personal faith in himself, his dream and his work increased immensely. If God is with you, who can be against you?

In September 2001, Dr Kalam visited the Dargah Sharif of Sufi saint Khwaja Moinuddin Chishti, called Gharib Nawaz at Ajmer. The simple teachings and message of Gharib Nawaz could penetrate even a heart of stone. Dr Kalam heard that Gharib Nawaz's compassionate gaze had silenced the fiercest of his enemies.

The teachings of Gharib Nawaz have been recorded in several books. Gharib Nawaz said that one who possesses the magnanimity of the river, the kindness of the sun and the humility of the earth is closest to God. One who is graceful in poverty, content in hunger, cheerful in grief and friendly in hostility, possesses the noblest character. According to the great saint, the surest way to avoid the punishment of hell is to feed the hungry, to redress the aggrieved and to help the distressed.

Dr Kalam always felt drawn to the spiritual teachings of great Sufi saints. His father once told Dr Kalam that his mother wanted to name him Aarif. She visualized her youngest child as enlightened, knowledgeable and devoted to Allah. She wanted to impart to her son a deep inner calling to inspire others for a higher cause. But his father saw his boy as a collector, and therefore they settled on naming him after the most respected Muslim of the era. That day while returning from Ajmer, Dr Kalam realized that he had indeed become what his mother wished him to be.

That he had become knowledgeable was also without question. On 1 November 2001, Tezpur University conferred an honorary doctoral degree on Dr Kalam, along with renowned musician Bhupen Hazarika and eminent mathematician Professor Jyotiprasad Medhi. After the convocation, Dr Kalam addressed a large gathering of young students. He chose the theme 'indomitable spirit' for the interaction. During the ensuing discussion, one student asked Dr Kalam, 'Why cannot water from the Brahmaputra, which is in flood most of the time, be diverted to Rajasthan, which suffers from a drought every year?' Dr Kalam later recalled how he was baffled by the manifest common sense of the question: 'Only children will have these innovative ideas. Grown-ups tend to see more impossibility. It was such a powerful question! I was completely beaten. I was sure even the prime minister would not have been able to answer it!'[4]

How could Dr Kalam answer this bright youngster, who was asking a valid, straightforward question? How could he explain that rivers are a pet issue for the states, and that they fight for imaginary rights over their waters, never minding that the rivers have flowed for millennia before the states were formed? The states make claims over the water with arguments that they are guarding the prosperity of their future generations, careless of the fact that in the meantime the water wastefully flows into the sea and causes floods every year. Galvanized by this most obvious but perplexing question, Dr Kalam made interlinking of rivers a mission at the PSA and pursued it at various forums – but in vain. As president, he would continue to speak of the virtues of linking the country's rivers:

> Interlinking of rivers could minimize flood havoc and provide water to drought-prone regions. The country has been utilizing very little of the quantity of water from the available 4,000 billion cubic metres. The country's food and water requirement has been growing because of the fast-growing population. Only planned and better water management (can) meet the challenge.[5]

In the same event, another student asked Dr Kalam a question for which he had no good answer. The student said, 'Sir, big leaders in any field don't come and talk to us. We see our prime minister often going to Chennai, Lucknow, and many other places. But he never comes here. We want him to come here; we want to talk to him. Is Assam not part of India?' Dr Kalam didn't shy away from the student's valid concern, and even made a point of conveying it to the prime minister: 'I later narrated this to the Prime Minister (Vajpayee). He conceded the point and said. "Children don't talk to me anymore. Maybe the security cordon has created a separation."'[6] Thereafter, Dr Kalam resolved that he would meet young children whenever and wherever he could possibly do so. He would remain firm on this throughout his presidency and later in his life; he even breathed his last while talking to young children.

On 3 November 2001, Dr Kalam delivered the Justice Harihar Mahapatra Memorial Lecture in Cuttack, Orissa, declaring: 'India will emerge as a developed nation in twenty years.' Justice Mahapatra was judge in the Patna High Court for a long period. He established Cuttack Eye Hospital, Utkal University and above all, worked to eradicate poverty in his area, living to a good age of ninety-two years. The Oriya translation of *Wings of Fire* was released on the occasion of Dr Kalam's lecture. After the function, one boy asked Dr Kalam about his favourite books. Dr Kalam's reply was as revealing of his character as it was frank: 'Four books in my life have been very close to my heart. *Man the Unknown* by Dr Alexis Careel, *The Thirukkural,*

Light from Many Lamps by Lillian Eichler Watson; and the Holy Quran is, of course, a constant companion.'[7]

There was no clutter in Dr Kalam's mind. Just four books, a book providing scientific outlook, a book the morality of his culture, a treasury of inspiration featuring hundreds of passages and quotations selected from the wisdom of the ages and the book of his religion.

3.3

Who Is Our Enemy?

> Genius is not that you are smarter than everyone else. It is that you are ready to receive the inspiration.
>
> – Albert Einstein
> Theoretical physicist and Noble laureate

Dr Kota Harinarayana had been Dr Kalam's closest buddy during his tenure as the chief of DRDO. Dr Kota was not a friend of Dr Kalam's like Y.S. Rajan. Neither was he his lieutenant like Sivathanu Pillai. He was hand-picked by Dr Arunachalam to head the Light Combat Aircraft (LCA) Development Programme in 1985 from HAL, where he was working as chief designer. Dr Kalam stood by his side figuratively throughout the ten years that they worked together and physically on 4 January 2001, when Wing Commander Rajiv Kothiyal soared into the sky with the LCA, designated as Technology Demonstrator 1 (TD-I) at HAL Airport in Bangalore.

The flight lasted about twenty minutes. Two support Mirage 2000 aircraft flew along with the LCA prototype. Leading from the front, Chief of Air Staff Air Marshal A.Y. Tipnis piloted one of them. With this accomplishment, India entered the elite class of countries with an indigenous fighter aircraft. The aircraft was given the code KH-1 to honour the great work of Dr Kota Harinarayana that made this success possible.

The LCA project was conceived in 1983 with the target of designing and developing an advanced technology, single-seat, single-engine and supersonic lightweight aircraft for air-to-air, air-to-ground and air-to-sea combat. It was the second prototype fighter of Indian origin, after HF-24 Marut, which was designed by a German team. The American-made GE F-404 engine was used in this aircraft, as the indigenously built Kaveri engine had been delayed.

LCA was the most ambitious project ever undertaken by the DRDO. There had been over eighty organizations and 300 small and medium firms committed to this mammoth effort. The project also faced loud criticism over cost and time overruns and whether the aircraft's technology would become obsolete by the time it was inducted into the Indian Air Force. And worse, the question was actually posed whether the country needed to embark on this exercise at all.

Dr Kalam used to pity the critics who never got their hands dirty in any engineering shop and who would willingly or gullibly play into the Western lobby's hands. He answered the naysayers in his usual measured manner, but with clarity hinting at bluntness: 'We have more advanced technology than the JAS 39 (Gripen) and as much advanced technology as EFA's (Eurofighter) Typhoon. We have pumped in so much advanced technology. I wish people would understand the reasons why we have taken more time. We were not laying a road; we were making a fighter plane.'

The point Dr Kalam had consistently made was that a country with a one-billion-strong population couldn't sustain itself by relying on goods from abroad. We can buy some things, but crucial military requirements such as strategic aircraft have to be developed here, and that has been our challenge and mission. We should not attempt to meet our defence needs by assembling aircraft with parts from abroad. What base could you create in the country from such activity? This country would forever remain poor if we relegate our engineers and scientists to the mechanic's shop, to use spanners and screwdrivers instead of their minds. Dr Kalam saw all too clearly that this was an issue of generating wealth – of the material and intellectual kinds. The LCA project, and those of a similar nature that he championed, are not merely about building an aircraft or a missile. They create jobs and stimulate the country's scientific advancement; and for this reason, they are indispensible.

From the LCA project, our country has fostered a series of technologies, leading to a multitude of spin-off benefits. Several companies that developed technologies for the LCA have exported them. There have been plenty of tears, tribulations and hard work, but that is par for the course. Technological development is by no means easy. Dr Kota Harinarayana explained the protracted nature of aircraft development to the media, bemoaning that critics had not looked at the time taken for foreign endeavours to field successful aircraft:

> Building of the F22 aircraft began in 1980 and it flew first in 1997 – after seventeen years. The Eurofighter was to make its maiden flight in 1990, but it flew in 1994. The UK, Germany, Italy and Spain have been involved with the EFA. Why is the media mum on this aspect? Western nations are continually working on prototypes and have more time, considering their technology. In the aircraft business, fifteen years is not a long time. But moving ahead should be faster – decisions are needed to enter production.[1]

Dr Kalam's face would beam with pride, however, when he talked about the LCA:

> The LCA is the smallest supersonic fighter in the world. It has performed beautifully. The touchdown was beautiful and the pilot said it did not feel like a prototype. We may have taken our time, but we have perfected it. When the Americans ran away with their software after Pokhran II, we tested our control laws and flight control systems for almost two-and-a-half years. We have tested it thrice as intensively as any European country or the US. There were no failures in the first flight. The design, evaluation, flight-testing and airworthiness teams did an incredible job. Why are we enemies of our own success?

Prof. P.V. Indiresan and Dr Kalam crossed each other's paths by chance. Prof. Indiresan, the former director at IIT, Madras, and a great champion of rural development, had developed a model called Providing Urban Facilities in Rural Areas (PURA). Dr Kalam as

PSA was looking for ideas that can transform India, particularly its 700,000 villages. On the sidelines of an event where they both finally met, Dr Kalam asked him, 'Tell me, sir, have the bureaucrats accepted your counsel on contentious issues?' Prof. Indiresan said, 'They seek the advice which they want, and not the guidance that they need!' Thus began a short but very intense collaboration between the two great scientists for transforming Indian villages. Prof. P.V. Indiresan saw pooling resources as a way forward for villages to sustain themselves and forge ahead: 'The problems of rapid urbanization can be overcome by "providing urban amenities in rural areas" through the PURA scheme and by working with clusters rather than individual villages.'[2]

Dr Kalam later recalled his immediate affinity with the concept: 'When my friend Prof. Indiresan came up with the idea of PURA, it struck a chord. I started detailed discussions with him and several other experts in the field who had a similar interest'[3]

Bearing in mind that most villages in India are too small to offer even basic amenities and cannot support schools, hospitals, markets and services that are currently available in urban areas, PURA was evolved as a solution as well as an ideal. PURA offered a way of transcending this isolation. It considered a village not as a disparate unit but saw the resources of a cluster of villages with a total population of at least thirty to fifty thousand; and this would be large enough to sustain many basic urban services.

On 30 September 2001, Dr Kalam was flying in a helicopter from Ranchi to Bokaro to attend a Jharkhand State Science and Technology Council meeting. Samaresh Singh, science and technology minister in the Jharkhand government, was seated next to Dr Kalam. There was violent turbulence, and the pilots said that there was something terribly wrong with the helicopter's rotor. Moments before landing at Bokaro at around 4.30 p.m., the helicopter engine failed, and it plummeted to the earth from a height of about 100 metres. Miraculously, everybody survived. Samaresh Singh recalled Dr Kalam's politeness and calm in the face of doom: 'It sounded like imminent death to all of us; Dr Kalam remained composed with his signature smile playing on his lips. He even advised the two pilots not to worry.'[4]

Despite being hurt, Dr Kalam effusively expressed his gratitude to the pilots, who were injured themselves, and told them they deserved awards for bravery. He then headed without delay to the Ramakrishna Vidyalaya in Bokaro for his scheduled programme, addressing the students there without any indication of his ordeal. At night, a panel of doctors sent by Samaresh Singh persuaded Dr Kalam to take a tranquillizer. That night, Dr Kalam had a vivid dream. He saw himself in a desert with miles of silvery sand shining under a full moon. Five men stood in a circle around him. The men were Emperor Ashok, Caliph Umar, Abraham Lincoln, Albert Einstein and Mahatma Gandhi, and they spoke in turn to him.

Emperor Ashok said, 'O Kalam, I learned after the Kalinga war that there is no victory in causing suffering to others. Triumph is a peaceful kingdom. You have done enough for weapons, now work for peace.' Caliph Umar said, 'O Kalam, I learned after I conquered Jerusalem that all men are indeed equal. There is no point in forcing others to follow your path. You will get only that which is ordained for you. God alone is the sovereign. Never seek favours of men.' Einstein said, 'O Kalam, you are a great scientist but be aware that science without religion is lame; religion without science is blind. Never deviate from your religion.' Finally, Abraham Lincoln said, 'O Kalam, nearly all men can stand adversity, but if you want to test a man's character, give him power. Be careful with your power.'

The next morning, Dr Kalam read in the newspaper that a plane carrying the young leader Madhavrao Jivajirao Scindia and a team of journalists, crashed on the outskirts of Mainpuri district of Uttar Pradesh, killing all on board. A shiver ran through his spine. What if the helicopter lost power a few seconds earlier? Was there a link in his surviving the mishap and the divine messages in the dream?

Upon returning to Delhi, Dr Kalam met Prime Minister Atal Bihari Vajpayee and requested him to relieve him from government service. Dr Kalam said, 'Sir, I have completed seventy orbits around the sun, may I take leave now?' The prime minister offered Dr Kalam a ministerial position, but he politely declined. After some silent moments, with unspoken words hanging in the air, the prime minister said, '*Jaisi aapki marzi*' (As you wish).

Prof. N. Balakrishnan at the IISc had been a friend of Dr Kalam's since the Cray supercomputer denial days in the late 1980s. He later established the Supercomputer Education and Research Centre (SERC) at IISc, one of the best high-performance computing centres in India. Balki, as Dr Kalam called Prof. Balakrishnan, felt that Dr Kalam should come to IISc. The high-speed aerodynamics laboratory at IISc had some of the first facilities in the country for the study of gas flow, and it had flourished because of the launch vehicle programmes of ISRO and the Agni missile programme.

Dr Kalam enjoyed the historical distinction of being the earliest scientist to harness the growing power of computers for aerospace development in India. He made it possible for new regimes of gas flow – high temperature, high speed, low density, etc., to be studied in detail numerically. His collaboration with Prof. Roddam Narasimha and his brilliant students at IISc and later at National Aerospace Laboratories, which at that time had the country's most powerful computer using parallel computation technologies, was advantageous not just for aerospace. A further spin-off benefit had seen an enhancement in national capabilities due to the requirements of the programmes that Dr Kalam was working on.

Dr Kalam played a key role in the creation of the Space Technology Cell at IISc headed by Roddam Narasimha. In his habits and lifestyle, Dr Kalam was a guerrilla commander in the disciplined barracks of IISc. His simple, almost monkish lifestyle offended the ways and manners of many internationally trained academicians at IISc, who would see themselves as martyrs, sacrificing their lives by working in the institute rather than living in more developed Western societies. Dr Kalam seemed entirely uninterested in chasing wealth or material comfort; but he was clearly driven by an extraordinary passion for designing and building ambitious technological systems. These characteristics, along with his great personal charm and obvious commitment to the project on hand made it very difficult for anyone to say no when Dr Kalam sought help. Prof. Sivaraj Ramaseshan, who was the director of IISc from 1981 to 1984, would say that Kalam could milk a tigress. Incidentally, Prof. Ramaseshan came from impressive Indian scientific stock: he was the nephew of Indian scientist and Nobel laureate Sir C.V. Raman and cousin of Nobel laureate Subramanyan Chandrasekhar. An acclaimed writer, his fair summation of his colleague Dr Kalam remains one of the most insightful ever written:

> He (Kalam) defied monocultural paradigms: he was a technologist with a big heart, a man who broke up the development of the nation to a large series of doable projects, an ascetic in his personal life, and a person who respected ability wherever he found it, with total disregard for wealth, power, degrees, position [and] class.[5]

The Indian Space Research Organization had set up the Brahm Prakash Memorial Chair at IISc, and Balki and many others like him at IISc were keen for Dr Kalam to take the chair. They met Dr Kalam at Delhi to this end, but he pointed out that he did not hold a formal PhD degree, and that would be requisite at IISc for such a position. But their enthusiasm for seeing him at the IISc campus made for an interesting discussion, and the group bolstered their argument by hearkening to the very conception of the institution.

They narrated to Dr Kalam a significant historic event that occurred in 1893. A ship called *Empress of India* was sailing from Yokohama in Japan to Vancouver in Canada. On board were two extraordinary Indians – Swami Vivekananda and Jamsetji N. Tata. Both were headed for Chicago on two different missions. Swamiji was to attend the World Congress of Religions. Jamsetji was going to see World's Columbian Exposition, a celebration of technology and industrial progress. On board the ship, Jamsetji discussed his plans to start a steel mill in India. Swamiji told Jamsetji that there were two parts to the challenge – manufacturing technology and the science of steel. The technology could be brought from abroad but the science had to be researched at home. This sowed the seed of an idea in Jamsetji Tata's mind to start the Indian Institute of Science at

Bangalore. He later wrote to Swamiji in 1898, asking for his support for the venture.

The coterie of Dr Kalam's supporters for the chair even showed him the facsimile of that historical letter. The exact words Jamsetji Tata used were: 'I know not who would make a more fitting general of such a campaign than Vivekananda.' Swamiji in turn wrote, 'I am not aware if any project, at once so opportune and so far reaching in its beneficent effects, has ever been mooted in India ... The scheme grasps the vital point of weakness in our national well-being with a clearness of vision and tightness of grip, the mastery of which is only equalled by the munificence of the gift that is being ushered to the public.' As events would transpire, Swamiji passed away in 1902 before the Indian Institute of Science eventually started functioning in 1909.

The team felt that an academic PhD was important; but it was no more than a selfish endeavour between a guide and a student, financed by some project and done to earn a livelihood by the student and sustaining one for the professor. In their view, IISc was losing its way; it was drifting far from the ideology of its founders. They felt it needed a breath of fresh air to lead the institution into working for society, rather than for itself or its faculty. Perhaps they were a little too close to the truth here, as the advocacy for Dr Kalam triggered a very strong reaction in the IISc establishment, as a contemporary article pointed out:

> The dons of IISc nixed the idea. 'We cannot encourage him to work out of IISc because there is a conflict of interest,' the director said. Ostensibly, IISc, which handles only postgraduate and doctoral students, did not want the 1,00,000 children that Kalam wanted to meet each year to instil the scientific temper in them on its campus.[6]

Dr Kalam took the controversy, which was widely debated in the country, in his usual stoic way. He was no Vivekananda, and IISc had long left behind the legacy of Jamsetji Tata. The institution appeared now to be inspired by the more worldly vision of becoming an Indian Harvard or MIT. The debate surrounding Dr Kalam's candidature – or at least the advocacy by his supporters – had, however, raised an important point about the responsibility of the Indian government to its scientists. The government should ensure that the scientists who commit their careers to national programmes are given time and support to earn academic credentials befitting their abilities. Nevertheless, Dr Kalam had been too busy building rockets and assisting military and nuclear programmes to commit himself to the rigmarole of a master's and PhD. And perhaps, in the final analysis, the nation was all the better for this.

In November 2001, Dr Kalam moved to the campus of his alma mater, Anna University in Chennai, and resumed his academic pursuits. He became involved in teaching and research tasks, which was something he had always wanted to do. But his official responsibilities never allowed him to teach. By that time, he felt he had a divine ordinance to inspire spiritually enlightened, skilful and hard-working youths – and that must be fulfilled.

At Anna University, Father Aathappilly Kuriakose George approached Prof. Kalam. He wanted to do a PhD after completing his Master of Computer Applications from Christ College in Bangalore. Dr Kalam asked him to select a topic that would eventually help people. After many weeks of deliberation, he came up with the idea of enhancing the capabilities of mentally challenged children by stimulation of their brains.

This topic resonated with Dr Kalam. A mentally challenged child typically suffers from his condition due to a deficiency in the quantity and quality of brain neurons. It is this deficiency that results in his intellectual ability being impaired. If a way of increasing the neuronal density by appropriate training in at least some areas could be found, it would lead to a better quality of life for the affected children. Aware that he was not qualified to guide his student – Dr Kalam was never one to overstate his knowledge – he involved Dr T.R. Raju at National Institute of Mental Health and Neurosciences (NIMHANS) in the research and to guide Father George. The research evolved methods for increasing the population of neurons through natural challenging of the brain, external stimulation, through the use of stem cells or with a combination of these.

The research proved that the shortening of paths by practice underlines the need for repetitions in the case of mentally challenged children. The role of both the hemispheres in the execution of tasks points to the requirement for training both the brain's hemispheres. The role of proper exercises to wire the brain underscores the need for proper exercises to enhance the brain's capabilities. Dr Kalam was fascinated by this work, and it expanded his understanding of learning:

> During this time I came across research done on the brain at Harvard University. I learnt that there is converging scientific evidence for four systems as the foundations of human knowledge and it hints at a fifth one. I knew now that a child learns by observing the objects if they are moving as connected and bounded together as flocks of birds, or moving on connected, unobstructed paths like trains on railway tracks, or the objects are influencing each others' motion when and only when they touch like billiard balls colliding with each other.[7]

Each interaction with students was advancing Dr Kalam on a spiritual path. As time progressed he became more the saint than the scientist. On my birthday in February 2002, Dr Kalam gave me a book: *Care of the Soul*. It dealt with the theme of adding depth and meaning to everyday life. He highlighted the following lines: 'Soul is revealed in attachment, love, and community as well as in retreat or inner communing and intimacy. When soul is neglected, it doesn't just go away; it appears symptomatically in obsessions, addictions, violence, and loss of meaning.'[8]

On 11 April 2002, Dr Kalam was invited to a function at the Anandalaya High School in Anand, Gujarat. When Dr Kalam reached Ahmedabad the previous evening, the city was under curfew. He went to Anand by road, escorted by police. The next day at Anandalaya High School, during the usual informal interaction Dr Kalam would encourage after his formal lectures, one boy asked him a question: 'Who is our enemy?' Dr Kalam did not have a prompt answer, so he passed the question to the other children present there. After a few moments of deliberation, Snehal Thakkar, a class twelve student, answered, 'Sir, our enemy is poverty.' Dr Kalam was thrilled by the clarity of her answer. He congratulated Snehal and later dedicated his book *Ignited Minds* to her. To Dr Kalam, this answer was like a burst of light, akin to the blazing sun cutting through dark clouds. Deep inside him, Dr Kalam knew that spiritual poverty is even worse than material poverty. The ignorance of soul is our real enemy.

3.4

Kingdom of God

> Know you all not that the unrighteous shall not inherit the kingdom of God? Be not deceived: neither fornicators, nor idolaters, nor adulterers, nor effeminate, nor abusers of themselves with mankind.
>
> – The Holy Bible
> 1 Corinthians 6:9

Dr Kalam's talents were widely sought, and he never had any thoughts of retirement. The National Aeronautical Laboratory had played a major supporting role in the design of Light Combat Aircraft. NAL had been the work centre for the National Control Law team, which spearheaded the activities leading to the Initial Operational Clearance (IOC) Standard Control Law and air-data algorithms for the LCA. NAL quickly renewed its association with Dr Kalam and made him the chairman of its Research Council (RC). One of his colleagues reminisced of his time there in his new role, with a more prominent status:

> Once again we saw Kalam in the NAL guesthouse, but this time escorted by gun-toting security staff because he was seen as a terrorist target. Curiously enough, the Z-class security made him an even greater celebrity ... As chairman, Kalam seemed brusque and impatient. He didn't encourage deep technical discussions. Kalam seemed somewhat shallow (compared to Satish Dhawan who had

> been the chairman of RC earlier), but made sure that decisions were made quickly and followed up rigorously.[1]

Despite the rebuff of the Indian Institute of Science, Dr Kalam's credentials and unparalleled experience in his field had led to his new post at his alma mater, Anna University. He met with Prof. A. Kalanidhi, the vice chancellor of Anna University on 29 September 2001. Prof. Kalanidhi had phoned him upon reading in the newspapers that he was planning to join the Indian Institute of Science in Bangalore. Prof. Kalanidhi felt that Dr Kalam should occupy a professor's chair at Anna University. After all, he was a former student, and surely the university had the first right over him. They had a long, amicable discussion which concluded with Dr Kalam promising to call back after thinking about Prof. A. Kalanidhi's offer. Prof. Kalanidhi left for the United States immediately after their meeting. A few days later, when he was at Boston airport on his way to Chicago, Dr Kalam confirmed his willingness to work at Anna University.

Prof. Kalanidhi told Dr Kalam that since he represented the scientific community of India, he couldn't exclusively represent the university and be limited to any one subject or department. He suggested a title of 'Professor of Technology and Societal Transformation' – perhaps one of the most apt titles Dr Kalam had ever been given – and Dr Kalam readily agreed. Prof. Kalanidhi told Dr Kalam that in Western countries, universities flourish with the help of their alumni but in India, alumni support is barely mentioned. He wanted to change this and develop an alumni network. He told Dr Kalam that his presence on the campus would motivate the alumni of the university, spread across the world, to support their alma mater. Some months later, his unassuming tenure at Anna University – which was to be cut short by the calling of the nation – was described by the vice chancellor:

> On 2 October 2001, Kalam occupied the chair. A room and two attendants were provided for a man who was known to be simple and hated ostentation. An office room, an Internet connection, two research scholars and two stenographers were all that he had at the

> university. Of course, he had to put up with the security personnel provided by the Indian government.[2]

Dr Kalam was accommodated in the guest house of Anna University at its sprawling campus in Guindy. The grounds extended over 100 hectares abutting the River Adyar on the north. There were no mess facilities at the guesthouse, and breakfast would come from the PG Hostel mess. Prof. Kalanidhi convinced Dr Kalam to accept meals cooked in his house. Stenographers T. Nagarajan and S. Balasubramaniam, working in the registrar's office, became his two office assistants. Years later, T. Nagarajan would reminisce of Dr Kalam's simplicity and humility:

> Kalam sir entered the room with one small leather bag, which contained three sets of his clothes, a pair of shoes and a few books. I was surprised to see a man of his stature living such a simple life. He was contented, concerned about people around him and their families, and was polite and punctual. Not once has he shown any pride or arrogance. I have never come across someone like him in my entire life.[3]

Though others may have viewed his lifestyle as austere, Dr Kalam enjoyed what he perceived as the luxury of living on Anna University's beautiful campus. There, he could spend his leisure time with the students, listening to their dreams and answering their questions. He could take his contemplative evening strolls through the grounds and courtyards, surrounded by its trees and lawns. He was near his ancestral roots, at least linguistically and culturally, and the balmy Chennai weather was as familiar as the sultry seaside climate of his youth in Rameswaram.

From an academic snub that his indomitable spirit had barely even registered, he had landed in a place of acceptance and comfort, where his talents were recognized and he could contribute to the future of the new generation. But this was not what destiny wanted of him. He would be soon taken away from what must have seemed to many as his perfect retirement job, to a greater, higher orbit. He would not merely inspire a few students: he would inspire a nation.

Spiritual inspiration in these years was an increasingly important theme for Dr Kalam, even while attending to his more temporal duties. Dr Kalam made his first visit out of Anna University to Amrita Institute of Computer Technology near Kollam in Kerala. N. Balakrishnan and G. Madhavan Nair, then director VSSC, accompanied him. Dr Kalam met Mata Amritanandamayi Devi. She told him, 'Spirituality both begins and ends with compassion. No one is an isolated island; we are all links in the great chain of life. Just as the right hand reaches out to aid the left hand when it is injured, the ability to feel the sufferings of all beings as our own, and an intense yearning to comfort them, should awaken within us.'

On 6 October 2001, Dr Kalam went to Kanchipuram. The Sankaracharyas of Kanchi organized a very important gathering of farmers from hundreds of villages to launch a knowledge-empowered rural development programme based on the PURA concept. When the meeting ended, both acharyas – Swami Jayendra Saraswathigal and Swami Vijayendra Saraswathigal – called Dr Kalam for a private meeting. Swami Vijayendra Saraswathigal said, 'Kalam sahib, you have realized the presence of the same atman in all living beings, thus malice towards people and other beings starts disappearing. The divinity has dawned in your heart. Go and spread compassion.' Dr Kalam once again remembered the prophetic words of Pramukh Swamiji that a great destiny awaited him and one day he would lead India.

Dr Kalam did not realize the depth of the transformation that was happening around him, though. He was too busy meeting students and visiting organizations doing service. In January 2002, Dr Kalam went to Sri Sathya Sai Institute of Higher Medical Sciences at Whitefield in Bangalore, to attend a conference on Medical Technology and Health Care. Prof. P. Rama Rao accompanied him. He was impressed to see the world-class tertiary health care hospitals established by Sri Sathya Sai Baba to provide patient care facilities to all irrespective of caste, class, creed, gender, religion or nationality – completely free of any charge. As with the acharyas a few months earlier, Dr Kalam was well received by Sri Sathya Sai Baba. Kalam recalled: 'When I finished my presentation on how technology would transform human life, he got up and blessed me, to the cheers of participants.'[4]

The following month, Dr Kalam visited the Brahma Kumari Spiritual Academy at Mount Abu in Rajasthan. Dr A. Sivathanu Pillai and Dr W. Selvamurthy were with him. Dr Kalam interacted with coronary artery disease (CAD) patients, called dilwals there, and the doctors at the Global Hospital and Research Centre of the Brahma Kumari Academy, headed by Dr Pratap Midha. Dr Selvamurthy and Dr Midha postulated, through years of clinical work and research in physiology and psychology of heart patients, that there is a very strong mind–body synchrony. Further, by the purification of the mind through meditation and cleaning of the body with diet and exercise, heart disease can be controlled and even cured. Kalam wrote later of a profound spiritual incident, occurring in the wake of a number of spiritual events around this time, which seemed to augur great happenings:

> I had an extraordinary spiritual experience ... The deity of the Brahma Kumaris, Shiva Baba, descended on one of the disciples, Dhadhi Gurrzar. Before our eyes, her personality changed: Her face became radiant, her voice became deeper as she talked about the four treasures of knowledge, yoga, virtue and service.[5]

On 10 June 2002, Dr Kalam got a message from Dr Kalanidhi's office that the prime minister's office was looking for him and that he should come to the vice chancellor's office to speak to the prime minister. Dr Kalam was perplexed, as he had had no contact with any government functionary for some time. When he arrived in the vice chancellor's office, he was connected to the prime minister's office, and after a few minutes, Prime Minister Atal Bihari Vajpayee came on the line. He said, 'Kalam sahib, the nation needs you as its Rashtrapati.' Dr Kalam thanked Prime Minister Vajpayee and requested an hour's time so that he could reflect upon his generous offer. Vajpayee said, 'Please do that. But I need only a "yes" and not a "no".'

By evening, Dr Kalam's candidature was announced at a joint press conference addressed by the National Democratic Alliance (NDA) convener, George Fernandes, the parliamentary affairs minister, Pramod Mahajan, the Andhra Pradesh chief minister, Chandrababu Naidu, and the Uttar Pradesh chief minister, Kumari Mayawati. A press article at the time described the bipartisan support that Dr Kalam's nomination received:

> Kalam emerged with the backing of an overwhelming majority of the establishment. The Congress, after two days of being torn between its natural inclination to oppose the NDA and a strong compulsion to endorse an eminent, apolitical member of the minority community, finally plumped for the Missile Man.[6]

Another commentator saw the nomination in political terms, as a clever ploy by the government to breach the opposition's ranks. Ironically, Dr Kalam, an apolitical, unaligned and almost universally approved candidate for the office of president, had been a pawn in a political intrigue, the reporter asserted. And it was for his very attributes that the intrigue had been successful: 'Unwittingly, Kalam became the weapon of a devastating political strike. In a matter of six days, Kalam's candidature saw the People's Front breaking up and the Congress sheepishly toeing the great consensus.'[7]

Till Dr Kalam received the call from Prime Minister Vajpayee, presidency was the last thing on Kalam's mind. He had prepared himself to dedicate his time to various projects that he could not fulfil during his career proper. In Chennai, he launched himself into his dream of interacting with at least one lakh students from across the country. He was also involved in trying to preserve and transform the traditional knowledge etched on ancient palm leaves into digital media for permanent storage and wider distribution through the Internet.

All these projects would have to be put on hold, then handed to trusted people to advance on their own undertaking. Dr Kalam had many practical matters ahead of him, and would address them in his characteristic practical manner. When Parliamentary Affairs Minister Pramod Mahajan called him up and asked him for an auspicious time for him to file his presidential nomination, Dr Kalam told him astronomy, not astrology, keeps the world going. He would continue to function in a similar manner to that which had sustained him all his working life; and this could be quite a surprise for some. For their part, the media was bemused and more than a little taken with the future president's positivity and sincerity, which was anything but politics as usual:

> There is a quiet innocence about Kalam as he comes to terms with the fact that he will be the next occupant of Rashtrapati Bhavan. India's president-to-be at his first press conference on 13 June was yet to shake off the hangover of having delivered fifty lectures in the last six months. So when he faced the motley crew of young men and women holding notepads, microphones and video cameras, he felt he was merely addressing another group of students. As he quoted from the Bhagavad Gita (Whatever happened has happened for the good, whatever is happening is happening for the good and whatever will happen will happen for the good), Kalam repeatedly asked his 'class' if they had understood what he was saying. He urged everyone to repeat the punchline after him – 'The nation is bigger than the individual.' His 'students' obliged![8]

Pramod Mahajan came to Anna University and escorted Dr Kalam to New Delhi. Defence Minister George Fernandes received Dr Kalam at the airport. He immediately went to the prime minister's office from there. He also met Samajwadi Party leader Mulayam Singh Yadav, his earlier boss in the defence ministry. In the evening, Dr Kalam opted to stay at the DRDO guest house in the Asiad Village, which was his 'home' from 1992 until the final year when he left Delhi to join Anna University.

Accompanied by Prime Minister Vajpayee and his senior cabinet colleagues, Dr Kalam filed his nomination papers in parliament on 18 June 2002. The first set of nomination papers was filed by the Congress party led by its chief Smt. Sonia Gandhi, followed by party members Shivraj Patil, Dr Manmohan Singh, P.M. Sayeed, Najma Heptullah, Ambika Soni, Arjun Singh and Ahmad Patel. Prime Minister Vajpayee, Home Minister Lal Krishna Advani, External Affairs Minister Jaswant Singh and Defence Minister George Fernandes filed the second set of nomination papers on behalf of the National Democratic Alliance.

When Prime Minister Vajpayee pointed out the matrimonial status column, which indicated that Dr Kalam was a bachelor, Dr Kalam quipped that not only was he a bachelor, he was also a Brahmachari. This sent everyone present into fits of laughter. Among the leaders of the parties supporting the NDA, Telugu Desam Party chief N. Chandrababu Naidu, Samajwadi Party chief Mulayam Singh Yadav, Biju Janata Dal chief Naveen Patnaik, Bahujan Samaj Party vice-president Mayawati and Trinamool Congress chief Mamata Banerjee were present.

In his first press conference on 19 June 2002, Dr Kalam succinctly put across the need for having an educated political class, with compassion as the cornerstone of political decision making. Veteran reporters were a little nonplussed but charmed by his candid approach to their questions:

> For hard-nosed journalists, used to short term strategies, crisp and straight-on-the-face answers, Kalam's lectures about the need to educate people and improve the economy to end violence were alien. However, in between his vague replies, Kalam slipped in a few suggestions about how he plans to conduct himself atop the glorious Raisina Hill. On any controversial issue he would consult the country's leading constitutional experts. Decisions on issues such as president's rule in states would be decided based on 'what people needed, rather than what a few people want' ... Dr Kalam's disarming candour and an almost fanatic rigour to avoiding anything remotely controversial left both the missile man and the reporters still smiling at the end of it all ...[9]

Despite robust support for his candidature across the political spectrum, Dr Kalam would not be elected unopposed. Octogenarian freedom fighter and Left Front nominee Lakshmi Sahgal filed her nomination papers for the presidential election on 21 June 2002. She was accompanied by former prime minister H.D. Deve Gowda, CPI-M leader Somnath Chatterjee, CPI leader J. Chittaranjan, Forward Bloc leader Debabrata Biswas, RSP leaders Abani Roy and Harishankar Mahale and West Bengal chief minister Buddhadev Bhattacharjee.

The president of India is indirectly elected by means of an electoral college consisting of the members of parliament and the legislative assemblies of the states and the Union territories. Dr Kalam took a nationwide tour to campaign as a presidential candidate. While in the south, Dr Kalam made two detours. On 9 July he went to his home at Rameswaram, and on 14 July he went to Puttaparthi to meet Sri Sathya Sai Baba.

Dr Kota Harinarayana accompanied Dr Kalam to Puttaparthi from Bangalore. Dr Kalam saw Sri Sathya Sai Baba as a spiritual icon celebrating the civility and grandeur of life. He spread amongst his followers the message of devotion in the face of a global culture that was increasingly based on violence, cruelty and unrestrained greed, concealed with beautifying niceties about progress. Dr Kalam never discussed the mystique or extraordinary power devotees perceived in the Baba, but revered him as a cultural force of incredible magnitude.

Perhaps inevitably, Dr Kalam's election campaign raised some debate on his religious practices. A comparison between Dr Kalam and former presidents Zakir Hussain and Fakhruddin Ali Ahmed was rejected; Dr Kalam was not seen as a Muslim in the common understanding of Islam. The sudden emergence of a veena-playing, Bhagavadgita-reading, Rameswaram-born Kalam struck many as an unreal happening. They were indeed baffled at Dr Kalam's elevation as a force for good, change, agency, self-reflexivity, critical thinking, action, service and love. Dr Kalam invoked the simple truth of India as a pluralistic society; and he challenged the carefully constructed stereotypes favoured by vote-bank-based Indian politics. Some media commentators swiftly recognized that Dr Kalam was in many ways the quintessential Indian Muslim of the ages:

> The Indian Muslim, like any other Indian, is a creature of his village, district, state, in every possible way ... Kalam is part of a continuing tradition which exists but about which we have developed an amnesia because of the obsession of the global media – and that of our own – with painting the Muslim in a monochromatic shade ... As for Kalam's familiarity with Hindu scriptures, was not Justice Ismail in Chennai the country's leading authority on the Kamban

> Ramayanam? And Kalam, for all his devotion to Rama, still has to catch up with Abdul Rahim Khan-e-Khana's verses in Sanskrit dedicated to Dasharath's son.[10]

On 18 July 2002, Dr Kalam was elected the eleventh president of India, and the first scientist president of the republic, by a thumping majority, winning 90 per cent of the votes polled. Secretary General of the Rajya Sabha, R.C. Tripathi, who was the returning officer of the presidential election, handed over a copy of the notification declaring Dr Kalam as the president-elect to Parliamentary Affairs Minister Pramod Mahajan.

Pramod Mahajan drove to the Asiad Village and handed over the declaration to Dr Kalam. Dr Kalam thanked Pramod Mahajan for being his election agent. 'So, funny guy, you made me the president!' Dr Kalam said joyfully. He then emerged to the large media contingent gathered outside:

> I am indeed delighted to get elected as the next president. I thank all my friends, parents, teachers and three great professors – Professor Vikram Sarabhai, Professor Satish Dhawan and Professor Brahm Prakash ... My message to the country is that we need a vision, a second vision for the nation to get India transformed into a developed country in twenty years.[11]

On 24 July 2002, Dr Kalam's elder brother A.P.J.M. Maracayer with the imam of the local mosque, A.C.M. Noor-ul-Huda, P.L.V. Shastri, an elderly priest from Rameswaram who was Azad's classmate, and thirty-four other members of family and friends arrived from Chennai by train. Maracayer was warm with his words, and spoke of his wishes for Dr Kalam's tenure: 'I am extremely happy. I always prayed for his success. He has made us proud. We had special prayers for a hassle-free presidential term for him. But I don't expect him to serve us. The nation is more important.'[12]

On 25 July 2002, outgoing president K.R. Narayanan escorted Dr Kalam to the central hall of parliament. Vice-President Krishan Kant, and Lok Sabha Speaker Manohar Joshi welcomed him. The Chief Justice of India, B.N. Kirpal, administered the oath of office and secrecy to the new president. Former president R. Venkataraman was pleased and proud to see that the presidency of his country was being bestowed on the man whom he had rightly trusted in 1982 to make India a missile power.

Dr Kalam invited all his friends to the swearing-in ceremony. Dr Varghese Kurien came with his wife. Y.S. Rajan, Sivathanu Pillai, D. Narayanamoorthy, R.N. Agarwal, R. Swaminathan, Dr B. Soma Raju, I and many others were there. For most of us it was our first chance to enter the Indian parliament, and in all probability our last. Snehal Thakkar, who 'ignited' Dr Kalam's mind in Anand a few months earlier, was invited to the ceremony as the new president's personal guest.

President Kalam was given a twenty-one-gun salute and taken to Rashtrapati Bhavan in a six-horse buggy, escorted by the mounted President's Bodyguard, an elite household cavalry regiment of the Indian Army.

In the evening, after the 'tea' ceremony was done with and all the guests had left, President Kalam stood inside the majestic Rashtrapati Bhavan. It is a mansion of four floors and 340 rooms, with a colossal floor area of 200,000 square feet, constructed by the British rulers in 1931 with heavy classical motifs in order to emphasize power and imperial authority. President Kalam looked into the space around him, as if oblivious of the opulent building, and told me: 'Buddy, if you only had eyes to see and ears to hear and wits to understand, you would know that the Kingdom of God is the sense of holiness, goodness and beauty. It is as close to you as your breath The Kingdom of God is where our best dreams come from and our truest prayers. I glimpsed it at those moments when I found myself being better than I was and wiser than I knew.'

3.5

Angel and Marshal

> What a piece of work is a man, how noble in reason, how infinite in faculties, in form and moving how express and admirable, in action how like an angel, in apprehension how like a god.
>
> – William Shakespeare
> The greatest playwright of the English language

The Appointments Committee of the Cabinet selected P.M. Nair, secretary, Department of Defence Production and Supplies, as secretary to the president of India. He came from the 1967 batch of IAS officers from the Union territories cadre. Dr Kalam knew Nair 'sahib' since the time of the SLV-3 project, when he was posted at Thumba. President Kalam asked Nair to fix a meeting with Vice-President Krishan Kant on 27 July 2002 as his first duty after assuming office; but the meeting never took place.

The vice-president passed away that very morning. The unpredictability of life once again confronted President Kalam. Before the National Democratic Alliance decided on him as their candidate for the presidency, Krishan Kant was one of the front runners for the post. Krishan Kant had served as governor of Andhra Pradesh for seven-and-a-half years, from 1990 until his elevation to the vice-presidency. It would have been only natural that Krishan Kant would have followed the path of Dr Sarvepalli Radhakrishnan, Dr Zakir Hussain, V.V. Giri, R. Venkataraman, Dr Shankar Dayal Sharma and

K.R. Narayanan, who all became presidents after completing their vice-presidential terms. However, there was no telling one's fate.

Dr Kalam's guests from Rameswaram stayed for two days at the DRDO Development Enclave Guest House and another three days in Rashtrapati Bhavan after he moved there. Dr Kalam's brother stayed with him in his room. Dr Kalam hired a private bus to ferry his guests to various places and events. No official car was used. He also paid for their food and stay. His simplicity and propriety was ingrained, and no amount of pomp and circumstance would change his approach.

The pressing needs of the time meant that he would only take a few short days to settle into his position before he embarked on some of the more important duties of his presidency. Dr Kalam had earlier been actively involved in Gujarat's rehabilitation and rebuilding efforts after the devastating Bhuj earthquake of 2001. The earthquake had plunged Gujarat into the gloom of death, destruction and sheer helplessness. Thousands of lives were lost. Hundreds of thousands of people were rendered homeless. Entire livelihoods were destroyed. As if that was not enough, within a mere five months the mindless communal violence of 2002 had dealt the state another unexpected blow. Innocents were killed; families were rendered helpless. Property built through years of toil was destroyed. The violence was indeed a crippling blow to an already shattered and hurting Gujarat, still struggling to get back on its feet from the natural devastation of the earthquake.

As president, Dr Kalam took a bold decision to visit Gujarat as his first duty outside the national capital. He knew that two railway carriages had been burned, and efforts to quell the flames had been deliberately hampered by riotous mobs. The fire killed fifty-eight passengers, including many women and children. A retaliatory bloodbath followed in many parts of the state. Does the real safety of the minorities lie in the goodwill of the majority? Had Delhi not understood the need to confront the evil of communal violence after its anti-Sikh pogrom in 1984? But it had to change. The nation can't be held hostage to the deranged mindset of mob killings. Dr Kalam had always been appalled by such happenings, and he felt that his visit as president was the least he could do for the nation under the circumstances. Dr Kalam's decision to address the issue was lauded in the press, which acknowledged the courage of his visit to Gujarat at this time:

> Being the first presidential visit outside the capital, the Gujarat trip acquires a symbolic dimension. Dr Kalam will get to see for himself the horrors of communal violence and will hear the charges of governmental complicity. In political terms, Dr Kalam's Gujarat trip should serve a notice on all those who thought they had got a pliable President.[1]

Prime Minister Vajpayee was, however, lukewarm about his visit, as Dr Kalam would recollect:

> Vajpayee asked me only one question, 'Do you consider going to Gujarat at this time essential?' I told the prime minister, 'I consider it an important duty so that I can be of some use to remove the pain, and also accelerate the relief activities, and bring about a unity of minds, which is my mission, as I stressed in my address during the swearing-in ceremony.'[2]

Central government officials cautioned Dr Kalam that he would face a cold reception and that there would be protests from many sides. But to his great surprise, when Dr Kalam landed at Ahmedabad airport on 10 August 2002, not only was Chief Minister Narendra Modi awaiting his arrival, but his entire cabinet and a large number of legislators, officials and members of the public were also present at the airport. He could see the fear neurosis at play in the minds of the people sitting in Delhi. Some influential people had created a script for Indian society, and every event must fit that script – even if it has to be distorted, exaggerated, minimized or even ignored.

Dr Kalam visited twelve areas – three relief camps and nine riot-hit locations where the loss of life had been particularly egregious. The chief minister indeed escorted President Kalam throughout the visit. President Kalam was able to suggest to him directly the urgent actions that were required apropos the petitions and complaints he received from the people.

After visiting the relief camps and riot-hit locations, Dr Kalam went to the Swaminarayan temple on Shahibaug Road to meet Pramukh Swamiji. As he entered the meeting hall, sadhus chanted the Shanti Path, a mantra for peace, harmony and happiness. Pramukh Swamiji Maharaj warmly welcomed the president and the chief minister with garlands, and offered his support and prayers:

> Swamiji said, 'Our society is going through a difficult time, and peace, as you say, has to prevail. There are thousands of victims, both Hindus and Muslims. Right measures need to be taken to alleviate their suffering. Life is sacred; peace is sacred. My *vintee* (petition) to Rashtrapatiji and Mukhyamantriji is to work for peace and unity of minds. I have only one earnest prayer to God. That never again should such cruelly unfortunate days come in the lives of any other person, society, state or nation.'[3]

Dr Kalam later visited Bhuj, wrecked by the earthquake the previous year. The Technology Information, Forecasting and Assessment Council (TIFAC) had constructed 500 shelters made of composite boards of jute and coir, and particle boards made of rice husks, with bamboo-mat veneers supported on steel channels and angles. They also made more than a hundred fibre-reinforced plastic modular toilet units. It was a superb example of how composite materials offer significant advantages over metals in some structural applications. The shelter design had demonstrated the flexibility and efficacy of various combinations of fibre reinforcement and resin materials. 'Knowledge purposefully applied indeed becomes a divine force,' said President Kalam.

It was during this period that Dr Kalam read a book *The Inner Journey Home,* written by A. Hameed Ali. He liked a 'thought experiment' described in the book, and compared the situation of communal violence to a situation of dim light and vision distorted by the colours and designs of shutter glasses. The conversation he had with me on this matter would later appear in the book *Guiding Souls*.

> Let us imagine that we are in a completely dark room, a room full of all kinds of objects. There is a light source in this room, with a dimmer

> switch that can be enhanced or reduced. We are also wearing clear eyeglasses with shutters of different colours. The coloured glass of each shutter has some transparent designs engraved on it. We begin to increase the intensity of the light by sliding the dimmer slowly, to the dimmest illumination. We begin to see the vaguest outlines of some of the objects in the room. We may misapprehend what we see, for we still cannot differentiate the shadows from the real objects. Our predicament is complicated further because of the multi-shuttered glasses. Our knowledge is incomplete because of the dim light and distorted by the colours and designs of the shutter glasses. But all of what we see is taken as knowledge. We turn the dimmer up slowly and steadily, and every once in a while, remove one of the shutters in our glasses. Basic knowledge increases steadily, becoming fuller and more accurate. Only if we remove the shutters, what we see would surprise us. Our knowledge would become complete and objective, full and truthful.[4]

Such a depth of understanding was sure to imbue Dr Kalam's presidency with a unique quality, and the nation watched intently at the very different approach taken by President Kalam. He showed his independent mind, his courage to do what he felt was right and above all, a desire to connect with the ordinary people by going to them. He was aware that the powerful electronic media was capable of creating a virtual reality. A good leader must not be swayed by what is shown by the television channels. While his first visit had turned out to be a balm for a hurting people, his second visit had all the potential to stir another hornet's nest.

On 5 September 2002, Dr Kalam visited Bhopal and went to the Bhopal Memorial Hospital and Research Centre. On his arrival at the hospital, Shakeela Bano, a victim of the Union Carbide factory gas disaster of December 1984, Justice A.M. Ahmadi, chairman of the Bhopal Memorial Hospital Trust and Union cabinet minister Sadhvi Uma Bharati welcomed President Kalam. The construction and management of the hospital had been mired in unsavoury controversies, and many citizens had pleaded with the president to intervene. The imbroglio was noted in the print media:

> The hospital was funded from the sale of the attached property of Union Carbide India Ltd, and its aim was to give free treatment to gas victims. Instead, the hospital gives favoured treatment to the rich as 30 per cent of the money they pay goes to doctors. The very purpose of the hospital has been defeated.[5]

Dr Kalam had a long discussion with Justice A.M. Ahmadi and the doctors. He told the learned judge and the doctors that managing perception was very important. Public perception is indeed at times more important than reality. He said that your reality will not be a happy one if the perception of the people about you is not good. Dr Kalam inaugurated a telemedicine link with Care Hospital, Hyderabad, set up by Dr B. Soma Raju at his behest and interacted with some gas victims undergoing treatment at a sub-centre in Ginouri.

In the evening, Dr Kalam inaugurated the National Judicial Academy in the presence of the Chief Justice of India Justice B.N. Kirpal, Union Minister of Law and Justice K. Jana Krishnamurthi, the chief minister of Madhya Pradesh, Digvijaya Singh, and six former chief justices of India. Dr Kalam appeared to be carrying his pain from witnessing the effects of the Gujarat carnage. He voiced his concern over the growing intolerance and contempt in some quarters for those of other religions, and spoke out against the all-too-common justification of lawless violence. Describing the judiciary as the 'angel and marshal' that ensures the survival of democracy, President Kalam said that it should not be a mute witness to the devaluation of human life in society: 'All of us have to work hard and do everything to make our behaviour civilized and to protect the rights of every individual.'[6]

Certain forces were meanwhile conspiring to subvert the tenuous communal peace that remained in the state of Gujarat after the rioting. On 24 September 2002, two heavily armed gunmen killed at least thirty-two people in an attack on Akshardham temple in Gandhinagar, Gujarat, before army commandos recaptured the temple and killed the terrorists. It was yet another international tragedy in which terrorists had taken the lives of innocent men, women and children – pilgrims quietly going about their worship – in a senseless act of violence. Their act of terror was even more acutely felt, since it was perpetrated in the midst of the very place that serves as an inspiration for peace, harmony and tolerance. Dr Kalam would always remember Pramukh Swamiji's compassion and spiritual leadership in the face of this horror:

> The attack was meant to stir communal riots and tear apart the fabric of society. But Pramukh Swamiji defeated these nefarious designs of the terrorists ... Swamiji encouraged his followers to pray, not punish ... I believe that his spiritual calmness and saintliness not only restored peace in Gujarat, but also provided a final seal on the perpetuating cycle of communal violence in the state.[7]

Dr Kalam had always avoided his birthday celebration. But now that he was a public figure, this was going to be difficult. He found a solution by being away from the capital. There was an invitation to attend the Buddha Mahotsava festival from the Union tourism ministry in Tawang on 15 October 2002, and he decided to go there. He had heard a lot about the sacred Buddhist monastery at Tawang in Arunachal Pradesh and felt that his prayers for communal harmony and peace in the nation would surely be answered there.

IAF helicopters flew the presidential entourage, which included me, across the mighty 4,200 meters-high Sela Mountain. We were given oxygen masks while flying over the peaks. The pass had hardly any vegetation and was completely covered under the snow.

Soon after our arrival, President Kalam proceeded to the monastery situated at an altitude of over 11,000 feet. This monastery is known as Galden Namgyel Lhatse. It is one of the largest lamaseries of the Mahayana sect in Asia. Dr Kalam offered prayers and met the Rimpoche (the local term for the head lama). Everyone was surprised to see an instant rapport between President Kalam and the Rimpoche. Their discussion became very famous in the course of the time, and was notable for its succinct honesty:

> Kalam: What advice can I take back for the people of India?
> Rimpoche: Put aside the violence.
> Kalam: And how can I do that?

Rimpoche: By sublimating your ego. It's ego that is the core of selfishness and from it stems all violence.

Kalam: But how can this be done? How can we control our egos?

Rimpoche: Learn to forget the 'I' and 'Me'.

Dr Kalam was taken aback by this simple, stark and short answer. The dimness was illuminated by Rimpoche's words and Dr Kalam could see the root of all trouble in human relations. President Kalam, as the supreme commander of the defence forces, met army personnel deployed in the area and laid flowers at the war memorial of martyrs of the 1962 Sino-Indian War. In the evening, Governor Arvind Dave and Chief Minister Mukut Mithi hosted dinner. As there was no large building to accommodate more than 200 guests, a large tent was erected and tens of bonfires were made to keep everybody warm.

Dr Kalam knew Governor Dave well from the time of Pokhran-II, when he was the director of the Research and Analysis Wing. They spoke about the dynamics of security in the region. Having understood the root of violence in 'I' and 'me' earlier in the day, Dr Kalam perhaps wanted to understand now from a military intelligence veteran, how armed conflicts developed and persisted over such long periods of time. The territorial disputes in this region have helped no one but have deprived the entire region of development. Mukut Mithi and some of us joined the discussion with Dr Kalam.

The roots of territorial disputation in this region reach back to the latter colonial times. In the sixteenth century, when the Tawang Monastery was built, the Indian and the Tibetan rulers were in harmony, and no border was ever drawn or enforced. But things would change. In 1914, Tibet was an independent country. British India negotiated with Tibet to accept that the region of Tawang and the area south of it belonged to India. Everyone was happy except China. Chinese representatives in the meeting withdrew, and since then China has refused to accept the accord arising from the meeting.

Most of the state of Assam had lived with a strong Indian cultural influence from ancient times, and in 1914 the Tibetan government signed an agreement acknowledging the region as part of India. When in 1950 China annexed Tibet, the Tawang Monastery remained the last bastion of Tibetan culture. In 1962, China warred over the region. But the geography clearly favoured India, and China pulled back from Tawang. Since then, India has established complete control over the region. It is now as Indian as any other part of the country.

The holy month of Ramadan began on 5 November 2002. At this time, in accordance with a long-standing Delhi tradition, the president, the prime minister, political leaders, ambassadors, businessmen – anyone of any note or public profile – would host Iftar parties, serving the evening meal when Muslims end their daily Ramadan fast at sunset. People from all religions would attend these parties. The Iftar parties had become something of a talking point in the gossip press: not only who attended a party, but who skipped it would be treated as news. Moreover, the parties, over the years, had become events around which political analysts constructed conspiracy theories, forecast alliances – and much more. But no one could ever argue that the food wasn't delectable at the Iftar parties.

A grand Iftar party from President Kalam was much anticipated. It was a regular practice for the president of India to host one; and Dr Kalam was a Muslim. Dr Kalam, though, asked Nair sahib why he should host a feast for people who were already well fed. He asked him to find out the cost involved in holding an Iftar party. It was estimated at rupees twenty-two lakh. Dr Kalam asked Nair sahib to donate that amount to a few select orphanages in the form of food, clothing and blankets. He left the selection of orphanages to a team in Rashtrapati Bhavan and had no role in deciding where the money would go and in what proportion.

After the selections for the bequest was made, Dr Kalam asked Nair sahib to come into his room. He placed a cheque for rupees one lakh in Nair sahib's hand. Dr Kalam said that he was giving this amount from his personal savings, and this should not be disclosed to anyone. P.M. Nair spoke of his gift, however, as he felt that people should know that here was a man who not only donated what he should have spent, but was giving his own money also. Though he was a devout Muslim, Dr Kalam did not host Iftar parties in any of his five years in Rashtrapati Bhavan. With typical self-denial, he abstained from this indulgence so that poor children in orphanages could feast for at least that one day in the year.

Nair sahib and the staff at Rashtrapati Bhavan quickly understood Dr Kalam's ascetic tendencies; but it was perhaps difficult for others, more used to the ceremonial of the office of president, to come to terms with his style. At the very least, his staff would have to prevail upon Dr Kalam to change his manner of dress, if nothing else. His trademark pale blue shirt and sports shoes, which he wore for their practicality and comfort, were simply not befitting his new station. From now, bandhgala suits would be the new mode of dress, and one of the most renowned tailors in Delhi was summoned to make Dr Kalam several of these suits.

The tailor was proud of his record for making fine suits for all the presidents of the previous few decades, and he was naturally very pleased to be outfitting the latest president in the costume of his office. He arrived and carefully took all of Dr Kalam's measurements. A few days later, the tailor and his assistants arrived, beaming, with four beautifully crafted bandhgala suits. Dr Kalam tried on his new uniform. The dark suit was a perfect cut for Dr Kalam's physique; the length and drop were exact, and the coat was square on his shoulders. I was taken aback at witnessing the somewhat unkempt, brilliant man I had known for two decades transforming into a statesman in front of me. The charm of a boss with tousled hair, runners and a lab coat that had endeared a generation of staff to this great man was gone, and in its place was the bearing of a world leader. A comb over the untamed silver locks, and the transformation was complete.

The man himself, though, was far from happy. 'I'm feeling strangled in this thing. How can I breathe? You have to remake it.' The tailor and his staff looked quite bemused and more than a little disappointed; for their part, they had done their job perfectly, and to their trained eyes the suit was a sublime fit. But their famous client was having none of it. He had been in the business of making things for his whole working life – to be granted, nothing in the world of couture – and he knew exactly what needed to be done. 'Cut it at the neck,' he said. And the tailor complied. Thereafter, Dr Kalam mostly wore what came to be known as a 'Kalam suit': a bandhgala suit with an open neck – which was, of course, a contradiction in terms.

The new president would also baulk at wearing a tie. He felt choked while wearing ties, just as he did by the closed round-neck collar, which he would insist on the tailors calling an 'Indian collar' after Nehru, rather than a 'Chinese collar' according to tailoring jargon. 'Be patriotic,' he would say. He would, though, wear ties under sufferance. Once, I found him cleaning his spectacles with his tie, and I told him he shouldn't do this. An eminently practical man, he said, 'This is an absolutely purposeless garment. Let me at least put it to some use!'

Further than the Kalam suits and the occasional tie, Dr Kalam would not burnish his image or alter his style, as some are apt to do when they assume a new role. His trademark unruly silver hair, which he had worn long since his youth, would need to be regularly tamed. But his humble demeanour stayed, and he was just as approachable to all and sundry as he had ever been. His staff could not effect a makeover on their charge; and he didn't need one. That he cut a distinguished figure in his suits and formal wear was more of his natural charisma; that, and his hallmark silver locks with an appealing, boyish face that had endured into his senior years. Dr Kalam had not been changed by becoming president, but the office of president would be changed by him.

3.6

Thinking Is Growth

Isolation is the sum total of wretchedness to a man.

– Thomas Carlyle
Scottish philosopher and teacher

President Kalam visited Tripura on 4 October 2002. He had been there earlier twice. In 1998, he had attended a Tripura State Planning Board meeting. Later, he visited Tripura to attend the Tripura University convocation on 31 January 2001. Dr Kalam established a strong rapport with Chief Minister Manik Sarkar. The son of a tailor, Manik was born in East Pakistan and his father later migrated to Tripura. Manik and his wife lived a very simple life. In 1998, at the age of forty-nine, he became a member of the politburo of the Communist Party of India (Marxist), better known as CPI(M). In the same year, he became the chief minister of the state of Tripura.

Dr Kalam sent me to meet him in preparation for his visit. He said, 'You will meet a true revolutionary. He is the only chief minister in India who doesn't have a house or car. I know you speak well but when in front of Manik Sarkar, keep your mouth shut. Listen carefully to what he wants for his people.'

I was surprised at the intensity expressed by Dr Kalam to do something really good for Tripura. It was public knowledge that in the run-up to the presidential election, the CPI(M), which had been ruling Tripura for a long time, had supported Lakshmi Sahgal for the presidency against Dr Kalam. Only after Dr Kalam's passing, the truth came out that Manik Sarkar was indeed a great admirer of Dr Kalam. But he had followed the discipline of the party in voting against Dr Kalam; and Dr Kalam understood this well. Dr Kalam all along knew the extent of party discipline's role in the matter, which was only acknowledged in the print media in the days following Dr Kalam's death: 'The CPM politburo's decision had not gone down well with the state CPM, which unanimously called for a reversal of the politburo's decision and support to Kalam. The politburo remained unfazed and "martial law within the party" ensured compliance.'[1]

The chief secretary of Tripura, V. Thulasidas, reciprocated fully Dr Kalam's warmth. He suggested a telemedicine link between Kailashahar and Agartala and from there to Hyderabad. He ensured the support of BSNL on a war footing and despatched me to Kailashahar with a senior health official in the government with an armed escort.

Kailashahar is the headquarters of the Unakoti district along the Bangladesh border. It was the ancient capital of the Tripuri kingdom. After Partition, the road link with Agartala was lost to the other side of the international border, and what formerly was a pleasant three hours' drive on a plain road was now taking a tortuous six to eight hours through insurgency-affected highlands.

President Kalam's day-long visit was most fruitful and widely followed. He opened a telemedicine centre at the state's GB Hospital and interacted with a fourteen-year-old boy in Kailashahar, who was suffering from a heart valve disease and needed immediate surgery. When Dr Kalam asked him his name, the boy answered 'Abdul Kalam'. The president said that was his name and again asked him his name. When the boy answered that his name was also Abdul Kalam, everybody burst into laughter. Later, that boy was shifted to Hyderabad and was operated on by the cardiothoracic surgeon Dr G. Ramasubramanyam at Care Hospital, Hyderabad. The boy is now a healthy young man approaching his thirties.

In deference to President Kalam's wishes, two interactive sessions with students had been arranged in Agartala. It was vintage Kalam:

radiating hope, vibrancy and positivity, while replying to the students' queries and encouraging learners with words of wisdom. President Kalam also laid the foundation for a factory at the Bodhjungnagar industrial hub to manufacture medicated powder from the state's abundant pineapple production. But it did not develop as expected, and farmers in Tripura continue to see their bumper crops rotting without sale. Later, Tripura artisans built a bamboo-cane hut with a thatched roof in Rashtrapati Bhavan for the President.

President Kalam went to Manipur the following day. He was shown black flags and the Manipur Peoples Liberation Front observed a twelve-hour general strike. They were protesting against the failure of the authorities to provide security along the Imphal–Dimapur NH 39 and Imphal–Jiribam NH 53, where lootings and crimes had been rife for many years. Dr Kalam took the black flags in his stride with his usual calm aplomb, acknowledging that the people were simply trying to raise an issue that was causing suffering to them, and he should not take this personally. The president then went to Leimakhong, about 28 kilometres north of Imphal to inaugurate a 38 MW heavy fuel plant built by the Bharat Heavy Electricals Ltd.

After the function, Dr Kalam raised the issue with BHEL engineers that the cost of the project was higher than hydro and thermal projects. Further, cognizant that the heavy oil used in the furnaces of the generators was such an expensive commodity, he asked why this costly option was selected. None of the engineers could adequately address these critical and ineluctable issues. It appeared to be a regular case of distant planning, where the person does not know for whom he is planning. Dr Kalam was a technologist as much as a scientist and had an uncanny, almost psychic ability to select the best technology for a given purpose. But in this instance, anyone with common sense could see the project's shortcomings. Many years later, the apprehensions President Kalam had about the project openly erupted in a public scandal. An article in *The Telegraph* in July 2010 reported that a prominent state politician described the plant as

> ... a 'useless sleeping lion' and demanded in the Assembly today to dismantle the project. The price of the fuel has gone up to Rs 35.95 per litre, making it impossible for the government to operate the plant. Whoever formulated the project did so to ruin Manipur and responsibility should be fixed. 'What kind of project is this?'[2]

Dr Kalam had been keenly aware for some time of the need for greater integration of the north-east with the rest of India. He felt that the people of this geographically and politically isolated region needed more of a voice in the halls of power; further, that their potential had been routinely overlooked. With this in mind, he invited Anil Mangotra of the 1978 IAS batch from the Manipur-Tripura cadre to the presidential secretariat. Mangotra had a sound understanding of problems of the north-eastern states, and provided the president with worthwhile insights. He was very candid in proposing that the data and information on the region were not sufficiently analysed and communicated between the region and the Centre, contributing to further misinformation, mismanagement and alienation.

The history of these reaches of the subcontinent had been characterized by a divide between the Central government and its people. The colonial rulers took nearly a century to annex the entire region, and administered the hills as a loose 'frontier area'. The result was that large parts of the north-eastern hill areas never became acquainted with the principle of a central administration. The allegiance to the newly formed Indian nation state that was somewhat half-hearted from the beginning was further diminished by the creation of East Pakistan, which engendered the loss of a major chunk of the physical connection between mainland India and north-east India. Mangotra pointed out that 99 per cent of the north-east's boundaries is international borders.

Dr Kalam felt that although the conflict in the region is ostensibly based on complex political and economic issues such as the struggle over natural resources, migration-related issues, displacement, social exclusion and so forth, the politics of identity should not be overlooked. He saw identity itself as lying at the heart of the problems of the north-east, and believed that this must be addressed along with the other extant issues. He said that our leaders must reach out to the different ethnic groups there and hold the hands of their leaders like brothers and sisters, not treat them as colonial subjects.

Unfortunately, the approach of the Centre has been not dissimilar to that of a bewildered colonial ruler. With widespread ignorance of the region, the official modus operandi for dealing with its ills seems to have been either to pump in money or send in the army. The prevailing thought in New Delhi is that if there is economic development, all problems will disappear. But the generic challenges of governance in India – weak institutions, rampant graft and wasteful centralized planning – have made development elusive in Manipur.

On the long return flight from Imphal to Delhi, Dr Kalam told me we were not created to live our lives by ourselves. We were not given a sentence of solitary confinement and placed in a world of isolation. From the moment we enter this human experience, it is clear there is a world waiting to be discovered – people, creatures and experiences that are there for our interaction. And the spark inside us often has to be spoken to, to be touched by the soul of another. He felt that in a broad sense, the problems of the north-east relate to isolation and a dearth of meaningful interaction – the cause of many of man's conflicts. The north-east policy of the Centre was not just unfocused; it lacked any vision or understanding.

Dr Kalam returned to the north-east soon afterwards to address the National Symposium on Biodiversity at Shillong on 25 October 2002. Armed with a sound understanding of the region by now, and having developed the contour of his vision for the region, Dr Kalam gave a powerful mantra to the large gathering of scientists who arrived from all over the country. He could just as easily have articulated this at Anna University as professor of technology and societal transformation:

> Technology is the most non-linear tool that can effect the most fundamental changes in the ground rules of economic competitiveness. Science is linked to technology through applications. Technology is

> linked to the economy and environment through manufacturing. The economy and environment link technology to society. So there is an integrated relationship between science, technology, environment, manufacturing and society.[3]

Dr Kalam pointed out that India ranked among the top few nations in terms of having a rich biodiversity. Particularly in the herbal area, there were potential applications for developing a myriad of products for nutrition, and prevention and cure of diseases. Of the global herbal product market of USD 61 billion, China had a share of around USD 3 billion, whereas India's share was not even USD 0.1 billion. Dr Kalam pointed out that there was tremendous opportunity for growth in this area. It could only be achieved, however, if peace returned to the region, if scientists could come and work in the north-east without fear, if industries could set up their factories – and if investors bring in their money. It had to be done by the private sector, with full participation of the people living here. Setting up a furnace oil plant to generate power or installing a MRI (magnetic resonance imaging) machine in a hospital where the X-ray machine does not work to 'utilize' the budget can't be termed development. Such practices are indeed an insult to the sensibilities of the people of this region.

After his lecture in Shillong, President Kalam visited Nagaland. He first landed in Tuensang and then went to Kohima to attend a civic reception at Khuzama Public Ground. Before addressing the massive crowd there, Dr Kalam met Khuzama Village Council members. Soon after the programme ended, he chose to walk through the milling crowd, avoiding the VVIP car waiting for him in front of the rostrum, interacting with the schoolchildren eagerly waiting for him across the road at their small school compound.

Governor Shyamal Datta and Chief Minister S.C. Jamir were the president's constant companions on this visit. While interacting with the schoolchildren at Khuzama, he urged them to do their part to turn India into a developed and powerful nation. In this way, he was igniting their will for transformation, just as he had intended to do in his duties at Anna University. Assuming the mantle of president of the country had only made his campus of students immeasurably larger. And here, he became a role model to many young Naga students, who were thrilled to freely and frankly talk with him, sitting little more than an arm's length away from him. It was this unassuming manner of Dr Kalam that would endear him to the people of the country in general and children and students in particular. Chief Minister Jamir would recall this in his reminiscences years later:

> We reached the village and he went straight to the school. He interacted with the students and teachers for hours. He had questions, some plain and simple, and some really peculiar, which seemed ordinarily extraordinary. In the beginning, the students were overawed by the enormity of the occasion. However, as seconds rolled into minutes and minutes into hours, the students, younger and older, were somehow trapped into believing that they were NOT interacting with the President of India, rather they were with a friend, a very intimate and learned one! During the session, ideas were exchanged, intricate questions raised and answered.[4]

Dr Kalam expressed his thorough satisfaction that the village council comprised a teachers' representative, a parents' representative, a village representative and a government official. It was a sort of check-and-balance way of ensuring student attendance, teachers' presence, quality work for infrastructure and overall improvement. It was this kind of self-empowered approach that Dr Kalam favoured as a model for the nation's growth, and it relied on participation, forward thinking, a common purpose and the willingness to believe in human potential.

At a civic reception in the evening, a very pleased Jamir warmly addressed President Kalam as the 'Father of Nagaland'. Everybody gave a standing ovation, and it took a while for the applause to subside. When Dr Kalam's turn came to speak, he said, 'We all are the children of Mother India,' and called Jamir his beloved brother. This was what was needed; and it was here that the Centre had been failing.

Upon his return to Delhi, President Kalam shared this experience with Prime Minister Vajpayee. He told that him that neither Smt. Indira Gandhi nor Rajiv Gandhi had ever visited Kohima as prime minister and urged him to visit Nagaland, which he did on 28 October 2003. During Prime Minister Vajpayee's visit, he not only recognized the 'unique history' of the Nagas, but also admitted that mistakes had been made by the government. Moreover, he expressed his sorrow for the needless spilling of blood in the state.

In November 2002, President Kalam participated in the celebrations of the 1950th anniversary of the arrival of St Thomas and the 450th death anniversary of St Francis Xavier at Kochi in Kerala. He later spoke of his affinity with the divine in all world religions:

> Celebrations connected with any religion to my mind have a special significance. This is basically because all religions in their true form are one and the same. All are based on truth, fellow feeling, humility and the greatness of life in any form. It is people like us who have made religion subservient to our own selfish ends, corrupting religions from their pristine pure form to those that suit us, for our own specific purposes.[5]

St Thomas was one of the twelve disciples of Jesus. After Jesus Christ rose from the dead and came to the other disciples, St Thomas was not there. And he did not believe the others when they said that they had seen Jesus Christ. St Thomas said he wanted to see Jesus for himself before he would believe the good news. So Jesus Christ appeared to him and showed St Thomas his hands and sides, which had holes in them from his crucifixion. St Thomas is said to have exclaimed aloud, 'My Lord and My God', and spent the rest of his life telling the good news to all in faraway parts of the world.

St Thomas is believed to have brought Christianity to India more than 1950 years ago, which in due course became one of several major religions followed by Indians. St Francis Xavier, born in 1506 in the Spanish kingdom of Navarre, came to Goa in 1542 and went on from there to Kanyakumari. According to the legend, St Francis spent three years working among the pearl fishers or Paravas. He brought with him nothing but his all-consuming love for God and for the souls of his fellow men.

Dr Kalam never took any interest in the quibbling and controversies that might cloud the perception of any religion. He always celebrated the positive contribution that the believers of all religions had made to Indian society, particularly in the fields of education and medicine. His own teachers had been an eclectic mix of Hindus of various beliefs, Muslims of his own creed and Christians of several denominations, and he felt all the more privileged for this. Dr Kalam held that for a nation like India, which is rich in its unity of diversity, the contributions made by each religion are to be looked upon with gratitude and reverence.

Communal harmony and peace has been the mainstay of Kerala's society and, without exaggeration, the progressive state has been the envy of many on the subcontinent. For millennia, the region was the gateway to India for foreign seafarers, who brought new ideas and religions here. Perhaps this has facilitated a more pluralist society. Unlike many other parts of India, schools and other institutions here have catered for all those who resided in a particular area, irrespective of their caste or religion. This contrasts with the tradition of education in north India, where religious denominations founded exclusive schools and other institutions. The state of Kerala has given to the rest of the country a great lesson in tolerance and respect for diversity. Dr Kalam praised Kerala's excellence in universal education, and exhorted its people to continue to show leadership to the rest of India in this area: 'I appeal to the enlightened people of Kerala to sustain and reinforce that great tradition, built assiduously on these values from time immemorial and continue to be a beacon for the rest of the country to follow. I have no doubt that with such a high level of education and literacy in the state, my appeal will not fall on deaf ears. I am sure I shall not be disappointed in my expectations.'

Dr Kalam spent twenty years of his life in Kerala. During this first visit here as president of India, it was only natural that he opened up his heart and celebrated the uniqueness of Kerala's society. To him, the state was a model of harmony and aspiration, with the people striving for a better future through hard work and education. Those from Kerala may thus be seen pursuing careers in all the states of India and indeed, many countries of the world.

On 18 November 2002, President Kalam launched a 'bridging the digital divide' campaign called Akshaya. He also used this occasion to unveil his knowledge society and national development visions, which he would expound for the rest of his life. Dr Kalam always believed in the power of information and communication technology. He saw that it could generate massive economic growth, creating direct employment opportunities and transforming the entire socio-political economy of India.

The Akshaya mission was aimed at making at least one person in every family functionally IT literate, thereby making Kerala the first 100 per cent IT literate state in the world. Under this project, the government would develop multipurpose information technology centres within a 2-km radius of any household through private sector participation. This was a groundbreaking endeavour. It later transpired that these centres contributed to the employment of more than 50,000 youths and attracted Rs 500 crore of investment to the state.

President Kalam declared that day that becoming a knowledge power within a decade was a very important mission for the nation. While a knowledge society has a two-dimensional objective of societal transformation and wealth generation, a third dimension emerges when India has to transform into a knowledge power. That day also marked the birth of an idea that would later become the Aadhaar card. Seven years later, the Unique Identification Authority of India (UIDAI) was set up by the Government of India. Dr Kalam was an early proponent of the concept:

> We need to take on a mission for bringing out a national citizen card for usage as a voter ID card, a ration card, to operate a bank account and many other applications. The national citizen card/smart card has to be an integrated approach from multiple departments and industries.[6]

Dr Kalam spoke at length on competitiveness and cited the report prepared by the World Economic Forum that defined competitiveness as the ability of a national economy to achieve sustained high rates of economic growth. As per this definition, different countries were ranked as of April 2001. United States ranked first, Singapore second, Australia eleventh, Taiwan eighteenth, China thirty-third and India forty-first. As world competitiveness was decided by a triangular combination of progressiveness of industry, technological advancement and judicious governmental deregulation, an integrated approach assimilating and adapting technology to local needs must be a national mission. 'India must evolve such systems to improve its competitiveness in a global marketplace and to be in the first ten countries in the globalized world,' declared the great visionary president. He was unequivocal in advocating India's young minds to effect this improvement:

> Thinking is growth. Non-thinking is destruction of the individual or organization or the nation. India has to have a second vision. Seventy per cent of India's population is young. Only the vision of the nation can ignite its young minds. The ignited mind empowered with knowledge is the most powerful resource on the earth to bring about this transformation.[7]

The first three months of Dr Kalam's presidency had brought in the fresh air of hope and belief. He had successfully dispelled the gloom of communal violence, not by preaching religious harmony but instead by providing a vision for the country, to acquire knowledge and become an economic power in the globalized world. Through his extensive travel in different parts of the country and by meeting more than 100,000 people in the process, Dr Kalam had developed his own insights into the challenges facing the country. He identified the root of many of the nation's ills as the people's primordial identities, coupled with an insecure mindset of holding on to one's turf. He postulated that these had been conditioned by centuries of invasions and colonial rule.

3.7

Birth of a Humanist

> There is nothing I fear more than waking up without a programme that will help me bring a little happiness to those with no resources, those who are poor, illiterate, and ridden with terminal disease.
>
> – Nelson Mandela
> Anti-apartheid revolutionary and Nobel laureate

The 2001 Indira Gandhi Prize for Peace, Disarmament and Development was conferred upon Prof. Sadako Ogata of Japan, for her outstanding contribution in alleviating the pain of millions of refugees all over the world. She had been closely associated with the United Nations, in the area of human rights and refugees. Professor Ogata protected and assisted millions of people who had to leave their countries because of war, conflict and persecution.

Dr Kalam wanted to prepare well for this lecture. He called me for assistance. We sat inside the bamboo hut erected by the artisans from Tripura. Why had the history of the world been constantly ridden with conflict? No single century had passed so far without a major war happening somewhere between two or more groups of people. How did the imaginary lines of religion and national boundaries come to be drawn?

Dr Kalam recalled his discussion with Governor Dave in Arunachal Pradesh. There was no boundary between India and Tibet. They were living together as two colours in a rainbow – different but not separated by any line. Then some British official drew a line on the map. But outside, none of these lines tend to exist. As soon as you rise a kilometre into the skies and look down upon the earth, there are no national boundaries. Dr Kalam would say he never ceased to be confounded by the proclivity of these imaginary lines to draw blood from young soldiers. Furthermore, people are turned into refugees simply for being on the wrong side of these lines. Dr Kalam wanted to start his lecture with this thought but abandoned the idea after Nair sahib found it too radical for an international forum.

President Kalam instead started his lecture with a quote from one of Professor Ogata's speeches:

> 'The sources of security threats have emanated mostly from internal conflicts, most of the time caused by historical rivalries and animosities among different ethnic, religious and social groups.' The originators of these conflicts are mostly kings, priests and zealous ideologues. But the victims are primarily the civilians – ordinary men, women and children.

A sea change in basic humanitarian and developmental thinking and action is clearly called for. A realization was by now dawning on Dr Kalam that making policies and ensuring budgets for schemes was not going to change much. It was seven years since *India 2020* was published, and he could see hardly any progress. Dr Kalam saw this ceremony as a golden opportunity for a course correction, and was, true to habit, quite candid in expressing what he felt the country needed:

> What we get from (Professor Ogata's) message is: We should shed the differences in the name of religion and caste and in the name of haves and have-nots. Then only the mission of transforming our nation into a developed nation by 2020 will succeed.[1]

Where does socio-economic inequality hurt the poor most? Dr Kalam belonged to that rare breed of men who willingly engage in hard, solid thinking. He stood apart from the fraternity of people that are found in the corridors of power, peddling quick fixes, easy answers and half-baked solutions. Nothing pains some people more than having to think; but here Dr Kalam was thinking and caring for the answers to alleviate the suffering he saw around him. Two events to which Dr Kalam had been invited were like divine inspiration. It was almost as if they had been preordained to satiate his thirst for answers.

First, President Kalam was invited to the convocation of the Nizam's Institute of Medical Sciences (NIMS) at Hyderabad on 26 November 2002. Prof. Kakarla Subbarao was the director and vice chancellor of this deemed medical university. Prof. Subbarao had played a leading role in compiling a report on 'Healthcare in India' in Dr Kalam's days as principal scientific adviser. The report underscored the typical health problems facing Indian people and suggested possible solutions. The expert team proposed the eradication of three major diseases – tuberculosis, HIV and waterborne diseases – within the next decade. It also highlighted the threats posed by cardiovascular diseases, neuropsychiatric disorders, renal diseases and hypertension, gastrointestinal disorders, eye disorders, genetic diseases and accidents and trauma.

Dr Kalam saw that there were two major streams of development involved in addressing India's health care deficiencies. First, we would have to greatly augment our primary health care system, empower our secondary health care system and integrate both with the tertiary care centres. Second, we should see how the advancement in technology could be put to use to improve the healthcare system of the country. These two efforts would make modern medicine available and accessible. This would contribute to the nation's progress, as strong bodies and sound minds of its citizens are essential for progress.

Dr Kalam said in this convocation address that the vision of providing affordable and effective health care to the entire Indian population was much beyond the capability of any individual, institution or organization. Massive resources, both financial and in terms of human skills would be required. This vision needs to be developed into multi-organizational missions leading to the generation of thousands of goal-oriented projects. These projects would have to be supported and nurtured not only by the government, but also by our industry and philanthropic organizations. The most important ingredient of such a multi-organizational mission would be its leadership, which must be decentralized yet interlinked. Institutions which undertake research on various technological systems that are the tools for medical care, have to be fed with the latest clinical knowledge. Dr Kalam made it abundantly clear, by giving a tangible instance where indigenous medical technology had been successful, that this was no idle talk:

> I have just seen the indigenously developed digital Cath. Lab[2] at the CARE hospital. It demonstrates the success of multidisciplinary partnerships and technology integration ... the medico-technical knowledge must then go to the industries, which not only produce cost effective medical products but also profit share to make them available to the poorest of the poor at no cost.[3]

Dr Kalam enjoyed the rare distinction of having initiated numerous major projects that relied on bringing a diverse selection of people in different organizations together. It was thought impossible earlier that government organizations, academic institutions and industry could cooperate. Dr Kalam pioneered this approach during the missile programme and then at the Society for Biomedical Technology. He was now advocating this as the means of effecting a health care revolution in India.

The rewards for these collaborations could be rich. The interface between medical science, electronics, material science and engineering was facilitating the development of new techniques, both investigative and curative. These had provided the research worker with numerous tools to apply into the working of various physiological functions, right down to the molecular levels. Developments in biotechnology and molecular biology had made it possible not only to design drugs with specific properties, but also to deliver them to the specific sites in the body where they are most required. New imaging techniques had now made it possible to obtain real-time images of the various organs at a physiological and biological level. This would henceforth provide comprehensive data, invaluable for selecting the most appropriate treatment for a patient.

The second significant convocation for Dr Kalam was held a few days after that of the Nizam's Institute of Medical Sciences. In December 2002, ICRISAT (The International Crops Research Institute for the Semi-Arid Tropics) invited President Kalam for its thirtieth anniversary celebrations. President Kalam was, by this time, no longer seen as just a missile man. He was now seen more as a scientist who was committed to using knowledge for advancing society, particularly the marginalized poor. And his experiments in developing socially useful spin-offs of defence technology had, at least in some sense, compensated for his building of weapons. Dr William Dar, the Filipino director general of ICRISAT, aptly expressed the enthusiasm that the public felt for their genial scientist, social activist president: 'Sir, we are doubly graced by this visit – not only are you the head of state of this great country, you are also one of us – a scientist! We at ICRISAT share and support your dream of a food-secure India.'[4]

President Kalam was given a tour of the Sat Venture, which exhibits samples of the institute's many facets. Dr Kalam showed great interest in ICRISAT's genetic resources collection and was fascinated by the pyramid of institute crops, displaying from bottom to top the wild relatives, the farmer's landraces, the improved varieties and the hybrids. Another display which attracted President Kalam's attention was of photographs from the earthquake-affected areas of Kachchh, where ICRISAT gave relief aid, chiefly in the form of seed to help rebuild the area's agriculture.

President Kalam said that every Indian must have the physical, economic, social and environmental access to a balanced diet that includes the necessary macro- and micronutrients and safe drinking water. He moreover stated that everyone must have proper sanitation, environmental hygiene, primary health care and education so as to lead a healthy and productive life. The president highlighted the three interdependent dimensions: national or macro-level food security, essentially amounting to the domestic availability of food; household food security and individual food security. He said that while India had achieved national food security, there is the unfinished agenda of ensuring the physical and economic access to the available food by half of India's population.

India produces and stocks more than enough food to feed its entire population. Yet about 500 million people are food insecure. President Kalam was at pains to point out that despite the green revolution launched in the late 1960s, the country was home to one-fourth of the world's population of hungry and poor. In a manner that was consistent over many decades, he saw the development of technology for empowering the poor as a means of social upliftment:

> Another question I wanted to share with you, wherever there are people below the poverty line there is also the problem of the availability of water. It costs energy and money to bring water for specialized agriculture to such dry areas. What are the agricultural technologies and water conservation methodologies that can help uplift the people who are below the poverty line?[5]

Ably assisted by P.M. Nair, President Kalam was carefully choosing to connect with the best organizations that were truly working for the benefit of poor people and the marginalized sectors of society. When India gained Independence, the general perception was that developmental efforts and social service activities were purely the concern of the government. But as time passed, the government's role gradually diminished for various reasons and, appropriately, came to be regarded as more or less regulatory. It was important that non-governmental organizations (NGOs) came forward to weave a social safety net. On 30 November 2002, President Kalam visited Wagholi Educational and Rehabilitation Centre in Pune, an NGO that was indeed a harbinger of this wholesome and welcome change in the philosophy of development.

Dr Kalam was instantly drawn to the sagacious Shantilalji Gulabchandji Muttha, the chairman of Bharatiya Jain Sanghatana, Pune. When Dr Kalam asked Mr Muttha how he became involved in this mission, he said that in 1993, after the Latur earthquake, he initiated a programme to rehabilitate schoolchildren in the area. This gave birth to the Wagholi Educational and Rehabilitation Centre. He shifted 1,200 orphaned children of the fifth to tenth standard from Latur to this school-cum-hostel, where they were nurtured through to graduation. The same centre also accommodated schoolchildren from the 1997 Jabalpur earthquake. Dr Kalam liked his model of social service, disaster management and permanent rehabilitation through quality education. He congratulated the chairman, saying, 'Mutthaji, you are a divine person.'

Dr Kalam had always maintained that for the success of any such venture, the wholehearted cooperation and participation of the people affected were absolutely essential. His happiness derived from his observation that the Bharatiya Jain Sanghatana had helped the needy young children with full participation of their community and other people in society who mattered. Not only did Dr Kalam thereafter help provide them a nest to secure their childhoods, he empowered them with wings to soar high in their lives. He was most emphatic in his belief that the young would bring greatness to their country:

> I have no doubt that the future of the nation is in the hands of the younger generation ... They have their dreams, their aspirations, their vision, their expectations and hopes of a prosperous and developed India ... Developing them into citizens who would be capable of translating such dreams ... is the noblest task that can be undertaken in nation building.[6]

President Kalam presented the National Award for the Welfare of Persons with Disabilities at Vigyan Bhavan on 3 December 2002. The ceremony was held next to the building where he had his office as principal scientific adviser. He wanted to spend some time with his successor Dr R. Chidambaram in his old office, but presidential protocol would not allow this.

In his lecture, President Kalam recalled that when he was working in Anna University, he guided a doctoral research project to find a software–hardware integrated solution to achieve near-normal functioning of the brain of mentally challenged children. He said that when he saw some of the mentally challenged children performing certain activities like singing and painting, he became convinced that one day the convergence of information and communication technology, medical electronics, biotechnology and mathematical simulation could find a solution for their problems. He saw the potential of the disabled for a happy, productive life, just as he saw potential in the normally abled in society:

> I have been visiting various states and meeting children, people of all walks of life, including those who are in hospitals with pain, disabled persons in special schools and organizations and mentally challenged people. People with disabilities would definitely like to have a life like any other citizen and participate in all social activities and employment.[7]

President Kalam predicted on this occasion that the Internet would play a major role in rehabilitation measures for the disabled. He visualized a scenario in which all disabled people become part of the Internet culture. They would have access to information. Lack of access to the right information at the right time has been a barrier for the disabled in their growth. The Internet would provide a solution to these types of problems. He saw that online shopping and online transactions to pay various government service departments would greatly help the disabled to order their own lives.

Furthermore, Dr Kalam said the Internet would assist the disabled in having virtual interactions with people. In their working lives, this would obviate the necessity for physical mobility, which would be minimized or even eliminated by virtual office concepts. People would be allowed to work from their homes through computers and deliver their work output to their offices online. It is now clear that Dr Kalam's grasp of the potential of the Internet to better people's lives was uncannily accurate. One of his key strengths was, without question, to visualize people and technology in all their potential.

World Human Rights Day, 10 December, is normally marked both by high-level political conferences and meetings and by cultural events and exhibitions dealing with human rights issues across the globe. The Nobel Peace Prize is awarded every year on this day and on that day in 2002, Jimmy Carter, the thirty-ninth president of the United States, won the prize.

President Kalam chose the occasion to roll out his Empowered Human Life Vision in the function organized by the National Human Rights Commission. He said that he had visited numerous states and met people from all walks of life, including those who had been affected by communal clashes, poverty and unemployment. He raised the question: Is the perception of human beings different when viewed from an individual, national or global perspective? He predicted that future wars were rarely going to occur between nations; they would mostly involve smaller groups, often fighting proxy wars. Dr Kalam asserted that human rights in this new scenario would suffer grievously, almost beyond humanitarian comprehension. We can now see his sad prophecy coming to pass in various parts of the world, particularly in the Middle East.

He further said that the world in the twenty-first century was beset by international terrorism, and this was worse in some senses than the Kalinga war and the two world wars. It threatened the entire human community; people everywhere lived with constant fear and insecurity. He said that we had repeatedly witnessed human rights violations in terrorist strikes: during the World Trade Center attack, the attack on the Indian parliament, the Moscow theatre siege, the Bali hotel bombing in Indonesia and several plane hijacks. And ever more regularly, he stated, we saw mighty countries declaring war unilaterally, ignoring the United Nations. In an emotionally charged voice, he said,

> What are we doing, the great creations of God? Is it any more possible to realize a society in which a standard human being is a reality? Unlike in conventional wars, where war ethics have been defined in the Geneva Conventions, in proxy wars there are no codes of conduct. Innocent lives get caught in the crossfire and people are killed. Will the planet earth at any time see a no-war situation, at least in the future? It is indeed a big question ... With this background, can we evolve the creation of a standard human being?[8]

I was sitting near the press block and could hear the hushed voices of astonishment from the journalists. They were frantically scribbling on their notepads. Later I heard one senior journalist declaring that he had never heard such a passionate speech: 'This man is really different!'

Dr Kalam spoke for around an hour, which gave the captivated audience plenty of food for thought. No one present could harbour any illusion that he had assumed his lofty position to savour its fruits. This was no born-to-rule denizen of elevated company and sumptuous banquets, given to platitudes and self-congratulation. His dissertation on the evolution of human society from an agricultural to an industrial, information and the present-day knowledge society enlightened those present, and astounded them in equal measure. His delivery was a refreshing mix of one from a seer, university professor, scientist and statesman, the likes of which had never been seen in high office in the country.

President Kalam had now bestowed on his presidency an aura of idealism and vision, and his principles were reminiscent of those of Abraham Lincoln. He declared, 'Every citizen in the country has a right to live with dignity; every citizen has a right to aspire for distinction. Availability of a large number of opportunities to resort to just and fair means in order to attain that dignity and distinction is what democracy is all about. That is what our constitution is all about. And that is what makes life wholesome and worth living in a true and vibrant democracy.'

The humanist Kalam was born that evening.

3.8

Gem in the Lotus

> The heaviest penalty for declining to rule is to be ruled by someone inferior to yourself.
>
> – Plato
> Founder of Western philosophy and science

President Kalam was invited in January 2002 to the ninetieth Indian Science Congress at Bangalore. He had been attending the Indian Science Congress for more than a decade by this time. The Indian Science Congress Association owes its origin to the foresight and initiative of two British chemists, namely, Prof. J.L. Simonsen and Prof. P.S. MacMahon, who thought that scientific research in India might be stimulated if an annual meeting of research workers, somewhat on the lines of the British Association for the Advancement of Science, could be arranged. The first meeting of the Congress was held in January 1914 in Calcutta. One hundred and five scientists from different parts of India and abroad attended.

In 1976, it was decided by the Indian Science Congress to have a focal theme of national relevance and discuss it in every section, committee and forum during the annual session. In 2003, the focal theme was 'Frontier Science and Cutting-Edge Technologies.' Prime Minister Vajpayee by now had embraced the idea of India becoming a developed country by the year 2020. He was launching the new Science and Technology Policy 2003 with an understanding that science and technology, in all its true spirit, must be embraced to realize the dream of making India a developed nation.

The space summit was a unique event of the Indian Science Congress that year. President Kalam used the summit address to outline his vision for the global space community for a prosperous, happy and secure planet earth. He attended the Congress with his entire team of thoroughly prepared advisors that comprised Prof. P.V. Indiresan, Y.S. Rajan, A. Sivathanu Pillai, R. Swaminathan, D. Narayanamoorthy, Kota Harinarayana, Dr B. Soma Raju, Dr Tara Prasad Das and the newly inducted V. Ponraj. I was Dr Kalam's constant companion at the Indian Science Congress meetings since he called me to assist him in writing the historic 'Let My Brain Remove Your Pain' speech, which he delivered in the ninety-fourth Indian Science Congress at Jaipur.

President Kalam emphasized the need for GDP growth of 8 per cent as an important goal for India. In this context, he highlighted the role of technology; its relationship with the development and well-being of society and the need to transform Indian society into a knowledge society:

> In the twenty-first century, a new society is emerging where knowledge is the primary production resource instead of capital and labour. Efficient utilization of this existing knowledge can create comprehensive wealth for the nation in the form of better health, education infrastructure and other social indicators. Such a knowledge society has two very important components driven by societal transformation and wealth generation. The societal transformation has to be through large-scale development in education, healthcare, agriculture and governance. These in turn will lead to employment generation, high productivity and rural prosperity.[1]

In his address, President Kalam sharpened his focus on poverty. He asserted that global terrorism sprang from historical isolation, poverty, illiteracy and widespread unemployment and that these relate to a dearth of basic resources, such as water. He underscored the role space can play in solving the problem of water scarcity and thus in integrated and sustainable development. Isolated water-deficient regions could benefit from mainstream growth and prosperity with a judicious application of this technology, and the factors that give rise to terrorism would diminish. Moreover, Dr Kalam saw a role for energy from space as a growing possibility in the twenty-first century.

President Kalam envisioned international cooperation as a means of addressing common issues, including the cost of access to space and cost reduction strategies. He also outlined the need for strategies to combat dangers from asteroids and other space objects, which can threaten the existence of mankind itself. He even suggested there may be a requirement for an international space force for safeguarding assets in space, an idea that baffled almost everyone and was considered a little far-fetched. Dr Kalam, though, was reviving the dreams of his teacher Dr Vikram Sarabhai, who was a true global scientist who drew the best of the world's expertise in space science and technology to India. President Kalam felt it was time for India to lead.

President Kalam hosted the governors from all states and lieutenant governors of the Union territories at Rashtrapati Bhavan on 11 January 2003. It was a bright winter morning. Besides all the twenty-eight governors and three lieutenant governors in the two-day meet, the prime minister, the deputy prime minister and other senior ministers, as well as the cabinet secretary and the Union home secretary, were also invited. At the outset, President Kalam presented some aspects of national development and some thoughts on his visits to various states. He raised the issue of task team formation on river networking, and the need for progressing towards IT-enabled administration and management in governance. President Kalam called upon the governors to provide sage advice, beyond any political considerations, to the people and the government:

> In the last five months I have visited fifteen states. In each state I could visit remote districts and villages and was able to interact with common people and the younger generation. From this personal experience, I was convinced of the need for the governors of the states to reach the grassroots to understand problems and convey them to

> the concerned state government, and sometimes central government, for fast action to remove the sufferings of the common people.[2]

The burden of his exhortation was that without becoming a rival centre of power or authority, the governors could still be more than ornamental figures confined to the Raj Bhavans. Whether it be the issues of insurgency, communal tension or networking of rivers, the governors could play a salutary role in creating a climate of consensus among the states and the people. Additionally, the governors should play a key role in creating harmony between the Centre and the states.

After the president's spirited speech, the governors settled down for working sessions. The first session was devoted to the issue of militancy and insurgency. The governor of Chhattisgarh, Dinesh Nandan Sahay, the governor of Jharkhand, Justice M. Rama Jois, and the newly appointed governor of Andhra Pradesh, Surjit Singh Barnala, talked of Naxalite-related violence. This had become the bane of these states, and coordinating across state boundaries when facing a motivated, geographically widespread movement had proved extremely difficult. The perseverance of the Naxalite insurgency indeed posed the greatest internal security threat to India.

The Jammu and Kashmir governor, Girish Chandra Saxena said that the Jammu and Kashmir assembly elections in 2002 were seen as a victory of the ballot over the bullet. Electronic voting machines were used for first time, and the international community recognized the credibility of the elections and their results. The election saw power shift from one party to another after fifty-one years. Saxena said that people had participated in the elections in large numbers because they were keen to secure governance in key developmental areas. The new government was earnestly addressing the problems of education and housing, and this 'healing-touch policy' was working.

In the concluding session of the conference Prime Minister Vajpayee raised a vital issue. He said that all governors must play a proactive role with a total sense of partnership and become full-fledged participants in the development process. A few days after the conference, Dr Kalam told me in a reflective mood, 'When I met all the governor sahibs, I felt the time has come to review our system of governance afresh if India has to become functionally efficient, politically transparent and competitive in today's globalized environment. Distortions are visible to me in the way governors function.'

The government decided to invite the president of Iran, Seyyed Mohammad Khatami, as the chief guest at the Republic Day celebration. This is an honour customarily accorded only to India's closest friends, and was one of the first steps in recent years to build warmer relations with Iran, which is one of India's more influential neighbours. Seyyed Mohammad Khatami had enjoyed a distinguished career as a scholar before his appointment as president of Iran. In 1993, the influential American conservative political scientist Samuel Huntington provoked great debate among the theorists of international relations with his interrogatively titled article 'The Clash of Civilizations?' In this controversial piece, he attempted to legitimize the American-led Western aggression against China and the world's Islamic cultures. Seyyed Mohammad Khatami responded with the theory of 'Dialogue Among Civilizations.'[3] Indeed, his term of office was punctuated by numerous meetings with high-profile international figures.

India and Iran had historic ties. The Islamic Arabs invaded Persia and ended the Sasanian Empire in the seventh century. The local population unwilling to convert to Islam or accept dhimmi ('protected person' in Arabic) status was persecuted and fled to different regions of the world. The largest number of these people arrived in western India. Since this time, India has remained home to the largest Zoroastrian population of the world. In the modern era, the Parsi community have contributed significantly to India and Pakistan in the areas of politics, industry, science and culture. Prominent Indian Parsis included Dadabhai Naoroji, the three-time president of the Indian National Congress, Field Marshal Sam Manekshaw, nuclear energy scientist Homi Bhabha and the Tata family of J.R.D. Tata. Furthermore, Lucknow in Uttar Pradesh had been a major centre of Shia culture and Persian study in the Indian subcontinent. The ancestors of Ruhollah Moosavi Khomeini, later the Iranian Ayatollah, stayed for several generations there.

Dr Kalam spent many days studying the interactions between the people of two of the greatest civilizations of the world. He was struck by some marked similarities between their cultures. There are unmistakeable similarities between the Vedas and the Iranian Avesta. Sanskrit and Avesta languages share some likeness in respect of their terminology and phonetics. The rhythm and style of their poems were so similar that the Avesta language could be translated to Vedas using phonetic rules. God and the myths in Rig Veda and Avesta correspond closely. In fact, it could be argued that the Mitra in Rig Veda was a Misra of Avesta. The Indian and Iranian people both shared the practice of worshipping the sun, and beliefs in the holiness of fire and sacredness of the cow.

On the eve of the Republic Day, President Kalam gave his first address to the nation, which was eagerly watched by millions on the television. Beginning with the theme of developing India by creating a knowledge society, he spoke of ushering in a second green revolution, bringing urban amenities to villages and implementing electronic governance to weed out corruption and delays in servicing the citizens. He disappointed those who were expecting a homily on secularism, socialism and moral values.

President Kalam explained eloquently that during the last century, the world had undergone a change from an agriculture society, where manual labour was the most critical factor, to an industrial society where the management of technology, capital and labour provided the competitive advantage. He stated that we are now in the information era, where connectivity and software products have driven a sector of the economy of some nations, including our own. In the twenty-first century, a new society is emerging where knowledge is the primary production resource instead of capital and labour.

President Kalam gave a clarion call for India to embark upon a second green revolution, which would enable it to increase its productivity in the agricultural sector to meet the requirements of a growing population. The production of cereals needs to increase from the present 200 million tonnes to over 300 million tonnes by 2020. But the requirement of land for the increasing population as well as for greater afforestation and environmental preservation activities would demand that the present 170 million hectares of arable land will have to be brought down to 100 million hectares by 2020.

The net result of this is that all our agricultural scientists and technologists have to work for doubling the productivity of the land available for cultivation. The type of technologies needed would be in the areas of biotechnology, proper training to farmers and additional modern equipment for preservation and storage. The president respectfully remembered C. Subramaniam. As the minister for food and agriculture in the early 1970s, Subramaniam led the Indian green revolution along with Dr M.S. Swaminathan. Dr Kalam evoked his vision of graduating from grain production to food processing and marketing as the next stage of the agricultural revolution.

President Kalam used this occasion to share his concept of providing urban amenities in rural areas (PURA). He said that more than two-thirds of a billion people live in the rural parts of India. The vision of transformation to a developed India could only be realized if a tremendous mission for empowering the rural people is launched. He saw the solution in terms of connectivity:

> My visits to the rural parts of India have confirmed that the problem of rural India depends on the extent of connectivity available there. The connectivity has four components: Physical connectivity of roads; electronic connectivity of a reliable communications network; knowledge connectivity of vocational training centres and schools, and financial connectivity with the banks and the markets. All the four types of connectivity need to be pursued in an integrated manner so that economic connectivity will emerge, leading to a self-actuating people and economy.[4]

The president cautioned that PURA had to be a business proposition that was economically viable. It would need to be managed by entrepreneurs, local people and small-scale industrialists, as it involves education, health, power generation, transport and management. Government support should be in the form of empowering such management agencies, providing initial economic support and finding the right type of management structure and leaders to manage and maintain the programme.

President Kalam said candidly that India cannot become a developed nation if only the president or the prime minister desires it or the parliament makes a law. India can only become a developed nation if everyone contributes to the best of his or her abilities and capacity. For example, the student community can take up the task during holidays to make a certain number of people literate in the area where their schools or houses are situated. Teachers and parents can assist them in this task. Only a burning candle can light another.

Dr Kalam saw all sectors as having a role in development, and cooperation was key here. Research laboratories can provide technological support to our small-scale industries so that production can become more competitive. Large-scale industries have to increase their contribution to economic growth, particularly for the growth of the GDP. They can aim at becoming multinational companies in the areas of sugar and agricultural products, power, cement, manufacturing and knowledge-based industries. The farming community has to increase its productivity with advanced water conservation and innovative land management methods.

Dr Kalam's call for development unquestionably involved all of Indian society. He expressed his view that the media should become a partner, promoter and critic for national development. He stated that the fostering of a dynamic environment with motivation is the foundation for our vision of transforming India into a developed nation by 2020. *The Telegraph* on 26 January 2003 lauded President Kalam's address to the nation as a mix of 'politics, science and economics':

> Praise for the people, pat for governments, a word about those who worked the labs, and a call for another green revolution – President A.P.J. Abdul Kalam's Republic Day-eve address to the nation was a mix of politics, science and economics ... The President dwelt on the darker side, too. During the last six months, he had visited seventeen states ... 'I had the occasion to visit a large number of rural and drought-affected areas and I could share their concerns, grief and their aspirations,' he said.[5]

The next day, President Kalam and President Khatami took the salute at the grand Republic Day parade. President Khatami and Prime Minister Vajpayee signed the historic New Delhi Declaration, which boldly set forth the vision of a strategic partnership between the two countries. The two leaders also pledged to collaborate on energy, trade and other economic issues, to strengthen their cooperation on counterterrorism, and to broaden their strategic collaboration in third countries, which most analysts took to mean Afghanistan.[6]

Apart from the always vocal press and New Delhi's lively think tanks, India and its leaders had hitherto shown little interest in military or strategic issues. Strategic defence reviews like those that take place routinely in America, Britain and France, informed by serving officers and civil servants but led by politicians, were unknown in India. Two visionary leaders, President Kalam and Prime Minister Vajpayee, were changing that trend. Their aspiration was for a strong republic, well prepared militarily and strategically for contingencies within and beyond its borders. To the same degree, they concurred that the country should remain compassionate and responsive to its people.

For Dr Kalam, emphasizing two parallel, somewhat incongruous aspects of the nation's security was perhaps merely encompassing the nation's requirements in one comprehensive vision. It could be viewed just as easily as his perceiving the inherent need for symmetry, for equilibrium – in the man as much as the nation. He had dedicated most of his illustrious career to bettering the nation's defence capabilities, and had been personally involved in building the most lethal weapons the nation had seen. But he had advanced social causes with unparalleled zeal and vision at a time of his life where most seek leisure and personal comfort.

There was balance in the seeming paradox that was Dr A.P.J. Abdul Kalam: a peace-loving missile man, a doyen of military hardware championing the upliftment of the poor, an Indian of ardent patriotism who believed in the confluence of cultures, and whose reverence among his own people was matched by his esteem abroad. Dr Kalam knew well the capabilities of his weapons; he had designed and witnessed their destructive powers himself. He likewise knew that they were best kept in the barracks; but they were, at any rate, necessary for the order of the nation. As he would famously declare in a speech to the European parliament at the end of his presidency, '*When there is harmony in the home, there is order in the Nation. When there is order in the Nation, there is peace in the World.*'

Part Four
EXPANSION

A man who dares to waste one hour of time has not discovered the value of life.

– Charles Darwin
Founder of the scientific theory of evolution

4.1

Tamaso Ma Jyotirgamaya

> India of the ages is not dead nor has she spoken her last creative word; she lives and has still something to do for herself and the human peoples.
>
> – Sri Aurobindo

Dr Kalam first met Dr Govindappa Venkataswamy, a pioneer in mass eye care, in Madurai in 1990, when Dr Kalam's brother, A.P.J.M. Maracayer, required treatment for his eye. Dr Kalam had advised the apprehensive Maracayer to take the train to Madurai, and told him he would meet him there to accompany him to the clinic. He had heard many good things about Dr Venkataswamy and thought it fit to attend with his brother personally. That way, he would provide moral support to his elder brother and also meet the noble doctor.

At Dr Venkataswamy's Aravind Eye Hospital, Dr Kalam was astonished by the meticulous way in which the doctors attended to the patients. Moreover, he observed the impeccable courtesy and kindness shown to the patients by the hospital staff, and sensed an uncommon depth of concern for their welfare. Most significant, and doubtless the inspiration for this excellence, was Dr Venkataswamy himself. Everyone called him Dr V, an endearment which conveyed respect and love in equal measure. Dr Kalam felt that this elderly gentleman with an engaging smile radiated divinity, and found him even more impressive at their meeting than his illustrious reputation would suggest. A great friendship would develop between the pair. In spite of their different fields of endeavour, they were kindred spirits.

Dr V was taken aback that a renowned scientist such as Dr Kalam should come to meet him for such a small matter. Dr Kalam explained it was Dr V's eminence that drew him there. Dr V insisted that Dr Kalam and Maracayer share tea with him in his house before leaving, and together they walked to the small one-room cottage by the side of the hospital where Dr V lived. Dr V unfolded steel chairs and made tea for Dr Kalam and Maracayer while they talked. In a sense, Dr Kalam and Dr V were quite alike: they were both absorbed by their duty, and had little energy for sophistication. Dr V's simple furniture reminded Dr Kalam of the way his father had lived:

On the coast of Coromandel
Where the earthy shells blow,
In the middle of the sands
Lived some really rich souls.

One cotton lungi and half a candle –
One old jug without a handle
There were all the worthy possessions
Of these kings without a scandal.[1]

Dr Kalam asked Dr V how he became such a great eye doctor. Dr V said that he never wanted to be an eye doctor, but it was simply God's will, and so he became one. After medical college, he joined the military, but was bedridden for two years with severe rheumatoid arthritis. With almost preternatural will, he managed to return to medical training, battling the severe pain that was to be his companion for life. But his dream of becoming a gynaecologist and obstetrician was dashed. Arthritis had deformed his hands and fingers; he could only perform fine, delicate movements such as those for eye surgery.

Dr V continued his story. He retired from government service in 1976, aged fifty-eight. He was entitled to a small pension and could have retired in peace, as most people of that era did. Dr V, however, conceived a project that he believed in. He opened an eleven-bed eye clinic in a modest, rented house in Madurai. He had no business plan and meagre financial resources; but he had a powerful sense of duty and a vision perfectly aligned. He rejected business prudence, preferring to rely on Sri Aurobindo and the Mother for spiritual guidance, and named the hospital Aravind Eye Hospital after his guru. From this small base, he would venture to remote villages with his team, to perform vital ocular procedures for the most underprivileged in society.

At first, some derided him for his efforts. He was ridiculed for trying to popularize what colleagues disparagingly referred to as 'roadside surgery'. But he steadfastly persisted with his work in the areas of greatest need. 'I identified myself with the poor and destitute, suffering darkness in their lives. So what if I did not have a hospital? I had my skills, and so be it,' he told Dr Kalam. Dr V described his eye-clinic camps: 'My team and I would begin operating at five in the morning and work without rest until seven or eight in the evening. Only then would we eat. And all of them would sit together – the doctors, the nurses, the cleaning staff and the villagers. There was no segregation between "low-caste" menial workers from "upper-caste" professionals. We were doing rugged, bare-bones operations. We converted schools into operating theatres and sterilized the classroom. The more operations we did, the more the demand grew. The eye camps taught me the lesson that when you begin doing the work you are destined to do, unexpected resources will find you. Slowly, a powerful ripple of goodwill spread.'

A humble man despite his accolades and success, Dr V thanked Dr Kalam for leaving his important work for the nation and coming all the way to Madurai to meet him.

Dr Kalam and Dr V corresponded over the years, and they developed a powerful bond of friendship. Each of these great men possessed a humanity balanced between innate simplicity and a refined spiritual awareness, which united them with a concern for the welfare of others. It came as no surprise, then, that when a letter came from Dr Venkataswamy inviting President Kalam to open the Aravind Eye Hospital in Pondicherry, he promptly accepted. The date was carefully chosen to mark the 125th anniversary of the Mother's birth. The event, President Kalam told his personal secretary Sheridon, would allow him to fulfil his long-standing wish to visit Pondicherry. He had studied about this former French colony in Schwartz High School at Ramanathapuram, but had never had a chance to visit there.

I received a call from President Kalam sometime in mid-February, and he asked me to join him 'on a pilgrimage' on 21 February 2003. It was only after reaching Delhi from Hyderabad that I realized that he was taking me south again to Pondicherry. There, we would visit the Sri Aurobindo Ashram, and that is why he had called it a pilgrimage. But I later understood that my assumption was based on an incomplete picture: this tour was a pilgrimage for Dr Kalam on two counts. He deeply revered Dr Venkataswamy, and he saw his opening Aravind Eye Hospital as work for the divine.

The divine grace is infinitely more powerful than any worldly force, and it had guided Dr V's humanitarian endeavours from their inception. The Aravind Eye Care System flouted the usual rules of business to restore sight to the blind. It has, however, grown into a network of eye hospitals that has had a major impact in eradicating cataract-related blindness in India. As of 2015, Aravind has treated nearly thirty-six million patients and performed five million surgeries. The vast majority of these have been low-cost or even free, which has helped make Aravind the world's largest and most prolific eye-care service group.

The model of Aravind Eye Care hospitals has been widely acclaimed and has become the subject of numerous case studies across the world. It has also become a modern-day testimony to a socially responsible business model that is at once feasible, viable and competitive. Its success demonstrates that choices which seem naive or unworkable – when executed with wisdom and integrity – can yield bafflingly extraordinary results.

Dr V had a vision larger than other enterprises in the field: To see all as one; to give sight for all, and to eliminate curable blindness. There were some twelve million cases of blindness in India susceptible to reversal by medical treatment. The radical essence of Dr V's strategy was to provide free eye care to those least able to pay. The Aravind Eye Care System has thus treated more than a third of its patients, numbering in the millions, free of cost. Patients choose whether to pay. Those who could pay willingly paid. Those who could not pay gratefully received treatment without charge. There were no favours shown or obligations elicited. That Aravind's novel approach to its accounts has proved workable is almost as much a testament to the Indian people's integrity, as it is to Dr V's generosity.

An approach to mass medicine that appeared naive was in fact underpinned by eminently practical goals. Dr V, a keen innovator and proponent of inclusive progress, always recognized good health, especially good vision, as a major contributor to economic well-being. He authored three books in Tamil on eye diseases and diabetes. Efforts to duplicate the Aravind model have found success in many developing countries, and Dr V's vision was to start at least a hundred hospitals across the country.

To reach Dr V's hospital inauguration, we boarded a special aircraft in Delhi for the flight to Chennai, and took a helicopter a further 150 kilometres south from there to Pondicherry. There is a certain majesty in approaching a city in a helicopter. The forms of the buildings in Pondicherry, whitewashed against the greenery of its boulevards, now remain as a dream-like imprint on my memory. The chief minister of Pondicherry, N. Rangasamy, the lieutenant governor, K.R. Malkani, the French consul general, His Excellency Michel Segury and the vice chancellor of Pondicherry University, Prof. V.T. Patil, accompanied President Kalam. When Dr V greeted him with traditional folded hands, President Kalam responded with a warm hug; a rare gesture from a head of state.

President Kalam spoke in Tamil for a few minutes and then switched to English. He said that 30 per cent of the country's population lived below the poverty line, and medical care had to be provided to this large sector of the population. As ever, he was looking to the future:

> We have the best doctors and technologists in India. We have core competence in design and software engineering. Emerging

> technologies in virtual reality and micro machines will transform the healthcare scenario. This transformation should lead to helping the people who cannot afford modern medical care. If we remove their pain, God will bless us.[2]

Dr V had remained a bachelor like Dr Kalam, and he gave his entire life to serving his patients, without worldly comforts or pleasures. As with Dr Kalam, his work and service to people was its own reward. Dr Kalam had asked me to record six things that he felt made Dr Venkataswamy's Aravind Eye Hospitals one of the best social enterprises in the world. There could be many more than six, but I made mention of those that first came to my mind.

First, aspiration is always more consequential than resources. Dr V didn't have any venture capital or funds to make his initial project a sizeable endeavour. But he created a business model that allowed him to build, day after day, a sustainable social enterprise. When there were insufficient beds, he promptly added new ones. When there was not enough space, he simply built new floors. When the hospital could not cater to the increasing numbers of patients, he just built other hospitals. And when there were calls for hospitals outside India, he built them in seven different countries. This was his great aspiration – and it was so powerful, it transcended the usual imperative of business plans, capital backing and so forth.

Second, Dr V had taken control of his life, and his mission was to change the world as he could. This is a distinct characteristic of social entrepreneurs. If they see something that is wrong, instead of complaining, they do something about it. They change the prevailing reality. Dr V had an overriding conviction that there was a way to make things change, despite his want of material resources. And obviously, he was a great leader who was able to inspire people and convince them of his vision. In his hospital, he wanted to change the lives of blind people who could not afford their treatment, and he knew he could do this with a groundbreaking, commercially sustainable business.

Third, Aravind Eye Hospitals had an inspirational leader. There are different facets of ability in a professional context. You can be a highly capable individual, a contributing team member, a competent executive or an effective manager; but only leaders are able to change the world. Dr V built enduring greatness through a seemingly paradoxical combination of personal humility and willpower. He had a tremendous vision of combining social responsibility with innovative marketing and a revolutionary delivery strategy, which appears equally paradoxical by any standard business wisdom. He led by example: his simple lifestyle, his capacity for hard work and his encouragement of others' potential were an inspiration to his staff, not to mention his patients.

Fourth, Dr V had grown his organization from good to great. Dr V knew that an organization is indeed built by its people. He therefore focused on people and their development. He faced harsh realities, which would have discouraged even the most optimist entrepreneur. Youth was no longer on his side, and neither could he rely on family resources; he was fifty-eight and he didn't have any wealth to speak of. But he faced his situation; he would weave his fabric of success from the attributes that life had given him – his skills, his vision and his tenacity. Another crucial attribute in building his organization was his patience. He knew it would take a lot of time to realize his dream, but he wasn't the least discouraged by this, in spite of his advancing years.

Fifth, sound organizational values were the foundation of the hospital group. Dr V was guided by the principle of treating whoever came to his door. Even if patients did not have money, he found a way to cure them. That's how his cross-subsidizing model that takes money from one person out of three was conceived. He also possessed the necessary personal values to bring his rather novel vision to being. His practice was hallmarked by compassion, which translated into eye care for all and sensitivity to patients' needs, regardless of their status. Also, equity underpinned Aravind's operation: Dr V devised an amazing system of standardization that mandated a consistent level of care for all patients. Moreover, the manner in which the hospitals conducted business was transparent. Treatment was affordable, and the charges for those who could afford to pay were fixed across the organization for a given service.

The sixth and the most important aspect of Dr V's Aravind Eye Hospital was his ability to think like the big players. Dr V developed a franchise business model, with its advantages in economies of scale and manifold ways of optimizing efficiency. When he began the enterprise, the cost of an intraocular lens for surgery was USD 200. He applied the franchise model and managed to lower it to five dollars. Dr V followed the shift from sutured extra-capsular cataract surgery to small-incision cataract surgery. Phaco-emulsification with foldable lenses became the surgical choice. Dr V worked tirelessly to elevate the Indian intra-ocular lens industry. He firmly directed it away from cost-cutting manufacturing practices, to make it a quality-conscious, technology-driven and value-priced industry, competitive in the global market. This allowed Aravind Eye Care to export lenses to eighty-five countries.

In any event, the foundation of Dr V's life – and Dr Kalam's life, for that matter – was his faith in the divine. Dr V followed the venerable poet sage Sri Aurobindo. Dr Kalam was intrigued with the rather colourful life of Sri Aurobindo. Unlike other spiritual leaders who were born with a spiritual temperament or renounced the world in their childhood or youth, Sri Aurobindo's early promise was in the academic field. Far from being raised in a yogic tradition, his largely anglicized family was successful in every sense of the world, inhabiting the upper echelons of Bengali colonial society.

Young Aurobindo Ghose's father was the civil assistant of Rangpur district in Bengal (now in Bangladesh) and raised his children speaking English at home. Aurobindo and his two elder siblings were sent to the English-speaking Loreto House boarding school in Darjeeling, which was a centre of British life in India. The school was run by Irish nuns, through which the boys would have been exposed to Christian religious teachings and symbolism. Aurobindo studied for the Indian Civil Service at King's College, Cambridge, England, and successfully completed its required examinations. Life as a servant of the British Raj held no appeal to him though, and after returning to India, he took up various academic posts and civil service duties under the maharaja of the princely state of Baroda. He then began to involve himself in politics, for which he was to find fame and notoriety.

Aurobindo quickly became an ardent proponent of independence. His eloquent speech and scholarly articles brought him at odds with the British authorities, who accused him of involvement in revolutionary activities. He was imprisoned by the British colonial government, and held in solitary confinement for a year. It was during this solitary confinement that Aurobindo had a series of mystical and spiritual experiences that were to alter the course of his life. Despite being acquitted of all charges and released from prison, the colonial authorities continued their persecution of him, issuing warrants for his arrest for sedition on account of articles he had published. In 1910, to escape their wrath, he moved to Pondicherry, abandoning politics for spiritual work.

At the beginning of Aurobindo's stay at Pondicherry, there were few followers and little material sustenance, but with time their numbers grew, resulting in the formation of the Sri Aurobindo Ashram. After a few years, Mirra Richard, later known as 'The Mother', became Sri Aurobindo's close spiritual collaborator. The Mother was a French national, born in Paris on 21 February 1878. After meeting Sri Aurobindo during a brief stay in Pondicherry in the shadow of World War I, she returned and permanently settled there in 1920. Sri Aurobindo considered the Mother his spiritual equal.

When he retired to a life of renunciation and seclusion on 24 November 1926, Sri Aurobindo entrusted the Mother with the day-to-day running of the ashram and care of their disciples. From this time until his death, he communicated with thousands of his followers exclusively through letters. Sri Aurobindo died on 5 December 1950, and around 100,000 people attended his funeral. The Mother continued their spiritual work in the ashram, guiding their many followers until she passed away at the ripe age of ninety-five in 1973.

After we had attended the opening of Aravind Eye Hospital in Pondicherry, we made our way in the presidential motorcade along roads cleared of traffic to the ashram. I was privileged to sit next to Dr Kalam. It was, as usual, a noisy and stately affair. The presidential car was the third in a regal procession of fifteen to twenty cars: a pilot police vehicle with a flashing red light and wailing siren leading from the front, and an ambulance bringing up the rear. Police had carefully shepherded everyone to the sides of the roads, and saluted as we passed. President Kalam was not one for ceremonial; pomp and circumstance held little appeal for him. But this was part of the government machinery, and he knew he had to go along for the ride.

He was not entirely passive in cooperating with his minders, though. He would wind down his window and wave to the children who were standing on the roadside, hoping to catch a glimpse of their favourite Indian leader. This was against usual protocol, and created panic in his aides for the danger an open window could pose to his safety – the president would be an easy target for an assassin without the protection of bulletproof glass. I said to him, 'You shouldn't do that, it's not safe for you.' He replied, 'Funny guy, these are my children. They're not going to kill me,' and continued waving to the delighted youngsters. And he was right.

At Sri Aurobindo Ashram, the managing trustee, Manoj Das Gupta, received President Kalam. After going through various rooms in the ashram and laying floral tributes at the samadhi of Sri Aurobindo and the Mother, Dr Kalam went to the room where Sri Aurobindo had lived for twenty-four long years in seclusion. Is it really possible for a person to sentence himself to such a long solitary confinement? It is especially significant that he did so after suffering the brutality of solitary confinement at the hands of British colonial masters. Perhaps in this self-imposed imprisonment, he had found freedom. What would Sri Aurobindo have felt here? President Kalam asked to be left alone for a while in Sri Aurobindo's room and spent more than fifteen minutes there, deep in contemplation.

When he emerged from his meditations, a saying of the Mother displayed on the wall captured his gaze: 'Sri Aurobindo came to tell us: One need not leave the earth to find the Truth, one need not leave the life to find his soul, one need not abandon the world or have only limited beliefs to enter into relation with the Divine. The Divine is everywhere, in everything and if He is hidden, it is because we do not take the trouble to discover Him.'

When we returned to Delhi it was late in the night. President

Kalam asked me if I was tired and sleepy. I was. But curious upon his inquiry, I said, 'No, sir', and he invited me for a midnight walk in the Mughal Gardens. The waning gibbous moon was a little more than a luminous crescent in the sky. I heard perhaps the longest dissertation I had heard from Dr Kalam on that night. It was almost as if he had composed a didactic play, and was reciting it to himself and feeding me my lines.

Kalam: Do you know, buddy, why it is that of all the great civilizations that arose on this planet 5,000–7,000 years ago, it is perhaps the Indian civilization alone that has continued unbroken down the long and tortuous corridors of time?

Arun: Sir, there were other great civilizations that were even older, with magnificent structures and ruins, but these civilizations have disappeared.

Kalam: It is India – and to some extent China – that has maintained this continuity. Do you know why?

Arun: No, sir. Please tell me.

Kalam: There are two reasons. How many?

Arun: Two, sir.

Kalam: First, there has been a spiritual and philosophical foundation for Indian culture provided by the great scriptures. No other civilization has this kind of vast literature. Arabs had the Quran, Jews had the Torah, but thousands of years before these two great books, India had the Vedas and Upanishads. This literature sustained Indian culture even in the most terrible and tragic circumstances.

Arun: Yes, sir. The scriptures constantly gave Indian culture the capacity for regeneration and renewal over time.

Kalam: Second, a series of great men and women have articulated these truths. These philosophical truths are not merely intellectual constructs, but have been an inspiration for people in their daily lives. I have realized this today.

Arun: In Sri Aurobindo's room?

Kalam: Yes. You know, buddy, when I was there in the room, it suddenly occurred to me that three great souls were sailing in three different directions in 1893. Sri Aurobindo was sailing to India from England. Swami Vivekananda was sailing from Japan to Canada to attend the Chicago World Parliament of Religions. Mahatma Gandhi was sailing from London to Durban to start his career.

Arun: It is indeed true, sir. It never occurred to me.

Kalam: You are a funny guy. You are good at seeing. Develop the skill of feeling that is not visible. The hand of God was already making strokes that would create a new picture of India. Three great souls were launched on to their respective missions that would converge decades later into the Independence of India.

Arun: Sure, sir. What else did you feel in Sri Aurobindo's room?

Kalam: I felt that the nation is not only a political construct; it was in fact a divinity. I realized the meaning of Bharat Mata today, Mother India.

Arun: So it is a divinity into which one had to be prepared to offer everything as a sacrifice?

Kalam: Yes. This is what Dr Venkataswamy has done. He gave his everything for bringing light to the millions of blind people.

Arun: Perhaps it is for this reason he named his hospital after Sri Aurobindo.

Kalam: Dr Venkataswamy was not working to make a hospital for himself. He was doing a service. He surrendered his service at the feet of his guru Sri Aurobindo.

Arun: Sir, what can I put at your feet? You are my guru.

Kalam: I am not your guru. I am not anybody's guru. Another point that I want to tell you today is that Sri Aurobindo always placed India's freedom in the larger context of the destiny of the human race. This fact is very remarkable, because all over the world revolutionaries talk only about their own country.

Arun: But wasn't Sri Aurobindo a nationalist? He wanted India to be free.

Kalam: Sri Aurobindo had a deeper vision of what India should do for humanity. It is for this reason that India has to be free. Only a free India can play its role in the emancipation of the human race.

Arun: Did it happen?

Kalam: No. And that is my pain. That is what is not allowing me to sleep. The more I see the problems of my people the more I feel myself small, helpless and good for nothing.

Then, he suddenly turned away and started walking towards the mansion. I quietly followed his steps. He spoke no further. He did not turn even once and retired for the night.

4.2
Anjuman

> There is a candle in your heart, ready to be kindled.
> There is a void in your soul, ready to be filled.
> You feel it, don't you?
>
> – Jalal-ud-din Rumi
> Thirteenth-century Persian poet

Friday, 28 March 2003, was a special day for Hubli's Anjuman-e-Islam, the oldest minority educational institution in the state of Karnataka. It celebrated its 100th anniversary on that day. The historical background for the Anjuman-e-Islam dated to 1857, when the first war for freedom was waged against the country's British colonial rulers. After the war, Muslims openly expressed their resentment of foreign rule and most boycotted the English language, as they thought it was alien to their culture and tradition. An irked British government retaliated, launching a systematic campaign to exclude Muslims from mainstream activities and government jobs.

Predictably, the Muslim community began to fall behind in the race for employment and modern education. A visionary Mehboob Ali Khan, the brother of the Nawab of Savanur, felt that Muslims desperately needed a modern education to progress economically. He not only exhorted the Muslim community to take steps to further their own learning, but also spearheaded the education movement by founding the Anjuman-e-Islam. There are similar institutions in other parts of the country founded for the very purpose of the uplifting of the Muslim community through education. The Muslim community slowly started entering the mainstream, but the damage had already been done in the years since 1857. The community lagged behind. Apart from its contribution to education, Anjuman-e-Islam played a role in maintaining peace and harmony in the conflict-ridden Hubli–Dharwar region.

Hubli, also referred to as Hubballi, flourished under the Vijayanagara Empire. It became a major commercial centre dealing with the trade of saltpetre, iron and cotton. The city later came under the rule of the Adilshahis, a Shia Muslim dynasty that ruled the Sultanate of Bijapur. The Adilshahi rulers were forced to leave Hubli by the Mughals, and it came under the rule of the Nawab of Savanur. Then came the Marathas in the mid-1750s, followed by Haider Ali and his son Tipu Sultan. This period saw a number of shifts of power between various warring rulers, until the British East India Company conquered the city in 1817. The British had coveted this strategic centre for trade, and quite easily supplanted the disunited local rulers. Their ascent to power by exploiting divided loyalties and enmity between people followed a common pattern that occurred throughout the Indian subcontinent in that era.

On 28 March 2003, President Kalam, accompanied by the governor of Karnataka, T.N. Chaturvedi, and Chief Minister S.M. Krishna, arrived at the Nehru Arts, Science and Commerce College for its commemorative event. The college is among the most renowned in north Karnataka, and it is run by the Anjuman-e-Islam trust. Jabbar Khan Honnalli, president of the trust, received them. President Kalam told Jabbar Khan sahib that Najam means 'star' and Anjuman means 'a group of stars'. 'You are all stars of the great Indian civilization,' he said. He addressed the students with one eye on the past and the other on the fundamental values that sustain this great civilization:

> Dear young friends, when you are haunted with cultural invasions through the media and elsewhere, think of yourselves as children of civilizational bliss. We (the Indian people) withstood multiple

> invasions, and many dynasties have ruled us. Today, India is free from invasions and is independent. We cherish family values and spiritual life. Many developed nations are dreaming for such a full life.[1]

President Kalam evoked intense positive energy amongst the children by his simple narration. He explained that India, a multi-religious, multilingual and multiracial civilization based on the essential unity of culture amidst diversity, had kept her people united. The Partition of the subcontinent at the time of Independence had created a deep sense of mistrust and the narrow religious, regional and communal feelings lingered for a long time. This is because the politicians in the democratic framework that was adopted by the Indian Constitution saw their vote banks in every possible schism – between religions, between sects in a religion, between castes, languages – and even in mythical identities.

How can a fragmented vessel hold water? How can a family flourish under a roof that is torn asunder? Dr Kalam was passionate about this issue, and firmly expressed that our unity, integrity and solidarity cannot be compromised. Communal and clannish sentiments hamper the growth of the nation at every step. If the nation wishes to make sound progress in the socio-economic, political and scientific spheres, communal harmony has to be assured as a permanent feature of life. The forces trying to destroy social harmony by sowing dissent and promoting their vote banks should be isolated and shown the error of their ways. It is our duty to spread the message of communal harmony and hold on to the values of our great civilization.

A few days after his visit to Hubli, another opportunity appeared before President Kalam to speak on this issue, when he presented the Kabir Puraskar (communal harmony awards in the name of the saint poet Kabir) on 31 March 2003. Prime Minister Vajpayee and Deputy Prime Minister L.K. Advani came to the Rashtrapati Bhavan to attend the award ceremony. The winners included Tontada Siddhaling Swamiji, Farid Mazahiri, Raj Kishore Pandey and Syeda Naseem Chishti. President Kalam exhorted the highly influential gathering of social and political leaders to maintain national unity:

> We, a nation of a billion people, should think as a nation of a billion people. Indians are natural born leaders in critical situations and challenging environments for the reason they live in a multi-religious, multi-ethnic and multicultural society. I consider no other nation has the civilizational heritage to live a near-peaceful life like India. Indian minds have been capable of absorbing the best from numerous cultures. We have also evolved great qualities of leadership to manage the nation of a billion people with democratic systems and with various dimensions in every aspect of life. Now, we should not allow any religion or any individual fanaticism to endanger our nation. Because the nation is more important than any individual or party or religion.[2]

President Kalam was invited to a convention on the evolution of a good human being organized by the Brahma Kumaris Academy at Gurgaon. He called R. Swaminathan and me to discuss what a good human being means. Was there a definitive characterization? There has to be a clear-cut definition for this, otherwise any type of conduct could be deemed good and any organization may declare itself good and label others bad. Dr Kalam surprised us by opening a book right at the beginning. It was *Necklaces of Gems (Qada'id Al-jawahir): A Biography of Shaikh 'Abd Al-Qadir Al-Jilani.*[3] President Kalam read from the book the twelve special qualities that must be firmly established in the character of a good human being.

The two qualities come from God, who is always ready to pardon and forgive. A person who is endowed with them will always be ready to pardon (*sattar*), always ready to forgive (*ghaffar*). Two qualities come from Prophet Muhammad; a person who is endowed with them will be sympathetic (*shafiq*) and kind (*rafiq*). Two qualities come from the first righteous (*rashidun*) Caliph Abu Bakr; a person who is endowed with them will be both truthful (*sadiq*) and charitable (*mutasaddiq*). Two qualities come from the second righteous Caliph Umar ibn al-Khattab; a person who is endowed with them will be active in commanding what is right and fair (*ammar*) and active in forbidding what is wrong and unfair (*nahha*). Two qualities come from the third righteous Caliph Uthman ibn Affan; a person who is endowed with them will be an active provider of food (*mit'am*) and one who is devoted to praying (*musalli*) at night, when the rest of the people are sound asleep. Finally, two qualities come from Ali ibn Abi Talib; a person who is endowed with them will be both learned (*alim*) and courageous (*shuja*).These twelve qualities make a human being good. The absence of these qualities leads to unwholesome conduct.

The three of us had a hearty discussion that converged on the point that it is man's duty on earth to set himself the highest attainable goal, and to strive for this goal with all the powers at his disposal. But it must be done as a human being; and this is the challenge: to rise above material temptations. A good man does not trouble himself merely with food and drink; he does not allow himself to be driven by his basic instincts, like an animal. If a man's intellect strives only for worldly greatness or fame without keeping in view the general welfare and advancement of mankind, it cannot sustain a good human being – regardless of its prowess. Those with such consciousness have less value on earth than animals.

On 19 April 2003, President Kalam inaugurated the Om Shanti Retreat Centre with Rajyogini Dadi Prakashmani, the global chief of Brahma Kumaris. The centre is a sprawling 30-acre complex built in peaceful and verdant surroundings at Pataudi Road in Gurgaon. The governor of Haryana, Babu Parmanand, and the chief minister, Om Prakash Chautala, were present. Addressing a gathering of more than 2,000 people, President Kalam mentioned his core belief in *Wahadat-e-Insaniyat* – the unity of humanity. Basically, we are all connected. It was at this function that Dr Kalam recited for the first time a particular poem, which is an English translation of a proverb of the Chinese philosopher Confucius. It would later become his anthem:

Where there is righteousness in the heart
There is beauty in the character.
When there is beauty in the character,
There is harmony in the home.
When there is harmony in the home,
There is order in the nation.

When there is order in the nation,
There is peace in the world.[4]

On 31 May 2003, President Kalam was in Bodhgaya in connection with a function to celebrate the inclusion of Mahabodhi Temple in the UNESCO list of world heritage sites. It was here that Gautama Buddha attained enlightenment under what became known as the Bodhi tree, a massive peepul tree with heart-shaped leaves. The tree now at this very spot was grown from a sapling of the Mahabodhi tree in Sri Lanka, which itself was grown from a sapling of the original Bodhi tree, which had died due to old age.

A lover of children and a man with first-hand experience of poverty and deprivation, Dr Kalam expressed the desire to be with the inmates of the Gaya Muslim Orphanage at Cherki, about 15 km from Gaya town on the Gaya–Sherghati Road. S.M. Khan, the president's press secretary, conveyed his wish to the district officials. As the orphanage visit was not on the president's official itinerary, district officials scuppered the plan, pleading that the massive security arrangements needed for the presidential visit could not be made at such short notice. They even proffered the excuse that the orphanage was located in an area with a dangerous Maoist presence.

President Kalam would not give up so easily and insisted that he meet the children. In deference to the presidential wish, a group of children from the Cherki orphanage were hurriedly transported to Bodhgaya. Dr Farasat Hussain, the president of Cherki orphanage escorted the children and recounted his experience: 'The President played perfect guardian to the orphans and spent quite some time with them, ensuring the overawed orphans felt comfortable in his company.'[5]

S.M. Khan sahib briefed the president about the struggle of Enayeth Khan, who had established the orphanage in October 1917 with hardly any money and amidst stern opposition. He had showed great patience, perseverance and bravery in establishing this home, saving many children from the cruel fate of fending for themselves by the roadside. Enayeth Khan would tell children to be brave against the tormentor, but at the same time have faith in God and endure difficulties with patience. S.M. Khan recalled a couplet of Enayeth Khan and explained to Dr Kalam its meaning:

Bawaquar rahne ko, Barqarar rehne ko
Jung bhi zaroori hai, sulah bhi munasib hai.

To exist with dignity and stability
Battle is compulsory, and so is compromise.

In 1897, when Swami Vivekananda returned from the West, the citizens of Madras gave him a historic reception. Swamiji stayed at Castle Kernan, the house of advocate Biligiri Iyengar. It was a three-storey building situated at the Triplicane seaside. Swami Vivekananda sent Ramakrishnananda to Madras, where he started an orphanage for destitute children in this house. Over time, through the selfless service of volunteers and support from wealthy citizens, the orphanage grew into a large institution at Mylapore. On 19 June 2003, President Kalam visited Ramakrishna Mission Students Home, Mylapore, Chennai.

President Kalam shared with the students that two teachings of Sri Ramakrishna and Swami Vivekananda had been his guiding light, right from his childhood. Sri Ramakrishna said, 'As a lamp does not burn without oil, so a man cannot live without God.' Swami Vivekananda said, 'Imagination properly employed is our greatest strength. It goes beyond reason and it is only light that can take us everywhere.'

President Kalam interacted with the children here in a relaxed manner, without the pressure of his other engagements, and he was free to ignore the prodding of his staff. He said that when the British were ruling India, thousands of orphans and unparented children existed on the fringes of society, where they were at once more pathetic and more of a threat to social stability than children in even the poorest of families. Mothers in those times often died during or following childbirth. Young men in the prime of life could be struck down as well, especially when epidemics swept through

The initial objectives of the Indian space programme were to establish a modest sounding rocket launching facility and provide facilities to the international scientific community to gather data. While work was in progress, seven rocket engineers were sent for training with NASA. A youthful A.P.J. Abdul Kalam (second from left) was among them.

Vikram Sarabhai entrusted Kalam with the tasks of developing advanced composite materials and setting up India's first filament winding machine. His duty was to build non-magnetic payload housings for the two-stage sounding rockets and rocket motor casings.

Satish Dhawan oversaw Kalam's every step in the making of the SLV-3. It was successfully launched on 18 July 1980 when it carried the Rohini RS-1 satellite into orbit, thereby making India the sixth member of an exclusive club of spacefaring nations.

Satish Dhawan told Prime Minister Indira Gandhi that Kalam had shown exemplary leadership in the creation of SLV-3, which was a mammoth effort involving thousands of people over seven years.

The entire programme of military rocketry was reeling under a persistent mood of apathy. There was a leadership vacuum, and Raja Ramanna invited Kalam to assume a key role in the DRDL to give impetus to the missile programme.

On Republic Day 1981, the Padma Bhushan, the third-highest civilian honour of the country, was conferred on Kalam. He received the award from President Neelam Sanjiva Reddy.

Kalam, flanked by V.S. Arunachalam, showing Prime Minister Rajiv Gandhi the Agni missile in the making. Later, the prime minister laid the foundation stone of Research Centre Imarat (RCI), a facility for testing and evaluating completely integrated missiles. RCI's purpose would be to weed out design, fabrication and integration deficiencies in the missiles.

On Republic Day 1990, the Indian nation celebrated the success of its missile programme. Dr Kalam and Dr Arunachalam were awarded the Padma Vibhushan, the second-highest civilian honour of the Republic of India. Receiving the award from President R. Venkataraman, the visionary of the nation's missile programme, held particular significance for Dr Kalam.

Dr Kalam enjoyed direct access to Prime Minster Narasimha Rao, who was also the defence minister. After the Cold War ended in 1991, and with that the 1971 treaty with the Soviet Union, India was left vulnerable, without a superpower friend. There was little choice for India other than to become a nuclear-capable nation.

Defence Minister Mulayam Singh Yadav developed a great rapport with Dr Kalam. He would walk into Dr Kalam's office in the South Block whenever he needed to meet with him, instead of calling Dr Kalam to his chamber as was customary.

The Bharat Ratna, the nation's highest civilian honour, was conferred on Dr Kalam by President K.R. Narayanan in November 1997. This conveyed to the world a powerful message of India's commitment to national security. Dr Kalam was the first scientist after C.V. Raman to receive this award.

The Agni missile was successfully developed into a nuclear weapon delivery system. Defence Minister George Fernandes (centre) with Dr Kalam, his friend and right-hand man R. Swaminathan (second from right) and Agni Project Director R.N. Agarwal (far right).

On 11 May 1998 at 3:43:44.2 p.m., Indian Standard Time, the first three nuclear devices were simultaneously detonated underground at Pokhran Test Range. Two days later, two sub-kiloton devices were similarly detonated. A sixth device, which was installed and scheduled for testing, was taken back under orders from R. Chidambaram, as he felt that the team had obtained the results they required from the five blasts.

Dr Kalam filed his nomination papers for the office of President on 18 June 2002. The election was to be a one-sided contest, with Dr Kalam receiving support across the political spectrum and nearly 90 per cent of the vote.

On 25 July 2002, the Chief Justice of India B.N. Kirpal administered the oath of office and secrecy to Dr Kalam, making him the eleventh President of India.

Dr Kalam offering namaz with his elder brother A.P.J.M. Maracayer and members of their family in Rameswaram. Dr Kalam once said to me, 'If you only had eyes to see and ears to hear and wits to understand, you would know that the Kingdom of God is the sense of holiness, goodness and beauty. It is as close to you as your breath.'

Two visionary leaders, President Kalam and Prime Minister Atal Bihari Vajpayee, moved the nation away from servitude and fatalism. They envisioned an enlightened India, which possessed military might for its adversaries and compassion for its people in equal measure.

The Rashtrapati Bhavan was made ready for the swearing-in ceremony for Smt. Sonia Gandhi. Smt. Gandhi then told President Kalam that she would like Dr Manmohan Singh to be the prime minister of India.

The historic Indo-US Civil Nuclear Cooperation Agreement was signed during President George W. Bush's visit in March 2006. The way for India to procure uranium was effectively cleared, and the nation could now meet its acute energy needs as an emerging world power.

President Kalam asked, 'Dr Mandela, can you please tell me about the pioneers of the anti-apartheid movement in South Africa?' Nelson Mandela responded enthusiastically, 'Of course. One of the great pioneers of South Africa's freedom movement was M.K. Gandhi. India sent us a righteous barrister M.K. Gandhi. We returned him to you as Mahatma Gandhi.'

Dr Kalam was impressed with the way President Lula da Silva had raised Brazil's profile on the international scene and presided over Brazil's longest period of economic growth in three decades. Dr Kalam called President Lula a leader with integrity. President Lula inspired Dr Kalam to create his famous slogan, 'I will work with integrity and succeed with integrity.'

During his visit to Tanzania in September 2004, President Kalam came to know about the dismal plight of underprivileged Tanzanian children with congenital heart defects. Dr Kalam organized corrective surgeries for these children at Care Hospital, Hyderabad. Air India flew the children to Hyderabad with their mothers, free of charge.

On 13 February 2006, President Kalam was given a demonstrative excursion in INS *Sindhurakshak*, during which the submarine submerged and sailed in the Bay of Bengal for a few hours. The Chief of Naval Staff Arun Prakash accompanied him. Commander Pravesh Singh Bisht commanded the submarine.

President Kalam was the first Indian President to visit the Siachen Glacier, the highest battlefield in the world.

President Kalam fulfilled a childhood dream on 8 June 2006, when he flew the Sukhoi-30 MKI at the Lohegaon Air Force Base in Pune. President Kalam co-piloted the plane with Wing Commander Ajay Rathore.

President Kalam took the salute for the fifty-eighth Republic Day parade with Russian President Vladimir Putin. The strategic relationship between India and Russia had served not only the long-term national interests of both countries, but also effectively contributed to stability and security in Asia; and the world at large.

President Kalam's address to the European Parliament was the first of a President of India, and his speech received enthusiastic applause and a standing ovation. President Hans-Gert Pottering described President Kalam's address to the European Parliament as extraordinary: 'From a statesman, poet and scientist, this is unique.'

President Kalam met Mr Bill Gates in November 2002 in what was hailed as an exalted meeting of minds – the head of the world's largest software company and a visionary 'techie' president. The meeting, however, turned a little frosty when President Kalam made a case for open-source software, which was not at all to the liking of the software king.

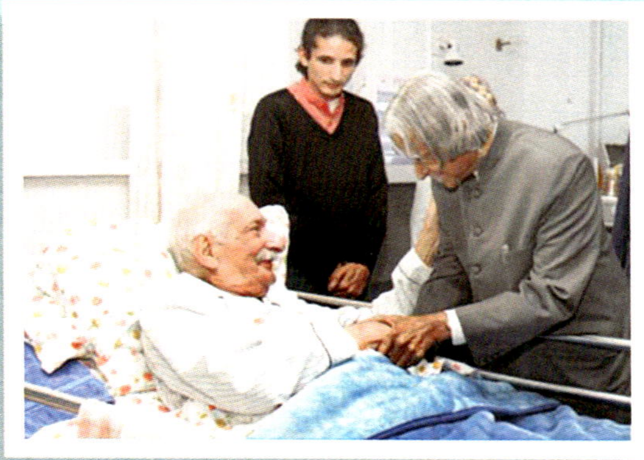

President Kalam called on the ailing Field Marshal S.H.F.J. Manekshaw, fondly called Sam Bahadur, at the Military Hospital, Wellington, on 24 February 2007. In his celebrated career of four decades, Sam Bahadur fought in five wars, including World War II.

The chief minister of Gujarat, Narendra Modi, invited Dr Kalam to address a conclave to discuss 'How government and business can change to provide Indian youth with the opportunities they deserve', at Ahmedabad on 29 June 2013. Dr Kalam gave Narendra Modi a signed copy of *Squaring the Circle*.

On 20 June 2015, Dr Kalam travelled to Sarangpur in Gujarat to present his book *Transcendence* to Pramukh Swamiji. As he handed the book to Swamiji, Dr Kalam said to him, 'You are a great teacher, a great spiritual teacher. I've learnt a great lesson from you: how to remove I-ness and My-ness.'

Dr Kalam was laid to rest at Rameswaram on 30 July 2015 at 11.30 a.m., with full military honours. Prime Minister Narendra Modi gave Dr Kalam the last salute. The sight of people from all walks of life – cutting across caste, creed and religion – bidding Dr Kalam a tearful goodbye in a peaceful and restrained manner, would be the envy of the mightiest of this world.

the overcrowded and unsanitary areas surrounding the factories in the cities. Half of all children would have lost one parent before completing adolescence. Many a young child was left without any support at all. It was institutions like Sri Ramakrishna Mission and Anjuman-e-Islam – and the indomitable spirits of the likes of Enayeth Khan, Dr Venkataswamy and Shantilalji Gulabchandji Muttha – who took up their cause. Great and selfless human beings have supported thousands of solitary pilgrims and wayward souls. Helping them grow to become good citizens and productive members of society has been their mission of the divine.

Dr Kalam's concern extended further than healthy young children. He was equally interested in the welfare of disabled youngsters, and had hoped for some time that technology would intervene to significantly improve their lot. Research such as that which he had sponsored with Father George during his short tenure at Anna University had shown promise. But there was still much work to be done in the area. In the meantime, children with disabilities needed love and care, and some of this would have to be specially tailored to their needs. Thankfully, there are souls who would dedicate their energies to this cause. Shyama Chona is one such soul. On 19 August 2003, President Kalam attended the inauguration of The School of Hope, a research, training and therapy centre for children with autism and multiple disabilities in Delhi. He brought smiles to the faces of the gathering of autistic children there, when he mixed with them and read out an inspiring poem.

Shyama Chona had been a blessed woman. Born in the family of the financial controller of the Government of India and married to an army officer, she was a teacher at the prestigious Delhi Public School. Then she gave birth to a girl with cerebral palsy. Shyama named her daughter Tamana. Cerebral palsy is a motor disability affecting as many as four in every 1,000 children. Tamana could not walk, talk or even swallow. She was like a doll given by God to Shyama as a half-finished job, as if she were to finish the rest. Shyama first experienced denial, then sorrow combined with anger; but then came a feeling that she could make a positive contribution to her daughter and society.

When Tamana grew up and needed to go to school, no school would take her. Society had turned its back on disability. Perhaps this is a matter of people expecting everyone to be like them and having no patience with those who are not. At any rate, a resolute Shyama Chona decided to create a special school for her daughter and hundreds of others like her. In 1984, she established a registered voluntary and non-profit society and named it Tamana.

Now there were three schools: Tamana Special School, Nai Disha and the School of Hope, educating approximately 500 mentally challenged and autistic children. About half of the handicapped children would come from poor families which would themselves need financial help. Shyama Chona would cater for their needs as best she could, and ensured the welfare of the handicapped children by providing them with special education, physiotherapy and occupational therapy. For the first time in the history of special education, there was a school providing integrated facilities for the disabled. But this had been no straightforward exercise for her, and she explained during Dr Kalam's visit the difficulties she faced in meeting the needs of mentally challenged children:

> In India, 10 per cent of the population is mentally challenged. The government has taken no initiative to take care of the special needs of these people. We have to run from pillar to post for managing funds for our institutes. With the help of the government, we could have made a huge difference in the lives of these children.[6]

Asking special children to spread their wings of imagination and soar high in life, Dr Kalam said, 'Love and compassion can move mountains, crush them or carve valleys where flowers of all colours bloom. Like any other normal child, if we nurture a special child with love and empower them with education, they can become rising stars and soar high in life.'

On 28 August 2003, President Kalam had a day out with politically empowered women. He addressed women sarpanches from eight states at the inauguration of a capacity-building workshop on 'From the Gram Sabha to the Lok Sabha', organized by the Guild of Service and the Public Affairs Department of the American embassy.

President Kalam began his speech in Hindi for the convenience of the audience, many of whom came from rural areas, and then switched to English. He then invited them to speak. Impressed by the brief speeches of the sarpanches, President Kalam remarked that some of them spoke like Jhansi ki Rani. He declared that they could all play a role in changing the face of Indian villages. 'The strength and wealth of India lives in villages. And when women become the leaders, the mission never fails,' he said.

A woman has the power to inspire a wholesome life for the village, which can in turn improve the district, state and nation. Referring to his favourite PURA scheme, Dr Kalam said that if roads, electronic and knowledge connectivity were given to villages, these would be transformed into cities. Righteousness too, he said, was important for eliminating corruption, and was essential for progress.

Dr Kalam evoked the memory of his mother Ashiamma and sister Zohara. He said that women, who comprise half of the total population, must have access to education, health, economic independence and political equality through panchayat. The progress of any nation would remain incomplete so long as women were not empowered, he said. Women should be provided their rightful place in all spheres – be it the Rajya Sabha, Lok Sabha, judiciary or executive. If women were empowered through panchayats, he averred, they would be able to rise to their place as leaders of this country.

By this time, Dr Kalam could see his priorities as the head of the Indian state: promoting the unity of minds by distilling the essence of world religions into universal spiritual tenets; reaching the marginalized poor and serving the disabled by synergizing government schemes with private efforts, and the application of technology for societal transformation. He had not set out these priorities. He took the pains to reach people and experience their situations – he heard their voices and felt their pain. It was this contact, which had not been initiated by any Indian leader after Mahatma Gandhi, that had defined these priorities.

4.3

Samagam

> Great things are done by a series of small things brought together.
>
> – Vincent van Gogh
> Dutch artist

In 2003, an order of Jain monks walked barefoot for more than 20 km to Rashtrapati Bhavan and presented President Kalam with the first copy of the book *Finding Your Spiritual Centre*. This is a book encapsulating the teachings of Acharya Mahapragya, the tenth head of the Svetambar Terapanth order of Jainism. It was compiled by Ranjit Dugar, the former president and CEO of Rajasthan Spinning and Weaving Company. Ranjit Dugar had been a philanthropist with a specific interest in helping underprivileged children. Expressing his surprise and admiration at the monks' fortitude and endurance, President Kalam received them with warmth and hospitality. When he realized they could not accept a meal, he offered them a glass of lemon water, which was the only refreshment they would take.

President Kalam inquired about Acharya Mahapragya, and after briefly perusing the book's contents, declared it holy and beautiful. He asked if it could be officially launched at Rashtrapati Bhavan. Upon receiving the monks' consent, he made arrangements to release the book on 23 June 2003. Eminent leaders – L.K. Advani, Dr Manmohan Singh and L.M. Singhvi – participated in the event. President Kalam referred to the great influence of Acharya Mahapragya had on his thinking and shared with the audience his first meeting with the Acharya.

Accompanied by Y.S. Rajan, Dr Kalam had met Acharya Mahapragya for the first time on 4 November 1999. Acharya Mahapragya had told him then, 'Kalam sahib, I bless you and your team, you have made a nuclear bomb to deter the enemies from attacking our country. *Ahimsa paramo dharmah, dharma himsa tathaiva cha*. Non-violence is the greatest dharma, so too is all righteous violence. But I have a second mission for you. Discover a system by which the nuclear bomb becomes irrelevant, insignificant and ineffective.'

These profound but manifestly realistic thoughts of Acharya Mahapragya led Dr Kalam to ponder the ramifications of his work in developing military hardware. He considered the role of nuclear missiles in the scheme of international geopolitics and, paradoxically perhaps, world peace.

Given what we know about the horrific capabilities of thermonuclear weapons, even the thought of contemplating their role in a peaceful world offends our moral sensibilities – and it seems to defy common sense. The world's nuclear arsenals hold a stupendous number of atomic bombs. There is somewhere in the vicinity of 20,500 nuclear warheads in the world today. If the average power of these devices is 33,500 kilotons, there are enough of these terrific devices to annihilate life as we know it on our planet, many times over.

Dr Kalam was no advocate of violence. But he also knew that one must come to terms with violence; and life cannot preclude death. Moreover, he was cognizant that the global nuclear challenge had changed dramatically over the preceding two decades. The bipolarity of the US–Soviet nuclear stand-off during the cold war has given way to a multilateral – and more unpredictable and perilous – structure comprising nine states that possess nuclear weapons. Several of these are situated in regions where intense geopolitical rivalries exist.

On several occasions, Dr Kalam had discussed with me his understanding of the changing threats to world peace. The dissolution of the Soviet Union, he said, foreshadowed the devolution of power from centralized state authority to institutions and organizations in the following decades. In this new scenario, smaller groups, including those of the terrorist variety, could wield great power. Thus, most of the armed conflicts in recent decades have occurred between small groups, sometimes involving non-state actors that are proxies for larger powers. In the chaos following the collapse of the Soviet Union, it is quite conceivable that nuclear weaponry of one sort or another had fallen into the hands of several of these smaller groups.

The odds, therefore, of a nuclear weapon being deployed today are indeed far greater than during the cold war, even as the prospect of an apocalyptic nuclear exchange between the United States and Russia has been drastically reduced. In the absence of a nuclear deterrent, India would have been vulnerable to all manner of military threats – not just from belligerent states, but from powerful non-state groups acting at their behest. With its full nuclear capability, India's military strength is unquestionable; any belligerent knows full well the nation's might before it acts against our nation's sovereignty. It is thus likely that India's having atomic weapons has forestalled numerous wars on the subcontinent, even in the last decade. Our enemies have been at pains to confine their aggression to isolated border skirmishing, in the face of Dr Kalam's team's missiles.

It can thus be seen that decades of tireless work by Dr Kalam and his colleagues – peaceful, well-educated and gentle scientists – have allowed our country to come to terms with violence and live in peace. While a pacifist missile man seems, at first glance, a contradiction in terms, we can see in truth that it is no more a paradox than sunlight and shade.

The Prophet of Islam (Peace Be Upon Him) said, 'Paradise lies under the shade of the sword.' Dr Kalam, in his learning, knew this well; those who would have peace must be ready for war. But he equally understood that the nuclear bomb can become irrelevant, insignificant and ineffective, as Acharya Mahapragya had asked, when the violence inside the heart of a person is cleansed. He remembered the story of Jibreel coming to the Messenger of Allah (Peace and Blessings of

Allah Be Upon Him) when he was playing with other boys. He took hold of him and threw him to the ground, then he opened his chest and took out his heart, from which he took a clot of blood and said, 'This was the Shaitan's share of you.'

Dr Kalam realized his fellowship with Acharya Mahapragya was similar to the fellowship of Jain Muni Raichandbhai Ravajibhai Mehta with Mahatma Gandhi. Like the other great seer and enlightened leader, Acharya Mahapragya and Dr Kalam believed in their spiritual principles finding expression in everyday life; their spirituality was practical, and they were willing to engage with the issues of the times. And there was a deeper and larger undertaking unfolding between them that was, in essence, a confluence of visions. President Kalam's conception of a fully developed India with a more prosperous and harmonious life for its citizens resonated with Acharya Mahapragya.

The Acharya expressed his desire to invite President Kalam to Surat, Gujarat, on 15 October 2003, Dr Kalam's seventy-second birthday. Acharya Mahapragya also suggested that spiritual leaders of different faiths be present at this occasion for a conclave, which could further their spiritual aims by establishing a broad consensus for interfaith dialogue and celebration; and, above all, cooperation and kinship. The gathering would evolve a coordinated action plan based on shared spiritual principles, with the purpose of creating enlightened citizens and realizing a unity of minds among India's diverse population.

India's is perhaps the largest and most diverse society in the world. India's people speak more than 300 languages and dialects in twelve distinct language families, which are codified in more than twenty scripts. All the major religions – Hinduism, Buddhism, Christianity, Jainism, Islam, Sikhism, Judaism and Zoroastrianism – have followers in India, making it the world's most complex and comprehensively pluralistic society. Furthermore, it is home to a vast variety of castes, tribes, communities, religions, languages, customs and lifestyles. Doubtless, one of the biggest challenges of the Indian nation has been how to learn to live in proximity with difference – different religions, different beliefs within a religion and within a belief, different ways of life. How do we peacefully relate to and negotiate with people with whom we may bitterly disagree on some key issues?

After many rounds of discussions and multiple meetings with prominent spiritual leaders in the country, fifteen leaders consented to attend this single-platform, interfaith event. Dr Kalam had much to be grateful for in the efforts of Y.S. Rajan in successfully garnering support for the conclave across the spectrum of religions. Dr Kalam had an enduring sagacity concerning matching the talents of those around him for a particular duty, and he had wisely entrusted this task to Y.S. Rajan. Rajan had tirelessly visited a significant number of religious leaders who were actively engaged in social work. His intellectual eminence and his Rabindranath Tagore – like appearance – his flowing steel-grey hair and beard and penetrating eyes – lent him the gravitas to break the ice with the numerous leaders. The inspiring message from Acharya Mahapragya and Dr Kalam did the rest.

The assortment of religious leaders who had agreed to attend the conclave may have appeared diverse in appearance and beliefs, but they had much in common. All shared a commitment to universal spiritual values; they were willing to look beyond their own faith's teachings to acknowledge the truths in other faiths. Each of them was learned. Moreover, they all were willing to reach out to their fellow Indians of other religious persuasions for the common good. All saw the inherent sense in Acharya Mahapragya's and Dr Kalam's endeavour of building inter-religious partnerships for the betterment of the Indian people.

Hinduism in the conclave was represented by Sri Balagangadharanatha Swamiji, the seer of Sri Adichunchanagiri Math, in Mandya, Karnataka; Jagadguru Shivaratri Desikendra Mahaswami, the twenty-fourth pontiff of Sri Suttur Math, Karnataka; and Swami Jitatmananda Maharaj, one of the most renowned monks of the Ramakrishna Mission.

Sri Balagangadharanatha Swamiji had provided humanitarian services – including catering to the basic necessities like food, education and health – for lakhs of people over the preceding three decades. A graduate in science, he had chosen the spiritual way of life at the age of nineteen. Swamiji had unerringly focused on practical service to the community as a spiritual duty; he saw duty to the people as the greatest means of attaining spiritual fulfilment. Swamji's concept of 'Service Before the Self' had won him the hearts of millions, including those of people belonging to different faiths. At the time of the conclave, he was working as the president of the highly respected JSS Mahavidyapeeth Educational and Cultural Institutions.

Like Balagangadharanatha Swamiji, Swami Jitatmananda Maharaj was a science graduate before receiving his religious calling. Swami Jitatmananda Maharaj received his degree in science from Presidency College, Calcutta, and postgraduate degree in English from Jadavpur University. Swamiji had been the editor of the *Prabuddha Bharat* journal started by Swami Vivekananda before becoming a monk in the Ramakrishna order.

Shiekh-e-Tarigat Hadrat Syed Muhammad Jilani Ashraf, the twenty-eighth descendent of Hadrat Ghuthe-Azan Syed Abdul Qadir Jilani, Maulana Wahiduddin Khan, Islamic scholar and peace activist, and Prince Huzaifa Mohyuddin of the Dawoodi Bohra, a sect of Shia Islam as propagated by the Fatimid Imamate in medieval Egypt, represented the Islamic religion.

Syed Muhammad Jilani preached human, moral and spiritual values and promoted peace and unity of faith and international brotherhood. He had established a spiritual complex in Dargah Kichhachuvi Sharif in Faizabad, Uttar Pradesh. Maulana Wahiduddin Khan had translated the Quran into simple and contemporary English and written a commentary on the Quran. In this commentary, he presented to the world the real face of Islam – based on peace, tolerance and coexistence. He established the Islamic Centre in New Delhi. Prince Huzaifa Mohyuddin is the son of H.H. Dr Sydena Muhammad Barhanuddin, the fifty-second incumbent of the august office of Dā'ī al-Mutlaq –the unrestricted missionary. The prince is an accomplished scholar, an illustrious philanthropist and head designate of the Dawoodi Bohra community, which has followers all over the world.

Bishop Dr Thomas Dabre, the Secretary General of the Council of Catholic Bishops of India and Archbishop Stanislaus Fernandes, S.J., the Archbishop of Gandhinagar, represented the Christian religion. Bishop Dr Thomas Dabre had been appointed auxiliary bishop of Bombay in 1990. In 1998, he became the first bishop of the newly created diocese of Vasai. Bishop Dabre did his doctoral thesis on the God experience of Sant Tukaram and a study in religious symbolism. Archbishop Stanislaus Fernandes, S.J., was ordained a Catholic priest in 1968 and professed in the Society of Jesus in August 1973. He was appointed Bishop of Ahmedabad in 1990 and Archbishop of Gandhinagar in 2002.

Dr Homi B. Dhalla represented Zoroastrianism, the pre-Islamic religion of Persia. He had been the founder of the Zoroastrian Cultural Foundation in Mumbai. He represented the Parsi community in various national and international forums. He had done his master's in oriental languages and literature at Harvard University and his PhD at Bombay University.

Yuvacharya Mahashraman Muni Mudit Kumar and Sadhvi Pramukha Kanakprabha represented Jainism. Yuvacharya Mahashraman Muni Mudit Kumar, the designated successor of Acharya Mahapragya, had guided the youth wings of the Terapanth order since 1997. Sadhvi Pramukha Kanakprabha had been declared the ninth Sadhvipramukha (head of nuns) in 1972 and Mahashramani (head of shramanis) of the Terapanth order in 1979. She had been an editor and author in the Sanskrit, Prakrit and Hindi languages.

Rev. Ezekiel Isaac Malekar of the Judah Hymn Synagogue, New Delhi, had been a distinguished scholar, a human right activists and a priest. He had represented the Jewish community in India and also written for national and international journals. He has authored many articles and books on meditation and national integration through education, his book *Education for Global Society – Interfaith Discussions* being the latest.

Ven. Rahul Bodhi represented Buddhism. He was the founder president of Bhikku Sangha United Buddhist Mission-Sarvodaya Maha Buddha Vihar, Mumbai. This organization operates throughout India and is spreading the message of brotherhood, love, kindness and compassion for the service of humanity.

Brahma Kumari Sudesh Didi had been a teacher and administrator with Brahma Kumaris World Spiritual University. She has actively promoted and encouraged women to play a leading role in the social and spiritual development of humanity. Currently the director of sixty centres in the United Kingdom and Germany, she has been an outstanding lecturer and broadcaster on human development, mediation and the creative abilities of the mind.

Dr Jaswant Singh Neki, an outstanding Sikh theologian, was decorated with the Order of Khalsa Award on the three-hundredth anniversary of the Khalsa, celebrated in Anandpur Sahib on 13 April 2000. He had been director of Post Graduate Institute (PGI), Chandigarh and head of the Psychiatry Department at the All-India Institute of Medical Sciences (AIIMS), Delhi. Perceptive critics have described his book *Ardas* as an all-time classic. An outstanding metaphysical poet in the Punjabi language, he received the Sahitya Akademi Award in 1980.

The conclave was a manifestation of the innate sense of oneness that Indians possess, even amongst the obvious diversity of the country's population. Indians retain their particular Indian quality, in tandem with their astounding range of beliefs. It is this very quality that has sustained the nation through the trying early years of Independence. Even after the country's Partition along religious lines, India chose to remain a staunchly secular country. Its secularism did not engender any absence of religion, or irreligiousness, however. Indians are perhaps among the most religious of all nationalities. Rather, it meant the nation would remain faithful to an illustrious history of multi-religiousness.

The conclave itself was an unqualified success. I was privileged to attend it, and have never yet experienced such a highly charged spiritual atmosphere. For more than three hours, ideas and dialogue flowed like a river of grace. President Kalam's patronage of the event demonstrated his far-sightedness in the need for inter-religious dialogue. As he arrived, he greeted his eminent spiritual colleagues as he always did: his eyes looking directly into theirs, his hands pressed together and with a gentle smile. A 'namaste' from him was no empty gesture – it truly embodied the humility of the word itself. Dr Kalam interacted freely with the gurus and scholars, and chaired the meeting at the end of the conclave.

Dr Kalam had chaired literally thousands of meetings in his unusually long professional career. He was a master at crystallizing ideas and areas of agreement – that might otherwise float into the ether unrealized – into a workable consensus. For Dr Kalam, the unity of minds that the conclave sought to establish should never rely on tolerance and compromise. Unquestionably, these are worthy modes of human behaviour, and have their place in many areas of human relations. But Dr Kalam felt they are not the correct basis for interfaith dialogue and the peaceful coexistence of religions. What really is needed, he would tell me, is respect – for others and their beliefs, and for the truth that others hold their beliefs in similar esteem to that in which we hold ours.

It was this essential understanding that had allowed Dr Kalam's father Jainulabdeen, a devout Muslim, to help Hindu visitors to Rameswaram on their pilgrimage and assist them in their devotions whenever the need arose. It had allowed him to sit for hours discussing philosophy with his close friend, Pandit Pakshi Lakshmana Shastrigal. And it had allowed him to talk with Father Bodal about the concerns of the fishermen of their island. Dr Kalam had been thoroughly tutored in harmonious interfaith dialogue; he was amply qualified from his childhood experience alone.

The inter-religious harmony of Rameswaram that Dr Kalam knew as a child was quintessentially Indian. Sadly, there are forces at work in India in these times that would carve our society into fractious segments of religion and ethnic identity. In our country, certain regions are presently being subjected to the tremendous stress of violence – that of the physical and more subtle kinds. If we study India's history over a period of 3,000 years, we will inevitably conclude that the country has always stood for peace. It worked for peace; it prayed for peace to live in peace. But in these times, peace seems to be endangered due to the fomenting of communal and regional sentiments for political gain. So, how does one bring back peace?

Paradoxically, the 'I' in us wants peace. Nevertheless, to attain peace one has to first transcend the 'I' and 'me' in accordance with our scriptures. This may be a tough proposition. For, virtually every sentence, every thought is dictated by 'I' and 'me'. As it is said – and as Dr Kalam was to regularly remind me – if we remove 'I' and 'me', the ego will vanish. When the ego vanishes, hatred fades away. When hatred fades away, any violence in the mind and body will disappear. Therefore, peace prevails when you forsake 'I' and 'me'. The spiritual goal of every religion is indeed for the individual to be free of violence – in mind and body – thereby allowing the creation of a peaceful society. Furthermore, it is axiomatic that with the renunciation of 'I', 'me' and violence, poverty loosens its grip on society.

We realize that the 300 million young citizens who are below twenty years of age in India want peace, prosperity, happiness and safety. It is our responsibility as religious and spiritual leaders to carry out a mission of conquering poverty for our people. Fortunately, there is a road map to use – *India 2020*, our national dream. That entails working intensively on five important areas. These are agriculture and food processing, education and health care, information and communication technology, infrastructure development (including networking of rivers) and providing urban amenities in rural areas.

The fundamental truth that Dr Kalam told me is this: If the individual prospers, the villages prosper; if the villages prosper, the states prosper; if the states prosper, India can prosper. Acknowledging this network of prosperity is extremely important in realizing the vision of the nation. Defeating poverty entails addressing several related elements, like tackling illiteracy and providing good governance. The latter is vital to ensure that funds allotted for the poor and the earnings of the poor people are not frittered away in various forms of corruption. This is where the making of an enlightened citizen is crucial. This acquires a moral, ethical and spiritual dimension, and it was Pramukh Swamiji's unofficial contribution to Dr Kalam's vision for India. Therefore, another component for prosperity is ineluctably religious and spiritual partnership. We have considered how this partnership can be developed.

Religions are exquisite places of refuge for the soul, places of surpassing beauty and tranquillity. They provide comfort for the soul and the spirit; but they are islands nevertheless. If we can connect all these islands with bridges of love and compassion, we will have a peaceful, happy and prosperous India. The conclave at Surat demonstrated that there are universal truths embodied in each religion that can be agreed by open-minded religious leaders. These would help to form bridges between religions, thus reinforcing our basic unity as human beings. Further, there was unanimity in support for value-based education, which would help to disseminate the universal truths common to all world religions. The representatives were equally resolved that value-based education must be instituted in schools.

Value-based education in schoolchildren provides the spiritual foundation for the proper use of knowledge-based education. And education itself must extend beyond schoolchildren. A significant impediment for progress is the yawning intellectual gap between the opinion-making class and the masses. This gap may only be closed by increasing the knowledge base of every citizen in vital aspects of their lives. As the number of enlightened citizens increases, the ability to cope with and transform their lives also increases.

In order to achieve this, in addition to concentrating on the education of the country's youth, there is also a pressing need for the continual education of the adult population. Education and intellectual activities are vital for all citizens, not just schoolchildren. Education can extend to values and understanding the basic spiritual unity of all religions. Additionally, values need to be sponsored by religious and community leaders, through specific inter-religious projects. These would bring people together, irrespective of their social background or religious beliefs.

Religious and community leaders would also need to open to change. The conclave was unanimous that there is much to reform in the manner in which religious education is conducted. Dr Kalam later made mention of the spiritual leaders' deep concern for promoting a spiritual education, beyond the all-too-familiar indoctrination that is foisted on most school children:

> I met fifteen spiritual leaders ... they belonged to various religions including Hinduism, Buddhism, Christianity, Islam and Sikhism. The religious leaders were concerned that education in the majority of the schools, particularly in the small towns, is taming the young minds with dogma and obsolete concepts rather than empowering them with freedom of enquiry ... The idea of 'to shape' the student to the 'template' by the time his or her formal education concludes is indeed ominous. Spirituality instead must form a vision of that which stands beyond, behind and within the passing flux of immediate things. Can we define spirituality to a young student without introducing religious terms?[1]

The leaders at Surat were able to share a vision, and agreed on several key issues. A significant outcome of the conclave was the envisioning of the Five Garland Projects. This was ratified in what came to be known as the Surat Spiritual Declaration. It proposed, inter alia, inter-religious festivals and multi-religious projects

Every month in all parts of India there can be a multi-religious gathering to convey the core message of religion in a prayer of peace and discuss the basic truths contained in various religions. Such a prayer should be preceded by prayers from all religions practised in that part of the country by respective religious and spiritual leaders in the presence of the people. Each month the day selected could be a holy day from one religion: Islam, Hinduism, Christianity, Sikhism, Zoroastrianism, Jainism, Buddhism, etc. Regular conduct of such meetings by all religious leaders and people from different religions respecting holy days of other religions will send a powerful message.

If possible, such gatherings can take place at the religious centres where all people from other religions can also gather on that day. People should also exchange pleasantries and sweets during these meetings, as is the practice in some parts of the country where unity of minds prevails. Additionally, in order to spread the message of equality to everybody on that day, langar (community kitchen and eating) can be arranged so that all people eat common food, sitting side by side.

So far, religious groups have made many efforts towards the removal of poverty and its associated misery, in large or small-scale undertakings; but always in isolation. It was decided at Surat to launch a number of multi-religious projects in education, health care and water supply as well as for generating entrepreneurship and employment, to help the poor. People would thus see for themselves that religions are working together for the common good. These efforts will elevate religions in the minds of the people and the nation will benefit.

All religious educational institutions operating in different parts of the country should enrol children from other religions, in numbers beyond tokenism. The real purpose and the unity of religions should be imbued in the minds of the students. Children are the pillars of tomorrow; given careful guidance early in their lives, they will help foster peace and amity between communities in the next generation. To this end, value-based educational material should be disseminated through various forms of media.

In addition to the projects directly benefiting the common people, it is also necessary to maintain continual interfaith dialogue between the religious and spiritual heads, as well as religious scholars. This dialogue can address a myriad of issues if it is approached correctly. President Kalam had seen very early in his life the manner in which religious leaders in society can cooperate through regular discussion for the common good. His father Jainulabdeen, Pandit Pakshi Lakshmana Shastrigal and Father Bodal would never have thought to term their discussions about the welfare of Rameswaram's people 'inter-religious dialogue'. But their communication was no less effective for this.

The dialogue may need to be more formal in these times, and the Internet may be a worthy venue for disseminating outcomes of such discussions. Furthermore, the existing models for interreligious dialogues that are available in some other countries could be explored and adapted for our own unique circumstances. Apropos his own personal faith, Dr Kalam would remind me of the practices of Prophet Muhammad (Peace Be Upon Him), who could truly be called one of the early proponents of interfaith dialogue. The Prophet (Peace Be Upon Him) regularly met with leaders of other faiths, and made numerous agreements with Christian citizens of lands under Muslim rule. He even sealed pacts guaranteeing their freedom to worship according to their customs, which the Christians gratefully accepted, given his impeccable reputation for integrity.

Finally, the religious and spiritual leaders at Surat came to the unanimous conclusion that a national-level autonomous organization should be set up. This organization was named Foundation for Unity of Religious and Enlightened Citizenship (FUREC). President Kalam later launched FUREC on 14 June 2004, the eighty-fourth birthday of Acharya Mahapragya, at the Rashtrapati Bhavan. FUREC combined the objectives of the Surat Spiritual Declaration and *Vision 2020*.

4.4

The World Machine

> After two world wars, the collapse of fascism, nazism, communism and colonialism and the end of the cold war, humanity has entered a new phase of its history.
>
> – Hans Kung
> Swiss Catholic priest and author

President Kalam's first official foreign tour began on 19 October 2003. The seven-day tour took him to the United Arab Emirates (UAE), Sudan and Bulgaria. Vice-President Bhairon Singh Shekhawat and Deputy Prime Minister L.K. Advani came to the airport to see him off. Arun Shourie, the Union minister of disinvestment, communications and information technology, and members of parliament Suresh Prabhu and Sarla Maheshwari, both members of parliament, accompanied the president. Dr Kalam's state visit to the UAE was the first of an Indian president in over two-and-a-half decades, since President Fakhruddin Ali Ahmed's trip there in 1976.

The UAE was home at this time to more than a million Indian expatriates. The UAE consists of seven emirates and was founded in 1971 as a federation. Indian workers have played a crucial role in its nation building. Mostly hailing from the southern states of Kerala and Tamil Nadu, the Indians in the UAE comprise in excess of 30 per cent of the total population of the federation. Today, the UAE is a modern, oil-exporting country with a highly diversified economy. Dubai in particular has been developed into a global hub for travel, tourism, retail, and finance; and it is home to the world's tallest building, the largest man-made seaport and the busiest international airport. Over the preceding few years, there had been a phenomenal rise in IT exports from India to the Middle East, with the UAE, Saudi Arabia and Oman topping the markets for Indian software solutions.

In Dubai, President Kalam visited GITEX 2003, the Middle East's largest and most important information technology event – much to the delight of organizers Dubai World Trade Centre. Dr Kalam was impressed by the size and scale of the event and the number of exhibitors who participated at the event from India. There were representatives from the Indian hardware industry, software and services sector, with over forty companies participating in the show. Sheikh Ahmed bin Saeed Al Maktoum, the son of the former ruler of Dubai, accompanied President Kalam.

Dr Kalam took the time to address a large group of Indian students at the Indian High School's Shaikh Rashid Auditorium and at the Birla Institute of Technology and Sciences (BITS) at the Knowledge Village. Dr Kalam said that the twenty million non-resident Indians living in various countries around the world can contribute to igniting the youthful minds of the 300 million Indians below the age of twenty in India. Further, they can become a powerful resource in achieving the great vision of development of India, and also help in the emancipation of their 260 million compatriots from the grip of poverty. For this, their minds were their greatest attribute: 'I suggest, thinking should become your capital asset, whatever ups and downs you come across in your life. Thinking is progress and non-thinking is stagnation to the individual, organization and the country.'[1]

The students hailed the visit of the Indian president, some of whom claimed it was an unforgettable moment of their lives.

President Kalam's visit to Sudan was a landmark event in the history of Sudanese–Indian relations. He was the first Indian president ever to visit Sudan. Sudan is estimated to have some of the largest oil reserves in the world, and it could prove to be a major source for energy-starved India, which depends on imports for 70 per cent of its petroleum requirements. For several months, India had been pursuing diplomatic initiatives. It achieved a major success in June 2003, when ONGC Videsh, the arm of the Oil and Natural Gas Corporation for activities outside India, bought 25 per cent equity from Canada's Talisman Energy, Inc., in Sudan's Greater Nile Project. Later, India acquired stakes in Sudanese projects from the Austrian oil and gas group, OMV.

Sudan was home to numerous ancient civilizations, most of which flourished along the fertile riparian plains of the great Nile. For much of Sudan's history, the nation has suffered from rampant ethnic strife, descending into the chaos of civil wars in more recent times. For much of Sudan's history, its fate was inextricable from that of Egypt, and with the opening of the Suez Canal in 1869, Egypt and Sudan's economic and strategic importance increased enormously. Sudan attracted the imperial attentions of the great powers, particularly the British, who governed the country as a colony from 1899. After Sudan finally won its independence in 1956, a civil war erupted between the northern and southern parts of the country. The fighting lasted for seventeen years, resulting in the death of somewhere in the order of half a million people. Civil war again broke out in 1982 and raged for more than two decades, only ceasing a little more than a year after the time of President Kalam's visit.

The civil war in Sudan had been the most vicious kind of war, polarizing the country into north vs south, Muslim vs Christian and Arab vs sub-Saharan African. Yet, beneath the obvious religious, cultural and racial differences that had in part fuelled the war – and manifested in brutal ethnic cleansing – there had been a bitter struggle over control of Sudan's rich oil reserves, and the wealth that this control entailed.

Addressing the parliament of Sudan on 22 October 2003, President Kalam said, 'The time has come for our two nations to consolidate these developments since independence and forge stronger bonds between creating public and private institutions and businesses to bring prosperity, happiness and freedom from insecurity to the people.'[2] Dr Kalam was most optimistic for a mutually beneficial relationship between India and Sudan:

> One among the key resources of Sudan is the hydrocarbon. With a large part of the country still unexplored, hydrocarbon contribution to the national economy is likely to increase significantly in future. The national oil companies of India and other countries are participating in the discoveries of oil and gas in Sudan. India and Sudan can work together in building capability for oil exploration, refining, marketing and value added oil based products. Exploitation of natural hydrocarbon and other natural resources by Sudan with the assistance of India could fuel economic growth of Sudan through many mission mode projects like the Vision 2020 of India.[3]

Sadly, the end of the civil war in January 2005 and the formation of South Sudan in July 2011 did not quell the violence in the country. In December 2013, civil war again broke out, this time in South Sudan. India, one of the first countries to recognize the new state of South Sudan, has continued to pledge its support for the country. It has offered assistance in developing infrastructure, training officials in health, education and rural development in return for oil resources. Much can be accomplished through cooperation, and ultimately, little from war.

Thankfully, the country of Dr Kalam's next visit had enjoyed a much more peaceful recent history. But the trip itself was to be challenging for him. When President Kalam landed in Sofia, the historic capital city of Bulgaria, on 23 October 2003, he was running a fever and suffering severe body pain. His back was burning with inflammation of the skin. Nevertheless, he carried on with his engagements; Dr Kalam was never one to let personal discomfort keep him from work. Sofia welcomed India's president with a twenty-one-gun salute. Bulgarian President Georgi Parvanov presided over a special ceremony at the square in front of Sofia's grand St Alexander Nevski Cathedral.

The Sofia University, called St Kliment Ohridsk, was founded in 1888, ten years after the liberation of Bulgaria from the Turkish Ottoman Empire, to serve as Bulgaria's primary institution of higher education. Sofia University had an Indology section, which since 1983 has been conducting courses at graduate and postgraduate levels. A sizeable crowd of students at the university greeted President Kalam. He was told that Indian culture has enjoyed considerable popularity in Bulgaria in modern times, right from the days of Rabindranath Tagore's visit to Bulgaria in 1926. Yoga, Ayurveda, Indian television serials and the spiritual heritage of India are increasingly gaining currency in Bulgaria. The Indian expatriate community, though, was very small, numbering around 250. A portion of this number were students studying medicine in the medical universities of Sofia, Pleven, Plovdiv and Stara Zagora. They all, however, turned out to greet Dr Kalam. Along with a discussion of common economic and cultural interests between the Indian and Bulgarian peoples, Dr Kalam spoke of a more spiritual endeavour:

> I feel that education systems around the world will have to work to generate enlightened international citizens who would then be able to work together as citizens of the planet earth to solve such problems together. How does one produce an enlightened international citizen? I feel this can be done through a combination of education with a value system. The second important component will be religions graduating into a spiritual movement. Third and the most vital component is poverty eradication by attainment of economic prosperity by the developing countries. This will result in raising the living standards and will result in bringing peace to the individual, to the family, to the nation and would thereby result in peace on the planet earth.[4]

Bulgaria's population of over seven million people is predominantly urbanized. Most commercial and cultural activities are centred on the capital and largest city, Sofia. The strongest sectors of the economy are heavy industry, power engineering and agriculture, all of which rely on local natural resources. President Kalam was familiar with Bulgaria's proven strengths in mathematics, physics, computer hardware and precision manufacturing from his years at the DRDO. Indo-Bulgarian cooperation in many of these fields had been continuous since the Soviet era. President Kalam and President Parvanov proposed cooperation in computer software and hardware. Indian expertise in software and Bulgarian strength in hardware production infrastructure could make a great combination outside the Western bloc. But it never happened. Bulgaria joined NATO in March 2004 and the European Union in April 2005.

President Kalam returned with cherished memories of his visit to the Rila monastery. He had much to tell from his interaction with Bishop John about its history, religious and cultural heritage and its contribution to spiritual life in Bulgaria. Bishop John informed President Kalam that in the ninth century, Tsar Boris I converted to Christianity and appointed an archbishop from Constantinople, the capital of the Eastern Roman Empire, and that is how Christianity came to Bulgaria. For nearly five centuries, Bulgaria was under Turkish domination, and the patriarch of Constantinople administered the church through a Greek clergy.

The hermit St Ivan of Rila founded the monastery. The hermit actually lived in a cave, without any material possessions, not far from the monastery's location. His students, who came to the mountains to receive education from St Ivan, built the great complex. They prayed together that all religions could come together to spread goodness, mercy and charity.

Along with other church properties, the monastery fell under the direct control of the post-war communist regimes. Unlike most other religious sites, however, Rila was granted protected status in 1961 by the Bulgarian government. In 1983, UNESCO (the United Nations Educational, Social and Cultural Organization) declared the monastery a World Heritage site. The Bulgarian Orthodox Church regained its title to Rila subsequent to the fall of the communist government in 1989, and the succeeding government formally reinstated the complex as a monastery in 1991.

By the time President Kalam returned from his week-long trip, it was obvious that he was in poor health. He attended the Army Research and Referral Hospital, New Delhi, the apex medical institution of the Indian Army Medical Corps, for an examination. Tests revealed that he had contracted a viral infection, probably while travelling; and it was now fully aggravated. Dr B. Soma Raju, Dr M.A. Saleem and Dr J.M.K. Murthy from Care Hospital, Hyderabad, joined the team of doctors attending him.

Even after Dr Kalam was discharged from the hospital after three days, he continued to suffer with severe pain. He described the pain to me as burning and stinging, and told me it was almost unrelenting. He did not sleep for many nights. One of those days, Dr Kalam shared with me that he cried alone, asking why his pain was unending and his wounds grievous and incurable. Then he heard Prophet Aramaya[5] speaking to him.

Aramaya:

O Kalam
Your pain is a cry
From your soul,
Do not become a prophet.

Kalam:

O Prophet Aramaya!
My Prophet is Muhammad.
I am only a teacher,
and my throat is parched.

Aramaya:

Why teach the ignorant
Worshipping false gods,
Toiling, procreating.
Stop teaching them!

Kalam:

No.
My people are innocent.
Gullible they may be,
But children will listen.
I love my people too much.

Aramaya:

Then suffer your love.

Kalam:

So I shall. O Prophet Aramaya!
Tell God Almighty that I am suffering for the love of my people.

It took about a week for President Kalam to fully recover. He resumed his normal schedule, but something had drastically changed in his inner world. It would soon appear in his speech on the occasion of the award ceremony for the Indira Gandhi Prize for Peace, Disarmament and Development, on 19 November 2003.

After more than a year in Rashtrapati Bhavan, meeting some brilliant minds from across the world – scholars, political leaders, social workers, philanthropists and business leaders – Dr Kalam had developed insights into the dynamics of power in world politics. During the intense pain and sleepless nights of his illness, those insights gave way to revelations.

He explained to me that there is a global elite that doesn't just possess great wealth, but basically controls every major bank and every major corporation on the entire planet. This elite has created the central banks of the world, and then used those central banks to ensnare the governments in endless cycles of debt, from which there is no escape. The ultra-wealthy have also played a major role in establishing other important international institutions, treaties, conventions and sanctions; and a myriad of other instruments of control. With their influence, people-to-people services have become jobs, transactions have become business, companies have become corporations – and multinational conglomerates have grown bigger than many governments and more powerful.

Giant corporations own television networks, cable channels, movie studios, newspapers, magazines, publishing houses, music labels, telecommunications companies and drug and food companies. They control most of what people watch, hear and read, talk, write and consume every day of their lives. They have conditioned people's minds to consumption, recreation and procreation.

Wars are created to sell armaments and manufactured in the massive military-industrial complexes owned by the global elite. To fund war efforts, to quell revolts and insurgencies, to police and control their indulgent moneyed classes and the deprived and angry poor, governments borrow massive sums of money from the banks. By supplying credit to those of whom they approve and denying it to those of whom they disapprove, international bankers can not only create booms or busts to support or undermine governments, they can also determine outcomes in a country's economy.

Corporate interests expanded their power and wealth exponentially, after acquiring government and national assets by privatization. Drives to increase exports of various commodities have led to wholesale deforestation in parts of the world. Timber companies have razed old forests, leaving semi-barren land useless for much but raising cattle to supply beef to the rich nations. Similarly, prime agricultural land has been exploited for the growing of cash crops for consumption in wealthy countries. This has reduced staple food production for local consumption. The result is price imbalances and people being forced out of the rural economy into urban money machines, creating crime and slums. Can it all be said? Would anyone listen?

President Kalam conferred the 2002 Indira Gandhi Prize for Peace, Disarmament and Development upon Sir Shridath Ramphal. Sir Shridath was the former foreign minister of Guyana and the Commonwealth Secretary General from 1975 to 1990, an unprecedented decade-and-a-half tenure. He had also been chancellor of three universities – University of Guyana, University of the West Indies and the University of Warwick. While the Commonwealth of Nations can be perceived as an insulting reminder of Britain's colonial past, it has gone some way towards ameliorating the excesses of those times by its efforts in the last half-century. Sir Shridath Ramphal passionately used this institution to support self-governance in newly independent nations.

Before the gathering of international diplomats, President Kalam unequivocally said that violent conflicts were indeed the outcome of the dynamics of greed. Further, a lack of development in large parts of the world was the outcome of overdevelopment and excessive consumption of resources by a small minority of nations. He alluded to the challenges globalization posed to developing countries and the environment, and expressed the need for a more equitable, peaceful global order:

> From our ancient times we (the Indians) have celebrated the cause of peace. It is only in conditions of peace and security that people and countries can effectively pursue development. Violent conflicts are an enemy of development. We too as a nation firmly believe that for a better tomorrow, interaction amongst nations must be based on coexistence not conflict, cooperation not confrontation and concord not coercion.[6]

President Kalam arrived in Tirupati on 20 November 2003 to participate in the golden jubilee celebrations of Sri Venkateswara University. In his extempore address lasting nearly thirty minutes, the president dwelt at length on what he envisioned as his 'law of development' to make developing nations like India join the elite club of developed nations. Outlining a strategy to accomplish the task, he suggested a three-dimensional approach – cost-effectiveness, quality and in-time supply – to make Indian products competitive in the international market. He said each university should have on its agenda a development component; one for its own region and another for the entire nation. Later, he addressed the All India Vice Chancellors conference at senate hall.

In the afternoon, President Kalam reached Sri Venkateswara Swamy Temple atop the Tirumala hills, accompanied by Governor Surjit Singh Barnala and Chief Minister N. Chandrababu Naidu. Upon arrival at the main entrance of the temple complex, they were received with traditional *Isti Kapal* temple honours. This, with the accompaniment of traditional music, amid the melodious chanting of Vedic hymns by the temple priests.

Later, priests escorted the president to the sanctum sanctorum of the temple, where he stood in front of the deity for about ten minutes and paid obeisance. The temple priests, who presented all the three dignitaries – the president, the governor and the chief minister – with the *Sesha Vastrams* of the Lord, also explained to the president the significance of the temple and its history.

Dr Kalam also deposited offerings into the sacred temple Hundi, as is the general practice. While dropping some folded currency into the Hundi he told me, 'God knows that my hundred-rupee note is a thousand time more valuable than the hundred-rupee note coming from a rich man's pocket.' Noticing that I did not offer any money, he said, 'Funny guy, whatever you offer to God, he adds many zeros to that amount and returns it to the true devotee whenever he needs it. Do not lose a chance to multiply your money.'

Later, at the Ranganayakula Mandapam, situated inside the temple complex, Dr Kalam was given Vedasirvachanam, a recited blessing from the temple's priests. Much to the surprise of the priests, Dr Kalam asked them to conduct Asirvachanam for the welfare of the nation and its people. He sat on the floor and ate the prasadam served in a bowl made of plantain leaf. I could see tears of joy welling in the eyes of the priest who served him the prasad. It was a great lesson for me in humility.

Humility is indeed the true key to success. Successful people can lose their way at times. They are apt to embrace and overindulge the fruits of success. Humility nullifies the allure of this arrogance and self-indulgence trap. Humble people share the credit for their triumphs and wealth, remaining focused and hungry to continue the journey of success. In all the time I knew Dr Kalam – extending thirty-three years and throughout his meteoric career in the public eye – I never once witnessed overindulgence or arrogance. This is not to say that he was without faults. But overindulgence and arrogance were simply not in his make-up, and this allowed him to serve his country impeccably. He was unerringly focused on the greater good; his gratification was his country's progress and the profound connection he maintained with its people.

Our president was, though, prepared to be stern, and he could even be so when the mood was festive. On 7 December 2003, President Kalam addressed a mega peace festival and grand assembly on 'World Peace through Spiritual Power'. The festival was organized by the Prajapati Brahma Kumaris Ishwariya Vishwa Vidyalaya. Vice President Bhairon Singh Shekhawat and Rajyogini Dadi Prakashmani, the chief of Brahma Kumaris, were present. Singer Mahendra Kapoor enthralled the audience with his soul-elevating devotional songs.

Dr Kalam was not deterred by this pleasant ambience, however. Despite his penchant for diplomacy, he would say what he felt needed to be said; and in some ways, he was becoming more resolute in doing so. President Kalam surprised almost everyone at the festival with his very plain words about the perils of indulging in corruption and cruelty in the affairs of the world. And he was not advising any more – he was warning: 'People who are in high and responsible positions, if they go against righteousness, the righteousness itself will be transformed into a destroyer. Whoever deviates from righteousness, whether they are individuals or states, they are responsible for their own actions.'[7]

4.5

The Deserted Village

> Ill fares the land, to hastening ills a prey,
> Where wealth accumulates, and men decay:
> Princes and lords may flourish, or may fade –
> A breath can make them, as a breath has made:
> But a bold peasantry, their country's pride,
> When once destroyed, can never be supplied.
>
> – Oliver Smith
> Eighteenth-century English Poet

In spite of its burgeoning metropolitan cities, India is still overwhelmingly rural. Seven out of every ten Indians live in villages, and every fifth person in India lives in a village of 2,000–5,000 people. In the country as a whole, the proportion of villages with less than 1,000 people might have fallen, but the proportion in larger villages has risen commensurately. And this pattern changes from state to state. Nonetheless, what remains is Indians' enduring bond with their rural heartland. Their connection to the land of their forefathers is mostly stronger that the allure of the nation's centres.

The village demographics too, from state to state, tell a story, and it is one of comparative development. In Bihar, it's villages with more than 2,000 people where the change has occurred. In Jharkhand and Orissa, villages with more than 500 people are still growing. In Tamil Nadu, the number of large villages, with more than 5,000 people, is growing still. And in Kerala, it's a mega-village story. We often read of the country's rapid urbanization. A concrete jungle of multilevel apartments and shopping complexes towering over crowded streets is doubtless the order of the day in India's sprawling metropolises. The real India, however, will continue to persist more or less in its current form for nearly fifty more years, according to UN estimates. Dr Kalam's PURA mission – with its goal of linking villages and connecting them with services and technology – is consequently the most relevant vision for the nation.

Details of the UN report entitled '2007 Revision of World Urbanization Prospects' were given some mention in India's media:

> Breaking the urbanization myth ... the UN said that though most countries would see rapid urbanization, India would continue to have the largest rural population in the world until 2050 ... 55 per cent of India's population will be living in urban areas, amounting to 900 million people only by 2050.[1]

On 24 December 2003, President Kalam was scheduled to visit Saifai. Saifai is the village of Mulayam Singh Yadav, the chief minister of Uttar Pradesh, his former boss in the defence ministry and since then a close friend. Saifai village is in the Bundelkhand region. Spread over 70,000 square kilometres in thirteen districts of Uttar Pradesh and Madhya Pradesh, the Bundelkhand region is considered the least favourable area of the country for agriculture. Faced with the choice of continuing to depend on erratic rainfall for their regular summer crops or invest in irrigation infrastructure, the farmers of Bundelkhand have mostly opted for the latter.

The issues for water conservation in Bundelkhand reflect a modern trend throughout the world. The basic principle that large-scale extraction of water from aquifers must allow for their replenishment has been ignored in recent years. Along with overfishing of our oceans and wholesale harvesting of precious rainforests, technological advancement has allowed the abuse of our most vital resource. The situation in India, though, has the potential for particularly grave consequences, given our population and reliance on agriculture to feed our ballooning population. Moreover, with the arrival of highly efficient water pumps and tube wells, traditional maintenance of water sources has fallen by the wayside.

Tank systems – which had been preserved for centuries as models of water management most suitable for this region – have been neglected, encroached upon, eroded and destroyed. At the same time, canal networks have become dilapidated; canals remain silt laden, choked with weeds and broken in many places. Worse still, distribution of water is anything but equitable. Irrigation needs of tail-end villages have been largely ignored in the Bundelkhand region. Influential and prosperous farmers in upper areas have employed guns and muscle power to grow even water-intensive crops in times of drought. In recent years, the demand for irrigated water has outstripped supply, with harvests inadequate to cover even capital outlays. Farmers have sunk into a debt trap. Once known for the valour of its people, Bundelkhand has become distinguished by its hunger and desperation.

These were the thoughts Dr Kalam expressed when he asked me, an Uttar Pradesh guy in his team, to write a pertinent speech for him. He wanted me to capture the issues of the people in this ailing hinterland. 'The people of Bundelkhand were once famous for their role and sacrifices in the freedom struggle – now they need help. What could be the way out?' he asked. An impenetrable fog led to the cancellation of the trip to Saifai at the last moment, disappointing villagers, who had gathered en masse to interact with the president. But the president, eager to visit his friend's village, was perhaps even more disappointed.

On 5 January 2004, President Kalam addressed the ninety-first session of the Indian Science Congress at Chandigarh, attended by nearly 4,000 scientists from India and abroad. Dr Kalam began his address by saying that he loved visiting Chandigarh because he had a particular fondness for the city. While Le Corbusier's crafted vision of modernity in his design of Chandigarh was the antithesis of the India he loved, Dr Kalam could appreciate its beauty. Dr Kalam told the scientists that from 1985 to 1999, he was a frequent visitor to the city due to his work at a strategic laboratory there. During those days, he stayed at the Punjab University Guest House. Some of the chapters of his first book were written there.

Dr Kalam highlighted about a dozen major programmes which he felt should be taken up on a priority basis by scientists and technologists. He stated that these were necessary as steps towards India becoming a developed nation in less than two decades. The first task he identified was providing food and nutritional security for India's population. Dr Kalam pointed out that whereas the 'green revolution' had taken place in the 1960s and was for the most part successful, the time had come to start working on the 'second green revolution'. This was needed to double the nation's grain production to 400 million tonnes by 2020. The challenge before the scientific community was to develop foodgrain seeds that provide a greater yield in an array of soil types. This had first been achieved, Dr Kalam said, under the visionary leadership of Dr M.S. Swaminathan. There was now a need to further this development.

Moreover, Dr Kalam was fully aware that while the first 'green revolution' had indeed achieved a dramatic increase in foodgrain production – particularly in Punjab, Haryana and western Uttar Pradesh – this was not without serious ramifications. Some critics had forewarned of the green revolution's dangers at the time of its launch; and many have been vindicated by events as they unfolded. In any case, the ill effects of the revolution have even been accepted by the programme's proponents in recent times.

The green revolution focused almost exclusively on developing and promoting the high-yielding varieties of mostly wheat and later rice seeds, which required intensive irrigation, chemical fertilizers and pesticides in order to guarantee the expected yields The widespread adoption of these has not proved to be sustainable. Soil fertility has declined with the overuse of inorganic fertilizers, and irrigation of areas beyond prudent levels has led to waterlogging and soil erosion. Furthermore, the lower-yielding but more hardy indigenous varieties of grain have been lost, and pesticide use has spiralled like a drug habit. At the same time, capital-intensive farming and mechanization have dispossessed large sectors of agricultural society.

Dr Kalam often cautioned against the notion that all problems can be overcome by technological solutions. Technology cannot alone be considered independent of societal or structural dimensions. He was adamant that technology is only relevant when it is properly contemplated in relation to those who would use it:

> One of the problems with some of our laboratories is that they will always say, 'I have already done it.' I would call this the laboratory syndrome. This is because many underestimate the 'last-mile' problems in taking the technology from the laboratory to the field. The last mile is so simple that we think that we know precisely what has to be done, yet so difficult when we actually get down to doing it. The technological development is complete only when the technology is transferred, absorbed and applied to the needs of people.[2]

Dr Kalam freely interacted with the scientists after his speech at the congress. No other leader had generated such enthusiasm among the scientific community. Dr Kalam was quite frank in telling a group of biotechnologists that his advocacy for biotechnology as the answer to the problems of agriculture and human health was not blind. He told them that he was working to evolve proper checks and balances to regulate developments in the biotechnology sector. The situation that the top ten multinational companies controlled more than 80 per cent of the pesticide market and had 53 per cent market share in the world pharmaceuticals market was not a happy one, he told them. In the food retail business, the top ten companies were controlling 57 per cent of the world's market. He asked, 'Where are we?'

Clearly, scientific and technological solutions to problems are never unique; there are always multiple paths to choose from. Equally, there are no comprehensive solutions, as problems are never one-dimensional; they are often of a structural or systemic nature. Tempering a scientist's dreams with realism must be done without losing heart, and it should be remembered that criticism and openness to it has always served to advance science. As a man who had seen the highs and lows of a scientific career in the public eye, Dr Kalam spoke with authority when he discussed the vagaries of life in the lab:

> I would like to convey some information based on my experience while working in various science and technology laboratories for nearly four decades. I have seen happiness and pain. I have seen happiness when you succeed; also I have seen pain when you don't.[3]

President Kalam also interacted with the children and shared with them his 'thinking mantra' that would later become a regular feature of his speeches in student forums:

> Thinking is progress.
> Non-thinking is stagnation to the individual, organization and the country.
> Thinking leads to action.
> Knowledge without action is useless and irrelevant.
> Knowledge with action brings prosperity.[4]

President Kalam asked children to note that the human mind is a unique gift. But one can enter into marvels of the universe only through curiosity and thinking. He said that thinking should become one's capital asset, regardless of the ups and downs in life. He said to them, 'Look at the sky. We are not alone. The whole universe is friendly to us and conspires only to give the best to those who dream and work.'

India would have general elections in 2004. On the eve of Republic Day, President Kalam virtually set the agenda for the Lok Sabha poll. He did this by asking all political parties to clearly state in their manifesto their vision, action plan and approaches for making India a developed nation by 2020. President Kalam called upon the political parties to move beyond blind criticism of the government on the developmental front. He asked them to outlay their alternative action plan and vision for development. And the least the political parties could do, he thought, is field candidates with a clean record in the ensuing Lok Sabha election.

Referring to the fifty-four-crore-strong youth of our country, President Kalam said India today is a youthful country, adding that the country's youth want to live in a developed and corruption-free India. He said that a developed India must be built in a timely manner to prevent instability in society. Dr Kalam was of the firm opinion that the manifestos of political parties should take into account the aspirations of the country's youth. The manifestos should be drafted in order to meet the dreams of the young and resonate with their aspirations by proposing cogent missions and an action plan.

President Kalam made reference to the peace process that was gaining momentum between India and Pakistan. He said that nations have realized that low-intensity proxy wars, deterrence-based build-ups and real wars are prohibitively expensive detractors from true development. He said, 'The country will be grateful to successful peacemakers.' President Kalam quoted poetry:

> When guns are silent,
> Flowers blossom on the earth;
> Fragrance engulfs good souls,
> Who created beautiful silence.

President Luiz Inacio Lula da Silva of Brazil was invited as the chief guest for that year's Republic Day parade. President Kalam had heard anecdotes of his guest's humble beginnings. As a child, Lula worked as a shoeshine boy and did not learn to read until he was ten years old. As a teenager, Lula worked as a metal worker, and lost one of his fingers at work while operating a machine press in an automobile parts factory. When President Kalam greeted President Lula, he noticed his missing little finger of his left hand.

When I asked Dr Kalam what he found unique in President Lula, his answer was quite revealing of the attributes he admired:'Lula da Silva's perseverance is outstanding. It took him four attempts before he was elected president of Brazil in 2002, and was re-elected for a second term in 2006. I see in him the embodiment of integrity. Lula came to power promising major reforms to the country's political and economic system. He vowed to eradicate hunger and create a self-confident, caring, outward-looking nation and lived up to his words.'

Dr Kalam called President Lula a leader with integrity. President Lula inspired Dr Kalam with his famous slogan, 'I will work with integrity and succeed with integrity.' He was very impressed with the way President Lula had raised Brazil's profile on the international stage and presided over Brazil's longest period of economic growth in three decades. Embraer, a Brazilian company, had become one of the largest aeronautical companies in the world. There were over 5,000 Embraer aircraft operating in eighty countries, including India. Embraer aircraft had become a preferred choice to connect small cities with metros, all over the world. A developing country has indeed joined the big league of aircraft manufacturing nations. Dr Kalam saw their rise in the international aeronautical field as worthy of emulation by the larger players in the Indian industry.

With the Agni-II intermediate range ballistic missile on the mobile launcher passing in front of him at the parade, Dr Kalam was beaming with pride. He conceived it at the beginning of the missile programme in 1983, successfully tested it in 1989; and now this nuclear-warhead-capable missile was a part of the Indian Army as their most credible strategic defence asset.

After the parade, the visiting Brazilian president and other dignitaries were invited for the traditional 'at home' party at Rashtrapati Bhavan. President Kalam was a genial host as always. Despite having no appetite for the finer material things in life, he exuded a sincere charm that put everyone from the waiters to the highest officials of the land at ease. After the guests departed and he rested for a while, President Kalam took me for a late-night walk around the sprawling Mughal Garden lawns. Rashtrapati Bhavan was decorated with lights that etched its golden silhouette on the Delhi night sky. It felt to me like an ambience from dreams of some fantastic paradise. Dr Kalam was still captivated with the personality of President Lula. His humble bearing, his fight, his perseverance – and above all, his success in taking his countrymen out of the poverty left behind by its colonial rulers – was the story that Dr Kalam had scripted in his mind. In President Lula, he saw the hero of his story in the flesh. I broke the magical silence of the still garden to press Dr Kalam on his thoughts:

Arun: Sir, what do you see that is common with India and Brazil?

Kalam: First and foremost, both countries are peace-loving. Though Brazil has ten neighbouring countries, it has never attacked anyone. Both countries suffered colonialism and both countries have been predominantly agrarian economies. Of course, Brazil became a republic in 1889, which was much earlier than we managed. During the cold war between the United States and the Soviet Union, Brazil was under the rule of military leaders like many other Latin American countries. But today, Brazil is a vibrant democracy. Brazil and India are in a similar stage of newly advanced economic development and are members of the BRICs group of countries, along with Russia, China and South Africa.

Arun: What can India learn from Brazil?

Kalam: India can learn a lot from Brazil in making development inclusive. Two social programmes of President Lula stand out as worthy of replication. In the *Bolsa Familia* scheme, a family allowance is given to very poor people and cash is provided to meet certain contingencies. In the *Fome Zero* (zero hunger) scheme, access to basic food for everyone is ensured. It takes a number of forms, ranging from financial aid to the poorest families to diverse strategies, such as water, low-cost restaurants, free vitamins and iron supplements, family farming and microcredit. All this was accomplished not with aid or loans but by creating real growth and a budget surplus.

Arun: Is it ever possible in India?

Kalam: I don't know. The elections will now happen. The present government is telling everyone that India is shining; but I do not see the shine when I go to villages. The ongoing development in the country lacks a humane face.

Arun: Sir, you say India today is a youthful country. There are fifty-four crore youth in our country.

Kalam: That is my worry, buddy. The curse of unemployment is one grave aspect of the problem. Today, more than eighteen crore young people are unemployed. They are at a loss to understand how they can contribute to the nation's regeneration.

I realized that night the prophet in Dr Kalam. The most respected leader of our times was happy to say, 'I don't know'. If a leader has the answers to all the questions, that is the proof that God is not with him. It means that he is not speaking the truth. He is using the name of God for himself. The great leaders of the people of God – even Moses – have always left room for doubt. We need to leave room for the Lord, not for our certainties; and we must be humble.

Around this time, Pramukh Swamiji invited Dr Kalam to the Suvarna Bal Mahotsav at Akshardham, Gandhinagar. The celebration was planned as a tribute to Yogiji Maharaj, the founder of BAPS Children's Forum. When Dr Kalam arrived at the Akshardham Mandir on 8 February 2004, orange, green and white balloons filled the sky, and children ecstatically cheered him. Spiritual vigour was reflected in the children's faces. The peace chant by 20,000 children, '*Om, dyoho shanti*', resonated in the air. Overwhelmed with joy, Dr Kalam told Pramukh Swamiji, 'You know, Swamiji, I had a great meeting with you in Delhi, and the words of that meeting still echo in my mind, and there is always divine radiation, divine vibration in me. I feel as if you are always near me.'[5]

At this glorious function, President Kalam felicitated successful entrepreneurs, social workers, police officers, pilots, soldiers, singers, sportsmen and scientists who had made a difference as leaders at the international level. Each one of them had been inspired as a child attending BAPS children's activities. Dr Kalam reminisced years later: 'I saw my dream of igniting minds manifesting before me.'[6]

Another friend was waiting for him in Uttar Pradesh. President Kalam visited Saifai on 16 February 2004, and paid tribute to the importance of villages in India:

> The heart of India lies in its villages, as there are 5,33,000 villages in our country and around 70 per cent of our population reside in these villages. Hence, the villages have to become economically developed in the country. The next two decades or even less are very important for India for transforming from a 'developing' country to a 'developed' nation. The development of the villages is the foundation for the national progress.[7]

President Kalam laid the Foundation of the Etawah–Mainpuri rail line project in the presence of Union Minister Nitish Kumar in February 2004. Once Mainpuri is connected to Etawah, about 56 km away, a new world of opportunities and development would open up for the people living here.[8]

He reminded the huge gathering of the intellectual leadership that Uttar Pradesh, the largest state of India, had provided to the country:

> Uttar Pradesh inspired the country with leadership in education. Pandit Madan Mohan Malaviya, Sir Syed Ahmed Khan, and Maulana Abul Kalam Azad were responsible for creating famous educational institutions in this part of the country. They inspired many such movements elsewhere and provided knowledge leadership for the nation. In the Bhakti Movement, luminaries like Tulsi Das, Vallabhacharya, Surdas, Kabir Das, and Ravidas were born here; from them spiritual wisdom emanated for the entire country.[9]

On our way back to Delhi, we had a discussion that would later appear in our book *Squaring the Circle*.[10]

I told Dr Kalam, 'Youth are not interested in agriculture. The trend is to migrate to the city.' The fact that agriculture is not expanding at the same rate as the rest of the Indian economy is truly worrisome. It is well acknowledged that every rupee contributed to the nation's GDP from farming is twice as effective as other interventions in alleviating rural poverty. Agriculture is an indirect growth driver, as a growth rate of 4 per cent in agriculture translates into robust demand for other sectors. Samuel Johnson wrote, 'Agriculture not only gives riches to a nation, but the only riches she can call her own.'

Dr Kalam said, 'Building up the agricultural sector is central to the real growth of our economy. Almost half of India's geographical area is used for agricultural activity and about 60 per cent of the country's workforce labours in fields, and yet agriculture and allied sectors like forestry and fishing account for not even one-fifth of the total GDP. The GDP will rise beyond 8 per cent, its current level, only when agricultural production rises to about 25 per cent of the GDP.' He also identified low yield rates in India as the main reason for youth shunning farming: 'Yields per hectare of foodgrains, fruits and vegetables in India are far below the global average. Our rice yield is one-third of China's, and about half of Vietnam's and Indonesia's. Even India's most productive states lag behind the global average. The nation needs a second agricultural revolution.'

4.6

Nation Builders

> We talk foolishly against a material civilization. The grapes are sour. Material civilization, nay even luxury, is necessary to create work for the poor. Bread! Bread! I do not believe in a god who cannot give me bread.
>
> – Swami Vivekananda

President Kalam was invited to the seventy-fifth anniversary of harmony between the steel major and Tata Workers' Union (TWU) at Jamshedpur, Jharkhand. The story of Tata Steel is the story of steel in India. India was left slightly dazzled and overwhelmed in the wake of the Industrial Revolution in England. Our people were astounded by the superiority of the machines that the colonizers brought here. Indian intellectuals of the nineteenth century believed that if India were to keep pace with the world it would have to master the modern scientific methods of the West. Indians cannot be left looking at the goods of modern civilization like beggars peering through the glass at shopfront window displays.

It was this vision of constructive change that would lead Jamsetji Nusserwanji Tata to embark on a journey of growth that paved the path for industrialization in India. Within his lifetime, Jamsetji was to witness the birth and rise of a revolutionary Indian nationalism. This would only culminate in the emergence of independent India, though, more than four decades after his death. J.N. Tata was spellbound and driven by three guiding ambitions – building an iron and steel company, generating hydroelectric power and creating an institution that offers the finest education in science. Tatas issued shares in 1907, some three years after J.N. Tata's death. For the first time in the financial history of the country, the Indian people – the masses and the affluent alike – joined hands to back this, the first truly Indian enterprise. The Tata family held 11 per cent shares of the Tata Iron and Steel Company Limited.

The steel company obtained its first colliery in 1910, adding six more in the course of time. Several mines were spread over the states of Bihar, Orissa and Karnataka. The Tatas became the first to own a fully mechanized iron ore mine in India. The coal beneficiation plant at West Bokaro undertook beneficiation of low-grade coal, thus helping in the conservation of the fast-dwindling reserves of high-quality coal. The collieries, the iron ore mines and the quarries together furnished the bulk of the raw material requirements of the plant.

By the Second World War, Tatas' production capacities had expanded enough to make their prices lower than those of steel produced in England, raising them to a commanding position in the market. Post-Independence, the Tatas decided to focus on the Herculean task of nation building. The much-required steel for the newly devised 'Five-Year Plans' came from the Tata factories. The company undertook supplies of iron and steel to the Howrah Bridge in Calcutta, the Bhakra Nangal Project and the Damodar Valley Corporation, the port at Kandla, the city of Chandigarh and many other important projects.

Speaking at a function that took place on 13 February 2004, Dr Kalam said India is among the largest producers of iron ore in the world. As much as 30 million tonnes of iron ore is exported from here annually. The need of the hour is to produce more steel, because steel is the foundation for the growth of a nation. President Kalam said that for India to become a developed nation, the industry has to be cost-effective and quality-conscious, and must stick to just-in-time delivery schedules. 'Competitiveness is the final determinant between a developing nation and a developed one,' he said, adding that the domestic industry must be globally competitive to facilitate India's transition from a developing country to a developed nation by 2020.

President Kalam predicted that the basic fabric of Indian society, including industry, would undergo a change in the next ten years. Management will depend 'more on delegation rather than direction'. Workers' skills will become 'less structured and more flexible, more software-driven instead of just hardware-driven'. The economy will become knowledge-driven instead of industry driven, and society will focus on empowerment instead of merely the fulfilment of basic needs.

Describing seventy-five years of industrial harmony at Tata Steel as 'an important milestone' for the Indian industry, Dr Kalam said the achievement is the result of a 'combination of technology, leadership, knowledge and an inspired workforce'. He called upon the Tatas to create a cluster of ancillary industries in and around Jamshedpur, with a view to generating employment and social upliftment of its residents.

The governor of Jharkhand, Ved Marwah, the governor of West Bengal, Viren J. Shah, the chief minister of Jharkhand, Mr Arjun Munda, and Dr J.J. Irani, director of Tata Sons and a former managing director of Tata Steel, were also present for the occasion. The event was called an 'example before the entire world'.

Upon our return to Delhi, I asked Dr Kalam whom he would pick as the greatest nation builders. This led to a three-hour discussion sitting in the bamboo hut in the Mughal Gardens, the very one gifted by Tripura Chief Minister Manik Sarkar and named 'Sant Kalam ki Kutiya' (St Kalam's hut) by Prime Minister Vajpayee.

Dr Kalam said of course Gandhiji was the father of Indian nation who ignited the minds of Indians to achieve freedom. He picked from the spark already created by Swami Vivekananda and Balgangadhar Tilak. Many great leaders and hundreds of thousands of patriots gave their lives to the cause of Indian freedom. Then our first prime minister built the foundation of India on humanism and scientific spirit. 'I will put the Tatas, particularly J.N. Tata and J.R.D. Tata, as nation builders of equal importance,' Dr Kalam said.

Arun: Why do some families succeed in creating legacy and others do not?

Kalam: It is all about transfer of personal excellence to the next generation with a purpose as a family value. Jamsetji Tata was successful in enabling Dorabji Tata who in turn enabled J.R.D. Tata to create institutions and not merely generate personal wealth.

Arun: So when institution building becomes the purpose of a business, it makes all the difference.

Kalam: Concern for society is fundamental to a good business. While the Tatas were doing what they were doing they also made Asia's first cancer hospital, the Tata Memorial Centre for Cancer Research and Treatment in 1941; the Tata Institute of Social Sciences (TISS) in 1936, and the Tata Institute of Fundamental Research (TIFR) in 1945.

Arun: Why we do not see many more such examples?

Kalam: Like strength, respect strength, goodness attracts goodness. The excellence of Tata Memorial Centre for Cancer is rooted in the genius of Dr Ernest Borges. I see a gap between good people and wealthy people now; it was not there earlier. Also, excellence has been sidelined for short-term profitability

Arun: What is responsible for this?

Kalam: The culture of greed.

Arun: How did it happen? It was not originally an Indian trait.

Kalam: Independent India had stumbled somewhere on its developmental path.

Arun: But you said greed?

Kalam: Greed is a very complex force. It does not confine to money alone. It is about power and control. Greed is so destructive. It destroys everything.

Arun: You mean the greed for profit and power came in the way of not many institutions like Tata Memorial Centre for Cancer being created?

Kalam: Yes. With India's hundred richest, all billionaires, with

> combined wealth of $346 billion, why are there not even a hundred institutions like the Tata Memorial Centre for Cancer?

Dr Kalam had obviously taken great pains to read India's history – along with that of other countries – and he had learned its lessons well. He was always passionate about bringing technology and progress to the people. And he was much enamoured of mass education, which is why his response to an invitation from a friend was something of a surprise. Prof. N. Balakrishnan, a close friend of Dr Kalam's, came to invite Dr Kalam to inaugurate the International Conference on Digital Libraries (ICDL 2004) in New Delhi. Dr Kalam bluntly questioned the relevance of a digital library for the millions of people who had yet to be reached by the 'printed library revolution' initiated by Gutenberg.

The response, at any rate, satisfied him of the merits of their project. Dr Kalam was always one to see reason. He happily inaugurated ICDL 2004 on 24 February 2004. It was the first such conference in India to be organized on a truly international scale, and it attracted more than 740 registered participants from thirty-three countries in Asia, Africa, Europe, America and Australia. He gave a forty-minute well-informed discourse on the impact of digital library developments on the emerging Indian knowledge economy. President Kalam convincingly highlighted to the international delegates the effort his country of a billion people was putting into technological development.

While interacting with foreign delegates over tea, President Kalam candidly told them they needed to be patient regarding Internet connectivity. Internet connectivity had been one of the subjects of discussion for several of the speakers. Dr Kalam explained that there are things that most people in the developed world could take for granted, like the water and electricity supplies to their homes. India, he reminded them, still had millions of households without these fundamentals. We are on the job though, he assured them. He stated that major telecommunications problems needed addressing before truly egalitarian access to digital libraries, or any other applications and services that depend on a reliable ICT (information and communication infrastructure), can be possible. We can now recognize that some of these issues have been dealt with – at least to some extent – in the intervening years.

Dr Kalam delivered an off-the-cuff dissertation on some of the interesting socio-technical projects he had been involved with, leaving the delegates more than a little impressed by his versatility. These included a mobile digital library complete with solar power, a satellite dish Internet connection and a small-scale printer and bookbinder that can bring a choice of books-on-paper to the remotest village. These technologies could bring learning to a significant proportion of the world's population who have yet to make their first telephone call.

On 2 April 2004, President Kalam became the first Indian president to visit the Siachen Glacier, the highest battlefield in the world. The Siachen Glacier is located in the eastern Karakoram Range in the Himalayas, just where the Line of Control between India and Pakistan ends. At 76 km, it is the longest glacier in the Karakoram Range and the second longest in the world's non-polar areas. Both India and Pakistan continue to deploy thousands of troops in the vicinity of Siachen, and attempts to demilitarize the region have been unsuccessful.

This may be as much due to the significance of the region for the national resources of both India and Pakistan, as to disputation about the international border. The glacier's meltwater is the main source of the River Nubra in the Indian region of Ladakh, which drains into the River Shyok. The Shyok in turn joins the 3,000-kilometre-long Indus that flows through Pakistan. Thus, the glacier is a major source of the Indus and feeds the largest irrigation system in the world.

Visiting the glacier is no small matter, least of all for a man in his senior years. Perhaps as much as 97 per cent of the army's casualties at Siachen have not occurred due to fighting, but the region's excessive altitude, inhospitable weather and challenging terrain. The altitude of around 6,000 metres (20,000 feet) is more than enough to incapacitate many. More than 2,000 people have died on the world's highest battleground.

To reach the Indian military base at Siachen, President Kalam first flew to the Indian Air Force's Thoise airbase near the Siachen Brigade Headquarters in Partapur. Army chief Gen. N.C. Vij, Northern Army Commander Lt Gen. Hari Prasad and Corp Commander Lt Gen. Arvind Sharma were present to receive President Kalam, the supreme commander of the armed forces. The airbase is located in one of the most beautiful areas on earth. Glorious ranges carved from the inhospitable earth reach into the heavens, giving way only for the confluence of the Shyok and Nubra rivers that flow through a broad valley lying north of the Khardungla Pass. Thoise – an acronym for Transit Halt of Indian Soldiers Enroute (to Siachen) – lies on a grassy plain in this valley, well north of the town of Leh in Ladakh. The hostility of much of this region to human existence is legendary. The Shyok literally means 'the river of death' in Yarkandi Uyghur.

President Kalam was well versed in the technical challenges that the rarefied atmosphere and harsh conditions at Siachen posed for aviation and military manoeuvres. He had, after all, pioneered, with Group Captain Narayanan, the RATO solution for turbojet aircraft to negotiate the short runways in the Himalayas, early in his career. He was eminently and unusually qualified as head of the armed forces to take stock of the machines and technology deployed to assist soldiers here. President Kalam saw numerous areas for improvement, and was forthright in expressing his expert opinions.

He said that the high-altitude capability of the indigenous 'Dhruv' helicopter should be improved, so that the Indian Air Force does not have to handle several variants. Moreover, he stated that helicopters and other types of aircraft should be fitted with advanced technological aids, such as ground-penetration radars to make patrolling safer for jawans. These devices could detect crevasses and taking cloud-penetrating photographs. Additionally, he suggested that a helicopter be converted into an ambulance.

Strategically, President Kalam also saw a greater role for technology. He mooted the deployment of high-altitude spy planes for reconnaissance operations. Since one of the most important aspects of mountain warfare is timely reconnaissance, the president wanted their vital intelligence to supplement the input from remote-sensing satellites.

From Thoise, President Kalam flew into the Siachen base camp in a helicopter, at a height of over 18,000 feet, where he mingled with the hardy jawans and officers alike. He spoke to them as if he were an ordinary man, lauding them for their commitment and endurance in defending the country in such hostile conditions. The troops and officers were amazed by his presence at Siachen; no president had ever come to the glacier, and that too, in his seventy-third year.

Addressing the soldiers, President Kalam said the technological tools to assist foot patrolling in the extremely treacherous terrain should be improved and the procedure for airlifting victims of avalanches, frostbite and enemy fire toned up. He assured them that the nation realized that they encountered not one adversary but two – one across the border and the other, inhospitable nature. He stated that it was the duty of the nation to ensure their welfare and happiness. Further, he made special mention that they were not only defending India's territorial integrity and water resources. They were also partnering in and fuelling the economic development mission of the nation. As had become quite regular with President Kalam – and was perhaps to be expected from the head of state of our most religious country – he gave our soldiers spiritual food for thought:

> I would like to share with you a philosophical thought, in this divine Himalayan ambience. I believe God creates every living being with a mission and specific purpose. You are fortunate to have been blessed to be in a position to perform a noble mission of defending the nation as soldiers. When I see you, you all look very smart, you look combat ready and through gracious smiles on your faces I can see that you are winning.[1]

President Kalam was now an equal proponent of the spiritual and technological aspects in Indian life, but his belief in indigenous military hardware never waned. The defence sector usually operates at levels of technological sophistication higher than those available in the civil sector of any country. Since 1992, Dr Kalam had been seen publicly as a crusader for indigenous technological development. At every forum, he argued for the creation of industrial capabilities in defence. Dr Kalam enjoyed the historic distinction of having promoted India's quest for self-reliance. And this was not merely in defence: the ventures he promoted in military hardware immeasurably advanced the science and technology base and industrial capability of the country.

India had been kept de-industrialized for over 200 years by the British. When the Industrial Revolution was taking root the world over and resulting in tremendous growth in technology and industrial capability, Indian industry was systematically hobbled by the colonial rulers. There could be no other motive for this than to guarantee the products manufactured in Great Britain a captive market in India. Furthermore, the British Raj rigorously followed a policy of retaining strategic capabilities while only allowing native Indians to participate in the practical dimension of most endeavours. Even as the need to transfer industry increased due to rising costs of labour in the British homeland, strategic industries and facilities were not established. At least, the colonial rulers of India would not look beyond basic infrastructure such as the railways and ports needed to rule the country.

At Independence, India faced the unenviable situation of needing to achieve self-reliance from an economy that was, for the most part, lagging at least a century behind its Western counterparts. Indian leaders were pragmatic in opting for an incremental path for its vital needs in defence. For self-reliance to be achieved, it was deemed necessary to continue meeting urgent requirements through imports while pursuing indigenous capabilities. It took a decade for IITs to be in place and another decade for the establishment of industrial complexes with the capability to produce modern armaments.

Bharat Electronics Limited was envisaged as part of the strategy for incremental self-reliance in defence hardware. It was set up in 1954 specifically to manufacture electronic products for the Indian armed forces. Likewise, the Electronics Corporation of India Limited (ECIL) was set up in 1967 by the Department of Atomic Energy. Its mission was to generate a strong indigenous capability in the field of professional-grade electronics used in the nuclear energy sector.

On 21 April 2004, President Kalam had a thirty-minute video interaction with the BEL community on the occasion of its golden jubilee celebrations. The products of BEL are diverse, spanning from communication systems to complex radars and sonars from modularized common communication systems to electronic warfare systems for the three services. Additionally, BEL also manufactures microwave components, application-specific integrated circuits (ASICs) and very-large-scale-integration (VLSI) semiconductor devices. While addressing the high-tech needs of the defence sector, BEL has also kept in mind its commitment to society. Dr Kalam said that he was happy to see that several broadcast and telecommunication devices, electronic voting machines and solar products for civil applications were in BEL's catalogue. For Dr Kalam, it was either onward, upward or forward:

> When you are celebrating this golden jubilee, you must have a vision for the next twenty years and beyond. My dream is that you should become a multi-billion dollar company: an Indian electronics multinational corporation catering to the defence needs of our country and competing in other markets. Also, BEL should become a household name in consumer electronic products of certain types.[2]

On 25 April 2004, the navy's sail ship, INS *Tarangini*, returned to its base at the Southern Naval Command after a historic voyage around the world. The president and supreme commander of the armed forces, Dr Kalam, welcomed the ship and its crew at an impressive ceremony at the south jetty at the naval base at Kochi.

During its fifteen-month voyage, the ship had covered 33,000 nautical miles, or 61,000 kilometres, and visited thirty-six ports in eighteen countries. The Indian Navy believes that training onboard these ships is the best method of instilling among its sailors an indefinable 'sea-sense' and respect for the elements of nature. These attributes, the navy command believes, are inseparable from safe and successful seafaring. INS *Tarangini* was constructed in Goa and launched in December 1995.

Addressing a gathering of naval personnel, their families and other dignitaries, President Kalam said that INS *Tarangini*'s 458 days of voyaging around the globe would ensure that there was never again a subjugation of Indian territory or danger to its seaborne economic activity. For the student of history that was Dr Kalam, the past was as relevant to the future as the present; it could help to predict future trends and dangers:

> Historically, if you look at our country, there have been many land-based invasions from Central Asia in the northern parts of India from numerous kings and warriors. These invasions led to a series of problems and pain for our people. But surprisingly, subsequent invasions which took place through sea routes in the name of trade engulfed the nation like wildfire. The Portuguese entered India in 1498 from the west coast. Later during the sixteenth century, both Danish and French came to India at Tharangambadi and Pondicherry respectively by sea. During the seventeenth century, the British came to India and formed a trading company again via the sea. They overpowered the Portuguese, French and Danish, and ruled India for over 250 years. Also, there were some isolated colonies of the other three European nations. This really reveals that economic war was waged from the seas, and also the war for ruling India was carried out through sea routes and sea journeys.[3]

Dr Kalam praised the officers, cadets and sailors of INS *Tarangini* for re-establishing the tradition of epic sailing voyages, and compared their efforts to those of Columbus. Columbus had taken about eight months to travel 3,000 nautical miles, in a bid to discover India. INS *Tarangini* covered more than 35,000 nautical miles in fifteen months. Dr Kalam told them, 'Columbus discovered a new continent through his mission, whereas you have travelled through all the continents and won the hearts of the people every where.. The sea was your classroom and elements of nature your teachers.'

The sea had cast its spell on Dr Kalam very early in his life, and it never lost its fascination for him. Wearing the cap of INS *Tarangini*, he beamed with pride.

4.7

We the People

> Let us never forget that government is ourselves and not an alien power over us. The ultimate rulers of our democracy are not a president and senators and congressmen and government officials, but the voters of this country.
>
> – Franklin D. Roosevelt
> The thirty-second president of the United States

Before the arrival of the British, India was the pre-eminent world economic power. Indian commerce accounted for more than 40 per cent of the global economy, and its roads and trade network were the envy of the civilized world. To wit: The Mauryan Empire connected Taxila and Patna, a distance in the order of 2,000 kilometres, 300 years before the Common Era. By the sixteenth century, Sher Shah Suri had extended the road along the Gangetic Plain to Kabul in the west and Chittagong in the east. This road was further improved by the British and named the Grand Trunk Road.

During British rule, India witnessed a massive expansion of transport infrastructure. By 1920, India's rail network was the fourth largest in the world, and macadamized roads penetrated to the village level. The motives for this British push for modern trade infrastructure were unquestionably in favour of their lucrative trade, and the expense was unfairly borne by the Indian taxpayer. But it cannot be denied that the rail network and roads actually helped in shaping modern India. After Independence from British rule, India embarked on socialistic policies that gave priority to Central planning and state-owned enterprises, due to which trade and road networks were sidelined. In fact, for the first fifty years after Independence, less than 500 kilometres of four-lane highways were built.

Prime Minister Vajpayee was to change this situation drastically. One of his first major announcements as prime minister in 1998 was the 6,000-kilometre highway project called the 'Golden Quadrilateral'. This network of roads would connect most of the major industrial, agricultural and cultural centres of India, including the four metro cities – Mumbai, Delhi, Calcutta and Chennai. Over the following five years, almost 25,000 kilometres of national highways were built, helping to fuel a period of economic prosperity unprecedented in modern India.

Owing in no small measure to the public approval of this vast infrastructure project, the BJP scored comfortable electoral victories in the 2003 state assembly elections in Madhya Pradesh, Rajasthan and Chhattisgarh. Prime Minister Vajpayee thought he could capitalize on the public mood which appeared to favour his party. He decided to prematurely dissolve the Lok Sabha in early 2004 to hold national elections over April and May of that year. Senior BJP leaders felt confident they could secure a further term of office, and the party optimistically launched an 'India Shining' campaign.

On 18 April 2004, President Kalam addressed the nation on the eve of the opening phase of the Lok Sabha polls. He appealed to voters to exercise their franchise 'positively', to elect members who would guide the destiny of the nation for the following five years. President Kalam said in his speech over Doordarshan and All India Radio that 'By casting your vote for a candidate who in your opinion can represent you in the Lok Sabha, you are sowing the seeds for the creation of a prosperous India, a happy India, a safe India, a secure India, and above all, an India with nobility'. This was the first time in the history of India's democracy that a president had chosen to issue such an appeal ahead of parliamentary elections. President Kalam further exhorted his compatriots to become involved in the democratic process:

> Dear voters, dawn of beautiful India is in your mind and then in your deeds. The deed for the day of the election for you is to cast your vote and be a proud contributor to the success of the spirit of democracy of the largest and most dynamic democracy of all democracies.[1]

General elections were held in various phases between 20 April and 10 May 2004. President Kalam cast his vote at the Government Co-education Senior Secondary School polling booth, minutes after the voting began at 7.00 a.m. in the New Delhi constituency. 'I feel beautiful to exercise my right to vote,' President Kalam said after casting his vote. Asked about the experience of using the electronic voting machine, the president said: 'Fantastic.'[2]

Always a careful planner, President Kalam had consulted constitutional and legal experts on the course of action to be pursued in the event that no party or pre-poll alliance won a majority in parliament. He had meetings with former Attorney General K. Parasaran and former Chief Justice of India J.S. Verma.[3]

The election results declared on 13 May 2004 came as a rude shock to the ruling NDA alliance. The number of people who had voted for Congress and the BJP had remained almost the same as in 1999. Approximately 10.3 crore people had voted for Congress in 1999. In 2004, around 10.3 crore people had voted for Congress again. In 1999, 8.6 crore people had voted for the BJP and in 2004, again around 8.6 crore people had voted for the BJP. But the number of seats won had drastically changed. In 1999, Congress had won 114 seats but in 2004, with almost the same number of voters, it won 145 seats. In the case of the BJP, in 1999, it had won 182 seats but in 2004, inspite of having the same number of votes, it managed to secure only 138 seats. With approximately the same sizes of their respective voter base, Congress managed to increase its seats by thirty-one, while the BJP's seats decreased by forty-four, ultimately leading to its defeat.[4]

President Kalam hosted a farewell function for the outgoing prime minister Vajpayee and his cabinet colleagues on 15 May 2004. Dr Kalam had enjoyed a relationship with Vajpayee that extended far beyond the realm of politics:

> The common thing between Vajpayeeji and me is poetry. I always cherish his poems. I would like to recall one of the poems 'Oonchai' which touched my heart. He says in the poem that the man achieves and achieves. The achievement takes him to heights ... it finally takes him to loneliness. Is loneliness as much a blessing as a curse? He concludes in his poem: 'My Lord, Never let me climb so high that I can't bend down to embrace another human. Deliver me ever from such arrogance.'[5]

In return, Prime Minister Vajpayee was all praise for President Kalam, saying, '*Jab jab main Kalamsahab se milta tha, man aanandit ho jata tha* (it was always a delight to meet Kalam).' The prime minister said he and his colleagues had learned a lot from the simplicity of the president.

On 15 May 2004, the Congress elected Smt. Sonia Gandhi its leader at a meeting in the Central Hall of parliament. The Election Commission of India constituted the fourteenth Lok Sabha on 17 May 2004, and submitted the requisite notification to President Kalam. On 18 May 2004, Smt. Sonia Gandhi, along with Dr Manmohan Singh, met with President Kalam. They brought no letters of support of other parties that would show they had secured a majority in the Lok Sabha. Rather, President Kalam informed them he had already received letters of support from the Samajwadi Party (SP) of Mulayam Singh Yadav and Rashtriya Lok Dal (RLD) of Ajit Singh. It was decided that they would meet again on the following day. Their next meeting would hold quite a surprise for Dr Kalam, as he would later recall:

> At the allotted time, 8.15 p.m., Mrs Gandhi came to Rashtrapati Bhavan along with Dr Manmohan Singh. In this meeting, after exchanging pleasantries, she showed me the letters of support from various parties. Thereupon, I said that is welcome. The Rashtrapati Bhavan is ready for the swearing-in ceremony at the time of your choice. That is when she told me that she would like to nominate Dr Manmohan Singh, who was the architect of economic reforms in 1991 and a trusted lieutenant of the Congress with an unimpeachable image. This was definitely a surprise to me, and the

Rashtrapati Bhavan Secretariat had to reword the letter appointing Dr Manmohan Singh as the prime minister and inviting him to form the government at the earliest.[6]

On 22 May 2004, President Kalam administered the oath of office and secrecy to Dr Manmohan Singh as the prime minister of India in the Ashok Hall of Rashtrapati Bhavan. The swearing-in ceremony was attended by outgoing prime minister Atal Bihari Vajpayee, former president K.R. Narayanan and former prime ministers P.V. Narasimha Rao, I.K. Gujral, H.D. Deve Gowda, Vishwanath Pratap Singh and Chandra Shekhar.

No prime minister in the history of modern India had the credentials of Dr Manmohan Singh. As a politician, he had been seasoned by an extended stint as leader of the opposition in the Rajya Sabha between 1998 and 2004 and in the 1990s, as finance minister. As a technocrat, there was barely an important post in government that Singh had not held. He had been chairman of the University Grants Commission, adviser to the prime minister, governor of the Reserve Bank of India, deputy chairman of the Planning Commission and chief economic adviser. President Kalam and Prime Minister Singh developed a harmonious relationship in the best tradition of the robust Indian system of government.

Two significant events took place in Bangalore on 23 July 2004. President Kalam inaugurated two conferences: the National Conference on Enhancing Learning in Elementary Schools, organized by the Azim Premji Foundation, and EDUSAT, the Indian Satellite in Education, organized by the Indian Space Research Organization and the Association of Indian Universities (AIU). The Indian nation was undergoing a strong and definitive transformation. Dr Kalam's call for making India a developed country by 2020 and his emphasis on transforming India into a knowledge nation had gained spontaneous support from governmental organizations as well as private establishments.

Dr Kalam had built a solid friendship with Azim Premji since he first met him in Bangalore in October 2000. Premji was the richest

Indian at that time, with a personal net worth in excess of USD 18 billion. Premji shared with Dr Kalam his desire to work towards improving the quality of education in the country. Dr Kalam gave him two suggestions: to focus on elementary education (Class I to VIII) and create a feasible model to elevate the quality of education, and to work with the government school system.

Soon after this meeting, Premji founded Azim Premji Foundation, a non-profit organization. The foundation's vision was to significantly contribute to achieving quality universal education; education that facilitates a just, equitable, humane and sustainable society. The foundation had since worked in the area of elementary education to pilot and develop 'proofs of concept' for effecting systemic change in India's 1.3 million government-run schools. Rural areas, where the majority of these schools were established, were a particular focus of the foundation.

Starting with Karnataka, the Azim Premji Foundation reached out to Uttarakhand, Rajasthan, Chhattisgarh, Pondicherry (now Puducherry), Andhra Pradesh, Bihar and Madhya Pradesh, in close partnership with the respective state governments. The foundation had worked largely in rural areas, helping to contribute to the improvement of quality and equity of school education.

Upon his arrival at Wipro, Azim Premji – flanked by the governor of Karnataka, T.N. Chaturvedi, and Chief Minister Dharam Singh – warmly received President Kalam. Premji did not shy away from raising some uncomfortable issues affecting the country in his subsequent speech:

> Why do we rank 127 among 175 countries on the Human Development Index? ... Why do we lack a sense of discipline while standing in a queue, throwing garbage or waiting at a signal? ... Why are we obliged to tolerate corruption on a daily basis? ... Why have we not achieved a modicum of social justice and equitability – equal opportunity for both the sexes, for rural and urban, for all citizens irrespective of caste and creed? It is imperative that our schools and educational institutes create an environment in which the intellectual, physical, social and moral attributes can be developed, cherished and

> nurtured in a way that our children can leverage their full potential to become bright, thinking, innovative, free and fearless citizens.[7]

Dr Kalam recognized the value of the work of Azim Premji and his foundation in furthering children's education. He spoke of his view that early education is the most powerful agent for moulding a human being:

> The prime learning period is between the age of six and seventeen years. Hence, the school hours for children are the best time for learning, and need the best environment and mission oriented learning with value based educational systems. This reminds me of the echo from Pestalozzi, a great teacher, saying, 'Give me a child for seven years, afterwards, let the God or devil take the child, they cannot change the child.' That is indeed the power of the teacher.[8]

On 23 July 2004 the Indian Space Research Organization organized a Conference on 'EDUSAT – the Indian Satellite in Education', jointly with the Association of Indian Universities and invited the president along with about 250 vice chancellors in the country, directors of Indian Institutes of Technology, heads of agricultural universities and medical universities, and other important educationists and administrators. The main objective of the conference was to appraise the educationists on the capabilities of EDUSAT – which was to be launched by ISRO in September 2004 – and how the various educational agencies could utilize it. With the success of the earlier INSAT-based educational project, a need was perceived for a dedicated satellite for educational purposes and the EDUSAT project was conceived by the ISRO in October 2002. President Kalam interacted via INSAT with students at Nashik, Ahmedabad, Bangalore, Belgaum and Mangalore, and shared his own initiatives:

> I would like to narrate our experience in tele-education piloted at Rashtrapati Bhavan for providing satellite connectivity for the PREVIK (President's Virtual Institute for Knowledge) members. The connectivity is through V-SATs provided by ISRO, Voice Over-IP and Internet. In this platform, the live virtual studio environment is created and it will connect a number of remote locations and provide

seamless, one to many connectivity, through multicasting modes in a collaborative environment. This also provides two-way connectivity.[9]

The EDUSAT satellite was built exclusively to serve the educational sector. It was mainly intended to meet the demand for an interactive satellite-based distance education system for the country. EDUSAT carries five Ku-band transponders providing spot beams, one Ku-band transponder providing a national beam and six extended C-band transponders providing national coverage beams. EDUSAT was later launched on 20 September 2004 by the first operational launch of the Geosynchronous Satellite Launch Vehicle (GSLV) from SHAR, now named Satish Dhawan Space Centre in Sriharikota. The satellite was placed in a 36,000-km-high geostationary orbit.

In the same month, President Kalam was invited to interact with heads of state of fifty-three African nations forming the Pan-African Parliament. He would be the only non-African leader to attend. Acutely aware of the conservation issues of Africa's game animals, President Kalam expressed his robust opposition to safaris in the savannah plains of Africa's well-known national parks. He viewed these as an anachronistic and cruel throwback to colonial times that could only serve to decimate Africa's remaining wildlife. He set himself a characteristically frenetic schedule in South Africa, Tanzania and Zanzibar. His goal, as ever, was to visit universities in these nations and interact with their youth. He was firmly convinced that in engaging and inspiring young minds, he could liberate some of their potential. After all, he would often tell me, children are the building blocks of progress in any country. On a more personal note, Dr Kalam was excited that he would be meeting Nelson Mandela, the liberator of South Africa.

President Kalam arrived in Dar es Salaam on 11 September 2004 at the start of his four-day state visit to Tanzania, where he was received by President Benjamin Mkapa. The name 'Tanzania' was created as a portmanteau of the names of the two states that unified to create the country – Tanganyika and Zanzibar – after the end of British colonial rule in 1964.

Indians have a long history in Tanzania, starting with the arrival of Gujarati traders in the nineteenth century. The leadership of Julius Nyerere ensured a peaceful transition of power post-independence, and equal representation for all Tanzanian people. The country thus escaped the conflicted path taken by Kenya and Uganda.

During the dinner hosted by President Benjamin Mkapa, Dr Kalam spoke with Dr Rajni Kanabar, who had worked with Tanzania's Ministry of Health for the welfare of the country's young heart patients. In 1979, Dr Rajni Kanabar pioneered a programme for helping underprivileged children with operable congenital heart defects travel overseas to receive treatment. Dr Kalam was deeply affected by the plight of these poor children, who would inevitably die without surgery. Dr Kalam felt moved by this non-resident Indian's love for his fellow citizens, and pledged to keep contact with Dr Kanabar.

President Kalam visited the archipelago of Zanzibar on 12 September 2004. In a pleasant surprise – further to the customary twenty-one-gun salute and an inspection of the guard – there were cultural troupes at the airport dancing to the rhythmic beat of their traditional musical instruments. The president was escorted by Zanzibar president Amani Abeid Karume, as they wended their way through the folk dancers and their lively accompaniment.

During the inaugural session of the Pan-African Parliament on 16 September 2004, President Kalam declared India's support to connect all the fifty-three nations of the African Union by a satellite and fibre-optic network. He stated that this would provide effective communication for tele-education, telemedicine, the Internet, videoconferencing (notably diplomatic communications and VOIP – voice over Internet Protocol – services) and also support e-governance, e-commerce, infotainment, resource mapping and meteorological services.

At the level of the African continent, the network would be made up of a hub earth station based in Dakar, Senegal. This would be linked via satellite with fifty-three VSAT stations installed in fifty-three national hospitals and VSAT stations likewise installed in fifty-three universities, facilitating telemedicine and tele-education services respectively. In India, the network would include one data centre in Delhi which would be linked to six Indian hospitals and six Indian universities to provide the network's services. India offered to fund the project with an estimated budget of USD 150 million and took up responsibility for capacity building through the education of doctors and nurses.

Then came Dr Kalam's cherished meeting with Nelson Mandela, whose peaceful liberation of his country had long been an inspiration to Dr Kalam. Dr Kalam would later recall their interaction:

> When I entered Nelson Mandela's house, I found him a bundle of cheerfulness. I was awed by the frail but towering stature of the man who had won freedom for South Africa from the tyranny of apartheid. When I was leaving his house he came to the portico to give me a send-off. While walking, he discarded his walking stick and I became his support.
>
> I asked him, 'Dr Mandela can you please tell me about the pioneers of the anti-apartheid movement in South Africa?' He responded spontaneously, 'Of course. One of the great pioneers of South Africa's freedom movement was M.K. Gandhi. India sent us a righteous barrister, M.K. Gandhi. We returned him to you as Mahatma Gandhi.'[10]

This visit provided answers to many spiritual questions that were concerning Dr Kalam particularly about the issue of landownership and the way it swayed the psyche of people across generations. Dr Kalam was intrigued by the great variations in the landscape and the differing contexts and conditions under which rural people live. During his visit to Africa he realized that Indians and South Africans share a common history of land dispossession and the manner in which European settlers accumulated capital and laid the foundations for their own well-being at the expense of the indigenous people.

Dr Kalam learned during this visit that the struggle to resist land dispossession and the systematic subjugation of indigenous people had been a long and bitter one. Africans fought fiercely to protect their land and defend their livelihoods and their way of life. Resistance took many forms, from outright war to events such as killing of cattle. Stories of the heroic struggles of indigenous people against colonial masters had been handed down from generation to generation.

Dr Kalam was more convinced than ever that land reforms must precede a meaningful development. After centuries of enforced cultivation through tenancy, the newly acquired ability to own land by a smallholder farmer becomes an existential issue. Indian farmers cling to their private ownership and bristle at all suggestions of land pooling or giving it away for development for any price whatsoever.

4.8
Creative Leaders

> The role of a creative leader is not to have all the ideas; it's to create a culture where everyone can have ideas and feel that they're valued.
>
> – Ken Robinson
> Author and educationist

In October 2004, as President Kalam's seventy-third birthday approached, another spiritual event was awaiting him. He received an invitation from Jagadguru Sri Shivarathri Deshikendra Mahaswamiji, the twenty-fourth Peethadheeshwara (pontiff) of Sri Suttur Math, in Mysore district, Karnataka. He was asked to attend the inauguration of a National Youth Conference, and he gladly accepted. The Suttur Math could be best described as an active ongoing movement to uphold the cause of social and economic justice, based on spiritual values and ideals.

Community life in India has always been closely linked with spiritual and religious institutions. Seers have been the beacon and guiding force for upholding moral values and for the progression of society as a whole. Adi Jagadguru Sri Shivarathreeshwara Shivayogi Mahaswamiji established the Suttur Veerasimhasana Math during the reign of the Chola dynasty in the eleventh century. When the twenty-third Peethadheeshwara Jagadguru Sri Shivaratri Rajendra Mahaswamiji came to Mysore in 1926 to pursue higher education, he observed that many rural students were in need of food and shelter.

He gave them shelter at his own place, and this marked the beginning of his offering education to poor students.

Later, Jagadguru Sri Shivarathri Rajendra Swamiji realized that instead of making students come to cities seeking education, it would be better to establish educational institutions in rural areas. To facilitate this, he started the Jagadguru Sri Shivarathreeshwara (JSS) Mahavidyapeetha in 1954. President Kalam lauded the JSS Mahavidyapeetha's comprehensive free educational programme:

> I find that the unique feature of JSS Mahavidyapeetha is that it caters to the educational needs of the people right from primary, secondary, graduate and postgraduate level including computer science, engineering and management. Also, a number of institutions have been created for providing vocational training to the needy students. Very few institutions in the country provide free education from class one to twelve, including boarding and lodging for large number of students. This is an important societal mission.[1]

On 18 November 2004, President Kalam inaugurated Nicholas Piramal's research and development centre in Mumbai. This venture came at a time when Indian pharmaceutical companies were increasingly looking to license their molecules to global drug companies. They were seeking to avoid the daunting expense of taking a drug through the process of testing and approval for the market. Chief Scientific Officer Dr Swati A. Piramal informed Dr Kalam that it takes about USD 1.7 billion to develop a drug.

President Kalam congratulated Dr Swati and her husband Ajay Piramal, the chairman of Nicholas Piramal India Ltd, for setting up the centre. Their undertaking would make it possible to locally pursue the research on a molecule and produce a viable drug for the Indian market, the prohibitive cost of developing a new drug notwithstanding. The benefit of value addition must not, Dr Kalam stressed, go to companies abroad. 'Molecule to drug is indeed the business of strong minds with the capacity to take calculated risks,' Dr Kalam told them and expressed his admiration for their bold step forward:

> On 1 January 2005, about forty-five days from now, the Indian pharmaceutical industry will face the challenge of demanding indigenous designs of drugs, which will have a profound impact on global competitiveness and business viability. As India comes into compliance with the TRIPS protocol mandated by the WTO, a new IPR regime will be enacted that will extend patent protection to new product inventions. The new product patent regime will affect a sea change in the way Indian pharmaceutical companies think and do business. I am happy to know that this centre is working on the concept of 'molecule to drug' as its mission, instead of selling the molecules to companies abroad.[2]

On 14 December 2004, President Kalam visited the Institute of Rural Management, Anand (IRMA) in Gujarat. The president cited the example of the Anand Milk Federation Union Limited (Amul) milk cooperative movement and the historical role played by the National Dairy Development Board (NDDB) in transforming the lives of villagers living in this region. The Amul programme had substantially benefitted in excess of one crore farmer members and resulted in self-sufficiency of milk and milk products in the country. Dr Kalam saw the Amul indigenous model for self-empowerment of farmers as part of a broader agenda for overcoming poverty and fostering development:

> The injustice that we have to fight today according to me is the societal and economic impoverishment and inequality in various aspects of life for a large number of people. India's movement in removing this impoverished state will become a trendsetter for the whole planet as in the past. When India got its freedom in 1947, many nations in Asia and Africa were inspired to fight for freedom and realize freedom for their nations. Hence the overwhelming question which I would like to reflect today is that – when will India become a developed nation? And show the way to the other developing nations. Will history repeat itself?[3]

Dr Kalam shared a deep bond with Dr Verghese Kurien, the founding chairman of the Gujarat Cooperative Milk Marketing Federation (GCMMF). Dr Kurien transformed India from a milk-deficient nation to the world's largest milk producer, surpassing the United States of America in 1998. Dr Kurien demonstrated that the generation of rural non-farm opportunities, along with the application of technology, can alone solve the problems of unemployment and inequality in India. Amul has grown into a 2.5-billion-dollar cooperative and Asia's top milk-producing brand. It is counted among the world's leading brands in any sector with one of the best recall values. Dr Kalam later likened his brilliance in using his expertise for the upliftment of the rural poor to the visionary influence of Gandhi:

> Kurien was ten years older than me. Born in Kozhikode, Kerala, he was a mechanical engineer with specialization in dairy engineering. He came to Anand in 1949 at the behest of the then Union Home Minister, Sardar Vallabhbhai Patel (1875–1950), to solve some problems of local farmers. He resolved the problems quickly and efficiently but never left Anand thereafter and lived a full life there.
>
> The story of Verghese Kurien has a common theme with Mahatma Gandhi, of using the educated mind and exposure to modern methods for the empowerment and sustenance of village people. Mahatma Gandhi – using his experience in law and familiarity with the ways of urban people – ignited the minds of Indian peasants and ordinary people with the aspiration to live in an independent country. Verghese Kurien developed a model of business where villagers were the producers; and their products, which they owned, were sold to urban dwellers, using the tools of a typically urban-centric business. He gave milk producers the control of procurement, processing and marketing and hired professional managers to do the business work. He turned the tables on multinational dairy companies and made economies of scale work for poor milk producers.[4]

The National Institute of Occupational Health (NIOH) of the Indian Council of Medical Research (ICMR) and the Nirma University of Science and Technology jointly hosted the ninety-second session of the Indian Science Congress at the picturesque campus of the Nirma University, Ahmedabad. The focal theme of 2005 was 'Health Technology as a Fulcrum of Development for the Nation'.

President Kalam addressed the Science Congress on 5 January 2005, and used the forum to highlight the role of political leadership in ensuring that the benefit of technology reaches the poor people. He firmly stated that we need science with a human face. There are about 5.8 lakh villages in the country, and most of them lack basic facilities. Therefore we need technologies, which are not only useful but are also affordable, so that a large number of people can benefit. Political will is necessary to create ecosystems connecting industry, universities, research institutes, professional associations, financial institutions and government. Dr Kalam demonstrated the power of indigenous technology in the missile programme and was strong in his conviction that health care costs could be halved if indigenous products are supported and promoted in this sector. He was adamant, though, that scientific advancement in health care required the sponsorship of politicians: 'Science has to be promoted through political systems. It is essential that technologies that give immediate benefits to the people directly or indirectly should be successfully put forward.'[5]

What he did not say but expressed fulsomely to me was his concern regarding the vice-like grip of multinational corporations over the burgeoning Indian market for medical devices and consumables. The initiatives he took part in ten years earlier through the Society for Biomedical Technology (SBMT) had all petered out. There was no visible effort anywhere to develop indigenous devices, and Dr Kalam was quite despondent that people were barely even talking about the issue.

Our president, though, was congenitally positive, and this reflected in his speeches. On the eve of the Republic Day, 25 January 2005, President Kalam started on a philosophical note in his address to the nation. He said, 'Everyone has inside of him or her, a piece of good news. The good news is, that you don't know how great you can be!' He balanced his innate optimism, however, with a realistic concern for the future of the nation's youth:

> I have met more than six hundred thousand children from all parts of our country, after becoming the president. During my interaction

> with them, they posed a series of questions, with affection. They asked: 'Mr President, you saw us smile, when we were five years old. We smiled because we were blossoming innocently. When we came to our teens, smiles slowly faded away and the signs of concern appeared. You said that it is because of our anxiety about our future. This anxiety almost took away our smiles. When we complete our education, the upmost questions in our minds were, what would I do after my education? Will I get employment? Our parents, who have spent all their savings on our education, also share the same concern. Mr President, will I get proper employment and be able to contribute to India, to make it a developed nation?' Their questions really made me think and think.[6]

President Kalam identified agriculture, education, health care, water and energy as the most important sectors for sustainable national development. Emphasizing PURA once again, he said: 'One of the ways by which rural agriculturists could increase their earnings is by value adding to the agricultural produce through processing and manufacturing. Farmers, either individually or through their cooperatives, would market processed and value-added items instead of marketing raw materials. This increase in value-addition taking place in rural areas itself is an indicator of society moving towards prosperity and a knowledge era.'

The Pune Institute of Engineering and Technology (PIET), formerly known as the Government College of Engineering, Pune (COEP), celebrated its sesquicentenary (150th anniversary) in 2005. President Kalam visited PIET on 1 February 2005. He addressed a large gathering and interacted with eminent alumni. A commemorative postage stamp was released to mark the historic occasion. The college's study model referred to in the early 1950s as the 'Poona Model' had been highly respected by industry and public utilities. Dr Kalam used this occasion to inaugurate his concept of creative leadership:

> One of the very important ingredients for success of the vision of transforming India into a developed nation by 2020 is the evolution of creative leaders. I am giving a connection between developed

> India, economic prosperity, technology, production, productivity, employee roles and management quality, all of which are linked to the creative leader. Who is that creative leader? What are the qualities of a creative leader? The creative leadership is exercising the task to change the traditional role from commander to coach, manager to mentor, from director to delegator and from one who demands respect to one who facilitates self-respect. The higher the proportion of creative leaders in a nation, the higher the potential of success of visions like developed India.[7]

On the same day, President Kalam visited another great institution: Gokhale Institute of Politics and Economics (GIPE). His schedule was punishing, but he never once resiled from his duty. On the contrary, he seemed to relish opportunities to talk to evermore people from all walks of life. At any rate, this engagement was particularly dear to his heart, as the history of GIPE had been closely linked with the history of the nationalist movement in India. The institute was located within the premises of the Servants of India Society, established in 1906 by the nationalist leader Gopal Krishna Gokhale, whom Mahatma Gandhi regarded as his political guru. The institute was established in 1930, and under its first director, Prof. D.R. Gadgil, it emerged as a major think tank on policy issues soon after Independence in 1947.

President Kalam spent some time in the library founded in 1905. The library is one of the foremost among specialized libraries in India in the field of economics and other social sciences. It is also the Indian depository library for all UN publications, as well as publications of other leading international development and financial organizations. Dr Kalam was captivated upon discovering the library's complete collection of all Indian parliamentary and legislative assemblies' records from 1924 onwards. Dr Kalam was told that Prof. Gunnar Myrdal actually spent considerable time at Gokhale Institute while he was working on his seminal work *Asian Drama: An Inquiry into the Poverty of Nations*. Dr Kalam was aware that Gunnar Myrdal's scientific influence was not limited to economics. He had earlier read the introduction in *Asian Drama* with the title 'The Beam in Our Eyes', a biblical expression. Myrdal indeed integrated social science, political science and economics as one practice, something that Dr Kalam was attempting in his own way. Dr Kalam spoke of the broad concerns of humanity, and like Gunnar Myrdal, he was visionary with his analysis and suggestions:

> There are many challenges in our planet earth of six billion people. There is shortage of water, increased atmospheric pollution leading to many diseases, depleting fossil materials and other natural resources, depletion of available land for agriculture and lack of availability of uniform opportunity to all citizens. Many nations are experiencing the problems of injected terrorism ... We have seen that the economic prosperity of a few nations alone has not brought lasting peace to the world. No single nation will be able to handle the situation by itself. Humanity will require mega missions for harnessing solar energy, drinking water from seawater through desalination processes and bringing minerals from other planets and also to bring space-manufactured products. In such a situation, the present reasons for conflict between nations will become insignificant and unwarranted. India can play a major role in developing a new model of an enlightened citizen–centric society, which will provide prosperity, peace and happiness to all the nations in the world.[8]

Despite the heaviness of many of the profound topics he discussed, our president always remained entertaining. The audience erupted when Dr Kalam said, 'Politics without nobility is similar to a balloon without air.' Unsurprisingly, he was given a standing ovation. Here was a head of state who would happily lampoon his own class – and he was sincere about it.

He was, though, nothing if not practical, and this was reflected in his next engagement's subject matter. On 24 February 2004, President Kalam gave away the first Nirmal Gram Puraskar (NGP) awards to selected Panchayati Raj Institutions (PRIs) functionaries in recognition of their outstanding efforts to eliminate the practice of open defecation in their respective panchayats. Forty PRIs from six states – Tamil Nadu, Maharashtra, West Bengal, Tripura, Kerala and Gujarat – were given Rs 130 lakh as cash awards. Dr Kalam outlined the scale and gravity of the issue:

> As per the 2001 Census, there are nearly 200 million dwelling units in the country of which nearly 140 million are in the rural areas. The sanitation facility is available only in nearly forty million dwelling units. Hence, there is an urgent need to provide sanitation facilities to over one hundred million dwelling units in rural areas. The lack of sanitation facilities is the greatest health hazard for our rural population. Waterborne diseases, hepatitis, leprosy, tuberculosis, etc., can all be attributed to non-availability of proper sanitation facilities. Hence, to improve the health condition of our rural population, it is essential to hasten up the process of providing sanitation facilities to all dwelling units, schools, hospitals and community halls in the rural areas.[9]

Dr Kalam's vision for rural areas was all-encompassing, and he felt that technology would be required to help feed our ever-expanding population. One early exponent of agricultural science, and truly an unsung hero for his work in using science to feed the world, was Dr Norman Borlaug. On 15 March 2005, President Kalam was delighted to present to Nobel laureate Dr Norman Borlaug, the first M.S. Swaminathan Award for Leadership in Agriculture, in a function organized by the Trust for Advancement of Agricultural Sciences (TAAS).

Dr Borlaug was ninety-one at that time, and sat amidst all the praise showered on him from those gathered there. When his turn came, he stood and highlighted India's advancement in agricultural science and production. He said that the political visionaries C. Subramaniam and Dr M.S. Swaminathan, pioneers in agricultural science, were the prime architects of the first green revolution in India. Even though Dr Norman Borlaug was himself a partner in the first green revolution, he did not make a point of this. He recalled with pride Dr Verghese Kurien, who ushered in the 'white revolution', drastically improving production and sales of milk products in India.

Then the surprise came. Dr Borlaug turned to scientists sitting in the third row, fifth row and eighth row of the audience. He identified Dr Raja Ram, a wheat specialist, Dr S.K. Vasal, a maize specialist, and Dr B.R. Barwale, a seed specialist. Dr Borlaug said that these scientists had contributed greatly to India's and Asia's green revolution. Dr Borlaug introduced them to the audience by asking them to stand, ensuring that the audience cheered and greeted them with great enthusiasm. Such a scene, Dr Kalam later said in his speech, he had not witnessed before in India. He referred to Dr Borlaug's acknowledgement of his colleagues as 'scientific magnanimity', and proceeded to laud Dr Borlaug's achievements:

> Very rarely in our planet, one single individual – particularly a scientist – makes the difference in multi-continents almost simultaneously. Dr Norman Borlaug is indeed the main architect of food production in many parts of the world through scientific work. The chairperson of the Nobel Committee for the Nobel Peace Prize 1970, had said, 'more than any other single person of this age, Dr Norman Borlaug has helped to provide bread for a hungry world'. Enhancement of food production will certainly result in world peace.[10]

Dr Kalam used this occasion to air his views to the esteemed scientific gathering on the still-unresolved debate on agricultural biotechnology. Dr Kalam suggested that effective communication focused on the current and potential benefits of agricultural biotechnology was essential if society has to benefit from these scientific advances. Sound science and regulatory review are only part of the process. Policymakers must also consider the political, social, ethical and economic dimensions of the debate on agricultural biotechnology. In any event, Dr Kalam was clear about the dire consequences of completely shunning agricultural biotechnology: 'According to Dr Borlaug, failure to use biotechnology for increasing food production could mean destruction of remaining forest area for crop cultivation, as the demand for more food is constantly rising. Biotechnology would facilitate increased crop production from existing croplands.'[11]

On 19 April 2005, President Pervez Musharraf visited India. A visit by the president of Pakistan is always a significant event in the country, and President Musharraf's infamy only added to the pandemonium in media and government circles. Everybody was wondering what President Kalam would tell General Musharraf, who was more known in India as the villain of the Kargil war than for anything else. But Dr Kalam surprised everyone by engaging President Musharraf with a thirty-minute presentation on rural development. He said, 'Mr President, like India you also have a lot of rural areas and don't you think we should both do whatever is possible to develop them on priority?'

General Musharraf was attentive throughout Dr Kalam's presentation and afterwards said, 'Thank you, Mr President. India is lucky to have a scientist president like you.' Dr Kalam introduced me to brief President Musharraf about the work we had been doing on making health care affordable by developing indigenous medical devices and consumables. President Musharraf held my hand for a long time and invited me to come to Pakistan and set up a modern hospital. I felt, though, that the offer had evaporated by the end of lunch.

President Kalam left on 22 May 2005 to Moscow on the first leg of his four-nation tour of Russia, Switzerland, Iceland and Ukraine. He would be the first Indian president to visit Russia after the disintegration of the Soviet Union in 1991. During his four-day stay in Russia, he would have the opportunity to meet many of his old-time friends from his missile development days. But there was something else in store for him; and it was a development that would put him at the centre of a big political storm.

Part Five

DISPERSION

When I stand before God at the end of my life, I would hope that I would not have a single bit of talent left, and could say, "I used everything you gave me".

– Erma Bombeck
American writer

5.1

Determination Is Power

All things are subject to interpretation. Whichever interpretation prevails at a given time is a function of power and not truth.

– Friedrich Nietzsche
Nineteenth-century German philosopher

The midnight proclamation issued by President Kalam from Moscow under Article 356 of the Constitution dissolving the Bihar assembly sent tremors across the nation. It also raised significant questions, not the least of which was whether the exercise of this power by the Union government was bona fide.

This was to become an issue of contention that would simmer over the following months, adding to the political uncertainty that had prevailed in Bihar after the hung assembly earlier in the year. Elections to constitute the new legislative assembly of Bihar were concluded in February 2005. No party or combination of parties was able to secure a majority. Governor Buta Singh explored all possibilities of government formation, but reaching the point where it was clear that no party or coalition of parties was able to form a stable government, he recommended the imposition of President's Rule in the state. The assembly was thus put in suspended animation. The cabinet, in its meeting held on 7 March 2005, recommended the same to President Kalam, and he signed the proclamation under Article 356 of the

Constitution the same day. Both houses of parliament later approved the proclamation.

The governor in May 2005 sent a report to the president recommending dissolution of the Bihar assembly. The report stated that he should do so in view of the allurements being made by the Janata Dal (United) (JD[U]) leadership to the Lok Janshakti Party's (LJP's) MLAs to form a breakaway faction. In offering allurements, the Janata Dal (United) leadership had hoped the MLAs would join hands with their party so that they could cobble together a majority, and thereby stake a claim to form the government in the state. The governor took the view that such undue influence over the MLAs would distort the will of the people. He felt that the house – in its state of suspended animation – should be dissolved to provide the people of Bihar with a fresh opportunity to exercise their mandate.

In its meeting late on 22 May 2005, the Union cabinet endorsed the assessment of the governor and recommended to the president the issue of a presidential order for dissolution of the Bihar assembly. By this time, President Kalam had already left for Moscow. Prime Minister Manmohan Singh spoke to President Kalam after he landed in Moscow and checked into the hotel. P.M. Nair would later recall Dr Kalam's concern over this serious matter:

> He was in his blue shirt and the characteristic smile, though the brow was more furrowed than normally. 'I had a call from the PM ... He spoke to me for about twenty minutes. This was about dissolution of the assembly of Bihar. The governor has sent a report about horse-trading going on, and the only way to save democracy is to dissolve the assembly. The Cabinet has considered the governor's report and the recommendation is coming to me to dissolve the assembly.'[1]

Notwithstanding the merit of Governor Buta Singh's allegations of horse-trading, the president of India is constitutionally bound to act on the aid and advice of the council of ministers. There were the reports of the governor, the recommendation of the council of ministers – and the twenty-minute call of the prime minister – advising the president. President Kalam was therefore duty-bound to dissolve the Bihar

Assembly, and he did so. It was now for the Election Commission to hold polls in Bihar, which it did in October–November 2005.

Dr Kalam had been a regular visitor to Moscow. The sight of the great River Moskva and St Basil's Cathedral, with its fairy-tale coloured domes, entranced him. He also appreciated its homage to nature. With over 40 per cent of its environs covered by greenery, Moscow is one of the more attractive capitals and major cities in the world, and it boasts the largest forest in an urban area.

In Russia, President Kalam held detailed discussions with the president of the Russian Federation, Mr Vladimir Putin. He also met the prime minister of the Russian Federation, Mr Mikhail Fradkov, and visited the Speaker of the Duma, Mr Boris Gryzlov.

In Moscow, Dr Kalam visited the Academy of Sciences, Moscow State University, Sukhoi Design Bureau, and NPO Mashinostroyenia, the joint-venture partner in BrahMos Aerospace Company. Rather than a protocol-bound presidential visit, it was more of an old alumni reunion. Dr Kalam had been a great admirer of Russian technology and scientific power, and found the Russian scientists and engineers thorough in their fields and trustworthy in sharing information. NPO Mashinostroyenia not only shared their ramjet engine technology openly, but also were most accommodating with inertial navigation, mission software and mobile launchers for Prithvi and Agni missiles for cruise missile applications.

On 25 May 2005 Dr Kalam went to St Petersburg, the second-largest city in Russia, located on the River Neva at the head of the Gulf of Finland on the Baltic Sea. In 1914, the name of the city was changed from St Petersburg to Petrograd and later after World War I to Leningrad; and in 1991, back to St Petersburg. The sentiment of the Russian people for their traditions seems to have persisted – as such sentiments have likewise done in India – despite changes of government and fortune. President Kalam met the governor of St Petersburg, Madam Valentina Matvienko, and visited the Laser Technology Institute and Arctic and Antarctica Research Institute.

From St Petersburg, President Kalam went to Switzerland. It was the first visit there by an Indian president in over three decades. As had been the trend during this three-day visit to Russia, the focus of Dr Kalam's sojourn here remained on science and technology. Dr Anil Kakodar, chairman of India's Atomic Energy Commission, joined him here and together they visited the European Organization for Nuclear Research (CERN).

Switzerland declared 26 May as Science Day in honour of the president and to commemorate his visit. The visit to CERN assumes significance in light of New Delhi's quest for access to nuclear technology and its plans for cooperation with one of the most advanced laboratories in the world.

President Kalam arrived in Keflavik on 29 May 2005 on his visit to Iceland, an island country between the North Atlantic Ocean and the Greenland Sea. With fewer than 400,000 people living in an area of 54,000 square kilometres, Iceland is the most sparsely populated country in Europe. Notwithstanding its isolation and its stark, frigid landscapes, Iceland has made great progress in developing green energy systems, and this would be the focus of President Kalam's visit.

Dr Kalam had talks with President Ólafur Ragnar Grímsson in Bessastaðir. Both the presidents attended a conference, 'Synergies and Strengths of East and West', hosted by the Icelandic Indian Chamber of Commerce. The key for them was the integration of Indian business initiatives, with a particular focus on pharmaceuticals and technology. Dr Kalam visited the University of Iceland and held discussions on warning and early information systems for earthquakes and other geo-hazards with Professor Páll Skúlason, rector of the university, Dr Magnús Jónsson, director of the Icelandic Meteorological Office, Dr Ragnar Stefánsson, head of the Icelandic Meteorological Office and Dr Steinunn Jakobsdóttir, head of the Geophysical Monitoring Section. He also visited the National Rescue Centre (Skógarhlíð).

The next day, 31 May 2005, accompanied by Prime Minister Halldór Ásgrímsson, Dr Kalam went to see Nesjavellir Geothermal Power Plant. Dr Kalam had a long discussion with Dr Guðmundur Þóroddsson, CEO, Reykjavík Energy, and Dr Alfreð Þorsteinsson, chairman of the board, Reykjavík Energy, to gauge the potential for

India to use this great green energy technology. In an interesting observation, President Kalam noticed a considerable number of women of Indian origin married to Icelandic men.

President Kalam arrived at Kiev, the capital of Ukraine on 1 June 2005. President Viktor Yushchenko received him. India has had a special relationship with Ukraine, even when it was a part of the Soviet Union. Many distinguished missile scientists of the USSR who helped Indian scientists were from Ukraine.

On 3 June, Dr Kalam travelled to Dnipropetrovsk, 500 kilometres from Kiev to visit the Yuzhnoye SDO, a facility engaged in the manufacture of space rockets. Yuzhnoye was established in 1954. It shot to prominence after the development of a missile based on radically new technologies of hypergolic propellant components and the use of a self-contained guidance and control system. Yuzhnoye SDO was one of the first companies in the aerospace industry to set up a Telemetry Data Processing Centre to carry out flight tests of strategic missiles and launch vehicles. After the break-up of the USSR and the declaration of the denuclearized status of Ukraine, the facility was assigned to a new programme of missile development, including an anti-aircraft missile defence system and airborne, seaborne, sea-based and surface-deployed missile systems.

The facility was also engaged in the development of various liquid-propellants for space rockets. Additionally, it has the distinction of pioneering a mechanism to facilitate the remediation of technical deficiencies while carrying out flight tests of strategic missiles and launch vehicles. The company, where 50,000 scientists and experts were employed, was working at that time on the Okean-O oceanographic satellite, Koronas-Fsolar observation satellite, Zenit 3SL three-stage launcher for sea launch projects and the Dnepr launch vehicle. Dr Kalam took the opportunity to engage with the scientists on their projects. The 'missile man' was indeed on his home turf. He seems also to have made a favourable impact on President Yushchenko, if his farewell was any guide:

> I developed an instant rapport with President Yushchenko, who survived an assassination attempt by poisoning. Dioxin, a lethal

> chemical and a contaminant in Agent Orange TCDD, was added to his food. He survived but suffered disfigurement as a result of the poisoning. While seeing me off at Kiev Airport, President Yushchenko asked me if he could touch me. We had a warm hug and I wished him good health and peace for his people.[2]

The first important event for Dr Kalam back in India was the governors' conference on 14 June 2005. The earlier governor's conference in 2003 was conducted against the backdrop of Prime Minister Vajpayee's commitment to ensure that India became a developed nation by 2020. The prime minister had outlined this in his Independence Day address from the Red Fort in 2002, immediately after President Kalam took over the presidency. Dr Kalam had no doubts about Prime Minister Vajpayee's sincerity in pursuing Vision 2020:

> The impressive speeches at conferences get forgotten. However, I placed great value on what was said, and continue to remember a serious commitment to faster development. Vajpayee stated that every part of the administrative system must recognize the need for development and further this cause, which would enable an earlier realization of our goals. This was something I could appreciate, having seen the difficulties that arise in motivating different departments to work for a combined purpose.[3]

Prime Minister Manmohan Singh attended the conference with all his cabinet members and held detailed discussions on the issues of education, terrorism, disaster management and the implementation of value-added taxation, based on the agenda structured by President Kalam's office. Dr Kalam later recalled that the prime minister gave his assurance that he and his colleagues would also make every effort for Vision 2020, guided by the inspiration provided by the president:'The prime minister announced at a governors' conference that the government would do everything to make "Vision India 2020" a reality. No political system can survive without a vision for the nation.'[4]

For his part, Prime Minister Manmohan Singh was a firm believer in the idea of the 'Indian century'. In 1991, when Dr Singh became the finance minister in the government of Prime Minister P.V. Narasimha Rao, India was on the brink of bankruptcy. Its fiscal deficit was close to 8.5 per cent of the gross domestic product; the balance of payments deficit was huge, with foreign exchange reserves of barely a billion dollars left in the treasury. In his maiden speech as finance minister, Singh had quoted nineteenth-century French writer Victor Hugo: 'No power on earth can stop an idea whose time has come.'

Dr Kalam had been a great admirer of Dr Singh and in particular how he had unshackled the country from the bureaucratic controls and the licence–permit raj. He had taken the economy to a high growth path of 6–7 per cent during his five-year stint as finance minister of India. Of course, Dr Singh had as many critics as admirers. Dr Singh had submitted his resignation thrice during his five-year tenure; but Prime Minister Narasimha Rao had not allowed him to quit.

The reforms introduced by Dr Singh had indeed provided the momentum to Dr Kalam's idea of Vision 2020 and as a result of the real progress achieved, it had reached a point of no return. India had to be strong and compete globally. Dr Kalam knew that the new order of a globalized world ushered in through the late 1990s would favour the strong and hurt the weak. India needed to strengthen its capabilities to withstand the forces of globalization. The international system of pricing fuel, rates of currency conversion cost of capital, global movement of commodities and pressures exerted through trade and environmental regulations were realities that the nation would have to contend with. 'The threat to our independence was never graver,' he later said.[5]

Dr Kalam had always been a strong believer in energy independence. Achieving energy independence is an immense technological challenge for the country. Energy independence has to be achieved through three different sources: renewable energy (solar, wind and hydropower), electrical power from nuclear energy and biofuels for transportation. Dr Kalam called nuclear energy an inevitable option, and the current capacity of generating a mere 4,000 MW grossly underutilized the great strengths of a world-class Indian nuclear establishment. The main issue here was the lack of availability of uranium.

In response to the Indian nuclear test in May 1974, the United States pressed for the creation of an informal group, the Nuclear Suppliers Group (NSG), to control exports of nuclear materials, equipment and technology. A series of meetings in London from 1975 to 1978 resulted in agreements on the guidelines for export of uranium. Initially, the NSG had seven participating countries: Canada, West Germany, France, Japan, the Soviet Union, the United Kingdom and the United States, but the participation was later expanded to fifteen countries in 1977. India's reserves of uranium represent only 1 per cent of the world's known uranium deposits; the NSG's uranium export restrictions fell squarely on Indian nuclear power generation capacity.

The importance of nuclear energy as a sustainable energy resource for our country was recognized at the very inception of the Indian atomic energy programme. Dr Homi Bhabha had chalked out a three-stage nuclear power programme, based on a closed nuclear fuel cycle. The three stages are natural uranium-fuelled pressurized heavy water reactors, fast breeder reactors and thorium-based reactors. India had reached the second stage, but progress had been impeded by a paucity of uranium. Dr Kalam visualized nuclear energy capacity rising to 20,000 MW by the year 2020 and found a great collaborator in Prime Minister Singh. The prime minister took the bold step of engaging the United States to break the uranium jinx.

5.2

Lend Me Your Ears

> The country that owns green, that dominates that industry, is going to have the most energy security, national security, economic security, competitive companies, healthy population and, most of all, global respect.
>
> – Thomas Friedman
> American journalist and author

Friends, leaders, countrymen, lend me your ears; I come to speak to you of truth, not to merely talk for your applause! President Kalam's tone and substance was gradually changing from suggestion to recommendation, from appeal to exhortation, and from enthusiasm to scepticism. In August 2005, he raised two important issues that were not getting a much-needed response in spite of his consistent appeal and persuasion.

He met the best of the Indian medical fraternity on 1 July 2005 to confer the prestigious Dr B.C. Roy National Awards for 2003 and 2004 on thirty-five doctors at a glittering ceremony at Rashtrapati Bhavan's Ashok Hall. This day has been celebrated in India as the National Doctors' Day in honour of Dr Bidhan Chandra Roy, who was born and departed on this day. Dr B.C. Roy was the chief minister of West Bengal for fourteen years, from 1948 until his death in 1962. A Karmayogi, Dr Roy continued his medical practice even as chief minister; he saw patients until his last day, and died in office.

Dr B.C. Roy is considered the architect of modern West Bengal. He passionately worked to establish five important cities – Durgapur, Kalyani, Bidhannagar, Ashoknagar, and Howrah – and transformed Bengal from a rural to urban society. Dr B.C. Roy was not only the first Indian president of the Medical Council of India, he was the guiding force and inspiring spirit for the Medical Council throughout his life. He was awarded the Bharat Ratna in 1961.

Corruption in the medical profession had become a public issue by 2005, and the Indian Medical Council itself was mired in controversy. President Kalam used this occasion to remind doctors that righteousness is an essential virtue in the medical profession. He touched upon a crucial point that righteousness is cultivated from childhood – and it starts with the family. Dr Kalam declared, 'Righteousness is important in whatever we do, be it social life or politics. Virtue is an integral part of making a strong family, nation and world. It is important that we build a strong foundation to work upon.'

With the opening up of 'five-star hospitals' across the country and high-cost equipment taking pride of place rather than the doctors themselves, Dr Kalam mounted a passionate argument for inclusive medicine:

> The poorest of the poor have as much right as anyone to less pain after surgery, reduced medication, less morbidity, shorter hospitalization and an early return to home, family and work. Minimal access surgery (is not) homage or a tribute to new technology, but the manifold benefits it gives to our patients and our people.[1]

Dr Kalam said that advances in medicine must reach the poor and not remain confined to expensive hospitals dedicated to serving rich patients.

The following week, President Kalam participated in the golden jubilee celebrations of Jadavpur University, Kolkata. The university had conferred upon him an honorary doctorate in 1990. Dr Kalam had worked extensively with Prof. Tapan Kumar Ghoshal in the areas of control and guidance of missiles and aspects of the Light Combat

Aircraft project. During his numerous visits to the university in the 1990s, it had become his second home.

Dr S.K. Chaudhuri, an alumnus of Jadavpur University, who would later become the director, Research Centre Imarat, ensured great collaboration between laboratories and academic institutions. Dr Chaudhuri also developed a strong emotional bond with Dr Kalam. While working on his speech, Dr Kalam asked Dr Chaudhuri to tell him 'one unique thing' about Jadavpur University.

Dr Chaudhuri waxed lyrical about the history of Jadavpur University being a true reflection of the evolution of scientific thought in India. It was here that education was honed as a tool to challenge the hegemony of the British establishment. The institution itself emerged out of the yearning of enlightened citizens of Bengal for scientific education for youth. Raja Subodh Chandra Mullick and Sir Rashbehari Ghosh gave away their personal wealth to create the institution. In 1910, the Society for the Promotion of Technical Education in Bengal institutionalized engineering and scientific education in Bengal, and by 1940 it was virtually functioning as a university. After Independence, it was bestowed the statutory recognition and identity of Jadavpur University in 1955. 'Wealth should never separate itself from education,' said Dr Kalam after hearing this story.

Governor of West Bengal, Gopalkrishna Gandhi, who was also chancellor of the Jadavpur University, welcomed President Kalam at the open-air theatre on the main campus of the university, which had been aesthetically decorated with fresh white flowers, a speciality of Bengali culture. Dr Kalam used this occasion to emphasize the role of education in empowerment:

> Education is not merely a tool for development of individuals. It must include the interests of the community and the aspects of nation building. Good education is indeed the foundation for our future. It is empowerment to make choices and emboldens the youth to choose and chase their dreams which must be taken up by the universities.
>
> When the child is empowered by the parents, at various phases of growth, the child transforms into a responsible citizen. When the

> teacher is empowered with knowledge and experience, good young human beings with value systems take shape. When an individual or a team is empowered with technology, transformation to higher potential for achievement is assured. When the leader of any institution empowers his or her people, leaders are born who can change the nation in multiple areas. When women are empowered, a society with stability is assured. When the political leaders of the nation empower the people through visionary policies, the prosperity of the nation is certain.[2]

President Kalam used the opportunity of the customary address to the nation on the eve of Independence Day to air before the people of India his forthright views on India's energy independence. He felt that despite his championing of the issue, common-sense approaches to India's energy issues were not being translated into policies and projects. He thought it best to bring this issue – which had otherwise become shrouded in technical jargon – to general public awareness. In his nationally televised address on 14 August 2005, President Kalam exhorted the country to become alert to the need for energy independence. It was a message of patriotism and empowerment he had been advocating, in various forms, for several decades.

Pointing out the unfortunate reality of India having 17 per cent of the world's population and only 0.8 per cent of the world's known oil and natural gas resources, Dr Kalam drew the nation's attention to the yawning gap between demand and supply of resources. He declared that the exigencies of energy and water would surely be a defining characteristic of our people's lives in the twenty-first century.

Why should energy independence not be our nation's first and highest priority? Dr Kalam called for a comprehensive renewable energy policy within one year. India has knowledge and natural resources, and all that was needed was planned integrated missions to achieve the goal, he said. President Kalam chose not to talk about any political, constitutional or economic issues facing the nation. For him, the nation's long-term energy quandary far surpassed any ephemeral issues in importance, even though its more serious consequences were not yet apparent.

In the immediate future, Dr Kalam felt that uranium-based nuclear energy was vital for sustaining the nation. Dr Kalam was aware that Prime Minister Manmohan Singh had made significant progress in assuaging the United States' concerns about its civilian nuclear programme, and a treaty was imminent in this regard. Dr Kalam pointed out that there would have to be a tenfold increase in nuclear power generation in order to achieve a reasonable degree of energy self-sufficiency.

Dr Kalam rationally argued for the development of nuclear power using thorium, as the nation has considerable reserves of this key resource. This was a key for energy self-sufficiency that had been proposed by Dr Homi Bhabha nearly half a century earlier. Crucially, thorium is not subject to the same international qualms about weapons proliferation that have hampered our uranium-based nuclear power regime. Moreover, Dr Kalam said, nuclear fusion research needs to be undertaken as an internationally cooperative mission, with the intent of developing the technology for this clean nuclear energy. Fusion could cater for a soaring population's energy needs when fossil fuels are depleted.

President Kalam concluded:

> We need to evolve a comprehensive renewable energy policy for energy independence within a year. By 2020, India should achieve comprehensive energy security and by 2030 there should be energy independence. This should address all issues relating to the generation of energy through wind, solar, geothermal, biomass and the ocean. The nation should also work towards establishment of thorium-based reactors. Research and technology development of thorium-based reactors is one of the immediate requirements for realizing self-reliance in nuclear power generation and long-term energy security for the nation.

Dr Kalam went to the north-east in September 2005. He had started his presidency with a resolve to connect with the people here, and had already visited Assam, Tripura, Manipur, Arunachal Pradesh, Meghalaya and Nagaland. It took a while for him to visit Mizoram and Sikkim to complete his connection with the contiguous parivar of seven sisters (Arunachal Pradesh, Assam, Meghalaya, Manipur, Mizoram, Nagaland and Tripura) and one brother (Sikkim).

The newspaper headlines proclaimed that it was not just the children, but even the weather seemed to be with President Kalam in Sikkim. He had gone there on a short two-day visit. Having rained incessantly for the previous two days, the skies cleared up just before the president landed at the Libing helipad on 22 September 2005. Governor V. Rama Rao and Chief Minister Pawan Kumar Chamling, along with his entire cabinet, received President Kalam on his first visit to the state. Dr Kalam developed an instant rapport with Chamling, the founder president of the Sikkim Democratic Front, which had governed the state since 1994. On the way to the capital, people gathered behind barricades on both sides of the heavily guarded highway to greet the presidential cavalcade, something not normally seen elsewhere. The president's overtures to the north-east had been noted, and the friendly people of this region were showing their appreciation. Gangtok city wore a festive look, with tricolours and flowers aplenty decorating its streets.

Sikkim had historically been the point where ancient Indian and Tibetan cultures met. A Buddhist kingdom was established in the seventeenth century here. Sikkim emerged as a polity in its own right against a backdrop of people coming from Tibet and Bhutan and settling here. Sikkim fell under British suzerainty quite early when the British East India Company sought access to the Tibetan market. After the British departed in 1947, Sikkim initially remained an independent country but merged into the Union of India in 1975.

President Kalam struck a chord with the children of Sir Tashi Namgyal Senior Secondary School immediately. 'I saw the beautiful rivers and mountain peaks from the helicopter, but what I saw in abundance were the smiles of the people of the state,' he said. In the afternoon, Dr Kalam addressed a special session of the Sikkim legislative assembly and made a presentation, 'Sikkim: Missions for Prosperity', before the members of the House.

In a big event in the evening, Dr Kalam inaugurated the 25,000-

seat Palzor Stadium. Football star Bhaichung Bhutia, a youth icon of Sikkim, sat by President Kalam's side for the duration of the engagement. The huge gathering sat in rapt attention throughout Dr Kalam's more-than-one-hour speech and cheered him with verve. As Dr Kalam's time in office progressed, an almost mystical resonance between this extraordinary president and the people was becoming apparent. Wherever his duties were taking him, a vibrant atmosphere of engagement would prevail. Stiffly formal events would take on more the ambience of a musical gala evening, with Dr Kalam the genial star signing autographs.

Such widespread adoration for a national leader had rarely been witnessed since Gandhi's time. His exploits in aerospace and in bringing the country into the 'nuclear club' were legendary. That he was accomplished outside the world of politics was beyond question, as was his patent sense of ethics. But his appeal was more than simple respect. India's people – noted equally for their sentimentality and ability to judge character – were showing their deep, sincere affection for their leader.

Dr Kalam visited the Enchey monastery of the Nyingma order of Vajrayana Buddhism. The monastery is built on a stunning ridge of a hill above the city of Gangtok. From here, the view of the snow-dusted peaks of Kanchenjunga, the third-highest mountain in the world, is a picture of creation's majesty. The deities worshipped in the monastery are the Buddha, Loki Sharia and Guru Padmasambhava, or Guru Rinpoche. Dr Kalam spent time with the monks and spoke like a saint:

> Most Indians – experienced and old, energetic and middle-aged, young and innocent – they all look to religion for solace and safety. I have also visited a great many religious places and houses of worship throughout the length and breadth of this great country, and I have met many of our religious leaders. The religions are like exquisite gardens, places full of surpassing beauty and tranquility, like sacred groves filled with beautiful birds and their melodious songs. They are enchanting islands, veritable oases for the soul and the spirit. But they are islands nevertheless. How can we connect them so that the

> fragrance engulfs the whole universe? If we can connect all the islands with love and compassion, in a 'garland', we will have a prosperous India and prosperous world.[3]

The next day, President Kalam inaugurated a conclave for HIV/AIDS at Shillong in Meghalaya. The conclave was organized by the Assam Rifles Wives' Welfare Association (ARWWA) for curbing the spread of the disease among defence personnel and security establishments, and for formulating an effective strategy for tackling the problem. Dr Kalam called for the sensitizing of Assam Rifles personnel and other armed forces to ensure that no further cases of this scourge would affect security personnel.

Governor of Meghalaya, M.M. Jacob, Union minister P.R. Kyndiah, chairperson of the National Commission for Women, Girija Vyas, Chief Minister D.D. Lapanng, director general of Assam Rifles, Lt Gen. Bhopinder Singh and director general of Armed Forces Medical Research, Thailand, of the Royal Thai Army (RTA), Maj. Gen. Sueb Pong Sangharomya participated in a public discussion on this highly sensitive social issue. They were discussing a stark reality: 90 per cent of the people with HIV remained untreated, and were dying of this disease.

One woman got up and said, 'Even though we have some blue sky now in our country, the sky could become cloudy again very soon.' Another woman, herself infected with HIV by her husband, said, 'The true learning in my life began when I had to face the reality of my situation. First, my husband's family turned me away from their home and later even my father told me to leave our house. I became like any other abandoned woman to face alone my destiny, as a fallen leaf would drift with the wind.'

Dr Kalam's eyes welled with tears. He put his hand on her head and said, 'God wants us to know that life is a series of beginnings, not endings.'

President Kalam reached Aizawl, the capital of Mizoram, for his first visit to the state on 24 September 2005. Governor of Mizoram, Amolak Rattan Kohli, and Chief Minister Zoramthanga received the president at Lengpui airport. From the air, the runway resembles a neat scar on the jungle-carpeted landscape. This, and the 36-km-long journey to Aizawl from the airport along a steep and tortuous hilly route, was enough to dispel any doubt about the state's remoteness.

If grievance ever had legitimate reason to be translated into political rebellion, it was in Mizoram. The Mizo National Front (MNF) was an insurgent group that emerged from the Mizo National Famine Front in 1959. The latter was a formation protesting the widespread famine caused by a regular failure of the bamboo crop and the subsequent failure of the Indian state to send adequate relief. Deprivation soon gave rise to open rebellion.

In 1986, Prime Minister Rajiv Gandhi and the MNF signed the Mizoram Peace Accord. Rebel leader Pú Laldenga – who had spent the better part of his adult life deep in the jungles of Myanmar fighting the Indian state – was appointed chief minister. Prime Minister Rajiv Gandhi made clear the Centre's position: The MNF violence had to end; Mizoram had to stay in the Union, forswearing conflict and committed to inclusive politics.

Today, Mizoram is a state that cradles several oddities. It is a Christian-majority state where the Presbyterian Church has immense influence over everyday life and politics. It is one of the few states enforcing prohibition due to intervention by the Presbyterian Church. It also boasts one of the highest voter turnouts in the country. It appears that electoral politics have taken a healthy, competitive turn after two decades of violence.

Addressing the Mizoram assembly, President Kalam presented seven missions for Mizoram prosperity – a biofuel mission, a bamboo mission, a horticultural mission, a mission for preparing paramedics and technicians with quality training, a tourism mission (including general, spiritual and ecotourism), a mission for creating a secured exclusive economic zone and a mission for the establishment of PURA for rural prosperity – and explained each of them with the passion of an evangelist. 'Production of biofuel plants in the 260,000 hectares of barren land in the state itself can generate employment for more than a lakh people, besides providing earnings to the tune of Rs 325 crores a year,' he said.

Dr Kalam visited Sairang, a picturesque village of about 5,000 people. While answering the queries of schoolchildren there, Dr Kalam told them that he had become what he was in life as a result of his teacher, who taught him how birds fly. 'I learned not only how a bird flies, but also how one flies in life.' Villagers addressed their grievance to the president, that they were denied access to resources of the area by vested interests in the state government. Years later, they would tell how a few days after his visit, the oppressive system that favoured a wealthy few from the city was abolished. Their village subsequently progressed.

At the conclusion of all the official engagements in Mizoram, it was evening. I was ready for a good night's rest, and arrangements had been made for a morning flight to take the president and his entourage back to Delhi. But Dr Kalam was restless, and decided we would return to Delhi that night. The local Indian Air Force (IAF) station's head was summoned and informed of the president's wish to fly to the national capital. 'But there are no facilities for taking off from the airport at night,' the IAF officer said, thinking that the matter was settled. Dr Kalam, though, was singularly unimpressed, and remained adamant that they would fly. He said, 'What if there is an emergency? Will the IAF wait for the morning? Tell them I have to take off and all necessary arrangements should be made.'

Obeying the order of the supreme commander of the armed forces, the IAF personnel placed lanterns and torches and lit bonfires along the verge of the runway to facilitate the plane's take-off. When I asked the air force officer while boarding the aircraft around 9 p.m. if it was safe to take off, his answer sent a shiver down my spine: 'The aircraft will take off, but should there be some problem and if you have to return, it will not be possible.' But everything went smoothly, and we landed in Delhi without incident.

Back in the study at Rashtrapati Bhavan that night, I asked Dr Kalam why he took the risk. He pulled out the Bible from his bookshelf and opened at the page of the Psalm of David, the Lord is my shepherd, for me to read: 'Even though I walk through the valley of the shadow of death, I will fear no evil, for you are with me; your rod and your staff, they comfort me.'[4]

5.3

Instruments of God

> Lord, make me an instrument of Your peace. Where there is hatred, let me sow love; where there is injury, pardon; where there is doubt, faith; where there is despair, hope; where there is darkness, light; where there is sadness, joy.
>
> – St Francis of Assisi
> Thirteenth-century Italian Catholic friar

Dr Kalam turned seventy-four on 15 October 2005. He chose to be in Hyderabad for his birthday. During his visit to Tanzania in September 2004, he came to know about the heart-rending plight of families whose children, born with congenital heart diseases, were dying without treatment. He initiated a process of transforming some of these lives. For many, a birthday is a day of festivity and indulgence; but not for Dr Kalam. He started his day by meeting a group of Tanzanian children, who had undergone surgeries to correct congenital heart defects at Care Hospital, Hyderabad. Dr Kalam affectionately placed his hand on the head of each child, and presented every one of them with a box of gift-wrapped toffees brought from Delhi. He turned to Dr B. Soma Raju and V. Thulasidas and said, 'Beautiful job, God bless you.'

Governor of Andhra Pradesh, Sushil Kumar Shinde, Chief Minister Y.S. Rajasekhar Reddy and Telugu Desam Party president N. Chandrababu Naidu, who had come to greet President Kalam with flower bouquets at the Raj Bhavan, were waiting outside. They were astonished that he had given this event such priority. Words could scarce describe the joy on the faces of the children as they emerged from the room clutching their gifts. A few months earlier they had not known whether they would live to see their next birthday. Today, cured of their disease, they had received gifts and blessings from the president of India.

The best part of all this was that Dr Kalam was not even thinking about the miracle that he had masterminded in these children's lives. He was simply carrying out what he perceived as normal activity: his duty to the divine will. Perhaps, though, witnessing the youngsters' health and beaming expressions had been his secret birthday indulgence. There is some parallel here with his forgoing the customary Iftar parties at Rashtrapati Bhavan in favour of donations to orphanages: he would derive pleasure at the thought of children enjoying themselves rather than in his own indulgence.

Upon his return from Tanzania a year earlier, Dr Kalam had asked me to find some means of arranging free travel for children and their mothers from Dar es Salaam to Hyderabad. He suggested that I liaise with V. Thulasidas, with whom I had worked in Tripura to set up the Telemedicine services in 2003. V. Thulasidas was now the chairman and managing director of Air India. He most graciously agreed to assist. Dr B. Soma Raju, chairman of Care Hospitals, and Dr Gopichand Mannam, chief cardiothoracic surgeon, volunteered to provide free treatment.

Madam Eva L. Nzaro, high commissioner of Tanzania to India, travelled to Tanzania to identify needy children with congenital heart defects from poor rural families, with the help of the noted paediatrician Dr Helga Naburi. Twenty-four children with their mothers were flown free of cost by Air India from Dar es Salaam to Hyderabad, and Dr Naburi came to India with the children. Care Foundation organized free board and lodging for the group of fifty people, who stayed in Hyderabad for about a month. One noble thought of Dr Kalam brought out goodness from so many hearts. That was the true power of the man.

Later, on his seventy-fourth birthday, Dr Kalam launched a

pilot project with the aim of correcting refractive errors in 125,000 children, with his friend Dr Gullapalli Nageswara Rao. I was a constant companion of Dr Kalam during the various meetings they had since 1996, when I brought Dr Kalam to L.V. Prasad Eye Institute (LVPEI) for an eye examination. Dr Kalam was having difficulty reading. Dr Tara Prasad Das examined him. Very pleased to meet Dr Kalam, whom he had admired for years, Dr T.P. Das wrote the case sheet himself. He recorded Dr Kalam's name as 'Abdul Kalam Azad' and refused to charge a fee for the eye examination. 'You serve Mother India,sir. Today, a chance to serve you with what little I know is indeed a great blessing. Please do not label my seva with money,' he said. He then escorted us to Dr G.N. Rao, where a warm friendship brewed over a cup of coffee.

'Tell me your story, doctor,' Dr Kalam asked Dr Rao. Dr Rao surprised him by sharing that he had lived as a child by the house of Dr Kalam's friend, the great Dr Govindappa Venkataswamy. Inspired by Dr V, Dr Rao said that he had decided to become a 'doctor of the eyes', even before he started school. Dr Kalam was immensely pleased that they shared an admiration for Dr V; Dr Rao was like a child relaying stories of his hero. Dr G.N. Rao, who was one of the most charismatic people I had ever met, charmed Dr Kalam with his simple and yet profound narrative:

> My grandfather was a freedom fighter who gave away his wealth, but my uncle lived a life defined by a compulsive need to consume. My grandfather always wondered what he could give to others. My uncle always deliberated what he could take from others. I grew up amidst an ever-present polarity in life and learned early that you have to choose a path for yourself and live by your choice. If this is not done, you end up living a life of false comparisons and tormenting yourself every time you come around apparently successful and seemingly happy people. The doctors' community has many victims of this lifestyle disease. They enter the medical profession to serve but later get drawn into the rat race of greed and consumption. I was immunized against this disease right from my childhood.
>
> I returned to India after teaching at the University of Rochester

> in the United States, with a dream to start my own Aravind Hospital. My savings were not enough to buy land. Chief Minister N.T. Rama Rao promised me land, but his officials would not budge. Chief ministers come and go but officials remain, and it has never been easy to convert decisions into actions in our country. Then one day, one common friend took me to Ramesh Prasad, son of L.V. Prasad, the well-known movie director and producer. After discussions and going through the project proposal, he decided to donate one crore rupees and five acres of land. He pledged that there would be no interference – now or ever. Ramesh said, 'Please name the institute after my father', and that is how L.V. Prasad Eye Institute began.
>
> When President K.R. Narayanan developed a cataract, his secretary Gopalkrishna Gandhi called me. I dutifully examined the first citizen of India and recommended surgery. I suggested that my colleague would do the operation as I had stopped operating since I turned fifty-five. Gopalkrishna Gandhi told me to operate on the president as a special favour to him. I said, 'Sir, I am indeed doing you a favour by not operating on the president.'

President Kalam launched four vision preservation and restoration programmes – Children's Eye Health Initiative, Sight for Kids, Lions Diabetic Retinopathy and Phase II of Sight First Programme – at the LVPEI, as part of the World Sight Day celebrations. He presented the Melwyn Jones Fellowship to Tae Sup Lee, chairperson of Lions Club International Committee of Campaign Sight First Phase II programme, for his fund-raising efforts. Dr G.N. Rao said India had shown that it was capable of controlling blindness. There was drop of 25 per cent in the number of blind persons in the country between 1995 and 2005.

Dr Kalam understood it is not enough just to attend events and mouth empty platitudes about charity or social upliftment. For him, society's betterment had to be a matter of personal commitment of everyone with any means. He donated Rs 10 lakh of his personal money for restoring the vision of about 100 children, and administered an oath to the audience that they would strive for restoring the vision of at least ten people. The auditorium of the LVPEI glowed with the divine light. Nevertheless, I am yet to see the oath fulfilled by the many eminent people who were there and swore it.

On 6 November 2005, Pramukh Swamiji consecrated Akshardham Temple in Delhi. It was hailed as the largest Hindu temple in the world, and one of the modern architectural wonders. President Kalam was invited to the inauguration ceremony, along with Prime Minister Manmohan Singh and the leader of the opposition L.K. Advani. More than 40,000 people were present in the majestic temple complex.

Dr Kalam declared that Akshardham Temple had arisen at the dawn of the twenty-first century only with the commitment and dedication of one million devotees and volunteers. It inspired him and gave him the confidence that Indian people can take up big projects and succeed; that the realization of a developed India was eminently possible before 2020 with the millions of ignited minds of Indian youth.

After the ceremony, Dr Kalam asked Pramukh Swamiji, 'Swamiji, when I see Akshardham and your work, the team spirit and hard work of thousands are visible in this great spiritual centre. How are you able to attract such enthusiastic and spiritual workers? I am dreaming and dreaming of this type of spiritual leadership – purposeful leadership – which is essential for the India 2020 vision: the national economic development mission. Swamiji, you are the embodiment of true spirituality. The divine spirit is incarnate in you. You have so much divine power that I feel that anything is possible in this world. I want to work with you for a better India.'

Pramukh Swamiji said, 'We should work together. I pray that you too have this spiritual energy and may it increase. Your life from the beginning has been very pious. Divine power has worked through you for India.'

Dr Kalam suggested erecting a statue of the Tamil saint poet Thiruvalluvar in the temple complex, and presented to Pramukh Swamiji his poem 'The Mother Embraces Her Children' that he had composed for the occasion:

My journey commenced, in my ancestral home:
Loving families,
Multiple cradles,
The civilization of my nation!
My mother nurtured me with love,
My father gave me discipline as strength.
I wanted to be there forever,
But my parents sent me off to grow and excel.
I feel the tender love of my mother here
And the strength of my father's discipline
India can do it
The dawn of civilizational abode – Akshardham.[1]

Pramukh Swamiji heard the poem and looked at Dr Kalam with eyes full of loving compassion. Sadhu Brahmaviharidas, who was translating, added, 'There is a deep need for preserving the values and wisdom of Indian culture among the Indian diaspora.'

Back at home, we had a discussion on the glorious event we had attended.

Arun: Sir, you were beaming with happiness in the function today.

Kalam: Yes. I am very happy today. It is incredible that in less than five years' time such a wonderful building can be created. In 2001, I saw it on paper; today it was there in front of my eyes.

Arun: I understand that no cement or steel is used to construct such gigantic structures. Stones are interlocked together using the ancient Indian art of temple construction.

Kalam: I have never seen before such intricate stonework. In today's world of glass and steel buildings, Akshardham appears as a building returned from some golden age of the past.

Arun: How could it be done?

Kalam: I can see two things at work. First is the grand vision of Pramukh Swamiji. He sees what others can't. The second is the quality of his followers and the depth of their devotion.

Arun: What if our political leaders have a grand vision for our country and their followers raise their lives to higher standards!

Kalam: That can't happen without faith in God. This is what Pramukh Swamiji told me when I met him first in 2001. Add the sixth element of faith in God to the five elements of *India 2020* vision. I did not.

Arun: Or, you could not?

Kalam: Perhaps yes. I am yet to become an instrument of God.

I felt, as most would, that Dr Kalam was being self-effacing as usual. In any event, his work for the betterment of others continued. President Kalam was invited to the tenth convocation of the National Institute of Mental Health and Neurosciences (NIMHANS), Bangalore. This institute has emerged as a centre of excellence for patient care and academic pursuits in the fields of mental health and neurosciences. The rather bleakly named nineteenth-century Lunatic Asylum was given the more palatable title of Mental Hospital in 1925 by the Maharaja of Mysore. In 1954, the Government of India established the All India Institute of Mental Health. In 1974, the institute and the hospitals were amalgamated into the present form of NIMHANS. Service, manpower development and research were made express priorities for NIMHANS.

Dr Kalam asked me to sit with Dr W. Selvamurthy and gather his views on whether modern treatment of mental health was lacking compassion. Dr Selvamurthy had been Dr Kalam's friend for many years. He had undertaken outstanding research on the psychological responses of individuals in extreme environments, and on motivation. His study for the government on the alienation of local populations in Jammu and Kashmir was highly acclaimed. The recommendations from his studies on the prevalence of suicide and fratricide amongst troops were implemented by the armed forces.

We briefed Dr Kalam on the need for a middle path between the two extremes of compassion without scientific knowledge on the one hand, and scientific knowledge without compassion on the other.

When patients find their lives turned upside down by poor mental health, they turn to their friends and those of a religious profession as their first port of call for help. Many of these people may be kind and have the best intentions for the patient, but lack specialist knowledge required to guide the patient back on to the right path. Their efforts could thus have a detrimental effect, driving him further into his illness. The danger can then be that the patient suffers a complete emotional breakdown, with the resulting family trauma and loss of productivity for society.

Specialist care – which few patients receive – is usually adequate for most patients. But there are occasions where an utter lack of compassion has left patients reeling. Some doctors would simply pronounce that a patient has chosen to be affected by a phobic anxiety and he could choose to stop having it. There have been numerous instances in teaching hospitals where senior doctors have called their juniors to coolly observe the distress of their patients, without offering the patients one word, look or touch of compassion. For them, a patient had become an object of study and not a suffering human being. Dr Kalam decided to propose an agenda for reviving compassion in the mental health care system.

President Kalam arrived at NIMHANS on 21 November 2005. The Union minister for health and family welfare, Anbumani Ramadoss, and Dr D. Nagaraja, director and vice chancellor of NIMHANS received him. In his speech, Dr Kalam foreshadowed the challenges facing the mental health profession in coming years. He stated that according to the World Health Organization (WHO), brain disorders will be the gravest public health threat in the next few decades. He suggested that a comprehensive human brain project should be taken up with active participation of research institutions, including NIMHANS, government agencies, academia and the entire medical fraternity. Dr Kalam's speech was, as India's people had come to expect, a curious mix of sagacity and practicality:

> The confusion between mind and brain has always perplexed medical scientists. Answers to questions like 'What is the mind?' and 'Who

> am I?' don't lie in the domain of philosophers and psychologists alone. Molecular biologists and neurologists are formulating their own theories. This phenomenon leads to different types of situations. First, there is a presence of an energy system in the existence of a soul that enters and lives in a personality over a lifetime. This eternal entity is capable of both withdrawing into a slumber and tapping the universal energy of divinity and collective consciousness for its empowerment. Second, there is a heritable sensory and biological component to the personality and behavioural traits. Third, as I understand, no definitive psychopharmacological recommendations are available for specific groups of patients with personality disorders.
>
> If it is possible to analyse behavioural tendencies and derive an inclination or aptitude pattern of a person through rigorous and extensive research, especially at an early age, it will help the person to opt for that particular field. This will also enable early detection of negative emotions and projection of concealed destructive tendencies in a child, which can be set right at the early stage itself.[2]

Regarding mentally challenged children, the president wanted NIMHANS to create a vision incorporating the advances made in multiple disciplines of science and engineering. This should encompass new possibilities for treating genetic disorders. Father George's PhD thesis topic at Anna University had sparked an enduring interest in Dr Kalam, for seeking technological solutions to intellectual impairment: 'These disorders can manifest as mental disorders and create mentally challenged children. Stem cell research and gene chip application are going to play a vital role in reversing many of the brain disorders. Can the brain researchers from NIMHANS and the young who are graduating today take it as a mission of their profession?'

By this time, medicine and well-being had become one of Dr Kalam's many preoccupations. He could see the failure of modern medicine in alleviating the suffering of the poor. The success of modern medicine, with the advent of revolutionary surgical procedures and wonder drugs, was only one side of the story; and even here there were grounds for serious misgivings. Dr Kalam was becoming increasingly convinced of the relevance of Indian traditional medicine and the importance of prevention by adopting a healthy lifestyle.

On 17 December 2005, President Kalam visited the Ayurveda Hospital complex at Ernakulum in Kerala, and used this opportunity to deepen his own insights through interacting with the best of the minds there. Dr Kalam always treated conferences as great places of learning. 'What a year at college may not provide, a guru can give in a day; what a book cannot teach in a month, a guru can convey in an hour!' he would say with conviction.

Dr Kalam was told that even though during the later colonial period Ayurveda and other traditional healing systems were marginalized by the British, Ayurveda would endure under the sponsorship of enlightened local rulers. Even as Western medicine became more dominant, Ayurveda colleges offering diplomas were created in several centres throughout India. Some of these also offered courses of study of classical texts in Sanskrit. Moreover, a number of these institutions, particularly in Kerala, proffered a broad-based medical education that integrated Ayurveda and Western medical concepts of disease and wellness. In more recent times, pharmaceutical companies have begun to produce high-quality Ayurvedic preparations and other forms of traditional medicines.

After Independence, the Government of India made some efforts to raise the status of Ayurveda, Siddha and Unani, that had long been derided by a Western-oriented allopathic medical establishment. In 1964, a government body was formed with the aim of setting norms for the manufacture and control of the quality of traditional medicinal preparations. In 1970, the Government of India passed the Indian Medical Central Council Act. This legislation standardized Ayurveda teaching institutions, their curriculum and their diplomas. It would take another ten years before the Ministry of AYUSH (Ayurveda, Yoga and Naturopathy, Unani, Siddha and Homoeopathy) could be formed for the promotion of education and research in these 'alternative' health disciplines.

Kerala has been blessed by some visionary kings throughout its history. To keep pace with the growing influence of modern medicine, the king of Cochin, Rajarshi Rama Varma started an Ayurveda course at the Sanskrit College in 1926. Over the years, the department evolved into a college, and in 1959 was designated an institute and moved to the Royal Guest House at the Hill Palace. In 1973, the institute was shifted to the Puthiyakavu campus and became affiliated to Kerala University. It has since become a centre of excellence in Ayurvedic medicine.

Flanked by the chief minister of Kerala, Oommen Chandy, the minister for health, K.K. Ramachandran, and minister for education, E.T. Mohammed Basheer, President Kalam urged doctors to spend more time with their patients. He exhorted them to teach patients the importance of healthier lifestyles, rather than treat them as objects and dole out medicine without compunction. He saw the duty of the medical practitioner in spiritual terms:

> Since every one of you is involved in the noble profession of removing the pain of the people, you can also play a vital role in preventing ailments through proper health education to the patient as well as to his or her relatives and friends through lifestyle intervention. When you remove the pains of the people, the patient becomes part and parcel of you and considers you almost as God. Hence, the patient will definitely accept your health education, considering you as the most respected guru.[3]

Dr Kalam developed his own statistics based on his discussions and feedback from the huge network of his well-informed friends. He surmised that for a significant proportion of the Indian population, the risk of dying before the age of fifty is ten times the national average. In this group, adults have five times the average incidence of disabling heart disease, ten times the average incidence of visual impairment and six times the incidence of mental illness, mental retardation and nervous disorders. This assertion has never been contradicted, because few have really cared to delve into the problems of the poor in our country. Dr Kalam was the first president who had gone beyond signing papers, attending events and gracing state occasions. Our scientist president was asking uncomfortable questions and urging change, as if an instrument of God.

54

A Man's Compass

> There is a higher court than courts of justice and that is the court of conscience. It supersedes all other courts.
>
> – Mahatma Gandhi

On 25 January 2006, the Supreme Court came down heavily on Bihar governor, Buta Singh, for recommending the dissolution of the state assembly the previous year. In a scathing indictment of his actions, the court held that the dissolution was both unconstitutional and illegal and a mala fide exercise of the governor's power. Further – and perhaps even more damning – was the court's finding that the governor's actions were motivated only by a desire to prevent the Janata Dal (U) leader Nitish Kumar from staking a claim to government.

A constitutional bench of the Supreme Court, by a majority of three against two, also held that

> ... in the absence of the relevant material, much less due verification, the report of the governor has to be treated as the personal *ipse dixit* (perception or opinion) of the governor. The drastic and extreme action under Article 356 of the Constitution cannot be justified on mere *ipse dixit*, suspicion, whims and fancies of the governor.[1]

This deeply affected Dr Kalam, a man who had lived a life of unimpeachable integrity and whose moral rigour bordered on the ascetic. It was ultimately his order – one he had signed in the early hours of the morning in Moscow under the advice of the prime minister – which had given effect to Governor Buta Singh's recommendation. Hours later, in his presidential address on national television on the eve of the Republic day, Dr Kalam surprised many by telling the story of an honest child, Abdul Qadir, for more than five minutes.

The poor boy said he had forty gold coins hidden in his coat. The robber ripped through his coat and found the coins. The astonished robber asked Abdul Qadir, what prompted him to make this confession? Abdul Qadir replied. 'My mother made me promise to always be truthful, even at the cost of my life. Here, it was a matter of only forty gold coins. So I told the truth instead of betraying her trust in me.' The looters started weeping and said, 'You have adhered to the advice of your great mother, but we have been betraying the trust of our parents and the covenant of our Creator for many years.'[2]

The following day, President Kalam took the salute at the Republic Day parade with King Abdullah bin Abdulaziz al-Saud, the monarch of the Kingdom of Saudi Arabia. It was after a hiatus of more than half a century – since an exchange of visits by the top leaders in the 1950s – that the king of Saudi Arabia made a royal visit to India. It was for the first time in more than a quarter-century, after Prime Minister Indira Gandhi visited in 1982, that India gained direct access to the Saudi leadership. Until that time, the gulf kingdom had been hesitant to interact with India in anything but the most routine way. This was notwithstanding the considerable commercial interests of both countries: Saudi Arabia in selling oil to India, and India in securing employment for Indian workers in Saudi Arabia.

After overseeing the Republic Day ceremonies with his usual elan, Dr Kalam descended into a reflective mood, with long spells of silence and solitude. He discussed at length his wish to resign with all his friends and the senior officials at Rashtrapati Bhavan in view of the Supreme Court judgment. Sheridon, President Kalam's personal secretary and my friend since 1993, called me on 2 February 2006. He asked me to take an evening flight from Hyderabad to Delhi so that I could talk to Dr Kalam in person, and 'convince sir not to quit', which he feared he would do the following morning. By the time I reached

Rashtrapati Bhavan, it was almost midnight. Dr Kalam was in his sitting room, in casual attire; he rarely slept before 2 a.m. He was in a pensive mood. After our usual pleasantries, we sat together, and he got straight to the point:

Kalam: Buddy, I have decided to get out of here and do some good work.

Arun: Sir, your presence here is facilitating a lot of good work by thousands of people. That would collapse.

Kalam: My conscience tells me to quit.

Arun: Sir, is it your conscience or your ego?

Kalam: What is this new trap?

Arun: No trap, sir. You only teach me to live by the conscience so that it produces integrity and peace of mind. You only teach me it is better to displease people by doing what you know is right, than to temporarily please them by doing what you know is wrong.

Kalam: Yes. So?

Arun: Then why are you upset? That you did wrong in signing the dissolution paper in Moscow?

Kalam: No. I did the right thing. Anything else would undermine the authority of the Union cabinet. I went by my moral compass.

Arun: The Supreme Court said that the papers must not have been put to you by the cabinet. So where do you come into this? Of course your ego is hurt.

Kalam: You are a funny guy. Go and sleep.

It is indeed true that ego focuses on one's own survival and pleasure. It is selfishly ambitious to the extent of exclusion of others. Conscience, on the other hand, elevates ego to a larger sense of the group, to the greater good. It sees life in terms of service and contribution. Conscience has patience and wisdom guiding it. It is capable of adaptation. Ego micromanages, reduces one's capacity and excels in control. Conscience reflects the worth and value of all people and affirms their power and freedom to choose. Ego is threatened by negative feedback. It perceives all data in terms of self-preservation.

When in February 2006, President Kalam reviewed the Indian Navy's fleet and witnessed its operational prowess in the port city of Visakhapatnam, he was radiating the energy of conscience; the unblemished mirror of his pure heart was reflecting the divine light.

On 13 February 2006, President A.P.J. Abdul Kalam became the first Indian head of state to sail in a submarine, when he took to the water aboard INS *Sindhurakshak* during the craft's deployment in Vishakhapatnam. He was given a demonstrative excursion, during which the submarine dived and sailed in the Bay of Bengal for a few hours. The chief of naval staff, Arun Prakash, accompanied him. Commander Pravesh Singh Bisht commanded the submarine.

INS *Sindhurakshak* travelled about five miles off the coast of Visakhapatnam and dived to a depth of 50 metres. Commander Bisht explained to the president the functioning of the submarine. He was also taken around the five compartments of the boat, so as to give him first-hand knowledge of the submarine's operations. When President Kalam thanked Commander Bisht while disembarking, the officer paid him an emotional tribute: 'Sir, I joined the navy when I was a boy. The navy looked after me like my mother. It fed me, took care of me and gave me wonderful opportunities. Today I am feeling my father had visited my mother.'

President Kalam, as the supreme commander of Indian armed forces, stood on the deck of INS *Sukanya* as it sailed past ships lined up in four columns off the Ramakrishna beach. Ten warships followed the presidential yacht on its two-hour inspection trip. As the presidential yacht passed between the rows of warships, the crew lined the upper decks in white ceremonial uniforms and doffed their caps in unison. It was indeed a stunning spectacle, one of the more attractive and dramatic ceremonial gestures of Dr Kalam's presidency.

The Eastern Naval Command showcased India's maritime prowess, comprising around fifty ships and fifty-five aircraft, including aircraft carrier INS *Viraat*, Talwar-class missile frigates, Delhi-class missile destroyers, Godavari-class frigates, stealth frigates, three submarines, naval sea fighters and helicopters like TU-142 maritime patrol planes, Sea Harrier jets, Sea King and Kamov helicopters. The review culminated with a fly-past featuring forty naval aircraft.

Also in February 2006, President Kalam paid state visits to Singapore, the Philippines and to the Republic of Korea. Dr Raghuvansh Prasad Singh, minister of rural development and Smt. Sumitra Mahajan accompanied him.

After meetings with President S.R. Nathan, Prime Minister Lee Hsien Loong, Defence Minister Teo Chee Hean, Trade and Industry Minister Lim Hng Kiang and Foreign Affairs Minister George Yeo, President Kalam visited the Nanyang Technological University (NTU) on 2 February 2006. He felt right at home at the NTU campus, with its greenery and the smooth lines of its postmodern architecture. Its style was uncompromisingly contemporary, with none of the ivy and cloisters of traditional universities; but it had an ambience of an institution looking to the future. After a quick tour of NTU's work on earthquake, tsunami and water research, he met fifty faculty members.

President Kalam gifted 'Bio-Suite' – a comprehensive state-of-the-art software package that caters to all aspects of computational biology from genomics to drug design – to the NTU. Tata Consultancy Services (TCS), under the New Millennium Indian Technology Leadership Initiative (NMITLI) programme, sponsored by the Council of Scientific and Industrial Research, developed this bioinformatics product. Dr Kalam suggested collaborative endeavours between India and Singapore in the nano-bioinformatic domain.

With his lifelong passion for aeronautics and his zeal for national progress, Dr Kalam always had an eye out for opportunities for the Indian aircraft manufacturing industry. He suggested that with India's proven competence in designing, developing and manufacturing both civilian and military aircraft, the aerospace communities in India and Singapore should cooperate to advance the region's industry. He suggested a collaborative project for developing ASEAN's first passenger jet, to support the huge demand for travel in various parts of the world in the coming decades.

Dr Kalam gave a very warmly received lecture to the NTU students. He spoke at some length about the history of scientific developments in India and its achievements in this sphere. It was a vibrant atmosphere, with young students alternately breaking into cheers and rapturous laughter. Praising the upbeat vibe of the NTU campus, Dr Kalam said he would have liked to have done his PhD here, had he been younger. After the function, Dr Kalam stepped over the security cordon and shook hands with eager students. It was almost like a pop idol being mobbed.[3] NTU president Dr Su Guaning noted the 'rock-star-like buzz' Dr Kalam created: 'Plunging in to engage young people, he showed all of us why he had received the accolade of "People's President".'[4]

President Kalam's first engagement in the Philippines was a visit to the College of Nursing, an institution that had sent its graduates across the globe. His insistence on going there had earlier surprised the visit's planners. They were at a loss to understand why the president of India would want to see a nursing college. But they were dealing with a great humanist whose reality was different from the drama and glitter of pompous ceremonies. One had to see the enthusiasm and pride in the faces of the nursing students and their teachers, as I did, to understand that. And there was purpose in Dr Kalam's visit. He knew that this engagement had at least as much relevance for his people as any state function. The man of vision that he was, he saw the potential for his nation in their work:

> You have introduced some unique courses to make nurses into doctors for rural areas. I want India to take a clue from this and make changes in the nursing syllabus there. I will take it up. This work carries the seeds of agenda for the future nursing community. Well-prepared nurse leaders may assume positions of power and influence on key decision-making bodies. I can see great possibilities of Indian and Filipino nurses and paramedics working together and emerging as the most powerful human resource in the world ... Empowerment of the nursing community is very important ... this includes increasing the economic value of nursing in the healthcare industry, nurse-piloted hospital systems, direct public relations and communication and self-regulatory culture and education.[5]

During his meeting with the president of the Philippines, Gloria Macapagal Arroyo, on 4 February, President Kalam symbolically handed over the foundation seeds of improved peanut and sweet sorghum, developed by the International Crops Research Institute for the Semi-Arid Tropics (ICRISAT). Dr Kalam's friend Dr William Dar was standing by his side. Dr Kalam told President Macapagal Arroyo, 'Dr Dar is a great gift of your country to Indian smallholder farmers. He gave a human face to agricultural research in India.' In one state visit, Dr Kalam had encompassed the two primary concerns of human existence: food and health. His understanding of priorities could never be faulted.

At any rate, President Kalam could just as easily walk the red carpet as deal with the pressing issues of humanity. President Macapagal Arroyo hosted a banquet in honour of President Kalam in the Rizal Hall of the Malacanang Palace on 4 February 2006. The word 'Malacanang' in Tagalog, a Filipino language, means, 'there is a noble man there'. The Malacanang Palace has indeed stood witness to the history of the Philippines. This great whitewashed mansion on the bank of the Pasig reflects on the river's calmly flowing water, just as it has mirrored the changing fortunes and rulers of the country. Malacanang Palace has been occupied by eighteen Spanish Governors General, fourteen American military and civil governors and later, each of the presidents of the Philippines.

From Siachen to ceremonies of state, our president was comfortable in almost any given situation, but I can never forget Dr Kalam's blushing face and shyness in President Arroyo's presence. For all of his life, Dr Kalam had been used to demurely attired Indian ladies. He had only ever encountered women from other lands in sober, formal settings. President Arroyo, though, was simply dazzling in an aquamarine off-the-shoulder brocade gown with a diamond necklace adorning her bare décolletage. Her glamorous demeanour was quite a culture shock for Dr Kalam. His usual calm aplomb deserted him, and he stood bashfully next to President Arroyo at the banquet while she proposed a toast to him.

The day following the banquet, President Kalam visited the International Rice Research Institute (IRRI) in Los Baños in Laguna Province of the Philippines. Dr M.S. Swaminathan was the director general of IRRI during 1982–88, and the IRRI–India partnership under his guidance had been an outstanding exercise in collaboration. Because of its symbiotic nature, this partnership had not only endured but thrived over the preceding half-century, advancing both global rice science development and India's rice production. Dr Kalam liked the idea of salted eggs grown there using genetic engineering, and chatted with poultry farmers about this novel product.

President Kalam addressed a joint session of the Philippine Congress in Manila, on 6 February 2006, flanked by the Senate president Franklin Drilon and the House Speaker Jose de Venecia. Convinced that in the following decades Asia would become the hub of the world's trade, he urged that ASEAN countries ready themselves: 'No doubt that the future of global business interaction would be in Asia, and members of the Association of South East Asian Nations (ASEAN) should take steps to make the region an attractive and viable marketing proposition.'[6]

Though Korean brands, like Samsung, LG (Lucky Goldstar), and Hyundai had reached millions of Indian homes, President Kalam was the first Indian president to visit the Republic of Korea, popularly known as South Korea. While the setting up of a joint task force to develop a comprehensive economic partnership agreement with a far-reaching charter was the central agenda of this visit, Dr Kalam used this opportunity to meet the giants of Korean industry. He wished to experience first-hand Korean technology and to understand why Japan was losing its manufacturing edge to South Korea.

President Kalam addressed the four major Korean business associations. He was briefed by the president of Tata Daewoo Commercial Vehicles about their operations in Gunsan, 200 kilometres south-west of Seoul on the mid-west coast of the Korean Peninsula, and the chairman of Hyundai Motors about their plant at Sriperumbudur, near Chennai. Dr Kalam was given a presentation by Korean steel major Pohang Steel Corporation (POSCO) on their activities later in the evening, including the investment of USD 12 billion they would make in a plant in Orissa.

Next, Dr Kalam travelled to Daedeok Innopolis, the research and development district in the Yuseong-gu district in Daejeon, 150 kilometres from Seoul. Daedeok Innopolis grew out of the research cluster established by President Park Chung-hee in 1973 that marked the beginning of the high-technology era in South Korea. Dr Kalam visited the Samsung Semiconductors Facility at Gi-heung, as well as the Korean Research Institute of Bioscience and Biotechnology (KRIBB) and the Korean Aerospace Research Institute (KARI). On the way back to Seoul, we took a bullet train, travelling at speeds of up to 300 kilometres per hour.

In the evening, Dr Ok Jung Lee, professor of sociology at the Catholic University at Daegu, visited Dr Kalam. She had translated *Wings of Fire* into the Korean language about a year earlier. When Dr Kalam asked Lee what could be the reason behind the popularity of *Wings of Fire* in Korea, she replied, 'Your book has provided a new perspective of patience and generosity to Korean youth growing in a highly competitive society. Your love for your parents and teachers, particularly your mother, has brought tears to many Korean eyes. Koreans have historically derived inspiration from the western pure land – as India is known here. Right from Gautam Buddha and the princess of Ayodhya, who married Korean King Suro in the first century, to Rabindranath Tagore and now you, India is seen as a beacon of light. We see in you Sir, the image of our King Sejong, who energetically promoted learning throughout his thirty-two-year reign in the fifteenth century.'

Dr Lee heaped further praise on Dr Kalam in media 'Kalam's celebration of his family, teachers and hard work in *Wings of Fire* is identical to King Sejong's statement: "All that I am, or will be, I have learned from my family, my friends, my teachers, and training with my sword." Kalam has emerged as the guiding soul of Korean youth, and *Wings of Fire* has made a profound impact since its publication, which is reflected in its excellent sales in the areas around universities. The impressive scientific achievements of Kalam remained rooted in his righteous simplicity, and that is what has made him a role model over so many other successful heroes of contemporary history.'[7]

President Kalam addressed the Republic of Korea National Assembly on 8 February 2006, where he presented his idea of the World Knowledge Platform and e-business network that will take 'both our nations' economies into a higher trajectory of growth'. On the flight back to India, President Kalam summarized his experience saying, 'I enjoyed so much the snow, the mountains, the people, the buildings, the roads – everything has entered into me. We need to build a strong bridge between our people with a vision to build peace and prosperity in Asia and thereby in the world.'

President Kalam was invited to the eighty-eighth convocation of Banaras Hindu University (BHU). He involved me in the preparation of his convocation address saying, 'I am going to the great city of Kashi, and I must prepare well for this lecture. There is a beautiful spiritual connection between Kashi and Rameswaram.' I recalled that he had said to me exactly the same words when he visited Kashi in 1991 to deliver the convocation of the Indian Institute of Technology (IIT) at BHU. In that convocation, Vibhuti Narayan Singh, the maharaja of Kashi and chancellor of the university, introduced Dr Kalam to the audience by stating that he had come to the land of the Ganga at Kashi from Rameswaram Agniteertham. After many days of work, Dr Kalam finalized his evolution of enlightened citizenship plan that he would unveil at the great city of Kashi.

Perhaps the idea of enlightened citizenship was an inevitable corollary of Dr Kalam's quest for progress. Dr Kalam knew that man is ineluctably a moral creature, and progress without a moral element would be meaningless and even destructive. The idea for a concerted effort towards enlightened citizenship had, in any event, been given shape by a fateful visit with Swami Ranganathananda, the thirteenth president of Ramakrishna Math, on 1 October 2004 at Belur Math near Kolkata. Dr Kalam had asked Swami Ranganathananda the solution for India's endless social problems, and Swamiji had told him of the need for starting a mission to enlighten the citizens of India. Swamiji explained to Dr Kalam that man's journey of evolution is a three-stage journey. The first stage deals with man's relationship to objects and acquisitions. Stage two deals with man's relationship to man. The third stage is of man's relationship to the divine. Swamiji's message had a profound impact on Dr Kalam: 'We exchanged thoughts on various national and international issues. One important thought propounded by Swami Ranganathananda was: the message of India has nothing creedal, dogmatic or sectarian about it, for it speaks in terms of man's development, his progress, his achievement of highest excellence. It is universal and human. The nation cannot be happy just with economic prosperity; the people would also need spiritual enlightenment. Swamiji realized that the people's salvation does not lie in material wealth alone. They need a righteous, spiritual path for evolution.'

Dr Kalam wanted to develop the idea of enlightened citizenship in order to create a bridge between worldliness and spirituality. 'This would be a very powerful vision for people and provide a strong ideal for every individual to hold on to', he told me.

President Kalam arrived at BHU on 3 March 2006. Union minister of human resource development Arjun Singh and the BHU vice chancellor Prof. Panjab Singh received him. His speech was, as his life's work had always been, a brilliant amalgam of vision and common sense:

> Inquiry, creativity, technology, entrepreneurial and moral leadership are the five capacities required to be built through the education process. If we develop in our students these five capacities, we will produce the 'Autonomous Learner' – a self-directed, self-controlled, lifelong learner who will have the capacity to both respect authority and at the same time question authority, in an appropriate manner.
>
> These enlightened citizens would work together as a 'self-organizing network' and transform any state into a prosperous state. The most important part of the education is to imbibe the confidence among the students in the spirit of 'we can do it'. These capacities will enable the students to meet the challenges of our national mission of transforming the nation into a developed country by 2020.[8]

A renaissance man had emerged in Dr Kalam, and he felt a strong moral duty to serve his nation for its own renaissance. He understood that Indian civilization must reinvigorate its core values, and this would take a concerted effort. It would involve two aspects. First, it would require the ability to have a compelling and powerful dream or vision of betterment for the one billion people of India. Second, it would require a disposition to do the right thing and influence others also to do the right thing.

5.5

I Will Fly

> A dreamer is one who can only find his way by moonlight, and his punishment is that he sees the dawn before the rest of the world.
>
> – Oscar Wilde
> Nineteenth-century Irish author and poet

It was a cold Delhi morning on 2 March 2006. I stood in the forecourt of Rashtrapati Bhavan, where President George W. Bush would soon alight from his limousine. Rashtrapati Bhavan can overwhelm nearly anyone. Its dome reaches into the Delhi sky like a perfect geographical formation as one ascends Raisina Hill: a glimpse of the Jaipur column, then the building itself – an astonishing monument of majesty and exquisite proportion in two shades of sandstone. It is one of the few wonders of colonial times – the architects who designed this glorious complex truly understood and captured the greatness of India. When President Bush arrived he was accorded the ceremonial welcome India grants visiting heads of state; and George Bush was, I guess, unprepared for the pomp and pageantry awaiting him. Looking at the presidential bodyguards, all over six feet tall, astride their awesome steeds, President Bush acclaimed loudly, 'It is fantastic. The men and their horses must be so well trained.'

In the historic Indo-US Civil Nuclear Agreement signed on that day, India agreed to a phased separation of its civil and military nuclear facilities and to bring its civil nuclear facilities under the International

Atomic Energy Agency (IAEA) standards. President Bush not only assured India that it will help in achieving full civil nuclear energy cooperation, he also agreed to work with the Nuclear Suppliers Group (NSG) to enable full civil nuclear energy supply and trade. President Bush described India as a 'responsible state with advanced nuclear technology' and acknowledged India's strong commitment to preventing the proliferation of weapons of mass destruction. He further declared that 'India should acquire the same benefits and advantages as other such states'. This effectively cleared the way for the transfer of civilian nuclear reactors to India to meet its acute energy needs, as it grows exponentially as an emerging economic power.

In the evening, President Bush returned to Rashtrapati Bhavan for a tête-à-tête with President Kalam, followed by a banquet. Dr Kalam had had some considerable bearing on this historic day. Without his personal intervention in the matter, it is doubtful that the Indo-US Civil Nuclear Agreement would have transpired at all. And without access to cooperation in procuring the materials for nuclear power in the current energy scenario, India's energy programme would have been in dire straits.

President Kalam gave a forty-minute PowerPoint presentation to President Bush on India's energy needs. The dinner was held in the awesome setting of the Mughal Gardens under a clear sky and a crescent moon, the heavens witness to a day when the historical alliance conceived nearly eight months earlier was finally consummated. The meal was set against the backdrop of Rashtrapati Bhavan, aglitter in lights. Each of the fourteen tables at the dinner was named for a flower that adorns the Mughal Gardens in full bloom. Usually, the presidential palace is lit up only for Republic Day and Independence Day. This was the first time Rashtrapati Bhavan was illuminated for a visiting head of state.

The two presidents sat at a table named 'Yellow Rose'. Others at the table included First Lady Laura Bush, Prime Minister Singh and his wife, Smt. Sonia Gandhi and US Secretary of State Condoleezza Rice, Chief Justice of India Y.K. Sabharwal, Defence Minister Pranab Mukherjee and Home Minister Shivraj Patil. I was seated on the table named 'Jasmine' with Dr B. Soma Raju and several dignitaries. I could not help but think that this evening was a fitting celebration for the birth of a new India. The resurgent nation, that had endured the ignominy of centuries of colonial repression and decades of lassitude, was now asserting its leadership in South-East Asia.

President Kalam began his three-day state visit to Myanmar on 8 March 2006 at the invitation of Senior General Than Shwe, who had visited India in October 2004. Union minister of state Kumari Selja and Foreign Secretary Shyam Saran accompanied him. This visit was about bilateral cooperation; India and Myanmar signed three agreements in the petroleum, space and education sectors. Since his days at the DRDO, Dr Kalam had been instrumental in a myriad of collaborative projects. Now, his diplomatic touch always served to give international agreements a final blessing – sealing the deal, as it were – even if he was not actively involved in negotiations.

While he was in Myanmar, President Kalam visited the historic Shwe Dagon Pagoda, an awesome golden structure that tapers to a point, aspiring to the heavens. It enshrines the sacred hair of Lord Buddha. According to legend, soon after Lord Buddha attained enlightenment more than 2,500 years ago, his relics were divided into eight equal parts and enshrined in the great stupas built at the time. In Myanmar, stupas came to be known as pagodas. The Shwe Dagon Pagoda is located atop a hill 58 metres high and is thus an indelible aspect of Yangon's skyline.

President Kalam made the first-ever visit by an Indian head of state to the historic city of Mandalay, and spoke at the University of Traditional Medicine. He offered to develop links for traditional medicine between Myanmar and India. An advocate of combining traditional medicine with biotechnology, Dr Kalam pointed out that most of the herbs being used in Myanmar were found in India's north-eastern states. Therefore, he suggested that the countries join hands to counter the common problems they faced in making traditional medicine available to the world.

The president also took the time to pay homage at two imposing ancient pagodas in the city. At the Maha Muni Pagoda, Dr Kalam pasted gold leaves at the base of Buddha's statue, in line with the tradition of gilding gold to the bronze idol. Dr Kalam also visited the Kutho Daw Pagoda, which houses rows of 729 small temples, each hosting a stone slab on which are inscribed the entire Tripitaka or the whole of the Buddhist scriptures. These inscriptions have been described as the world's biggest book.

Dr Kalam inquired about the jail where Tilak Maharaj was incarcerated during 1908–14 in Mandalay. The jail was just a few kilometres away, and in fact can be seen from the Kutho Daw Pagoda hill. The security detail, however, would not allow the president of India access to the jail, on grounds that it was a restricted area. Y.S. Rajan narrated to Dr Kalam how Tilak Maharaj requested his jailor to give him a pencil and stationery. As if mesmerized with the towering persona of Tilak Maharaj, the jailor could not refuse. Tilak Maharaj wrote a manuscript of more than 400 pages in the jail. It was published as *Gita Rahasya* in 1915 after Tilak Maharaj returned to Poona. Tilak Maharaj defended the ethical obligation to the active principle or action – even violent action including killing – as long as that was selfless and without personal interest or motive. In this sense at least, his approach was diametrically opposed to the principle of non-violence espoused by Mahatma Gandhi.

Back in Yangon, President Kalam visited the mausoleum of Bahadur Shah Zafar, the last emperor of India, who was exiled to Rangoon, as this city was called then, after the British victory in the First War of Independence. I explained to Dr Kalam the desolation of Bahadur Shah Zafar and the couplet he wrote while living in exile here:

pade faatihaa koi aaye kyuun,
koi chaar phuul charhaye kyuun
koi aake shamma jalaye kyuun,
main vo bekasi kaa mazaar huun.

Why should anyone come to sing a requiem
Why should anyone come to offer four flowers
Why should anyone come to light a candle
I am the tomb of that destitution.

The president wrote in the visitors' book. 'O Emperor of India. I have come here today and recited Surah Fatiha. I have offered flowers and lighted a candle here. It is not the tomb of a destitute; it is the mausoleum of the Emperor of India. May your soul rest in peace.' Before leaving the place, I glanced through the visitors' book and saw the entries made by Muhammad Zia-ul-Haq, the sixth president of Pakistan, and Hussain Muhammad Ershad, the tenth president of Bangladesh. There is a historic continuity that binds all of us. There are certain things that do not wither away; they live beyond individual lives, regimes and even ages.

From Yangon, President Kalam proceeded by flight to Mauritius. Prime Minister Naveenchandra Ramgoolam received him at the Port Louis airport on 11 March 2006. He would be the chief guest at the country's National Day function, which also commemorates the seventy-sixth anniversary of the Dandi March. Later, President Kalam called on the President of the Republic of Mauritius Sir Anerood Jugnauth at the State House.

Tracing the footsteps of the first Indian immigrants in Mauritius, President Kalam visited the Apravasi Ghat, the place where nearly 450,000 indentured labourers from India arrived between the 1830s and 1920s. The place symbolizes one of the greatest waves of migration in recorded history, which has had a determining impact on the demographic profile of the present-day Mauritian population. President Kalam placed a wreath on the plaque dedicated to 'the unknown immigrant'.

During the long flight from Port Louis to New Delhi, Dr Kalam initiated a discussion on what Mauritians of Indian origin think of India. A majority of the population in Mauritius originated from India, although composed of diverse religions and ethnicities. Although Mauritians have moved on in terms of cultural transformation, religious growth, educational achievements, etc., they cannot forget their ancestry, which probably has given them their drive, the substance of their dreams.

Our ancestry is like our shadow. We cannot prosper and achieve success if we forget our roots and if we are afraid of our shadows. Our observation was that Mauritians of Indian origin were very proud of their cultural heritage and of their ancestors' achievements. Those Indian pioneers of the nineteenth and the early twentieth century worked hard for paltry wages, remained docile and forbearing – and were always very grateful of the minimal recognition the government accorded them.

Back in Delhi, a political and constitutional fracas was soon to erupt that would test the mettle of the people's president. The political establishment and Dr Kalam were headed for a very public contretemps that was by far the most dramatic incident of his term of office. Any misconception that our genial scientist president was a 'rubber stamp' for the government of the day would be unequivocally dispelled; and the nation would see a clear demonstration of Dr Kalam's commitment to ethics in public office.

On 16 March 2006, President Kalam accepted a recommendation of the Election Commission to disqualify Smt. Jaya Bachchan of the Samajwadi Party from the Rajya Sabha for holding an office of profit while being a member of the parliament. Smt. Bachchan's standing as an MP had been questioned by a Congress party worker from Kanpur in a petition to Dr Kalam. Dr Kalam subsequently referred the matter to the Election Commission of India for its advice as ordained under Article 103 of the Indian Constitution. Dr Kalam acted strictly according to the opinion of the Election Commission in issuing a disqualification order against Smt. Jaya Bachchan.

A stray complaint and a decision thereon opened a can of worms, as it were. For their part, the Samajwadi Party did not take kindly to the loss of their prominent member. Far from being cowed by the disqualification, the party canvassed and received support from other opposition parties, and would later renominate Smt. Jaya Bachchan for re-election to the same seat. Subsequently, other cases from the ruling combine – including that of Congress president Sonia Gandhi holding the position of the chairperson of the National Advisory Council of the United Progressive Alliance – came under the scanner.

Before long, the Election Commission of India had received complaints of more than forty cases of MPs and 100 cases of MLAs holding offices of profit that invited disqualification. This clearly indicated a pervasive tendency in politicians to seek the fruits of power while in executive office, beyond being the people's representatives in parliament. It indeed revealed a pronounced craving of politicians for forms of power or remuneration, other than those associated with the satisfaction of the functions that their public offices assigned them.

The matter of Smt. Jaya Bachchan's disqualification promptly made its way to the Supreme Court, which dismissed her challenge to the president's order. A central plank of the plaintiff's case was that Smt. Jaya Bachchan had never actually received payment for her apparently innocuous duties as the chairperson of the Uttar Pradesh Film Development Council. The Supreme Court held, however, that it was immaterial whether a person thus disqualified had actually received any pecuniary gains from the office. Under the relevant provision, the very fact that a member of a legislature held such an office was valid grounds for disqualification.

Governments, especially coalitions, appeared to be doing everything in their power to retain legislators in their flock, and offering plum positions to legislators had emerged as one method of forestalling their potential dissidence.

Whatever might have prompted the complaint against Smt. Bachchan, it became clear that this phenomenon affected all the parties, which have customarily used the granting of such offices to please their legislators. And since every legislator took enjoying executive offices for granted, no one ever thought that any provision of the Constitution was being violated.

As was expected, the Samajwadi Party and the Bharatiya Janata Party did not lose a moment in dragging Sonia Gandhi's position as the chair of the National Advisory Council of the UPA into the controversy. In order to deflect the opposition onslaught, Sonia Gandhi resigned her Lok Sabha seat from Rae Bareli and sought re-election, which she convincingly won in May 2006.

None of the parties or the leaders was the least bit apologetic regarding the flouting of Article 103 of the Constitution. Removal of every qualification – or, in this case, disqualification – was the very basis of the concentration of power. It appeared that the purity and independence of legislative membership were the targets of every political party, so that their people could enjoy more than one position without threat of 'disqualification'. All the political parties were more or less in the same situation as the Congress and the Samajwadi Party. Hence, there was likely to be unprecedented unity and consensus among all the parties in this matter, to protect their present and future political interests. With forty-three members from different parties facing likely disqualification from parliament and 200 others from state legislatures facing similar sanction, there was a cross-party consensus that the Constitution should be amended.

On 17 May 2006, the parliament passed a bill seeking to exempt fifty-six posts, including the post of chairperson of the National Advisory Council, from being considered offices of profit and hence attracting disqualification for parliamentarians. The Rajya Sabha approved the bill through a division. On 25 May 2006, President Kalam received the Parliament (Prevention of Disqualification) Amendment Bill, 2006, duly passed by both houses of parliament for his assent under Article 111 of the Constitution of India. On 30 May 2006, President Kalam returned the bill for reconsideration by parliament on three grounds: first, that it could not be applied in retrospect from 1959; second, that there was a need to define transparent criteria for exemption from disqualification; and third, that the question be raised as to why there should not be a comprehensive bill that applies to all states. Dr Kalam had taken a stand that was based at once on ethical and legal grounds, and felt that the bill struck at the very esteem of the Constitution:

> I felt the manner in which exemptions were given was arbitrary. The office of profit concept was developed by the founding fathers of the constitution, who believed that parliament should and must question the executive. But since ministers and a few members of parliament may also hold executive posts while in parliament, the idea of giving select and careful exemptions to some offices held by them had been devised. The bill contained more than forty exemptions. Most experts

> advised me that the bill, as it was drafted, subverted the principle behind the original concept of giving careful and select exemptions. I felt the exemptions list in the bill must be purposeful. Why amend the very Constitution of our country merely to accommodate a few politicians who may risk losing their membership of the house?[1]

While these dramas were playing out, President Kalam fulfilled a childhood dream. On 8 June 2006, he flew the Sukhoi-30-Mk 1 fighter plane at the Lohegaon Air Force Base in Pune, co-piloting the plane with Wing Commander Ajay Rathore, commanding officer of the Lightning Squadron based at Lohegaon. Rathore took the flight to about 7.5 kilometres above ground level and flew at 1.25 Mach (one-and-a-quarter times the speed of sound). The flight went into twists and turns and also stalled mid-air in order to give Dr Kalam a first-hand experience of the fighter plane's capabilities. He was exhilarated by the experience and could barely contain his joy afterwards:

> I went up. I went down. I took right and left turns. I did everything that Commander Rathore told me to do. He is a great teacher. I feel proud that our country has such great and good pilots ... I want to give a message to young Indians that they should join the Indian Air Force.[2]

The president took control of the flight for roughly five to ten minutes. 'He had absolute control over the flight in mid-air,' Wing Commander Rathore said. Asked what they spoke about on the flight, Rathore said, 'I was giving him more technical instructions on how to operate the plane. He also told me how eager he was to fly an air force plane since his childhood.'

Back in Delhi, parliament reconsidered the bill and as thought fit by them, passed it again without any amendment. Of course, the government – with due respect to the president – resolved to refer the matter to a Joint Parliamentary Committee (JPC). This committee would define what constitutes an office of profit as stated in Article 102 of the Constitution. The bill came back to President Kalam for assent on 1 August 2006.

President Kalam did not sign the bill immediately. He waited for a good seventeen days for better sense to prevail. There was no attempt made by the JPC to discuss the issue. To silence the speculations that the president would sit over the bill till his tenure ended the following year – or that he would ask for a legal opinion as demanded by the opposition National Democratic Alliance, and precipitate a political situation – Dr Kalam eventually signed the bill on 18 August 2006. His presidential secretary P.M. Nair, who had not wished the president to take such a stance on the bill, would later write: 'Finally, the Constitution prevailed over conscience.'[3]

For Dr Kalam, however, this was a matter of principle and probity, and he felt duty-bound to raise his objections, even if he was not strictly empowered to influence the matter. He was deeply conflicted by the issue:

> During this period, I experienced an intense moral dilemma: should I have signed or should I have resigned? I needed spiritual guidance: an assurance about my decision to sign the bill, to enact legislation, which I was convinced, was flawed.[4]

Dr Kalam went to see Pramukh Swamiji at Akshardham on 11 September 2006. While walking with Pramukh Swamiji around the temple compound, Dr Kalam saw the beautiful Gajendra Pithika sculpture, depicting the story of five blind men trying to describe the shape of an elephant. None of these blind men was able to discover the true shape of the elephant. Their descriptions and definitions were partial and incomplete.

What does the parable imply? One's subjective experience can be true, but is not such an experience limited by its failure to account for other truths or a totality of truth? Is not relativism, differences and limitations in the expressions of truth, the hallmark of this world? Dr Kalam immediately felt unburdened of his personal qualms surrounding the matter:

> The opinions of experts vary because of their different perspectives, each one seeing his truth. In my personal dilemma of whether to sign or refuse the bill, I had been flooded and confused by expert

> opinions – all well meaning, but partial truths nevertheless. Hence, my decision to follow the Constitution and bow before the supremacy of the parliament was indeed right.[5]

Dr Kalam went to Sri Adichunchanagiri Math on his seventy-fifth birthday on 15 October 2006 and received blessings from the seventy-first pontiff Jagadguru Sri Balagangadharanatha Swamiji. Swamiji had headed the Math from 1974 – a commendable period of service but a mere interlude in the greater scheme of the Math. Situated in Mandya district of Karnataka, the Math is a socio-spiritual centre with a remarkable history of 1,500 years. According to legend, Lord Shiva blessed the Kshetra (dominion). When Lord Shiva was performing penance at Sri Kshetra, he devoured two demons, Chuncha and Kancha, who had been ravaging the area for a very long time. At the end of his austerity, Lord Shiva entrusted a siddayogi to establish a 'Natha tradition' and guided him to inculcate righteousness in society.

President Kalam was invited to the 702nd Urs celebrations of Amir Khusrau in New Delhi. Amir Khusrau was an iconic figure in the cultural history of the Indian subcontinent. He was a mystic and a spiritual disciple of Nizamuddin Auliya of Delhi. The renaissance man that he was, Dr Kalam could appreciate poetry as much as he could engage in scientific debate. Moreover, he understood the significance of Amir Khusrau's work beyond the aesthetic beauty of his words and meter:

> Each one of us has a page in history. Everyone has a religion, a family, a supporting society and a dream. We do not have time to observe what is happening around us. We generally tend to revolve around ourselves. The earth revolves around itself and orbits the sun. The choice before us is of revolving around ourselves to die, or of revolving around the sun in order to live. Hence, our thoughts, ideas and actions have to constantly change and expand. Now it is the right time for all of us to think of the nation beyond boundaries – as visualized and demonstrated by Ameer Khusro. Many called Khusro the father of Sufiana Kalam in India, many called him the father of the Urdu language, many others called him a great Sufi saint

> and poet; but besides all these I would also prefer to call him a poet of purpose, who turned the world around simply through his poetry and music.[6]

Dr Kalam was in the last year of his term as president, and in a matter of months, he would leave Rashtrapati Bhavan. Many are those for whom holding public office is an imperative, an addiction. Such people never relinquish power gracefully – they attach their personalities, their very existences and identities to their offices – and there are those who even seem to lose their souls. Dr Kalam was the very antithesis of this kind of career politician.

In a sense, Dr Kalam was not a politician at all; indeed, he had never actually sought public office. Doubtless, he approached his duties as president with a verve and assiduousness that could barely be surpassed. But he was never attached to his post. Just as he had always remained unaffected by his success, he was totally unchanged by his term as president. And after signing the Parliament (Prevention of Disqualification) Amendment Bill, Dr Kalam appeared to have become even more determined than before of his destiny. He would continue with his many orbits of the sun, but he would soon draw away from gravitational pull of Delhi's political scene.

5.6

What Can I Give?

> Arise, awake, and stop not until your goal is achieved.
>
> – Swami Vivekananda

After the imbroglio over the issue of office of profit, President Kalam was more than ever aware that Indian political and bureaucratic systems had been conditioned to maintain the status quo. Over the years, those in power had evolved ways and means to remain in power. The government itself had become reduced to serving electoral politics, and the bureaucracy had become entangled in the games of its political masters. The Indian nation had been taken over by its political parties, and they in turn were focusing on their own growth and welfare. The long-term interests of the nation and people had been firmly side-lined in favour of personal and partisan interests. This was surely not a system whereby the Indian people could hope to see their nation joining the ranks of the developed world.

In his last address to the nation on the eve of the Republic Day in January 2007, President Kalam invoked a topical and powerful question. His request to the people of India was reminiscent of President John F. Kennedy's inaugural address to his nation forty-six years earlier, where the American president had implored his people to 'ask not what your country can do for you, ask what you can do for your country'. Dr Kalam's question carried a similar sentiment, but was more engaging and personal, as our president was apt to be. He asked: 'What can I give?' Everybody appeared driven by what he or she could take from the system, snatching away from others, furthering individual interests, mindless of the cost to society. Dr Kalam identified the root of all maladies in the madness of 'what can I take' and saw the cure in a personal introspection of 'what can I give'.

> Developed India by 2020 is a mission of a billion people. Every one of us has a role to play. It will be a reality if everyone 'Gives – What I can give', through individual, societal and nationwide participation in a national movement facilitated by the government. My interactions with our citizens in India and abroad, particularly the youth, demonstrate to me the positive energy flowing from individuals which makes them eager to give all they can to make India developed. The attitude of giving by every citizen and each group will definitely be an enriching factor for the whole nation, leading to an accelerated development process.[1]

President Kalam also called for participation of youth in the political system for a developed India by taking up politics as their career in large numbers. Our great democracy had to work for the people. Its political parties and their leaders – who were united in their own development and welfare but divided in having a vision for the country – would need to adjust or stand aside to facilitate development.

It was most satisfying for Dr Kalam to take the salute at the fifty-eighth Republic Day parade with the Russian President Vladimir Putin as the guest of honour. The strategic relationship between India and Russia had served more than just the long-term national interests of both countries. Their alliance had also effectively contributed to stability and security in Asia, and the world at large. This would be Dr Kalam's last salute as president. Having the president of Russia by his side indeed was a fitting finale to his life in public office, in view of Dr Kalam's work with the Russian space and defence establishments.

Soon after, on 30 January 2007, President Kalam conferred the 2005 Gandhi Peace Prize upon anti-apartheid campaigner and Nobel laureate Archbishop Desmond Tutu. Archbishop Tutu had observed that the war against terror could not be won till the conditions that made some people desperate enough to take violent action are addressed. He said, 'disagreements' should not be met by 'force of annihilation' but with 'forgiveness, negotiations and compromise'. 'There is need for seeing points of view of others,' he said.

Noting that there have been people like Adolf Hitler, Mussolini and Gen. Alberto Pinochet who seemed 'invincible', the South African leader emphasized the need for learning lessons from history sooner rather than later. He pointed out that nobody remembers such leaders – except on account of their brutality – but leaders of peace and tolerance like Mahatma Gandhi, Mother Teresa and Nelson Mandela are revered and held in high esteem by the world 'because they are good'. Hailing Mahatma Gandhi's ideology of non-violence, he said it was as relevant today as it was a century ago, and emphasized that 'practices of injustice' can never have the last word.[2]

President Kalam shared at the function that during his recent visit to South Africa, he traced the train journey of Mahatma Gandhi on 7 June 1893. He said he boarded a train at Penrich railway station near Durban for a journey to Pietermaritzburg, where Gandhiji was forcibly ejected from the train because of his skin colour. Gandhiji spent the winter night on the platform. That night, Gandhiji vowed to stay and fight the disease of racial prejudice. His idea of active non-violence was born on the railway platform. Dr Kalam said, 'The path of ahimsa is a great innovation of the human mind, and it was a very powerful non-violent tool that was instrumental in achieving our country's freedom.' He then underscored the historic relevance of Archbishop Tutu's work of washing away the feeling of hatred and revenge from the black majority people towards their white rulers after South Africa abolished apartheid.

> In 1994 after South Africa's first multiracial election President Nelson Mandela suggested Archbishop Tutu to chair the Truth and Reconciliation Commission, investigating the human rights violations of the previous thirty-four years. In this appointment, Archbishop Tutu counselled forgiveness and cooperation instead of revenge for past injustice. It is indeed a beautiful message for every political system on planet earth: Forgive and go forward with the development of the nation.[3]

Nelson Mandela and Archbishop Tutu ensured that the end of apartheid in South Africa not only marked the liberation of the country from a long period of colonialism followed by white domination, but their efforts also ensured that South Africa would see the restoration of peace, unity and human dignity. The two wise leaders encouraged offenders to take responsibility for their actions, to repair the harm they had done – by apologizing, returning stolen money or community service. Why could this not be done in India?

Dr Kalam celebrated the spirit of 'what can I give' during the inauguration of Kakarla Subbarao Radiological and Imaging Educational Sciences Trust (KREST) in Hyderabad:

> I am delighted to see Prof. Kakarla Subbarao, a pioneer in radiology, who has been known to me for over two decades. The more I understand his life, the more I am inspired. He brought tertiary health care to India. Part of his own house has been transformed into a school. Now he has given the other part of the house for KREST. Recently in the Republic Day address, the topic of my talk was 'what I can give to the nation'. Here, in front of me I see Prof. Kakarla Subbarao: giving his lifetime to the care of his patients, to his medical students in teaching and research, and giving resources and time for the education of children. Prof. Kakarla Subbarao is indeed an embodiment of giving.[4]

President Kalam gave a very inspiring lecture before the young scientists of Defence Research and Development Organization on 21 February 2007. He defined the five dimensions of a good scientific career through the examples of five Nobel laureates, each one possessing a special trait which he symbolizes. He described them as the values, lifetime commitment, universal outlook, converting challenges into opportunities and an attitude of magnanimity.

He shared the story of Sir C.V. Raman, who was in the first batch of Bharat Ratna award winners in 1954. President Dr Rajendra Prasad invited Sir Raman to be his personal guest at Rashtrapati Bhavan. Sir Raman politely declined the invitation, as his PhD student, who was valiantly trying to wrap up his thesis, needed his presence. Here was a scientist who gave up the pomp of a glittering ceremony associated with the country's highest honour to do his duty for his student. His was a rare trait of giving value to science over everything else.

Then Dr Kalam talked about Subrahmanyan Chandrasekhar. Two of Chandrasekhar's students in 1947, Tsung-Dao Lee and Chen Ning Yang, were doing particle physics research. Working at Yerkes Observatory in Lake Geneva, Wisconsin, Chandrasekhar would regularly drive 100 miles to Chicago to guide and teach Lee and Yang and others every week, frequently in difficult weather conditions. In 1957, these two students won the Nobel Prize in physics. Science indeed was a lifetime commitment for Chandrasekhar.

Prof. Bert Sakmann, a German medical doctor, realized that living organisms could be understood in engineering terms. He collaborated closely with electrical and computer scientists, and established the basic mechanism of vision and the existence of ionic channels in cell membranes. This in turn unlocked the mystery of conditions like diabetes, epilepsy, cardiac diseases and certain neuromuscular disorders. In Prof. Sakmann, we can see a doctor with the capability of working in multiple laboratories simultaneously and becoming a team scientist, sharing his research, sharing his work – and sharing its rewards too. He exemplified the borderless, universal nature of science.

Dutch scientist Prof. Paul Crutzen was awarded the Nobel Prize in chemistry for demonstrating that the chemical compounds of nitrogen oxides accelerate the destruction of stratospheric ozone, which protects the earth from the sun's ultraviolet radiation. From a young age, Prof. Crutzen was beset by adversity. The World War II and compulsory military service disrupted his education, and his family situation was challenging. It was extraordinary that even though the circumstances of his early years did not permit him to take up the study of science, his inherent passion for the subject drove him to achieve at the highest levels of his field. He converted his challenges into opportunities. He is indeed an example of how a strong mind can overcome disadvantages and succeed.

Dr Kalam then talked about the scientific magnanimity of Prof. Norman Borlaug. Nearly two years earlier, Dr Kalam had presented Dr Norman Borlaug with the first M.S. Swaminathan Award for Leadership in Agriculture at a function organized by the Trust for Advancement of Agricultural Sciences. It was at this event, attended largely by young scientists, that Dr Kalam first administered an oath on courage that would later become his hallmark:

Courage to think differently,
Courage to invent,
Courage to discover the impossible,
Courage to travel on an unexplored path,
Courage to share the knowledge,
Courage to remove the pain,
Courage to reach the unreached,
Courage to combat problems,
And succeed.[5]

Courage is not the foremost characteristic associated with Dr Kalam, but it was with him aplenty throughout his life. He was not one for bravado, and it is perhaps on account of this – and his sensitivity and concern for others – that a steely resolve in Dr Kalam was often overlooked. He had, though, proven his courage many times over in his public life, most recently in his stand-off with parliament in the office-of-profit debacle. More often, people would witness his care for people, which was given ample expression even while he occupied the office of president. Stories of Dr Kalam's kindness are legion, but his humanity never descended into mawkishness.

One of the delightful expressions of Dr Kalam's kindness was that he would take time away from his tightly packed schedule to give support where he felt it was needed – whenever he could. President Kalam called on the ailing Field Marshal S.H.F.J. Manekshaw, MC,[6] fondly called Sam Bahadur, at the Military Hospital, Wellington, near Udagamandalam (Ooty) on 24 February 2007. In his celebrated career of four decades, Sam Bahadur had fought in five wars, including World War II. President Kalam spent about fifteen minutes alone with the ninety-three-year-old veteran, whom he called 'a great son of India', and a person he admired. Kalam told Col R.T. Draper, who was commanding the hospital, to 'look after' Manekshaw, who was suffering from various age-related health complications.

During this time, I spoke to Sam Bahadur's personal attendant Bikram Singh Thapa, a subedar in the 5th Gorkha Rifles (Frontier Force), an infantry regiment of the Indian Army. When I asked him how he had come to be there, such a great distance from his home, he told me that Sam Bahadur had commanded the 5th Gorkha Rifles in 1950, and he would be taken care of by the regiment for the remainder of his days. The subedar proudly told me that his regiment has six battalions, and it has seen active service in virtually every major campaign the Indian Army has undertaken in its four wars with Pakistan.

Sam Bahadur was equally famous for his military genius and trademark frankness – this latter trait would get him into trouble and the former out of it – throughout his decorated career. He once faced a court of inquiry for his unseemly bluntness in a disagreement with Defence Minister V.K. Krishna Menon; but he was acquitted of any wrongdoing. He was even willing to face down the prime minister on tactical matters. Not only would he again emerge unscathed but Prime Minister Indira Gandhi would award him a Padma Vibhushan the following year.

According to legend, in a cabinet meeting towards the end of April 1971, Prime Minister Indira Gandhi asked army chief Manekshaw to go to war with Pakistan. Manekshaw flatly refused. When Smt. Gandhi asked the cabinet members to leave the room and the chief to stay, he offered to resign. She refused to accept his resignation, but rather sought his advice. He then said he could guarantee victory if she would allow him to prepare for the conflict on his terms, and set a date for it. The prime minister agreed to both these conditions. In December 1971, the Indian army under Manekshaw's leadership roundly defeated the Pakistan army. The war, lasting under a fortnight, saw more than 90,000 Pakistani armed forces personnel taken prisoner, and the unconditional surrender of Pakistan's eastern half, resulting in the formation of Bangladesh.

President Kalam wrote in the visitor's book at the hospital:

'Military Hospital, Wellington is always contributing the best. Please take care of our great wealth, our only Field Marshal Manekshaw.'

Later in the day, addressing the students and faculty members of Defence Service Staff College, Wellington, President Kalam raised a critical question. It was an issue that he had raised on several occasions, and it had always confounded him. He brought the question to the attention of the young aspiring staff service officers, because it was most relevant for the nation's future defence policy:

> I must share with you this question, which is bothering me. If you look from the time of Alexander, our nation has been regularly invaded. Many people invaded, one after the other. Even the Afghans invaded. Then the British came, the French, the Dutch, the Portuguese and ruled us. Now, why India has always been invaded? On the other hand, during the last 2,500 years, has India anytime invaded any nation? No. Why?
>
> This is something which you have to address yourself, before evolving big philosophy, big strategy, big national plans ... We have to change probably, we have to re-engineer our thoughts, concept and philosophy, because history shows we have always been invaded.[7]

President Kalam was now in the final months of his term. Although he had undoubtedly savoured his experience of Rashtrapati Bhavan – the grounds with abundant greenery and animals were a particular delight for him – he was quite prepared for his departure. He would miss his walks in the Mughal Gardens and the assortment of wildlife that had made the expansive grounds home. I doubt, indeed, if any president could have enjoyed the gardens more than our nature-loving Dr Kalam. The Mughal Gardens were host to an exquisite display of roses of all hues at this time of the year, and the scent of the flowers themselves was intoxicating.

One morning, Dr Kalam and I took a stroll through the Mughal Gardens, along its stone paths. The flowers were a kaleidoscope of colours, and the greenery itself exuded the fragrance of the brief Delhi spring. Dr Kalam was in a pensive mood, and was considering his options after his term. As we walked, a well-fed white cat walked nonchalantly across our path, barely acknowledging our presence. Dr Kalam gave a broad smile – neither of us was the least superstitious about such occurrences – and said, 'That cat will still be here after July, unlike me, who comes and goes after five years. These animals are the real permanent residents here.' I had to laugh. His humour and humility – not to mention his clear philosophical perspective – were so disarming that you could forget with him that he was bearer of the highest office of the land. That moment will stay with me, as will so many others from my cherished time with Dr Kalam.

I knew that Dr Kalam would truly miss those permanent residents of Rashtrapati Bhavan – a whole range of animals from peacocks to deer and domestic animals – at least as much as its grounds. I couldn't say that he would miss his quarters, for he only occupied one room, and he was never much attached to physical comfort. But his attachment to the animals of Rashtrapati Bhavan was another matter altogether. Earlier in his term, he had noticed a stricken fawn, barely mobile with its leg broken. He immediately became preoccupied with its welfare. Little did this young animal know that it had now found a most powerful saviour. But the staff knew soon enough: they were promptly charged with a mission to nurse the fawn back to health – and no questions were to be asked. Veterinary specialists were summoned, and Dr Kalam was not quite at ease until he saw the fawn happily walking again.

Perhaps it was fitting that in the last few months of his presidency, Dr Kalam would address the most prominent international gathering of his term of office. President Kalam had accepted an invitation to address the European parliament when President Josep Borrel Fontells, the twenty-second president of the European parliament and Spanish leader, visited him in October 2006. The parliamentary staff had wanted him to attend in January 2007, but President Kalam's tight schedule could not accommodate this. Under the rotational presidency of the European Union, President Josep Borrel's term ended in January 2007, and German leader Hans-Gert Pottering took over as twenty-third president of the European parliament. The invitation was renewed, and President

Kalam's address was fixed for 25 April 2007. Twenty-five minutes was allotted for the address.

What could be his message to the European parliament?

President A.P.J. Abdul Kalam departed on 24 April 2007 for a five-day visit to France and Greece. Besides the speech at the European parliament, Dr Kalam would visit the International Space University in Strasbourg. The vice-president of the European Union, Mario Mauro, the precept of the Strasbourg region, Gene-Paul Savgere, and India's ambassador to the European Union and France received President Kalam. Strasbourg had been the capital and principal city of the Alsace region, on the west bank of the Rhine adjacent to Germany and Switzerland. The city had suffered greatly in the past from historic decisions, wars and strategic politics of the great powers in Europe. But in more recent times, Strasbourg has become the seat of several international organizations and bodies, including the European parliament when it was created in 1962.

Soon after his arrival, Dr Kalam left for the International Space University (ISU) to give a lecture. The ISU is an international institution of higher learning, dedicated to the development of outer space for peaceful purposes. The ISU president, Prof. Michael Simpson, briefed Dr Kalam about the philosophy of 3-I's, which meant providing an Interdisciplinary, Intercultural and International environment for educating and training space professionals and postgraduate students.

President Kalam hailed the arrival of India on the global scene of space science and technology. He outlined the scope of India's aerospace programme to the students at ISU:

> Today, India with her 14,000 scientific, technological and support staff in multiple research centres, supported by about 500 industries and academic institutions, has the capability to build any type of satellite launch vehicle to place remote sensing, communications and meteorological satellites in different orbits, and space applications have become part of our daily life.
>
> India has today a constellation of six remote sensing and ten communication satellites serving applications like natural

> resource surveying, communication, disaster management support, meteorology, tele-education (10,000 classrooms) and telemedicine (200 hospitals).
>
> Our country is in the process of establishing 100,000 common service centres across the country through public–private partnership model for providing knowledge input to rural citizens.

After his lecture, Dr Kalam interacted with the students. Bijal 'Bee' Thakore, an Indian student doing her master's in space studies, asked Dr Kalam how long he thought it would be before the world would see the first Indian woman land on the moon or on Mars.

Dr Kalam answered matter-of-factly: 'Three of the astronauts who have taken on space missions have been of Indian origin – Rakesh Sharma, Kalpana Chawla and Sunita Williams. Two out of three are women. Hence the chances of Indian women landing on the moon or on Mars pretty soon are high.'

The next day, President Kalam was at the European parliament buildings, located outside the city centre of Strasbourg. The main parliament building is a very modern-looking curved structure dominated by glass. The sun was shining and the building was beautifully reflected in the waters of the River Ill. It was the first time that a president of India was to address the European parliament. President Kalam had a short preliminary meeting with President Pottering, and they walked together into a packed European parliament hall. This hall is much bigger than the Central Hall of the Indian parliament. After a concise introduction of less than two minutes, President Kalam took the podium.

Dr Kalam began with a Tamil quote from the Sangam[8] period that the world is one big family, and said that the European civilization has a unique place in human history. Its people were valiantly engaged in the adventure of exploring the planet earth, resulting in the discovery of many ideas and systems. Europe had seen the birth of modern science, leading to quantum leaps in technology. But Europe had also been the theatre of conflicts for hundreds of years among and between its nations, including the two world wars. It was against this backdrop and with these dynamics that the European Union was born with a vision for peace and prosperity for the entire region. The European Union had become an example for connection among nations. There was now no probability of war, and there would be lasting regional peace.

President Kalam said that the European Union had demonstrated to the world that it was possible to build a strong union of nations without compromising national identities. The European Union had become an inspirational model and an example to emulate for every region in the world.

> I have brought from India, a message: a message to start three important Indo-European missions which can contribute to global peace and prosperity. These missions, I am putting forth based on India's experience and the dynamics of the European Union.
>
> 1. The evolution of enlightened society – for evolving a citizenry with a value system, leading to a prosperous and peaceful world.
> 2. Leading to Energy Independence –a three-dimensional approach for energy choice toward realizing a clean planet earth.
> 3. A World Knowledge Platform – for synergizing the core competence of the European Union and India in certain areas for providing solutions to critical issues like water, healthcare and capacity building.[9]

Towards the end of his forty-five-minute speech, Dr Kalam recited an English poem composed by him,'A Message from Mother India,' about the European Union. The poem captured the essence of European geography, as well as the adventurous, creative and methodical spirit of the people who lived here.

Beautiful environment leads
To beautiful minds
Beautiful minds generate,
Freshness and creativity

Created explorers of land and sea
Created minds that innovate
Created great scientific minds
Created everywhere, why?

Gave birth to many discoveries
Discovered a continent and unknown lands
Ventured into unexplored paths
Created new highways

Then the poem turned to the conflicts in Europe's past, where countless bloody wars were waged in the name of religion; the Jews were persecuted, colonial campaigns were unleashed upon nations across continents and seas by its people – all this, and the two world wars, that brought unimaginable bloodshed and misery.

In the minds of the best
Worst was also born
Generated seeds of battle and hatred
Hundreds of years of wars and blood;

Millions of my wonderful children
Lost in the land and sea
Tears flooded many nations
Many engulfed in oceans of sadness

After establishing the two polarities – the best of the minds and the worst of the deeds – President Kalam positioned the European Union as the golden mean of human possibilities.

Then, then came, the vision of European Union,
Took the oath,
'Never to turn human knowledge,
Against ourselves or others.'

United in their thinking,
Actions emanated,
To make Europe prosperous and peaceful,
Born, the European Union.

That 'Glad Tidings' captivated
The people of the planets of my galaxy.
O! European Union, let your missions
Spread everywhere, like the air we breathe.

The way President Kalam held the mirror before more than 700 leaders from twenty-eight European countries was truly amazing. When he finished saying 'namaskar' with folded hands, the parliamentarians gave him a standing ovation and greeted him with rounds of applause. President Hans-Gert Pottering, of the European Parliament termed President Kalam's address to the European parliament extraordinary, the likes of which they had not heard before.[10]

5.7

Awakening

That is the real spiritual awakening, when something emerges from within you that is deeper than who you thought you were. So, the person is still there, but one could almost say that something more powerful shines through the person.

– Eckhart Tolle
Spiritual author

President Kalam arrived in Greece on 25 April 2007 late in the night. India's ambassador to Greece, Dr B. Balakrishnan, and the Greek chief of protocol received President Kalam at Athens airport. The following day, he was given a ceremonial reception at the Presidential Palace. Dr Kalam, escorted by the Greek president Karolos Papoulias, inspected the guard of honour. National anthems of both the countries were played. The Greek national anthem is called 'Hymn of Liberty' to honour the struggle of Greeks for independence in the eighteenth century after hundreds of years of Ottoman rule. Its words are passionate and optimistic in equal measure:

From the graves of our slain,
Shall thy valour prevail,
As we greet thee again,
Hail, Liberty! Hail![1]

President Papoulias had a surprise item for President Kalam. He showed Dr Kalam a coin depicting the figure of King Milinda and a symbol of the umbilical connection between the ancient civilizations of India and Greece.

Every child in India knows the battle between the Indian king Porus and the the Greek king Alexander the Great 2,400 years ago. Alexander overran the Persian Empire and reached the Jhelum, the western boundary of Porus's kingdom that stretched up to the Ganga in the East. The valour of King Porus blunted the courage of Alexander's army and it refused to march further into Indian lands. Alexander returned leaving behind Greek forces, which established themselves in the city of Takshashila. More than thirty Greek kings ruled and perished there, often in conflict with each other, before Chandragupta Maurya defeated King Seleucus and signed a treaty. Seleucus married his daughter to Chandragupta Maurya, and marriages between Indian and Greek families thereafter became a practice in the Indian ruling class. Greek troops even assisted Chandragupta Maurya in toppling the Nanda dynasty. Several Indo-Greek kingdoms ruled over the region from the Hindu Kush Mountains in the west to the Ganga–Yamuna plains in the east and the Vindhya Mountains in the south. Most of these kingdoms followed Buddhism.

President Kalam delivered a keynote address to a distinguished gathering of intellectuals organized by the prestigious think tank, the Hellenic Foundation for European and Foreign Policy (ELIAMEP).[2] Dr Kalam spoke on 'Dynamics of Peace and Prosperity'. A large number of Greek students of Hindi and Indian history and culture were present. He gave them food for thought, the kind that is rarely uttered by Western leaders: 'Without peace in our hearts, prosperity in our homes will not come. Without peace in our homes, prosperity in our society will not come. Without peace in our society, the nation will never prosper. If your neighbouring nation is not prosperous, your nation will not remain peaceful for long.' Dr Kalam's simple thoughts won the hearts of even the most seasoned of the academics there.

President Kalam took a detour to the Hellenic Aerospace Industries complex (HAI, Elliniki Aeroporiki Viomichania, or EAB in Greek), the leading aerospace company of Greece, 65 kilometres north-west of Athens. Over the years, the company had undertaken a great deal of subcontracting work with major international aerospace companies including Dassault Aviation, Lockheed Martin, Boeing and Airbus. Dr Kalam had shown a keen interest in the original designs of the Pegasus, an unmanned aerial vehicle developed here. He mingled with the engineers working in the assembly shop of the Mirage 2000 fighter jet and where the retrofit of ten existing Mirage 2000-E to Mirage 2000-5 was progressing at that time.

The next stop for Dr Kalam was the National Council for Scientific Research (NCSR 'Demokritos'). It is the largest multidisciplinary research centre in Greece, with international credentials in the fields of nanotechnology, energy and environment, biosciences, particle and nuclear science and informatics and telecommunications. Dr Kalam spoke on the 'Convergence of Technologies' and visited the institution's research facilities.

At the Hadzipatreion rehabilitation centre for children with cerebral palsy, Dr Kalam shared his own experience of working with similar organizations. He also spoke of his previous interactions with researchers of mental disorders like autism and permanent movement disorders. He presented ten computers in support of the centre's activities.

President Kalam went to the Phaleiron War Cemetery in Athens, and paid homage at the graves of Indian servicemen who died during World War II. In 1940, Greece was overrun by Germany, Italy and Bulgaria in an attack from 'all the four sides'. The three invaders divided the country between them, and their subsequent plundering of its resources for their war machines caused great misery to the Greek people. The 4th Indian Infantry Division sailed to Greece as part of the British force and liberated Athens in October 1944.

In the evening, at the banquet in President Kalam's honour, President Papoulias welcomed Dr Kalam in Sanskrit.

Rashtrapati Mahabhaga, Suswagatam Yavana Deshe

Respected President, You are welcome in Greece.

On 29 April 2007, President Kalam visited the Acropolis, the 'Sacred Rock' of Athens, which is considered one of the most important historic sites in the world. Dr Kalam spent about forty minutes at the Acropolis. The most famous of the buildings there is the exquisite Parthenon, dedicated to the goddess Athena, whom the people of Athens considered their patron. It was constructed more than 2,400 years ago. Walking through the stone-paved pathways, Dr Kalam freely mingled with the visitors.

When he met a large group of school children, he asked them to recite after him:'Dream, Dream, Dream because dreams transform into thoughts and thoughts lead to action.'He was always at work when it came to inspiring children. The children responded wholeheartedly, reciting the lines and clapping joyously. Dr Kalam presented an autographed copy of his book *Ignited Minds* to archaeologist Bennerie Ionne, who showed the president around the Acropolis. The visit was almost over when Dr Kalam inquired about Socrates: 'Where did he live?' He was told that it was here in a cave that Socrates was imprisoned, and ultimately sentenced to death by drinking poison. Dr Kalam insisted that he go there; and there was no way he could be refused.

Dr Kalam trekked to the nearby Philopappos Hill to the cave where Socrates had been imprisoned. It was dark inside. Dr Kalam sensed a strange serenity in the cave. He requested some solitude; the accompanying officials respectfully obliged. In the dimly lit cave he stood at the place where, declining the request of his friends to escape, Socrates had drunk the cup of poison as the punishment given to him for propagating inappropriate thoughts amongst youth, and thus sacrificed his life.

Dr Kalam later narrated his experience to me and we included it in our book *Squaring the Circle*. My mind was filled with many questions about what had transpired in the cave. He heard in his imagination Socrates telling him that 2,500 years had gone by and Kalam was the only leader who cared to visit his cave prison. That he had sacrificed his life for the cause of glory of human freedom and majesty of righteous life. Socrates said that he knew that Kalam was concerned for the future of humanity and he was seeking wisdom for the twenty-first-century planet earth.

> When I emerged from Socrates' cave, I realized I have a message to convey to the people. Humanity needs a great vision to forego all conflict and move towards a common goal of peace and prosperity for every human being. We foresee the birth of a world vision leading to a 'liveable planet earth'. This vision will be greater than any other goal ever aspired to by humanity.[3]

On 22 May 2007, President Kalam inaugurated a national convention on human values in education through 'Jeevan Vidya' at IIT, New Delhi. The 'Jeevan Vidya' concept was pioneered by Baba Shri A. Nagraj Sharma and propagated by Prof. Ganesh Bagaria and Prof. Rajeev Sangal, starting at the Indian Institute of Technology, Kanpur.

Dr Kalam met Prof. Rajeev Sangal during the formative years of the International Institute of Information Technology, Hyderabad (IIIT-H), which was founded in 1998 as an autonomous university. The idea of IIIT-H was born in the mind of Dabbala Rajagopal 'Raj' Reddy, an Indian-American computer scientist and dean of School of Computer Science at Carnegie Mellon University, Pittsburgh, Pennsylvania, USA. He convinced the chief minister of Andhra Pradesh, Chandrababu Naidu, who hailed from the same district, Chittoor, in Andhra Pradesh, where Prof. Raj Reddy was born. Chief Minister Naidu lent his wholehearted support to the idea and provided land and grants for the buildings. A governing council consisting of eminent people from academia, industry and government presides over the governance of the institution.

Prof. Raj Reddy invited Prof. Rajeev Sangal, working with him at the Carnegie Mellon University, to head the new institution and develop it as a research university, focused on the core areas of information technology. Information and communications technology was sweeping across the globe, and it was imperative that bright Indian minds were trained at an international standard without going abroad.

The institute structured itself not in the form of departments, but as a cluster of research laboratories in a host of areas, with computation or IT providing the connecting thread. Emphasis was placed on the development of technology and applications, which can be transferred for use to industry and society. It was also decided to carry out basic research that can be used to solve real-life problems.

The growth of information and communication technology has been bewildering. A new generation has found their world very different from that of their parents. But then, bewilderment is not a good mental state. The power of technology must be used with discretion. The Internet can be a window to the knowledge world, a dip into the Gyan Ganga, or a door to pornography and all manner of turpitude.

Youngsters armed with technology must know what is worthy in a prompt and efficient manner. It is not within the scope of technology to decide what is worthy. The Internet does not tell anyone what to seek. Who will decide what is worthy? Without discernment, technology is aimless, directionless and therefore can be put to any use – constructive or destructive. A student who is trained in information and communication technology without discretion – without a grasp of what is worthy – would be aimless and directionless. Moreover, he would be vulnerable to moral degradation; and perhaps prone to behaviour that is deleterious to himself and others.

The general public perception of the young IT community had been of youngsters with plenty of money: beer-drinking, fun-loving people with a liberal lifestyle. This image is at odds with the vast majority of IT professionals. Prof. Rajeev Sangal decided to challenge public misconceptions of the industry and change the conditioning of his students. He fostered a serene atmosphere at the institute, and ensured that appropriate attention was paid on campus to larger human and societal concerns. In 2005, Prof. Sangal designed a human values course around 'Jeevan Vidya', and made it a regular part of the academic curriculum at IIIT-H. Seeing its transformative effect on young minds, several other universities would later adopt this course.

Dr Kalam maintained regular contact with Prof. Rajeev Sangal. He understood 'Jeevan Vidya' as a programme concerned with addressing the basic causes of violence, corruption, exploitation, domination, terrorism and war. Violent and antisocial behaviour, unless it is dealt with compassionately and with due regard for its root cause, could indeed worsen. Dr Kalam saw the innate merit in Jeevan Vidya. He perceived this course as an effective means of addressing the causes of conflict of all magnitudes: 'I understand Jeevan Vidya is a "teachable human value-based skill" that can address inherent conflicts within the mind of the individual, within families, in organizations and in public life. Inner conflict is the very essence of violence.'[4]

Dr Kalam spoke as a prophet that day, radiating with divinity. He said,

> Conscience is the light of the soul that burns within the chambers of our psychological heart. It is as real as life is. It raises the voice in protest whenever anything is thought of or done contrary to righteousness. Conscience is a form of truth that has been transferred through our genetic stock in the form of the knowledge of our own acts and feelings as right or wrong.
>
> Conscience is also a great ledger where our offences are booked and registered. It is a terrible witness. It threatens, promises, rewards and punishes, keeping all under its control. If conscience stings once, it is an admonition, if twice, a condemnation. Cowardice asks, 'Is it safe?' Greed asks, 'Is there any gain in it?' Vanity asks, 'Can I become great?' Lust asks, 'Is there pleasure in it?' But conscience asks, 'Is it right?' Why have we become deaf to its voice? Insensitive to its pricks? Callous to its criticism? The result is corruption.
>
> Corruption is an assault on consciousness. The habit of taking bribes and seeking favours has become very common. People holding important positions do not consider their conscience. They pretend everything is all right. Do they not have any idea of the law of action and reaction? Have they forgotten how impressions of the subconscious mind and their force work? If you take bribes, your thoughts and actions are registered in the subconscious mind. Will you not be carrying forward your dishonesty to your next generations, causing them great suffering? It is a painful reality that corruption has become a way of life, affecting all aspects of living – personal as well as social.

After making some effort in seeing that President Kalam was not interested in seeking a second term in office, the United Progressive

Alliance on 10 June 2007 announced that the next president of India would be from their fold. The Election Commission of India issued the notification for the presidential election on 16 June 2007, and the election was scheduled for 19 July 2007.

On 14 June 2007, the United Progressive Alliance declared Smt. Pratibha Patil, the governor of the state of Rajasthan, as its candidate for the presidential election. The Left parties, the Bahujan Samaj Party (BSP), the Dravida Munnetra Kazhagam (DMK) and the Shiv Sena also supported her candidature. A valiant attempt was made by the regional parties to bring Dr Kalam back to the fray. The assortment of parties – the All India Anna Dravida Munnetra Kazhagam (AIADMK) led by J. Jayalalithaa, the Samajwadi Party led by Mulayam Singh Yadav, the Telugu Desam Party (TDP) lead by Chandrababu Naidu and the Indian National Lok Dal (INLD) led by Om Prakash Chautala – came together as the United National Progressive Alliance (UNPA). A delegation from the UNPA met Dr Kalam on 20 June 2007 and requested that he stand for the presidential elections. While Dr Kalam had received literally thousands of emails imploring him to seek a second stint as president, and was aware of the overwhelming public sentiment for him to stay at Rashtrapati Bhavan, he knew that it was time for him to depart from politics.

The next day, Dr Kalam saw the culmination of a project he had sponsored nearly a decade earlier. On 21 June 2007, President Kalam handed a replica of the mobile autonomous launcher (MAL) of the BrahMos missile to the chief of the army staff, General J.J. Singh, symbolizing the commencement of the delivery of the missile's land version to the army. The seeds of this joint venture were sown on 12 February 1998 when Dr Kalam, then scientific adviser to the defence minister, and N.V. Mikhailov, first deputy defence minister of Russia, signed an intergovernmental agreement. There had been fourteen launches of BrahMos missiles from India between June 2001 and April 2007, four of which were army versions.

President Kalam said that the time had come for BrahMos Aerospace Limited to work on the Mark II version of the BrahMos supersonic cruise missile so that India could still be the market leader in hypersonic cruise missiles. In the emerging network-centric warfare scenario, state-of-the-art fast-deployment hypersonic missile systems would be necessary to maintain our force-level supremacy, he said.

Flanked by the Minister of State for Defence Pallam Raju, Ambassador Vyacheslav I. Trubnikov of the Russian Federation, chairman of BrahMos Aerospace, Alexandre Dergachev, scientific adviser to the defence minister, M. Natarajan, and BrahMos CEO Dr Sivathanu Pillai, Dr Kalam inspected the mobile command post and the mobile autonomous launcher of the BrahMos system. The army personnel present explained the sequence of the launch system to him. The two stages of the BrahMos rocketry propel the missile to a mind-boggling velocity of 1 km per second and give it a range of 290 kilometres. At 9 m long, it is quite sizeable, and can carry conventional warheads weighing 300 kilograms.

While leaving the venue, Dr Kalam said he visualized long-range hypersonic cruise missiles not only delivering payloads, but also returning to base after a mission. He said this would lead to a reusable class of cruise missiles within a decade. Dr Kalam always took a long-term view!

On 22 June 2007, President Kalam made his formal announcement that he would not run for a second term. Party politics was never his domain: 'Once you are interested and you are a President, you have to propagate as a candidate. I did not want to damage the name of the Rashtrapati Bhavan, which has been made into a people's Bhavan during my tenure.'[5]

The National Democratic Alliance (NDA) eventually fielded the incumbent vice-president Bhairon Singh Shekhawat. In the election held on 19 July 2007, Smt. Pratibha Patil was elected as the twelfth president of India.

5.8

One Man's Bible

> There are basically two types of people. People who accomplish things, and people who claim to have accomplished things. The first group is less crowded.
>
> – Mark Twain
> Nineteenth-century American writer

The members of parliament hosted a farewell for Dr Kalam in the Central Hall of parliament on 23 July 2007. President Kalam thanked Prime Minister Manmohan Singh and his predecessor Atal Bihari Vajpayee, with whom he had worked during his five years of presidency. He also expressed his gratitude to Vice-President Bhairon Singh Shekhawat for his support throughout his term of office. But having dispensed with these obligatory niceties, he used the occasion for some plain talk and raised two very important points. He later published this speech in his book *Turning Points*.

> There is a general feeling and appreciation that the environment internal and external to India's system of governance has gone through rapid and apparently irreversible change. The challenges posed to national sovereignty, integrity and economic growth posed by these changes need to be addressed coherently and rapidly. Our social organizations tend to deteriorate and become crisis prone. As a social entity, India's system of governance appears to have entered a stage of crisis, and this is a clarion call for self-renewal and change.
>
> The fact that the Indian economy is globalizing has strengthened

> our economy. The nation is richer, but great vigilance is needed to enhance the power of parliament. International treaties now increasingly govern much of economic decision-making, and the Indian parliament is one of the few parliaments in the world that does not have a system of effective treaty oversight in place. These treaties are by and large a fait accompli by the time they come to parliament. Hence, the power to oversee and legislate on treaties and agreements with foreign nations is urgently required for parliament.[1]

Dr Kalam said that the future political leadership the world over has to rise to the challenge of sustainable growth, development, environment and resources. The national leadership has to radiate confidence in our people that 'we can do it', he added. Urging the MPs to debate his suggestions, Dr Kalam said that they should draw up a 'Parliamentary Vision for the Nation', similar to the framing up of country's constitution:

> This twenty-first century parliamentary vision for India needs to have a global and long-term perspective, and needs to be underpinned with implementation strategies, integrated structures and action plans for transforming India into a developed country by 2020 – with National Prosperity Index as a measure – and acquiring energy independence before 2030.[2]

On 24 July 2007, President Kalam spoke to the people on national television in his characteristic and by now very popular style: simple words, eye contact, and unabashed rendering of his aspirations of making India a developed nation. His conviction about the development of India and his belief in the people of his country was amazing, if not audacious. He, of all the nation's leaders, could understand that India's aspirations were inextricable from the personal hopes and dreams of each of its billion-strong citizens. And in this, only Dr A.P.J. Abdul Kalam could quote a Disney song's lyrics in a meaningful way:

> When you wish upon a star,
> Makes no difference who you are
> Anything your heart desires
> Will come to you.[3]

It is important that this speech of Dr Kalam is discussed here, because it puts on record the passion of a great visionary, which contrasts with the indifference of our system towards development and growing in stature as a nation.

Dr Kalam distilled ten messages out of his five 'beautiful and eventful' years in Rashtrapati Bhavan. Calling his last day in office a thanksgiving occasion, he said that he enjoyed every minute of his tenure. He stated that he had been enriched by the wonderful association with people of his country, hailing from all different walks of life – politics, science and technology, academics, arts, literature, business, judiciary, administration, local bodies, farming, homemaking, special children, media – and above all, from the youth and student community, who he said 'are the future wealth of our country'.

Dr Kalam enumerated the ten imperatives for accelerating development: to meet the aspiration of the nation's youth for living in a developed country; to empower the villages; to mobilize rural core competence for competitiveness; to develop the entire supply chain of seed to food as a backbone for agricultural growth; to defeat problems and succeed; to overcome problems through partnership; to have courage in combating calamities; to develop connectivity for societal transformation; to defend the nation, which he said must be our pride; and finally, to start a youth movement for Developed India 2020.

Dr Kalam recalled a question from a little girl – Anukriti of Sri Sathya Sai Jagriti Vidya Mandir School, of Darwa village in Haryana – when she came to visit Rashtrapati Bhavan on 22 May 2006. He said that Anukriti had asked him, 'Why cannot India become a developed nation before the year 2020?' Dr Kalam said that he had assured her that her dream would be taken to the highest institution of the nation, and we would work for it to be achieved before 2020. Dr Kalam said that this question reflected how the desire to live in a developed India has entered into the minds of the Indian children. He declared that

> The same feelings are echoed by over fifteen lakh youth, whom I have met so far and who represent the dream of the 540 million youth of

> the nation. The aspirations of the young to live in a prosperous, safe and proud India should be the guiding factor in whatever profession we contribute.

Dr Kalam made mention of his visit to Nagaland on 26 October 2002, soon after his assuming the office of president. He said it was a unique experience for him at Khuzama village to meet tribal village council members and discuss with them the village progress and the dream of village citizens. He was very happy to see the empowered village council functioning with financial powers and taking decisions. He saw a truly prosperous village, with abundant fruit and vegetable production. It was, however, a paradise in isolation. There was a need for providing a physical connectivity through quality roads for enabling faster movement of products from villages to the market. That meeting gave him a powerful message about the transformation which can take place for the 600,000 villages of India, if all the villages are empowered to deal with their development and are well connected among themselves and with the urban societies.

Dr Kalam then discussed the initiative of Periyar Maniammai College of Technology for Women at Vallam in Thanjavur. This programme is dedicated to providing urban amenities in rural areas involving sixty-five villages with a population of 300,000. It includes provision of physical connectivity, electronic connectivity and knowledge connectivity leading to economic connectivity. The programme has health care centres, primary- to graduate-level education and vocational training centres. This had resulted in large-scale employment generation and the creation of a number of entrepreneurs with the active support of 1,000 self-help groups. Two hundred acres of wasteland had been developed into cultivable land. The villagers were busy in cultivation, planting herbal and medicinal plants, generating power using biomass, food processing – and above all, running marketing centres. A credible development model for Indian villages was in operation.

He added that the villagers with technical support from Periyar Maniammai College of Engineering for Women had worked with experts from the Japan External Trade Organization (JETRO) on various products, for which core competence and raw materials were available in Thanjavur district. They had developed internationally competitive prototypes for fifty-five lifestyle products with the support of JETRO specialists and constructive feedback from exhibitions at Delhi and Tokyo. This cooperative venture had enhanced the innovative ability of the people of the villages, enabling them to develop and produce internationally viable products. He said this initiative proved that the urban–rural divide could indeed be bridged.

Dr Kalam shared his experience of meeting more than 6,000 farmers from different states and Union territories who had visited Rashtrapati Bhavan. The farmers evinced keen interest in the Mughal Gardens, the Herbal Gardens, the Spiritual Garden, the Musical Garden, the Bio-diesel Garden and the Nutrition Garden, and interacted at some length with the specialists managing them. The farmers gave many practical suggestions, which he shared with the agricultural scientists during a national symposium on 'Agriculture Cannot Wait'.

Dr Kalam said that there was no other way but to double the agricultural production with reduced land, reduced water resources and reduced manpower. He declared that we must improve the economic conditions of the nation through the principle of 'Seed to Food', since agriculture was the backbone of the nation. We should empower the farmers to protect and nurture the fertile land for the second green revolution. Meeting the scientists and farmers had given him the confidence that the nation is poised to increase the agricultural GDP growth by at least 4 per cent per annum. This would be possible through the partnership of farmers and agricultural scientists and industry, particularly for value addition.

Dr Kalam talked of meeting, at Coimbatore, Vidwan S.R. Krishna Murthy, who had no hands or legs. He recalled, 'On 24 February 2007 at Coimbatore, a smiling person in his late fifties was brought to me on a wheelchair. His radiant face was revealing his happy state of mind. I greeted him and asked him how this had happened. He smilingly said that it was from birth. He thanked God, his parents, teachers and many others for giving him confidence, training and help. I asked him, what I could do for him. He said, "I don't need anything from you. I would like to sing in front of you." I readily agreed. He sang melodiously Saint Thyagaraja's Pancharatna kriti *"Endaro Mahanubhavulu"*. I was moved with the brilliance of his voice.'

Dr Kalam asked, 'What is the message?' And answered it himself, 'Despite being physically challenged, the latent talent of music could blossom in this person with his positive attitude and perseverance. Now he wants to give, give and give his art to inspire others. I invited him to perform in the Rashtrapati Bhavan art theatre.'

Dr Kalam spoke about the indomitable spirit of the people of Jammu and Kashmir – particularly the children – in the wake of the devastating earthquake in 2005. He said, 'I visited Urusa village on 26 November 2005. I found that the school building had been severely damaged. However, the classes were being conducted in tents. I appreciated the courage of the people of Urusa in defeating their problems. Undaunted by their losses, they had mastered the problems and prevented the problems from becoming their master.'

Highlighting another society at the opposite end of the country, Dr Kalam mentioned his observations on the people of Car Nicobar Island. He said that in 2005, he met the people of Chuckchucha village there, while various reconstruction and rehabilitation activities were in progress after the tsunami. During discussions with members of the tribal council, he realized that the cohesiveness of their society had helped their people to survive the aftermath of the tsunami. Even though there were many human losses due to the tragedy of 26 December 2004, the people had taken possession of the affected victims as their children; there was nothing like an orphanage on Car Nicobar Island.

Talking about the importance of connectivity for societal transformation, Dr Kalam said, 'I addressed the Pan-African Parliament on 16 September 2004, at Johannesburg, South Africa. This was attended by fifty-three member countries of the African Union, where I proposed the concept of a pan-African e-network for providing a seamless and integrated satellite, fibre-optic and wireless network connecting fifty-three African countries, at an estimated cost of 100 million dollars. The pilot project on tele-education and telemedicine in Ethiopia has already been commissioned. Indira Gandhi National Open University has taken up the MBA course for thirty-four Ethiopian students of Addis Ababa and Harmaya Universities. As regards telemedicine, Dr Rajiv Menon, Cardiologist at CARE Hospital, Hyderabad, visited Black Lion Hospital, Addis Ababa, and thereafter he and his team have been connected live with their counterparts at Black Lion Hospital since November 2006.'

Dr Kalam recounted his visit to Siachen Glacier located at 17,000 feet above sea level, his underwater journey in INS *Sindhurakshak*, and his flight in the Sukhoi-30 fighter jet. Dr Kalam said, 'In these three experiences, I personally felt proud of our ever-vigilant soldiers, sailors and air warriors performing their tasks beyond the call of their duty, even in the most adverse circumstances – natural and man-made.'

Dr Kalam said that during the five years of his presidency, he had the opportunity to present colours to many regiments and participated in a number of passing-out parades. He also said he met troops who were going to undertake peace missions and interacted with the family members of our defence personnel. Dr Kalam said, 'The nation cherishes the valour, commitment and devotion to duty of our defence forces.'

Dr Kalam then spoke about the need of a youth movement for Developed India 2020. He mentioned a group of dedicated people who are putting into practice the aspiration of transforming our youth into enlightened citizens. He said, 'The Lead India 2020 Foundation created by Dr N.B. Sudershan is training thousands of students in many districts of Andhra Pradesh in partnership with the district administration.'

Dr Kalam said, 'I talked to Padma, a student leader from Andhra Pradesh Tribal Welfare School, Nalgonda. She related how she had weaned her father from smoking after imbibing the spirit of the ten-point oath from the Lead India Training Camp. This gives me an assurance that the youth of our country are on the right path through this mission-oriented programme. With the ignited minds of the 540 million youth below the age of twenty-five – which I consider is the most powerful resource on the earth, under the earth and above the earth – we have to empower the youth through value-based education and leadership.'

Dr Kalam concluded by saying, 'I was touched by the variety of Indian panorama, emotional content of the tune, cultural diversity and unity of minds in the vast land of ours. I have cited these examples just to give a glimpse of the richness of our tradition and effort being taken by different agencies to preserve it. Whomsoever I met, they constantly asked what they can give to the nation. We should constantly strive to empower such members of society. With this spirit, I am extremely happy that we are on the right path.'

He said in a tone reverberating with divine energy, 'My dear citizens, let us resolve to continue to work for realizing the missions of Developed India 2020. Let us make a nation where the rural and urban divide has reduced to a thin line, where there is an equitable distribution and adequate access to energy and quality water, where agriculture, industry and the service sector work together in concert, where education with a value system is not denied to any meritorious candidates because of societal or economic discrimination. A nation, which is the best destination for the most talented scholars, scientists, and investors, where the best of health care is available to all, where the governance is responsive, transparent and corruption free, where poverty has been totally eradicated, illiteracy removed and crimes against women and children are absent and none in the society feels alienated. A nation that is prosperous, healthy, secure, peaceful and happy and continues with a sustainable growth path; and above all, a nation that is one of the best places to live in, and is proud of its leadership.'

Dr Kalam thanked every citizen of India for showering upon him love and affection throughout the five years of his presidency, and for their cooperation and support. He declared that his mission in life is to bring a sense of connection to the billion hearts and minds of the people of India in our multicultural society, and to instil the self-confidence in the people that 'we can do it'.

President Kalam's farewell speech stands with the 'India's Tryst with Destiny' speech of Prime Minister Jawaharlal Nehru and the 'I have a dream' speech of Martin Luther King Jr. Or was it his 'one man's Bible', as I would know a little later?

Since the time we wrote *Wings of Fire* together in the 1990s, I have become Dr Kalam's literary assistant. He had been a voracious reader all his life, and there was not a day that he had not read at least one passage from a book; though I am sure he never read any book cover to cover. He amassed a sizeable personal library; but he was far from reverent with the books themselves. He would scribble on them without hesitation while reading; he would mercilessly fold a page to return to that point later and use his airline boarding passes as bookmarks.

It remained an enigma to me how he could come across a certain book and locate a particular line – somewhere buried in the middle of the book – as the most appropriate message at that point in time. When I asked him his secret, he said, 'I never chase books, the books find me.'

'And why should they find you?' I asked.

He answered, 'Because I am seeking them.'

Pitying my vexed look, he said, 'Buddy, good authors are indeed instruments of God, and great books write themselves. They carry messages for any soul that may be looking for some solution, some guidance, some solace.'

So when he gave me *One Man's Bible* written by Nobel Prize–winning author Gao Xingjian, I was eager to know the message it was bringing with it. I did not have to wait for long. In less than an hour's time, the message was in front of me: 'Whether in "beehive" offices in Beijing or in isolated rural towns, daily life is riddled with paranoia and fear, as revolutionaries, counterrevolutionaries, reactionaries, counter reactionaries, and government propaganda turn citizens against one another.[4]

After the swearing-in ceremony in the Central Hall of parliament on 25 July 2007, the former president and the new president proceeded to Rashtrapati Bhavan in a horse-driven carriage as per tradition.

Drama remains – only the actors change. It was an exact reprise of the ceremonial on 25 July 2002 when former president K.R. Narayanan brought the then new president A.P.J. Abdul Kalam from parliament. This time, former president A.P.J. Abdul Kalam was bringing the new president Smt. Pratibha Patil to her home for the next five years.

Eminent Indian jurist and parliamentarian Dr L.M. Singhvi proclaimed 'Welcome Citizen Kalam' in *The Tribune*. He wrote,

> President Kalam is completing his term in the midst of a countrywide accolade of affection for his intellectual calibre and warm human qualities. A glorious presidential term will soon be behind him. A peoples' president is how he will long be remembered. With no personal axes to grind, he occupied the august office and edifice of presidency with great distinction. He came to that office with no experience of political and constitutional intricacies and made no more than one untoward and innocent mistake. Innocence and humility are what mark the man whose warm heart and brilliant mind have carved a niche for him in the hearts of the people ...
>
> What does a president do when he retires? Kalam is energetic and in good health. I see for him the role of the nation's conscience and the civil society's voice. He tells me he will teach and write. That he must. But his voice should always be heard above the din of the distorted discourse of plotting and scheming politicians in our public life. His spiritual and moral energies should be harnessed in awakening India and realizing its spiritual, cultural, economic and social aspirations. The nation needs the sanity and equanimity of Kalam, the austere and ascetic citizen.[5]

It was time for Dr Kalam to move on. There were two suitcases he had brought here in 2002; and he left with two suitcases. Dr Kalam flew to Chennai in the evening. V. Ponraj, who by now had become his principal thought partner in matters of development and politics, and Anna University vice chancellor Prof. D. Viswanathan accompanied him. Some of us think holding on makes us strong; for Dr Kalam it was letting go.

Part Six

EMANCIPATION

I am a well in this great land
Looking at its millions of children
To draw from me
The inexhaustible divinity
And take it afar
Water drawn from the well.

– A.P.J. Abdul Kalam
Wings of Fire

6.1

Where Eagles Soar

> Great men are like eagles, and build their nest on some lofty solitude.
>
> – Arthur Schopenhauer
> Eighteenth-century German philosopher

Dr A.P.J. Abdul Kalam was, in a sense, never more in demand than in his retirement from national politics. At an age when most people are leading evermore sedate and limited lives, he seemed to be going from strength to strength – and he showed no physical signs of flagging. Unquestionably, he had good genetics: his father had lived an active life until his nineties, and his elder brother Maracayer was still going strong at a similar age. But it was a sense of mission that really drove India's most popular president. He felt that he had a duty to the nation – and in a sense to the world – and this gave him almost boundless stamina. And he would certainly need it for the following years.

Dr Kalam was now free to do what he enjoyed most: talking to our youth; inspiring them and urging them reach their potential. And the first request for his time would be exactly for this purpose. At the sixth convocation of the International Institute of Information Technology (IIIT), Hyderabad, on 28 July 2007, Chairman Raj Reddy announced – amidst an uproarious ovation by the students – that Dr Kalam would devote part of his time to teaching students there. He said, 'We want the institute, which is at the forefront of research, to have the potential to make a major social impact. Our innovative curriculum allows the students flexibility in selecting courses and projects, and Dr Kalam's presence here would create societally responsible technology leaders of tomorrow.'

Our former president was also in demand for social projects. The governing board of the Emergency Management and Research Institute (EMRI) resolved on 30 July 2007 to appoint Dr Kalam chairman emeritus. EMRI, a non-profit organization, had provided comprehensive emergency response services since August 2005. It had supported the Andhra Pradesh government's efforts to provide a free emergency response service of an international standard, to all citizens of the state.

At any rate, the rest of Dr Kalam's life would be spent in public service of one kind or another. On the occasion of India's sixtieth Independence Day, Dr Kalam hoisted the national flag at IIIT, Hyderabad, before an ecstatic gathering of more than 1,000 students. Later in the day, with Chief Minister Dr Y.S. Rajasekhar Reddy and Finance Minister K. Rosaiah of Andhra Pradesh standing by his side, Dr Kalam dedicated to the people of Andhra Pradesh the free 108 emergency service. He lauded the Emergency Management Research Institute (EMRI) for having saved 14,000 lives during the preceding two-and-a-half years and said it was a good model of public–private partnership for the rest of the country to emulate. 'It is time for putting in place a decentralized national emergency management mission on the lines of 108 in Andhra Pradesh to save lives in critical situations like road accidents,' he declared.

On this day, Dr Kalam gathered another in his growing band of disciples: EMRI chief executive officer Venkat Changavalli. Venkat would soon realize this dream; when Dr Kalam made a statement, it was blessed with impetus and power.

Dr Kalam was invited to speak at an international conference in celebration of the fiftieth anniversary of space exploration – 'Fifty Years in Space' – at the California Institute of Technology. This would give Dr Kalam an opportunity to meet the scientists at the Graduate Aerospace Laboratories of the California Institute of Technology

(GALCIT), Northrop Grumman Space Technology and NASA's Jet Propulsion Laboratory. He had been interacting with several of them, but had not had an opportunity to visit until now, as there was no presidential visit to America during his term.

Dr Kalam arrived in San Francisco late in the night of 18 September 2007. I travelled with him. It was a Delhi–New York Air India flight with a stopover at London. There was special status given to Dr Kalam, and the immigration officers at the New York John F. Kennedy Airport were most courteous and stamped our passports almost instantly. Embassy officials were present to take care of Dr Kalam during our stopover of about two hours before we boarded our flight to San Francisco. By the time we landed in San Francisco, it was past midnight there, and it was thirty-two hours after we had boarded the plane in Delhi.

Dr Kalam stayed at Taj Campton Place, San Francisco. The United States government had assigned Dr Kalam two high-ranking security officials to ensure his safety. They would be his shadow throughout his stay in the United States. These were tall, powerfully built men in suits, bearing automatic weapons. They were network-connected with GPS and in constant radio communication with the police department. Dr Kalam talked with them as he would with any of the people we met. He found this experience quite a contrast from that of India. For years he had been surrounded by twenty security officers wherever he went, yet he had never had any real opportunity to relate to his minders.

After a sleep to shake off the fatigue from the long journey, Dr Kalam began 19 September 2007 with a breakfast meeting with a group of professors from the University of California, including Prof. Bruce Alberts, a leading biochemist at UCSF (University of California, San Francisco), and S. Shankar Sastry, dean of UC Berkeley College of Engineering.

We then took a road trip to CISCO in San Jose. The CEO of CISCO, John Chambers, was standing in the lobby to receive Dr Kalam. I knew of John Chambers for his annual salary of twenty million dollars, and was thus pleasantly surprised by his simple demeanour and engaging manner. He exhibited a complete absence of the airs and graces that are so common in the Indian business world. Unless you were introduced to him, it would be difficult to differentiate him from anyone else in his offices.

Dr Kalam almost bowled him over by asking, 'So tell me, John, how did you take CISCO from seventy million to thirty-eight billion?' He took a moment to adjust to Dr Kalam's frankness and gestured him to the TelePresence System. 'I will tell you, sir, and more. Our guys in Bangalore are waiting to see you.'

CISCO TelePresence System had been recently introduced. It provided high-definition 1080p video, spatial audio, and a set-up designed to link two physically separated rooms so that they resembled a single conference room, regardless of the location. It was indeed an amazing experience: we faced the CISCO team at Bangalore as if they were sitting just across the table from us. It was quite realistic – we were hooked up to microphones to communicate, the image sizes exactly matched the body sizes of our opposites. It felt for me like a 'teleporting' experience from a science-fiction film.

In a sense, it was quite ironic, and even a little surreal. We had travelled most of the way around the world, deep into the western hemisphere, and here we were, sitting in a virtual office speaking to fellow Indians as if we were in an attractive office in Bangalore. Dr Kalam was, as usual, either at the cutting edge of technology, or anticipating it. At any rate, the Bangalore team secured Dr Kalam's acceptance to inaugurate CISCO's Globalization Centre East campus in Bangalore in the coming month.

John Chambers hosted a working lunch for Dr Kalam. Once again, there was no frills nor the false pageantry of hierarchy. Chambers picked up Dr Kalam's question about how he took CISCO from seventy million to thirty-eight billion without a reminder. 'I started my career with IBM selling computers. I was twenty-seven and did not know much other than talking sweet to my customers. Somehow they would buy whatever I was selling. After selling computers for about seven years, I moved to Wang Laboratories. They made me the vice-president of US Operations. It was in 1987, and I was just thirty-four years old. Nothing clicked there and Wang had gone from a USD

2 billion profit in 1989 to a USD 700 million loss in 1990. And then I came here. It is all about vision and hard work, sir. Vision without hard work is useless. Many of our friends in Europe are suffering from that. Hard work with vision is what billions of poor are doing around the world. No big secrets. Wang suffered from lack of vision; CISCO succeeded because we saw the future before others could even guess it.'

Chambers then asked, 'What is your vision, sir, if I may ask?'

I thought Dr Kalam would launch into his Vision 2020 monologue; but he had always been beyond my comprehension, and so he was that day. He said, 'Look, John, India's destiny is to show the world how to promote economic growth in a way that enhances social equity – this is what I am trying to do. There are three billion poor people in the world. The transformation that we do as one-sixth of the world's population will benefit all the other nations.'

In the afternoon we went to Stanford University. Dr S.V. Mahadevan, a specialist in emergency medicine at Stanford Health Care and the visionary behind the EMRI system launched in Andhra Pradesh, welcomed Dr Kalam. He escorted us to the chamber of the president of Stanford University, John Hennessey. A computer scientist, Hennessey was one of the founders of MIPS Computer Systems Inc. and had been dubbed 'the godfather of Silicon Valley'.

Leaving Dr Kalam and John Hennessey with their 'high-level' talk, Dr Mahadevan took me around the campus of one of world's most prestigious universities. We went to see the grand Stanford Memorial Church, called MemChuon campus, located at the end of the mile-long axis of Stanford University. I had never before seen the likes of its twenty large stained-glass windows. The filtering sunlight through vivid mosaics gave their subjects a life that transported me to another realm. The breathtaking scenes of *The Annunciation, The Home at Nazareth, The Sermon on the Mount, Christ Calming the Tempest* and *The Raising of Jairus' Daughter* seemed infused with a still power and being, their exultant figures communicating on another level. It reminded me of the spiritual essence of my mission with Dr Kalam. There always seemed to be a higher power guiding him now, as if he had been assigned a schedule of work from the divine.

Then came a wonderful evening – something of a homecoming in a foreign land. In every country, there are non-resident Indians, and despite our adaptability and resilience, or perhaps because of it, Indians always seem to retain a distinct Indianness. The sentimental attachment to the motherland endures, and our people never forget their heritage, regardless of the adjustments they make in their new homes. Just as India itself has subsumed so many cultures and yet remained, so too do Indians themselves assume other cultures and nationalities and remain Indian. On this night, scores of families – many of whom, including children, were resplendent in saris and shervanis – had come to greet Dr Kalam at the newly built 800-seat India Community Centre (ICC) in Milpitas, near the Silicon Valley. IISc's North American alumni, pan-IIT alumni and the desi network TIE (The Indus Entrepreneurs) co-hosted the event.

'Something seems to happen to you guys when you cross the Atlantic. You become changed personalities. I wanted to find out why,' said Dr Kalam. The large audience just loved the opening. The vibrant Indian community had been waiting patiently for many years to see this icon of modern India, but he had not been able to make it to the United States until now. Today, he was there in front of them, not talking about himself, but asking them the secrets of their success. He was vintage Dr Kalam – spontaneous, and radiating loving kindness. Maybe the young Indians assembled there saw in him the missing father, the grandfather, an inspiring uncle or an angel. Whatever people saw in Dr Kalam, there was something magical in his presence.

Dr Kalam's next stop was Los Angeles, where he would address the World Space Conference. The conference had been organized by the prestigious Caltech University to mark fifty years of space exploration. The 'space race' had begun with the Soviet Union's Sputnik endeavour successfully launching the first artificial satellite into earth orbit in 1957. Dr Kalam was visiting Los Angeles after twenty-two years. He had been here in 1985 for work at the Northrop Corporation, and saw that many changes had occurred in the intervening years. Dr Kalam found Los Angeles a truly global city. He felt that the diverse economy of Los Angeles in entertainment, culture, media, fashion, science, sports, technology, education, medicine and research is truly unparalleled in world history.

Caltech is often touted as one of the world's best universities. Though Caltech does not have a large campus like Stanford University – and there are other, grander 'Ivy League' colleges – the students and faculty here have won an astounding thirty-four Nobel Prizes. Years after year, a sizeable number of United States National Medals of Science or Technology are triumphantly brought back here. Furthermore, there is no national academy in the United States without a Caltech alumnus on its faculty.

Caltech has had a unique and integral relationship with the space programme. Closely linked to it is the Jet Propulsion Laboratory (JPL), which was the first laboratory in America to focus on technologies for exploration of the outer space. The JPL even preceded NASA. Dr Kalam called his participation in 'Fifty Years in Space' at Caltech and JPL a long-awaited pilgrimage. A further pleasure for him was the setting for this event. He found the open skies and picturesque downtown area of Pasadena, flanked by the San Gabriel Mountains, especially appealing.

Dr Kalam attended the keynote address by Michael Griffin, administrator, NASA, like an attentive student. He even scribbled some of Griffin's sentences on his notepad: 'To understand where we might go, we must understand where we have been, and I think we need a better understanding of our history than is commonly the case,' Griffin said. 'In the next fifty years we really can celebrate the one-hundredth anniversary of *Sputnik* with the twentieth anniversary of the first human landing on Mars. It is up to us to make it so.'[1]

Dr Kalam admired Griffin's far-sightedness. The other speakers included Yannick D'escatha, president of the Centre National d'Études Spatiales, France, Jean-Jacques Dordain, director general, European Space Agency. And then came Dr Kalam's moment. Everyone expected Dr Kalam to talk about ISRO, which he eventually did. But he first set his agenda about the imperative of a global perceptive of space research:

> Planet Earth has twin human needs. One is protection of the earth environment for living and the other is energy independence. Earth is experiencing both stratosphere cooling (due to the ozone hole) and troposphere warming (due to increased greenhouse gases). Energy production through fossil fuels leads to the generation of thirty billion tonnes of carbon dioxide annually. Can space science and space technology assist in meeting these twin needs?[2]

Dr Kalam cautioned that the geosynchronous orbit region was almost completely full, with 240 satellites from many nations. There were more than 800 active satellites currently in various orbits. The satellite population includes a number of military satellites for communication and reconnaissance. He stated that mankind's technological assets in space were extremely costly and quite indispensable. Protecting these assets and ensuring continuity of services, without any impediment or interference, was now of paramount importance.

The audience of scientists listened to his speech with an attentiveness that was more of emotional connection than intellectual engagement. Despite his intellectual vigour and scientific proclivity, Dr Kalam would often speak more from his heart than his scientific mind. He touched an emotional chord with everybody present there as he likened the worldwide fraternity of space scientists to a family:

> When I am with the space family, I am reminded of my joint family in Rameswaram, a small island in the southern part of India where a number of brothers and a sister lived together. I am the last fellow. I witnessed how my mother connected and brought together her sons and daughter, inspite of multiple variations in their needs and personalities.
>
> Similarly, during the last five decades, I have witnessed how successes and failures of space programmes connect the countries on the planet Earth. Wherever major space events take place, such as – man landing on the moon, the first series of communication satellites in geosynchronous orbit or remote sensing satellites in polar orbit or NASA astronauts including Sunita Williams descending to the earth on a rainy day; these capture the attention of the families and the children of the whole planet Earth.

> I will say the events in space and the actions in space have in one way integrated the whole world, like a mother unifying the family. Now, can we use space with motherly characteristics to transform the planet Earth – prosperity without poverty, peace without fear of war – and make it a happy place to live for the whole of humanity?[3]

Dr Kalam returned to the United States again in October 2007 and in fact celebrated his seventy-sixth birthday at Goddard Space Flight Centre of NASA at Greenbelt, Maryland. He had been here as a young man in 1963 and this visit was naturally nostalgic. Much had transpired in the intervening decades, and his career had taken him far beyond any of his imaginings from those times. But his energy and passion for life were still strong, despite his years; and he still nurtured hope, something that has long abandoned many in their senior years.

In any event, Dr Kalam was still learning, engaging, and receiving recognition. The Carnegie Mellon University conferred an honorary doctorate in science and technology on Dr Kalam in a special ceremony on 17 October 2007. 'As engineer, educator, leader of a great nation and world statesman, Dr Kalam has inspired millions with his commitment to science and technology as instruments of peace and global development,' said Carnegie Mellon president Jared L. Cohon. 'We especially honour his unswerving belief in the transformative power of learning.'[4]

Sunil Wadhwani, chief executive officer of iGate Corporation and a vice chairman of Carnegie Mellon's Board of Trustees, lauded Dr Kalam as both a statesman and an educator. 'He is truly a remarkable human being, who sets an inspiring example of how much can be accomplished in one life. President Kalam has shown it is possible to have big dreams, make a difference and do it without compromising values.'

In his acceptance speech, Dr Kalam unveiled his idea of a 'societal grid'. This would consist of: a 'knowledge grid' interconnecting universities with socio-economic institutions, industries and research and development organizations; a 'health care grid' interconnecting the hospitals at different levels of care delivery, namely primary, secondary and tertiary care, with research institutions, educational institutions and ultimately pharmaceutical research institutions; an 'e-governance grid' interconnecting the central, state, district and town-level offices, and a 'rural development knowledge grid' connecting the rural development centres with the domain service providers.[5]

Earlier in the day, Dr Kalam presented the Carnegie Medal of Philanthropy to Ratan Tata in an awards ceremony at the Carnegie Music Hall in Pittsburgh. 'It is a great honour and happiness for me to witness the scene of Ratan Tata receiving the 2007 Carnegie Medal of Philanthropy,' Dr Kalam said, and he was speaking from the bottom of his heart. He had been a great admirer of the house of Tata, and saw the family as among the great visionary builders of modern India. He told me later in the night, 'A nation is not defined by its borders or the boundaries of its land mass, and a nation builder is not some political leader holding on to a high office. Rather, a nation is defined by different people who have been unified by a cause and a value system. And nation builders are the people who are committed to a vision for the type of society they wish to live in and give to the future generations to come.'

At the Rice University in Houston, Texas, on 18 October 2007, Dr Kalam called for the creation of a World Space Council to speed development of extra-terrestrial travel and industry. Speaking before a near-capacity crowd in the Stude Concert Hall, he outlined World Space Vision 2050, his vision for using space as a stimulus for international cooperation and problem-solving. Combining large-scale societal missions with low-cost access to space, comprehensive security and exploration and current application missions could have a profound effect on mankind, he said. 'Achieving extraterrestrial projects that will benefit all of society will require reducing the cost of access to space. There is definitely a need for spacefaring nations to work together to develop reusable launch vehicles, which can bring down the cost of payloads in orbit. More global interdisciplinary and inter-institutional research is also needed to realize ideas like delivering energy from space and desalinating seawater with solar power.'

For space technology to benefit life on earth, space must remain weapon-free, Dr Kalam said, and the international community must work diligently to keep geopolitical conflicts from spreading into outer space, which belongs to everyone. To this end, Dr Kalam suggested creating an International Space Force to protect space assets in accordance with international law and in the interests of international peace and cooperation.[6]

Before returning to India, Dr Kalam visited the University of Arkansas at Fayetteville on 19 October 2007. B.S. Prakash, the consul general of India in San Francisco at that time, best described these two groundbreaking visits to the Unites States:

> It was my good fortune as the resident diplomat to accompany (Dr Kalam) from function to function. We had started fairly early in the morning with one appointment after the other; he must have started his day even earlier; and it was now evening.
>
> At each venue he had been mobbed like a rock star. There were tumultuous demands for autographs, photographs, and nods of encouragement, words of wisdom. Throughout the day, Dr Kalam had obliged everyone, constantly smiling for photographs, remembering names and places which people invoked to remind him of a past connection, and above all, remaining receptive and curious.[7]

On his way back to India, an honour was waiting for Dr Kalam at London. The prestigious Royal Society King Charles II Medal was awarded to him at the Royal Society in the presence of Lord Karan Billimoria, Lord Swraj Paul, and Lord Meghnad Desai – three jewels of India in the United Kingdom. Lord Martin Rees, the president of the Royal Society of England, said,

> President Kalam had led India at a time when science and technology investment in the country had radically increased. He has played a major part in preparing a road map for transforming India from a developing into a developed nation. As a scientist himself, he has also made a great contribution to scientific advances in his country.[8]

In the plane on our way back to Delhi, we had a discussion which started like an appreciation of avian aeronautics, but was really much more profound:

Kalam: Buddy, have you ever watched an eagle soar?

Arun: No, sir.

Kalam: Funny guy. Visualize an eagle flying now. It is flying very high. It is gliding motionless on the winds, far above the gusts that whip the surface of the earth. Look at its movements! How graceful! Look how it is yielding to the flow of the winds and lets them carry it.

Arun: Yes, sir, I am visualizing.

Kalam: That's the way it is with faithful people. When we relinquish our lives to the movement of God's spirit as did Prophet Moses, Prophet Joshua, Prophet Muhammad, Gautam Buddha and Mahatma Gandhi, a great transformation happens.

Arun: Did you experience it?

Kalam: Oh yes. I can tell you from my own experiences the consequence of resisting God's presence in the innermost recesses of our lives, and the inexpressible changes that come when we yield to God's will.

God was never far from Dr Kalam's thoughts, even as his relentless schedule kept him moving here and there. As promised at the CISCO headquarters in the previous month via our curious 'teleporting' experience, Dr Kalam attended the company's event in Bangalore. There, he inaugurated the Globalization Centre East on 30 October 2007, with a beaming John Chambers standing by his side. Dr Kalam was now a global leader.

6.2

Into the Uncharted

> Don't keep forever on the public road, going only where others have gone. Leave the beaten track occasionally and dive into the woods. You will be certain to find something you have never seen before. It will be a little thing, but do not ignore it. Follow it up, explore all around it; and before you know it, you will have something worth thinking about.
>
> – Alexander Graham Bell
> Scientist and inventor of the telephone

The two visits to the United States made Dr Kalam realize the unique power of the Indian mind in the computer sciences. Indians were truly making waves in this exciting area. Not only had they acquired important positions in the industry, they had also made their mark in the computer business. Shiv Nadar was one such bright star in the world of computing. After establishing himself in the international market, he was setting up international technology centres across India. His first centre would be in Noida in Uttar Pradesh, which had become by this time something of a satellite town of New Delhi.

Shiv Nadar, a graduate in electrical and electronics engineering from PSG College of Technology, Coimbatore, started his business career selling digital calculators in the Indian market. In 1976, he founded HCL. Sensing a boom in the information technology sector much before anyone else, he expanded his information technology services business internationally. In 1996, Shiv Nadar founded SSN College of Engineering in Chennai in the name of his father Sivasubramaniya Nadar. He has since remained focused on developing the educational system in India through the Shiv Nadar Foundation.

Dr Kalam inaugurated the HCL Technology Hub at Noida on 1 November 2007, with the Union finance minister P. Chidambaram and the Union commerce and industry minister Kamal Nath. Dr Kalam made mention of Shiv Nadar's achievements:

> I am witnessing today, how the dream of six young entrepreneurs in 1976 – who left their secure corporate jobs with a dream that the 'microprocessor could change the world' – has brought them to the top three slots in the IT industry of India and number one position in the personal computer segment consecutively for six years ... among the Top IT industries in India, HCL tops the list with the per capita employee output of USD 82,000. [1]

HCL had started as a dream of a few young men, and its stellar performance on the world stage showed what Indian youth were capable of, given some direction. Dr Kalam had always advocated nurturing the talent of the nation's young. He increasingly felt at this time the importance of connecting with them; they became his highest priority. The political leaders had their own concerns, bureaucracy had their own systems and educational institutions had become both conditioned and commercialized. Someone had to reach out to the nascent creativity of young minds and encourage their innocent enthusiasm before it withered away. He could only speak at so many events and connect with so many individuals. How could he play a greater role as a mentor for children? Dr Kalam contemplated this for some time and, predictably perhaps, arrived at a technological solution.

Dr Kalam handpicked a number of journalists, scientists and technologists to oversee the content and design of an electronic newspaper, and launched it on 14 November 2007 at Karimnagar in Andhra Pradesh. The paper was named *Billion Beats* and uplinked to www.abdulkalam.com. Dr Kalam decided it would be a platform for highlighting success stories of Indians from all fronts: 'No politics, no crime, no negative news. Every Indian who is keen to put the country on the development track will have a say in *Billion Beats*.' He entrusted the management of *Billion Beats* to V. Ponraj and M. Anantha Krishnan. In the launch issue, Dr Kalam mapped the profile of a vibrant India in a ten-point plan and devoted it to the nation's schoolchildren.

In November 2007, Dr Kalam flew to Jakarta to speak at the national congress of the Indonesian Institute of Science. Dr Kalam was greatly inspired by the role that daring pilot patriot Biju Patnaik played in Indonesia's freedom struggle. He wondered how the bond between the two countries had weakened over the decades. He decided to emphasize the need for societal transformation before the congress:

> Emphasis in our societal transformation is on full utilization of the natural and human resources of the nation to meet the demands of the modern society. The natural resources include management of water, minerals and materials, multiple agro-climatic conditions and large bio-diversity ... India is attempting to fully utilize the five hundred and forty million youth by empowering them with quality education, with vocational skills and value-added employment in the agriculture, manufacturing and service sectors ... Certainly, this experience may be of use to Indonesia in its mission of societal transformation towards a knowledge society.[2]

Dr Kalam felt that there is much common ground between India and Indonesia. He was told that more than a million people of Indian origin live in Indonesia. They had merged and assimilated with the indigenous population over the centuries, and were now undistinguishable from native Indonesians. Furthermore, a large number of Indian nationals live and work in Indonesia. The Indian diaspora includes adventurous Oriya, Telugu and Tamil people, who had arrived there by sea many centuries ago. Indonesia had seen an influx of north Indians in the textile industry and Sindhi trading families in more recent times. Dr Kalam interacted with the students of Gandhi Memorial International School in Jakarta, and saw a mini India in front of him.

Dr Kalam was invited to deliver a keynote address by Google India at their 'Be the Change Employee Summit' in 2007. On 3 December 2007 at the Google Centre in Hyderabad, Dr Eric E. Schmidt, chairman and CEO of Google, received Dr Kalam amidst the thunderous applause of hundreds of young engineers. Dr Kalam recalled his meeting with Larry Page and Sergey Brin, the founder duo of Google, on 11 October 2004 at Rashtrapati Bhavan: 'They had been scouting for some of their global offices. They commissioned a centre in Dublin, Ireland, and were in India to set up another one. They were seeing services getting localized and catering to special requirements, particularly advertisements. They explained to me how Google could be used as a research tool for students and researchers.'

The audience erupted with raucous laughter when Dr Kalam said that Larry and Brin shared with him their adventure of touring Hyderabad in an autorickshaw to finalize the location of their centre. Dr Kalam recalled that gmail was not launched at that time, and Larry and Brin said they were still in the stages of testing it and improving its features.

In a jovial vein, Dr Kalam 'lamented' the drastic reduction of his support staff since leaving the presidency in July, and thanked Google's search engine for being a trustworthy 'friend' throughout the transition. Though Dr Kalam's lecture touched on many topics, he focused on how the ability to access, comprehend, and effectively utilize information can be an instrument of economic growth and national development.

Dr Kalam argued that delivering valuable information over the Internet can boost creativity, innovation and competitiveness, leading to the creation of a 'knowledge society'. 'The challenge is not the technology alone, but how the application and service are facilitated or delivered to the people as per their requirements,' he said. Further, he noted:

> In a knowledge society, we have to make innovations continuously. Innovations come through creativity. Creativity comes from beautiful minds. It can be anywhere and in any part of the world. Google is born

> out of creativity ... Google thought leaders, who have assembled here of course, are in search of creativity. Creativity is a process through which we can continuously improve ideas and find unique solutions by making gradual alterations and refinements to our works. The important aspect of creativity is: Seeing the same thing as everybody else, but thinking of something different.[3]

Dr Kalam offered three recommendations to the information and communications technology industry: First, industry should lead society's key stakeholders in broadly accepting the Internet as 'the new way of living, the way of learning, the way of trading and business, the way of socializing and the way of governance'; second, he encouraged the industry to facilitate the creation of local content online that could bring economic prosperity to a particular region, and third, he asked the industry to promote public policy changes that address issues such as authentication, security, intellectual property rights and the prevention of abuse on social networking sites.

Dr Kalam urged 'Googlers' to tackle some big problems: the development of speech-recognition and speech-production technologies that would create 'language-independent access to knowledge and information'; the creation of digital libraries of information for science and engineering students in the developed and developing worlds, and the building of a system that generates, collects and distributes clean energy. While we were leaving the Google centre, I overheard a young engineer telling his colleague, 'He's the dude that sparked a fire, and literally changed the balance of power in the Asia region!' I felt that this was a fair summation of Dr Kalam's work. Now, the rockets were gone from Dr Kalam's life, and he was sparking a different kind of fire.

Tata Consultancy Services (TCS) invited Dr Kalam to be with them on their fifteenth anniversary celebrations in the Benelux region on 5 December 2007, at Amsterdam in the Netherlands. A part of the Tata Group, TCS, had at that time over 100,000 of the world's best-trained IT consultants in forty-seven countries. These consultants generated consolidated revenues of more than USD 5 billion in the year ended 31 March 2007.

Without hesitation and with childlike curiosity, Dr Kalam asked, 'What is Benelux?' He was speaking with Girish Ramachandran, director, TCS Europe.

Ramachandran replied, 'Sir, Benelux is a politico-economic union of three neighbouring states – Belgium, the Netherlands, and Luxembourg. Actually, sir, the name Benelux is formed from joining the first two or three letters of each country's name.'

'Fantastic!' Dr Kalam said, and an instant bond developed, with smiles lighting up every face in the large gathering.'Who are your clients?' Dr Kalam asked. Ramachandran recited a litany of names, which included the most prestigious companies of Europe – Philips, Belgacom, ABN AMRO, Colruyt, Rabobank and the ING Group.

'What makes you unique?'

'Our success here has been built on the principles of integration within the local economy and community from where a considerable proportion of our staff is recruited,' said Ramachandran.

'You are good guys,' complimented Dr Kalam. In his speech, Dr Kalam chose to tell the incredible Tata story.

Dr Kalam also addressed the meeting of the Foundation for Critical Choices for India (FCCI) at The Hague. The FCCI is a think tank and focal point for initiating and implementing studies and programmes on issues of strategic importance to India in the social, political and economic fields by mobilizing the resources of Indians living abroad.

Dr Kalam said that people often voiced their concern to him about the large number of professionally qualified people migrating to foreign countries from India. They asked him if this 'brain drain' was a significant loss for the country. He said his answer had always been a resounding 'no!' Of the Indian population of more than one billion people, about twenty-three million are living abroad, spread across the planet. They have certainly been contributing to the nations where they have settled. But they have equally maintained their connection with their parents and the educational institutions of India, thereby enriching both their countries. He then recited a famous saying of Avaiyyar, the great Tamil poetess:

திரை கடலோடியும் திரவியும் தேடு

The mission of life should be to earn knowledge and wealth, even if it needs crossing the oceans.

Dr Kalam not only delivered a candid and inspiring speech at The Hague, he also highlighted his vision for a developed India afterwards. He interacted extensively with the sizeable audience that had come to listen to his inspiring words. Appreciating the work of the foundation, he suggested that we should all, like the foundation, pay attention to the social problems in India. The foundation has followed the compelling issues of security of women, civic awareness, urban development, water and waste management in India.

The Nyenrode Business University, Amsterdam, conferred upon Dr Kalam another honorary doctorate degree. In his acceptance speech, Dr Kalam spoke about 'National Prosperity and Energy Independence'. He said that nationalism and globalization could coexist and even become mutually advantageous, if the upliftment and prosperity of humanity as a whole becomes their guiding vision. He called upon the Nyenrode University to carry out research for the benefit of the entire world. He said that their international environment and experience in meeting challenges of national progress gave them ample qualification for this task.

In February 2008, South Korean president Lee Myung-bak hosted Dr Kalam during his inauguration as the chief executive, as a personal guest. Several months before becoming a presidential candidate, Mr Lee had travelled to India and called on Dr Kalam, who was then the president of India. He had wanted to know more about Dr Kalam's initiative for a world knowledge platform. This was a proposal that could bring universities together with 'core competencies' in different spheres. Mr Lee was now planning to set up an international science-technology-business entity that might be modelled on Dr Kalam's idea. While Dr Kalam was given pride of place at the function, Ambassador N. Parthasarathi formally represented the Government of India. After the ceremony, Dr Kalam visited the Korea Institute of Sciences and Technology in Seoul and met a group of scientists.

Wherever he travelled, Dr Kalam was inevitably sought after by various groups of the global fraternity of scientists, especially in the aerospace field. He felt an enduring affinity with his fellow scientists through the world, and seemed to have never lost the childlike wonder for new discoveries. His contribution to science now would no longer be practical or theoretical, though. It would take the same form of his work in all other spheres: exhorting, inspiring, prognosticating; giving a spark that would ignite a desire in individuals he touched to strive for greater aspirations.

From Seoul, Dr Kalam proceeded to Tel Aviv on a two-day visit to Israel. Dr Kalam had been invited as the keynote speaker at a conference in view of the reputation he commanded in aerospace sciences. Naturally, his contribution to strengthening Indo-Israeli cooperation was a factor in his invitation.

Addressing the Israel Annual Conference on Aerospace Sciences on 27 February 2008, Dr Kalam called for the creation of a 'World Space Council' to carry out tasks like large-scale societal missions and low-cost access to space. He said that aerospace science and technology had been a cradle for a number of innovations. It had fostered a culture of a number of disciplines working together, because this had been the only manner of achieving state-of-the-art systems. It had connected people from the remotest parts of the world. He also cautioned, however, that the dreams of aerospace research had created a mindset of unnecessary rivalry and possessiveness, and this has led to the underutilization of its potential. Dr Kalam emphasized cooperation at the global level and said, 'standing alone has caused certain feelings of insecurity and suspicion'.

Dr Kalam was invited to the twelfth annual Wharton India Economic Forum at The Wharton School in Philadelphia, USA. On 22 March 2008, around 1,000 people gathered to contemplate the ambition, frustration and development in the lives of a billion Indians. The conference theme of 'India I Imagine' was fitting for the country's zeitgeist of aspiration. The forum brought together an eclectic array of Indian leaders from across the political spectrum. Students, faculty, guests and speakers came together for a stimulating discussion about different aspects of the Indian growth story.

Dr Kalam spoke about the inception of the 'Develop India by 2020' concept in an optimistic government in the early 1990s, when the current rate of growth would have seemed quite implausible. He painted a picture of India as it is today, with its failures and his dreams for progress, and the will to achieve inclusive national prosperity by 2020. He spoke passionately about the need for an integrated action plan for developing India in the five areas discussed in this book already.

Unerringly genial with the press as with the public, Dr Kalam accepted an impromptu request for an interview from Knowledge@ Wharton, the school's online business analysis journal. Dr Kalam enumerated six essential qualities of a leader, and gave a powerful endorsement of renewable energy:

Knowledge@Wharton: How did you come to become India's president in July 2002? What leadership qualities does one need to lead a country as large, complex and chaotic as India?

Kalam: Well, I won't call India chaotic, because order comes from disorder. That is what is happening now. I was elected president of India – from 2002 to 2007 – through a well-structured election process. Any leadership – whether it is political leadership or leadership in technology – requires that the leader have six traits. What are those six traits? First, the leader must have vision. Without vision, you cannot be a leader. Second, the leader must be able to travel on an unexplored path. Normally, the tendency is for people to travel along well-laid-out roads. Third, the leader must know how to manage success, and even more importantly, failure. The fourth trait is that the leader should have the courage to make decisions. Fifth, the leader should have nobility in management. Every action of the leader should be transparent. And finally, the leader should work with integrity and succeed with integrity.

Knowledge@Wharton: If you could rewind and replay your years as president, what might you do differently? Is there anything you wanted to accomplish that you were unable to do?

Kalam: I came up with an idea that I should power the Rashtrapati Bhavan completely with solar power little late. For that, I worked on a proposal after completing four years of my presidential term, and at the beginning of the fifth year. But then the environmental agencies raised a lot of questions. Before I could answer them, my term ended. I would have liked the Rashtrapati Bhavan to be the first home in India to be powered completely by solar energy.[4]

On 24 March 2008, the University of Kentucky rolled out the 'blue' carpet for Dr Kalam. The term had come from the Bluegrass region in the state of Kentucky, where a majority of the state's population has lived and developed its largest cities. Before Europeans arrived here, this region was mostly a savannah of wide grasslands interspersed with enormous oak trees. Europeans named this region for the blue-flowered Poa grass that they found in abundance here.

The university conferred upon Dr Kalam an honorary Doctor of Science degree. Two Indian Americans – S. Melappalayam and Sowmya Vijayaraghavan – gifted one million dollars to establish the President A.P.J. Abdul Kalam India Studies Endowment Fund. Their gift would help to support endowed professorships for the proposed Centre of Excellence for India Studies, and support research in India business studies through the Gatton College of Business and Economics. 'The receipt of this gift is the next major step in allowing our curriculum to become truly international and helps to reinforce our "world-ready" theme at the Gatton College,' said the dean, Devanathan Sudharshan.[5]

In 1967, to commemorate the fiftieth anniversary of Finland's independence, the Bank of Finland made an endowment of 100 million marks for the creation of an organization by the name of SITRA. SITRA is an acronym for the *Suomen itsenäisyyden juhlarahasto* (Finnish National Fund for Research). SITRA was tasked with promoting Finland's stable and balanced development, economic growth and international competitiveness and cooperation. In 1991, SITRA was transformed into an independent fund that reports directly to the Finnish parliament. By 2008, SITRA endowment capital was valued at more than 600 million euros.

In 2005, SITRA launched an 'India Programme' with a view to expanding Finland's relationship with India. Over the ensuing three years, the programme had provided the Finnish public with information about India and presented Finnish expertise to Indians. Environment and health care had emerged as two win-win industries for which India had a need and Finland had corresponding competence. For the final seminar for the India Programme at the University of Helsinki on 15 April 2008, SITRA invited Dr Kalam to speak. He would share his views on the theme of inclusiveness and on how the fruits of Indian economic growth could be equally distributed to all segments of its society.

Dr Kalam arrived in Helsinki a day before the event to meet the Finnish prime minister Matti Vanhanen and his team. Vanhanen was known for being a teetotaller, and that became the first talking point between these two abstainers. Mr Vanhanen had been depicted in the media as a bland leader, lacking both charisma and personal charm, and he had been quoted as saying he never took advice. But all this seemed at odds with the gracious man who met Dr Kalam. A very tall Mr Vanhanen (at 6 feet 6 inches) stooped to shake hands with Dr Kalam, who was at least a foot shorter. He warmly sought Dr Kalam's views on social equity. Mr Vanhanen was flabbergasted that India, a country of more than one billion people, could contemplate a social equity programme, when no common will could be mustered in Finland, which had just five million people.

The next day Dr Kalam spoke on the topic, 'The role of technology in ensuring an inclusive and sustainable future'. His content was at once broad and enlightening, imparting sound principals for sustaining technological projects from conceptualization to realization:

I want to convey to you what I have learnt from these three

> programmes (space, defence, and nuclear) based on my personal experience. Wherever there is a dream in life, it transforms into a vision. High-level thinking transforms the vision into missions. Next is acquisition of knowledge from all sources, then working and working without boundary conditions till the realization of the mission brings success. Absorption of the failures and taking the responsibility and giving the credit for success to the team while executing the mission makes the success permanent.[6]

Dr Kalam had described a proven way of achieving enduring success in almost any endeavour. And he was answering the issue raised by Prime Minister Matti Vanhanen at their meeting. He knew how to take what seemed like quixotic ideas through to fulfilment; and he had personally experienced all the tribulations that this entails. That he could crystallize his experience into words that were truly meaningful, and not the least bit trite, was a tribute to the inspiration guiding the man. His gift was surely not from academic learning or some tapas (spiritual training) – it was a spring from a divine source. Dr Kalam had by now become a saint scientist.

6.3

Transformers

> The number one benefit of information technology is that it empowers people to do what they want to do. It lets people be creative. It lets people be productive. It lets people learn things they didn't think they could learn before, and so in a sense it is all about potential.
>
> – Steve Ballmer
> CEO of Microsoft (2000 to 2014)

Dr Kalam flew from Finland to Toronto. He had been invited by the Canada-India Foundation to present 'Chanchlani Global Indian Award' to Satyanarayan Gangaram 'Sam' Pitroda. Dr Kalam gladly accepted the invitation, for he had admired Pitroda's missionary zeal in using technology for the public good. Years earlier, he had read Pitroda's book, *Exploding Freedom: Roots in Technology*, and admired his insights into the application of technology for societal transformation. Pitroda's principles had instantly resonated with his own personal calling around the same time, of developing civilian spin-offs of defence technologies. Dr Kalam had highlighted the following lines in the book, as he felt as if these were written for him:

> In my personal advancement, technology gave me the tools to fight poverty, cut across caste and community barriers and bring pride in performance. Technology was helpful in not only generating personal wealth but also generating ideas and exploring new concepts related to products, services, markets, growth, developments, values and work.

> Technology taught me a great deal of discipline, good interpersonal relations, teamwork, management and a systematic approach to problem-solving with focus on clear objectives, measurable milestones and commitment to reach fruition.[1]

Sam Pitroda had travelled to Chicago in 1964 to study electrical engineering. Born in Orissa in 1942 in a small village, since early childhood he had nurtured dreams of living in the exciting world of cities and faraway lands. After going to the USA and then succeeding there, he had experienced the agony of disconnection that those living away from their Indian families experienced in those times. The lack of availability of telephones in India meant he could not even talk to his parents during their illnesses. And when he would visit them, he would be mostly unable to contact his family in Chicago.

Until the 1980s, the Indian telephone network functioned on an electromechanical switch system. Telephones were a privilege of the rich. There were barely 2.5 million telephones in the country, and almost all of them belonged to business people and government officials and leaders living in urban centres. The service was truly appalling. With no foreign exchange in the treasury to import digital switches from the US, Japan or Europe, the Indian government was helplessly looking for ways to modernize the nation's telecommunications.

Indigenization was to be the answer. A swadeshi approach had worked wonders in aerospace, and it would do so in telecommunications. In 1984, Prime Minister Indira Gandhi invited Pitroda to return to India. She asked him to develop a digital switching system suited to the Indian network. Pitroda suggested establishing a Centre for Development of Telematics that would be called C-DOT. Prime Minister Gandhi was firm with her support. C-DOT was promptly registered as a non-profit society, funded by the government but enjoying complete autonomy. By this time, Pitroda was a naturalized US citizen. But he renounced his US citizenship and resumed his Indian nationality in order to work in the Indian government. There was to be no looking back. Pitroda extended digital telecommunications to every corner of the country, including his village in Orissa.

Dr Kalam awarded the first Canada- India Foundation Chanchlani Global Indian Award to Sam Pitroda on 18 April 2008, in the presence of the prime minister of Canada, Mr Stephen Harper. Dr Kalam called Sam Pitroda's work in transforming the Indian telecom system a long walk to freedom. He quoted Nelson Mandela from his book of the same name, 'And as we let our own light shine, we unconsciously give other people permission to do the same. As we are liberated from our own fear, our presence automatically liberates others.'[2]

The following day, Dr Kalam visited the Swaminarayan temple in Toronto. Sadhu Jnanpriyadas welcomed him amidst thunderous applause from thousands of Indo-Canadians, both young and old. The temple trustees guided him and the Attorney General of Ontario, Hon. Chris Bentley, through the Canadian Museum of Cultural Heritage of Indo-Canadians located in the temple. Dr Kalam was very pleased to see his dear friend Pramukh Swamiji's photograph in the temple. Pramukh Swamiji was also reaching millions of people suffering the misery of spiritual isolation, and connecting them with the divine.

Speaking at the University of Toronto, Dr Kalam proudly declared that India today possessed a constellation of six remote sensing satellites and eleven communication satellites. These were serving applications like natural resource surveying, communication, disaster management support and meteorology. Moreover, satellites supported a comprehensive tele-education system connecting 27,000 classrooms, and a telemedicine network connecting 250 hospitals in remote areas to large teaching hospitals in the metropolitan cities. 'Our country is in the process of establishing 100,000 Village Knowledge Centres across the country through public private partnerships to provide real-time knowledge input to rural citizens using space and ICT,' he said.

Dr Kalam visited Meerut in Uttar Pradesh, about 70 kilometres north of Delhi, on 27 May 2008. He was there to address a National Seminar on Total Quality Management (TQM) in pedagogy at Meerut Institute of Engineering and Technology (MIET). The Ministry of Human Resource Development had rolled out a Technical Education Quality Improvement Programme (TEQIP) that entailed systemic transformation of the technical education system – and Dr Kalam was playing a crucial role in this mission.

I received a call from Dr Kalam to join him. He remembered that it was my birthplace and wanted to meet my mother. I hesitated and said that she lived in a small house and would not be able to handle the visit of a celebrity like him. Dr Kalam airily brushed aside my concerns, saying, 'Her house can't be smaller than my house in Rameswaram.' We descended on my humble ancestral home with the usual motorcade and security detail, which was incongruous with the sleepy small town ambience of Meerut outskirts. The entire population of the suburb emerged from their homes and abandoned their works for the spectacle of this great man's visit.

As always, however, the sound and fury surrounded him; but he was himself the eye of calm in a storm of activity and wonder. He told my mother, 'Your son is a good guy.' He ate the kheer she had prepared and happily mingled with my siblings – my sister Seema and brothers Varun and Salil – and their families. That day, I understood the meaning of Saint Augustine's saying, 'It was pride that changed angels into devils; it is humility that makes men as angels.' As my mother said later, 'God in human form has visited my house today.'

In June 2008, the Liverpool Hope University in the United Kingdom invited Dr Kalam to the Global Youth Congress, 'The Big Hope'. More than 600 young men and women from fifty-five countries attended the event. The vice chancellor, Prof. Gerald Pillay, said,

> Many of you are considered to be your communities' future leaders. So what is The Big Hope? All the strands will consider three questions: how we develop a humane global society; how may we ensure that there is integrity in public life; and what can the individual do? Dr Kalam is here because he made an indelible impression on millions of young minds to improve their communities.

Dr Kalam said,

> Now the question is: How do we inculcate righteousness in the heart? In my opinion, there are three sources that can build a youth with righteousness in the heart. One is mother, the second is father

> and the third and the most important is the teacher, particularly the primary-school teacher. Also to provide righteousness in the heart to the young minds, we should have an environment of great education and a spiritual way of life and spiritual environment.

In his own simple way, Dr Kalam had pinpointed the very factor that Western society was missing in its homes. He continued touching on emotionally sensitive topics throughout his speech. His words brought tears to the eyes of many of the youths in the audience, and defying the 'stiff upper lip' that pervades British public life, they were not hiding them. Their tears were not the mark of weakness, but of power that Dr Kalam had helped to revivify. They were indeed the messengers of their grief – and of love that needed expression.

Back in India, a political commotion was threatening to turn into an outright revolt. The issue of contention was the Indo-US civil nuclear agreement. An assortment of political parties and activists were staunchly opposed to the agreement, right from the day its framework was announced on 18 July 2005. In accordance with the framework, India agreed to separate its civil and military nuclear facilities and to place all its civil nuclear facilities under the International Atomic Energy Agency (IAEA) safeguards; and in exchange, the United States agreed to work towards full civil nuclear cooperation with India.

The primary opposition to the nuclear deal in India had come from the Left parties. They had been hoping that it would not progress beyond discussion, and the powerful anti-India forces in the United States would strike it down before it became operational. President Bush, though, ensured it was endorsed by the United States establishment. Now known as the '123 Agreement', it needed ratification by the Indian parliament. On 9 July 2008, the Left Front withdrew its support to the UPA government under Prime Minister Manmohan Singh in protest; the nuclear deal – indeed the government itself – was in peril. Prime Minister Manmohan Singh later recalled this crisis, and the role that the pragmatic elder statesman Dr Kalam played in resolving it:

> When I faced a vote of confidence, he was not the president but he still played an important role ... the situation was difficult ... I was discussing these matters with Amar Singhji, and Mulayam Singhji ... with great difficulty we managed to persuade them to relook at their stand. It occurred to me that Mulayam Singh had great regard for Kalam ... (I) then urged the SP leaders to meet Kalam. They went to see Abdul Kalam ... he told them this deal is in the national interest ... and we won the vote of confidence.[3]

Dr Kalam would lend his support to the government again regarding nuclear power, but this time in his home state. Villagers at Kudankulam in Tamil Nadu had launched a series of bitter and highly charged protests in October 2011, demanding the halt of the upcoming Russian-built nuclear power plant project there. Dr Kalam visited the villages to allay their fears regarding nuclear energy. 'The people of Kudankulam do not even need to have a "nano-sized" doubt at the project's safety,'[4] Dr Kalam declared. 'We are all caught too much with the disease of fear and danger. Cowards do not make history. Sheer crowd size cannot bring about changes. Only those who think everything is possible can create history and bring about changes,' Dr Kalam said after visiting the Kudankulam plant on 6 November 2012.[5] He had played a vital role in the history of the Indian nuclear energy programme, and was consistent throughout in his support of nuclear energy as a means of facilitating development.

Less contentious, but nevertheless significant, duties awaited Dr Kalam. The prime minister of Malaysia, Dato Seri Abdullah Bin Haji Ahmad Badawi, invited Dr Kalam to Malaysia's fiftieth anniversary of independence. On the eve of the celebrations, Dr Kalam went to George Town, Penang, to meet the Indian community. Flanked by Chief Minister Lim Guan Eng, Second Finance Minister Tan Sri Nor Mohamed Yakcop and Indian high commissioner to Malaysia, Ashok Kantha – and followed by more than a hundred local people – Dr Kalam visited each one of George Town's ten famous religious establishments. These are located along the road often referred to as the 'Street of Harmony'. There were lion dances, lively tunes of nadaswaram and a percussion brass band playing during his halts.

It was a vibrant demonstration of inter-religious fellowship, something Dr Kalam had always held paramount. A foreign Muslim dignitary visiting temples and churches and mosques with equal deference struck a chord in the hearts of many in Malaysia and was widely reported in the media:

> His humble acts of respect and reverence within the holy temples, mosques and church clearly echoes the glaring shortcomings within our own citizenry and leaders who have been instead making clarion calls along divisive religious and racial lines ... Our leaders must quickly learn and emulate what Abdul Kalam has come from so far to remind us of our God-given gift of 'unity' and 'harmony'.[6]

The Universiti Sains Malaysia (University of Science Malaysia) conferred an honorary degree of Doctor of Science upon Dr Kalam on 30 August 2008. Earlier, Dr Kalam had been awarded an honorary degree of Doctor of Engineering at Nanyang Technological University, Singapore on 26 August 2008.

India's most popular president had become something of an international ambassador of goodwill, and he would use his status to raise issues that he felt needed his influence. Dr Kalam delivered the fourteenth convocation address at Kathmandu University in Nepal on 18 November 2008. He used this forum to call for a paradigm shift in higher education. Dr Kalam raised an important question. While we are enjoying the fruits of technology – expanding physical travel and connectivity beyond any realm of imagination – and humanity could be proud of this kind of exponential growth of opportunity, are we up to the challenges that confront us today? Dr Kalam felt that universities needed to move in step with a changing world, delivering education to meet modern challenges:

> If we consider any issue be it energy independence or environment protection or understanding the atmosphere or exploration of outer space or increasing the outreach of science or equitable distribution

> of prosperity and wealth or dealing with deadly diseases or weaning people away from drugs or combating terrorism or preserving family ties, they all require the creativity of the best of minds from any part of the world.
>
> The question we have to ask ourselves is whether the universities provide an adequate breeding ground for such minds ... It is natural, therefore, that the university system itself has to meet new requirements in the twenty-first century. The universities, in my view, need to address four important criteria: The education has to address the needs of the citizen for contributing to the sustainable growth in various areas of national and global development; it has to meet the diverse cultural needs; it should ignite the minds towards research and enquiry; and it has to be cost effective for deserving students to take up subjects of their choice.

After the convocation, Dr Kalam visited Ka-Nying Shedrub Ling Monastery in Boudhanath and met Chökyi Nyima Rinpoche. He carried forward the questions he raised at the university to the revered monk.

Kalam: Revered Rinpoche! The rapid advances of technology have created the challenge of complicated changes in lifestyles, values, behaviours and work ethics. Because of the fast pace of life and demands of multitasking, people are confronted with greater uncertainty. What can be done?

Rinpoche: You are a very wise man, Dr Kalam. You have asked the most important question. Doing all the good, not doing all the evils, and purifying your mind are fundamental.

Kalam: What is good? What is evil?

Rinpoche: Good is that which produces good effects and relieves one of sorrow and stress; evil generates ill effects and prolongs the agony of suffering and stress.

Kalam: What kind of changes should be made in our education system?

Rinpoche: We have to give knowledge of various subjects, but also must teach a student how to live his life by developing his mind and equipping him to deal with reality. What use is the subject knowledge without this?

Kalam: And how could that be done?

Rinpoche: By making students live by discipline, by teaching them how to meditate and by sharing with them the ancient wisdom. This is fundamental. The rest is all acquisition of knowledge for earning money and to live in worldly comfort.

Kalam: What is discipline?

Rinpoche: Eat only when hungry. Sleep only when tired. Do not speak unless asked for.

Kalam: What is meditation?

Rinpoche: To know your feelings. To hear your inner voice.

Kalam: But there are two inner voices. One if of the soul, but the other is of Shaitan. You and I know the difference, but how does a child or an untrained person know which voice to follow?

Rinpoche: Follow the voice that says give, forgive, let go, move on. Do not follow the voice that says take, seek revenge, hold grudges and settle scores. There is nothing to settle. Accept what is as the final settlement.

In March 2009, Dr Kalam met about 1,000 students who came from 120 countries to the 'Education Without Borders' event in Dubai. The Higher Colleges of Technology (HCT) had been organizing this international student conference every two years. The theme of this conference was how to make the world a better place. Besides Dr Kalam, the CEO of Rolls-Royce, Sir John Rose, Princess Astrid of Belgium, and the first female self-funded space traveller and first Muslim woman in space, Anousheh Ansari, were the other guests invited.

In his inaugural speech, Dr Kalam raised the question: What could be the methodology for evolving a happy, prosperous and peaceful society on our planet? He then answered by calling this methodology the 'Evolution of Enlightened Society'. He said he shared these thoughts with many intellectuals in national and international spheres and articulated three components: education with a value system; religion transforming into spirituality; and economic development for societal transformation. 'Whichever nation adopts these three components in an integrated way, they will be able to evolve an enlightened society,' he declared with the finality of a prophet. He further aired his thoughts on a globalized world, and the need for greater responsibility in this new regime:

> Borderlessness doesn't come without a price tag. The economic crisis, which started in the United States because of borderlessness, affected many countries. It will continue to have ripple effects and sympathetic oscillations on other countries. Hence, it is important that in a connected world the members behave with responsibility and ensure that only good effects are propagated and communicated through the borderless system.[7]

In April 2009, Dr Kalam was invited by Bill Gates to meet Microsoft professionals and also the Bill and Melinda Gates Foundation team in Seattle. Dr Kalam had met Bill Gates years earlier in November 2002, in what was billed as an exalted meeting of minds – the head of the world's largest software company meeting a visionary 'techie' president. That meeting, however, turned frosty when President Kalam advocated open-source software. This is unquestionably a boon for users, but anathema to software moguls at the time. It would allow anyone with the technical knowledge to change a programme to suit their needs. Dr Kalam felt that open-source-code software in India has its place in ensuring benefits for all of our billion people. And he had been quite prepared to raise this with one the world's richest men, Mr Bill Gates; even if this did vitiate the atmosphere somewhat.[8] Perhaps Dr Kalam was simply ahead of his time; open-source software has become increasingly commercialized in recent years.

In any event, Mr William H. Gates, father of Mr Bill Gates, and Mr Jeff Raikes, CEO of Bill and Melinda Gates Foundation, had a private meeting with Dr Kalam on 22 April 2009. Dr Kalam raised three issues of particular importance – prevention of HIV/AIDS, creation of the PURA rural development and the Societal Grid. At the end of the meeting, the senior Gates presented Dr Kalam *Showing Up for Life*, his book scheduled for release in the ensuing week. In the foreword, Mr Bill Gates wrote, 'Dad, the next time somebody asks you if you're the real Bill Gates, I hope you say, "Yes." I hope you tell them that you're all the things the other one strives to be.' Dr Kalam addressed the Microsoft professionals the next day, and later met the faculty and students of University of Washington and members of the Greater Seattle area.

The president of Boeing India and vice-president of Boeing International Trading, Dinesh Keskar, took Dr Kalam around the Boeing Everett Factory on 24 April 2009. This factory is the largest building in the world by volume, at 4 billion cubic feet built area, situated on 100 acres of land. The wide-body Boeing 747, 767, 777, and 787 aircraft are assembled here. At the plant, Dr Kalam met the eighty-eight-year-old Joseph 'Joe' Sutter, who once headed the 4,500-member design team of the Boeing company and was dubbed the 'father of the 747' aircraft, the largest commercial airliner ever built. Dr Kalam was given a personal guided tour of the first Boeing 787 aircraft – the long-range, wide-body jet airliner. It was the first of the twenty-seven aircraft that were joining the Air India fleet and was called 'the Dreamliner'.

On 28 April 2009, Dr Kalam joined a veritable league of illustrious Americans, including three former US presidents, when he was given the prestigious Hoover Medal for 2008 for his services to humanity. He received the medal at a ceremony at the Columbia University in New York. He became the first Asian to receive the Hoover Medal, which is an honour that has been given annually since 1930 by the American Society of Mechanical Engineers. Beatrice Hunt, chairperson of the Hoover Medal Board, handed the medal and a citation to Dr Kalam.

In his acceptance speech, Dr Kalam talked about the challenges modern society is facing, and made mention of the fundamental role of biology in human suffering:

> Advances in genetics have demonstrated great similarities in the genomes of man and animals and showed that 'the limbic brain' perhaps is the cause for all conflict, within and outside. It could be seen more clearly now why human society, from its origin until now, has always been at war within and between groups – and this has led to two world wars. Presently, terrorism and low-intensity warfare are affecting many parts of the world.

Although such suggestions could appear fatalistic, Dr Kalam was at pains to point out that our intellect can rationalize past these atavistic tendencies:

> Simultaneously, the brain has intelligence to understand the price that humanity has paid because of such conflicts and if only this attention is diverted to development, the human civilization would have taken a shape leading to peaceful coexistence.
>
> We have to analyse why wars have occurred so far in human history and see how to avoid future conflicts. Paucity of resources, inequitable growth within countries and different parts of the world, deprivation, depleting resources, and ego are among the reasons for conflicts, along with remnants of hatred from historical fights. It becomes necessary to analyse potential sources of conflicts in the twenty-first century for us to spot problem zones and avoid conflicts, as far as possible. Man is fighting a war on all fronts – environmental degradation and diseases on one side, and terrorism on the other side,

Dr Kalam noted that inclusive and equitable development can facilitate peace in our world. He was now quite vocal with his belief: 'The improvement of quality of human life across the world is in the best interest of the entire humanity.' Dr Kalam's vision of India as a developed country had now transcended to using technology as a non-linear tool to make this planet more liveable and human society prosperous and harmonious. The spiritual ascent of Dr Kalam was reflected in his dream of the ascent of humanity. He was no longer talking about five projects or some integrated programme or a mission. He was talking about the victory of consciousness over blind forces – in nature, in society and in man himself.

6.4

Prove All Things

> Though my view is as spacious as the sky, my actions and respect for cause and effect are as fine as grains of flour.
>
> – Sogyal Rinpoche
> Tibetan lama

A visit to Trinity College at Dublin in Ireland on 12 June 2009 was like a pilgrimage for Dr Kalam. Since its establishment in 1592, Trinity College, Dublin, has endured over the centuries and even prospered, despite Ireland's historical tribulations, to become a modern university with an illustrious history. With more than 16,000 students representing in excess of ninety different nationalities, Trinity College is indeed a mini world. It has a connection with India dating back to 1762, when it established its chair of oriental languages. In the second half of the nineteenth century, when Trinity College hosted an India Civil Service School, it supplied over 150 graduates for the bureaucratic service that ran the British Raj.

When Dr Kalam entered the beautiful Trinity College campus escorted by Provost John Hegarty, its motto, *Panta Aokimazete To Kaaon Katexete* captured his attention. Forever a student – and never hesitant of asking questions about what he did not know – Dr Kalam requested the provost to explain the meaning of the phrase. Prof. Hegarty explained to him that it means: 'Prove all things; hold fast that which is good.'

'What is the idea?' Dr Kalam asked.

'It is a Biblical phrase. Men are prone to go to extremes in their beliefs. St Paul seems to have been guarding against this tendency when he wrote, "Despise not the prophesies; prove all things; hold fast that which is good."'[1]

The discussion continued over tea. In the early days of Christianity, there were those who claimed to prophesy by the Spirit, and actually did so. But there were also those who claimed to prophesy by the Spirit and did not. The result was that, at least, some despised all prophecy by reason of the false claims of the pretenders. Such a wholesale rejection of all prophecy was thought by St Paul to be unreasonable and even unsafe. It was neither justified to reject those who were truly prophesying by the Spirit because some were not, nor to accept those who were falsely prophesying because some were truly prophesying. St Paul indicated the safe course: 'Prove all things; hold fast that which is good.' As there has always been evil mixed with the good, this admonition is advice for the ages.

Dr Kalam was taken through the newly set up 75-million-Euro research institute for nano science. Speaking on 'The Vision Elevates the Nation', Dr Kalam presented a vision for transforming India into a developed nation by 2020, using the multidisciplinary specializations available in the country. More than 400 people attended his lecture. The university announced the establishment of an India chair and a post in Indian studies to commemorate Dr Kalam's visit.

After his speech in Dublin, Dr Kalam headed to Northern Ireland, and was conferred an honorary degree of Doctor of Laws for distinction in public service, at a ceremony at Queen's University in Belfast. Earlier, on 9 June 2007 Dr Kalam had been honoured with the International Medal of the Royal Academy of Engineering, one of Britain's top engineering awards, at a gala dinner in London. Former chief executive of British Petroleum and the Academy president Lord John Browne presented the award. According to the Royal Academy, the International Medal is awarded occasionally to an individual resident outside the European Union for his or her 'outstanding and sustained personal achievement in the broad field of engineering, including commercial or academic leadership'. The Academy's senior fellow, Prince Philip, husband of Queen Elizabeth II, was present at the dinner.

Wherever he went, Dr Kalam would find ideas and concepts that he felt could benefit his country. For him, these events were not exercises in self-congratulation as perhaps they were to some eminent people. He was meeting with some of the world's greatest minds, and he would make the most of every opportunity that he was afforded. Dr Kalam was particularly impressed with one practical scheme that he encountered when he was invited to the first convocation of the University of Information Technology and Sciences (UITS) in Dhaka, Bangladesh, in July 2008. While he was in Dhaka, he met Nobel laureate Muhammad Yunus at the Mirpur headquarters of Grameen Bank on 18 July 2008. Prof. Yunus briefed Dr Kalam about the activities of the Grameen Bank and the concept and practice of social business as ways to tackle poverty and other social problems in South Asia. Dr Kalam said he wanted to learn details of the workings of Grameen Bank so that the system could be implemented in India. Professor Yunus said that Grameen would be delighted to help set up microcredit programmes in India, as one was already in place in Kerala.

Professor Yunus raised the issue of strengthening the South Asian Association for Regional Cooperation (SAARC). He explored possibilities for SAARC passports and SAARC scholarships to facilitate the free flow of people for education. Additionally, he felt that joint water management and power generation for the countries of the region would greatly help improve their peoples' quality of life. Dr Kalam said he fully supported the idea of closer cooperation within SAARC. Professor Yunus was very pleased to receive the Hindi edition of his book *Banker to the Poor* from Dr Kalam.

Later, Dr Kalam attended a dinner hosted by Prime Minister Sheikh Hasina and President Zillur Rahman. The hosts knew about the vegetarian food habits of Dr Kalam and took great care to serve him food that was of his liking. Dr Kalam talked with Prime Minister Sheikh Hasina about her husband, nuclear scientist Dr M.A. Wazed Miah. He had been engaged in research work at the New Delhi–based laboratory of Atomic Energy Commission of India during 1975–82 and later became the chairman of the Bangladesh Atomic Energy Commission. Prime Minister Sheikh Hasina briefed Dr Kalam about the Rooppur Nuclear Power Project that was in progress.

President Zillur Rahman sat by Dr Kalam's side throughout the convocation. Dr Kalam saw the respectful homage paid to Srijnan Atish Dipankar, poet Rabindranath Tagore and scientists Acharya Sir Jagadish Chandra Bose and Satyendra Nath Bose, who were all seen as Bangladeshi icons. It resonated well with the theme of Dr Kalam's lecture:'Science is borderless'. Dr Kalam observed that in response to a more integrated world economy and improved travel and communications technology, almost every government around the world is making an effort to internationalize higher education. The number of internationally mobile students is expected to almost double to eight million by 2025.

Dr Kalam mentioned the success story of Indian private universities. With rapid growth in student numbers and constrained government budgets, there has been a shift towards funding higher education from private sources. India did not open its door to foreign universities, following a policy of self-reliance in higher education. Dr Kalam said that India would be among the top five global scientific powers by 2020, and there is no reason why India and Bangladesh should not become one great knowledge system.

Engagements at international universities would take Dr Kalam far and wide. In May 2011, the University of Technology, Sydney (UTS), conferred upon Dr Kalam an honorary degree of Doctor of Engineering. Founded in 1850, it is Australia's first university and is regarded as one of its most prestigious. UTS is ranked among the world's fifty most reputable universities. In 2011, it had more than 32,000 undergraduate and more than 16,000 postgraduate students. Vice Chancellor Professor Ross Milbourne announced the creation of the Dr Abdul Kalam International Scholarships to celebrate Dr Kalam's commitment to education, and his endeavours to support outstanding students to develop as future leaders. Since then, ten scholarships have been given to students for undergraduate and postgraduate coursework programmes every year. The high commissioner for India in Australia, Smt. Sujatha Singh was present at the ceremony.

Dr Kalam visited the Harvard Business School on 27 September 2011 to deliver the 2011 Harish C. Mahindra Lecture. He spoke on 'Empowering Three Billion'. Professor Drew Faust, the president of Harvard University, Tarun Khanna, director of the South Asia Institute, and Professor Jorge Paulo Lemann received him. Tarun Khanna would later reminisce of Dr Kalam's gift for delivering simple, powerful messages in his speeches, that could touch even the most erudite and sceptical audience:

> Mostly, his message was simple. In his Harvard talk .. he emphasized the importance of leadership, and kept returning to the idea that leadership was about being magnanimous, being compassionate, and creating an atmosphere where there was a win-win approach to problem solving. Not rocket science, this, even from the missile man. Yet, coming from someone who had accomplished so much, it did not degenerate into maudlin sentimentality. There was an air of authenticity.2

In March 2012, the Samajwadi Party led by Mulayam Singh Yadav won a thumping majority in the Uttar Pradesh assembly elections. This led to his son Akhilesh Yadav's electionas the chief minister of India's most populous state. At thirty-eight, he was the youngest chief minister the state had seen. He invited Dr Kalam to give Uttar Pradesh a vision for development and organized a conclave with the help of the *Hindustan Times*, the leading newspaper in north India. I was also invited to speak at the conclave.

Dr Kalam had always firmly believed in the power of India's people and the potential of its youth. Uttar Pradesh had plenty of both, and more. At the outset, Dr Kalam pointed out that the state of Uttar Pradesh had been the second-largest economy in the nation and was richly endowed in natural and human resources. With its 100 million youth, UP is the home to every fifth youth in the nation. Dr Kalam said that by 2016, of every 100 skilled jobs being generated worldwide, about eight could come directly from Uttar Pradesh alone. But Dr Kalam had his own wish for the state. 'How can the present per capita income of 26,000 rupees be increased to 100,000 rupees? This should be our mission,' he said.

Dr Kalam pointed out that Uttar Pradesh had never been a backward state, but a land where skills of different kinds had blossomed over the centuries. The carpets of Bhadohi, brassware of Moradabad, glassware of Ferozabad, mango products of Malihabad, scissors of Meerut, locks of Aligarh, ceramic pottery of Khurja, leather work of Kanpur and Chikankari of Lucknow had historically been industries of worldwide fame. Dr Kalam saw these as a wellspring of economic and social potential to be tapped: 'Had the fame of the product been matched by the economic activity? How many relatively unknown arts, crafts and cuisines had the potential to turn into a vibrant industry with support on technology and marketing fronts? We also need a carefully drawn economic map of the state across various districts and skill zones, according to the per capita income and human development index.'

Dr Kalam even exhibited a map showing areas for possible development. 'Superimposing the skill map and the economic map can identify the gaps between the potential and realization of the skill,' he suggested. Nobody could question his thoroughness. And he was aware that for progress, a multifaceted approach was called for:

> Finally, academia, industry and administration need to come together at the district level to plan on what is the sustainable method to bridge the gap between economic realization and skill potential across their respective districts. This may require targeted training across the industrial training institutes (ITIs), youth workshops, marketing and distribution support, investments into technological process enhancements and other interventions.
>
> In this way, each district will clearly identify its skill sets, its potential and how to go about achieving the mission of developing an economy based around the available skills. Also, they can benchmark themselves against each other, and find avenues of collaboration towards the common good of the state. This will lead to the formation of industrial hubs in many areas including Lucknow, Kanpur, Noida, Meerut, Mirzapur, Bhadohi, Moradabad, Aligarh, Agra and Sonebhadra.

Furthermore, Dr Kalam proposed the launch of a mission of social entrepreneurship for youth. This would require the setting up of a total of about 100,000 social enterprises across the state to serve its 200 million people in numerous crucial aspects. These would include food and nutrition; access to water (both potable and for irrigation); access to health care; access to income generation capacity; access to education and capacity building; access to quality power and communication applications and access to financial services.

Cognizant of the need for effective leadership for such ventures, Dr Kalam emphasized the need to develop creative leaders through nurturing talent, and promoting innovation in every sector. The emergence of creative leaders would facilitate global competitiveness and help in transforming the state. Moreover, he knew that all the imperatives and resources to attain success are here – in Uttar Pradesh as in India. His early successful indigenization endeavours had demonstrated this to him. There was no need to look outward for the solutions to Uttar Pradesh's problems – they are here:'You have everything, all ingredients of prosperity are here, resources, young people and proven skills. It is time to prove them to the world. The missing links are financial inclusion of the people and competitiveness of the local enterprise. Don't look outside and feel despondent, look inside, transform your potential into actuality, compete with the outside and conquer them.'

Despite Dr Kalam's unequivocal retirement from national politics, there were still attempts to lure him back to Rashtrapati Bhavan. In June 2012, the ruling United Progressive Alliance (UPA) declared Pranab Mukherjee their candidate in the forthcoming presidential elections. The opposition parties viewed Dr Kalam as their preferred candidate. Trinamool Congress chief Mamata Banerjee took the lead in attempting to persuade Dr Kalam to again stand for office. The Bharatiya Janata Party leader L.K. Advani and Samajwadi Party chief Mulayam Singh Yadav also met with him. The possibility that Dr Kalam could return to the presidency created euphoria amongst the nation's youth, and the media stoked public sentiment with speculation. The people had always been on his side, and many would have liked to see him in office again. He was seen as the peerless icon of modern India.

But Dr Kalam was having none of it. Breaking his silence, Dr Kalam on 18 June 2012 declared that he would not contest the presidential poll. 'I have considered the totality of this matter and the present political situation, and decided not to contest the presidential election 2012.' He seemed to have internalized the message he learnt at the Trinity College at Dublin, 'Despise not the prophesies; prove all things; hold fast that which is good.' Pranab Mukherjee was elected the thirteenth president of India and was sworn in on 25 July 2012.

Away from the hustle of New Delhi, Dr Kalam attended the first convocation of the Indian Institute of Space Science and Technology (IIST), Thiruvananthapuram, on 28 June 2012. The IIST was established by the Department of Space in 2007. Dr Kalam was appointed chancellor of IIST, which had become a deemed university in 2008, when the first batch of undergraduate students was inducted. The institute started three postgraduate courses in radio frequency and microwave, adoptive optics and soft computing for the degree of Master of Technology in 2009.

It was a dream come true for Dr Kalam to see the first batch graduating from the world's first space university. He could see his younger self in the fresh-faced graduates. Dr Kalam had been blessed with the finest education of his time at MIT, and this had prepared him thoroughly for the rigours of the pioneering years of Indian aerospace. From its humble beginnings, he and his colleagues had applied all the knowledge and energy they could muster in their quest to establish India's spacefaring capability. India's young scientists could now be afforded indigenous training that would propel the Indian space programme into the middle of the twenty-first century. And this engendered a myriad of exciting possibilities. Always forward-thinking, Dr Kalam's visions for aerospace in the following generations would differ little from the aspirations of his young charges:

> When I saw you all, I was asking myself, what type of missions you young graduates will get focused on and what type of innovative revolution you will create in space science and technology. Will

> you give leadership and new knowledge for spacecraft to reach geosynchronous orbit at an economic cost? Will you work for the creation of Space Satellite Service Stations for extending the life of satellites through in-orbit maintenance? Will you be responsible for building the launch vehicle to launch the spacecraft to reach Mars and the Moon for studying the possibility of new human habitats? Will you be responsible for building reusable launch vehicles that will result in the reduced orbital cost of USD 500 per kilogram instead of today's USD 6000? Of course, the challenges in space science and technology are many and you are uniquely fortunate, when India has established its credibility as a spacefaring nation.[3]

Dr Kalam attended the 150th birth anniversary celebrations of Swami Vivekananda on 11 September 2012, at the Ramakrishna Mission in New Delhi. He began his dissertation with the words spoken by Swami Vivekananda on this date in 1893 at Chicago: 'Help and not fight', 'assimilation and not destruction', 'harmony and peace and not dissension'.

In a speech with passion and idealism that would have made the saint proud, Dr Kalam gave a clarion call for a more harmonious world. He pointed out that the world is still beset with conflicts arising out of language, religion, cultural disparities and poverty encompassing around half the global population. Moreover, a shortage of water for a similar proportion of the world's people, a significant portion of the population suffering from new diseases – and most importantly, the planet suffering the effects of climate change phenomena due to indiscriminate use of fossil fuel – could give rise to greater, unprecedented conflict. Our country's great scientist and sage was concerned for the future of humanity with the trials he envisaged:

> In this environment of struggles, I am asking myself while remembering (Swami Vivekananda's) famous Chicago speech, can we collectively make it possible in every part of the world, people living in a green environment without pollution, having prosperity without poverty, peace without fear of war and a happy place to live for all citizens of the world?[4]

Dr Kalam visited Canada in October 2012 to deliver the inaugural Dhahan Memorial Lecture at Carleton University in Ottawa, and received an honorary doctorate from Simon Fraser University in Vancouver. He had by now created enthusiasm in the Indian diaspora about the India 2020 vision, particularly in North America. Hope was now replacing the earlier disbelief. Dr Kalam's numerous visits had generated a singular optimism in the overseas Indian communities. The mood was becoming 'Yes! Something good is happening back home; let us do our bit.'

Much of the optimism that Dr Kalam evoked lay in his quite unique combination of spirituality, technological prowess and inspiration. But more than that, he possessed a native wisdom and practicality that underpinned all his thinking. He identified the energy deficiency in the Indian economy as the biggest hindrance for its development. He was aware that no vision, no rhetoric, no mission or plan would make any real difference unless there is sufficient energy. India needed a good deal more energy to power its industry and bring water to its vast dry lands for agriculture.

Unquestionably, the Indian economy was bleeding from the costly import of large quantities of oil and gas. There had been delays and inefficiencies in the development of abundant indigenous coal reserves. The greater use of nuclear power was mired in international treaties restricting the supply of uranium. And the renewable resources of solar and wind power could not yet conceivably handle the quantum of the expanding requirement for electricity. Outdated power generation infrastructure continued to falter with an ever-growing demand, causing voltage fluctuations and regular shutdowns throughout the country. Worse, 300 million people still lacked access to the grid. The country's power generation regime simply did not match its aspirations for industrial growth and urban expansion.

Dr Kalam was naturally happy for any opportunity to provide further impetus for this crucial issue, and this was duly presented to him by The Economist Group. This British multinational media company is best known as the publisher of the highly regarded *The Economist* magazine. The company invited him for a keynote interview, followed by the launch of its White Paper in New Delhi on his eighty-first birthday. He was given an advance copy of the White Paper prepared by the Economist Intelligence Unit. The White Paper examined the prospects for India's future energy system, from source to generation to distribution to consumption.

The birthday boy Kalam converted the sombre gathering of experts and stalwarts – with their pinstriped suits and guarded stances – into a free-flowing conclave, with his characteristic spontaneity and his grounded approach. His presentation was eminently sensible.

He said that human society had seen four levels of fuel. The first fuel was wood, which began with the discovery of fire some one million years ago. The second fuel was oil and related petroleum products, which was as new as the late nineteenth century – only about 100 years old. The third fuel was nuclear, barely fifty years old. Now we are exploring the fourth fuel, termed green energy, like solar and wind, which has been becoming increasingly commercially viable and technologically feasible within the last two decades. 'Now, let me talk about the fifth fuel – which is not a hardware fuel in the conventional sense – it is energy efficiency,' he said.

Dr Kalam told the expert audience that building energy efficiency is indeed the most economically feasible and convenient way to 'generate' energy, simply by saving it. More than any form of technology, what is needed is the social awareness and incentives for industries and homes to save energy. In the distribution of power alone, the losses are in excess of 40 per cent in many states. There is also an immense scope for energy efficiency at the household level. Ranging from cooking fuels to smart buildings, up to 50 per cent of the energy consumed in homes can be saved with cost-effective and judicious innovations. And by merely replacing incandescent lamps with LED lamps, using analogue chips to start electric pump sets in agriculture, regulating domestic fans and making air conditioners and refrigerators intelligent, India could double its energy availability.

Dr Kalam was an agent of opportunity. Apart from his prognostications – such as those in the realm of space, many of which behold a distant future – everything he advocated was currently feasible and realistic. And much of what he suggested could be quite easily mandated or brought into being with some cooperation, effort and coordination. But with the system itself hampered by its own inertia and wedded to poor choices, there was little immediate prospect of improvement in most parts of the country.

6.5

Liveable Planet Earth

> We are in danger of destroying ourselves by our greed and stupidity. We cannot remain looking inwards at ourselves on a small and increasingly polluted and overcrowded planet.
>
> – Stephen Hawking
> British physicist, cosmologist

When an invitation arrived to give a special address at the Beijing Forum 2012, Dr Kalam could barely contain his enthusiasm. Since the publication of his two books in China – *Wings of Fire* in 2002 and *Guiding Souls* in 2007 – he had wanted to visit the country. China had been an enigma for him. He was impressed with the longevity of the Chinese civilization and intrigued at its rise as a world power in the preceding thirty years. The Beijing Forum is an international academic forum sponsored by Peking University, the Chinese Ministry of Education, and the Korea Foundation for Advanced Studies to promote academic development and social progress around the world.

As much as anyone, Dr Kalam was aware that progress can be hard to define. He had noted in *India 2020* that economic figures can themselves be deceptive, and hide all manner of human misery. Following the World War II, development largely replaced traditional concepts of prosperity, and GDP became the measure of progress and well-being of a nation. This served as a means of perpetuating the power of the war's victors. Since they had not only the power and resources to produce but also to determine prices, developing countries were cleverly subjugated as consumer markets. China's leadership understood the dynamics of the globalized economic system. They turned the tables on the Western bloc, and became the manufacturing hub of the world for low-priced consumer goods.

As briefly discussed earlier, there is an international elite influencing the affairs of this world. The World Economic Forum (WEF) is one venue that represents the elite's interests. It is a Swiss non-profit organization. Every year it invites people in business from all over the world to Davos, a mountain resort in the eastern Alps region of Switzerland. An opposing force is the World Social Forum (WSF), which is based in the city of Porto Alegree, Brazil. The WEF proclaims that accumulation of wealth by market rules is the only way for humanity to improve; and there is no other alternative. The WSF sees development as the antithesis of enhancing humanity's well-being. It fights to protect local forms of social, cultural and economic organization from the global market forces.

Perhaps a good measure of the Buddha's middle path here would yield lasting prosperity for humankind. Our scientist sage could see both perspectives, and would not subscribe wholesale to the views of either of these organizations. A thoroughgoing proponent of hard work, he supported development; but only that which was inclusive, sustainable and harmonious. His own efforts had helped bring prosperity to countless people through indigenization, and his natural pragmatism saw the benefits of development. Development, to Dr Kalam however, engendered much more than generating money.

He delivered the keynote address on 2 November 2012 in the presence of UN Secretary General Ban Ki-moon and former prime minister of the Republic of Korea Ro Jai-bong, among other distinguished speakers. Dr Kalam shared his vision of a Liveable Planet Earth as a global scale-up of his India 2020 development plan: 'Nations unite when they share a common urge. With pressures as pertinent as the climate and the environment, I urge delegates to consider a "Liveable Planet Earth", where we address problems of management, water, energy, healthcare, and education for seven billion people.'[1]

Dr Kalam sat through the lectures and captured the essence of China's rapid economic growth of more than thirty years. He realized that in its rapid economic ascent, China could scarcely avoid the knotty problems of urbanization. Rural areas in China were now confronted with sociological dilemmas: young people were migrating to its cities, and only old people and children were left in the villages to face bleak realities. Much arable land was lying uncultivated. The message Dr Kalam brought back from the Beijing Forum was that his PURA mission is not only relevant for Indian villages, it is also relevant throughout the world – and certainly in China.

Later, Dr Kalam visited the China Academy of Space Technology (CAST), the space agency of China under China Aerospace Science and Technology Corporation (CASC). The CAST designed and manufactured the Dong Fang Hong satellites. The name of the satellite means 'the east is red'. It was taken from a song that was the de facto anthem of the People's Republic of China during the Cultural Revolution in the 1960s. Dr Kalam was told that after reaching orbit on 24 April 1970, the Dong Fang Hong satellite transmitted the song '*The east is red*' continuously for twenty-eight days. The People's Republic of China was making its point. It was a remarkable day for Dr Kalam. He saw much of China's aerospace history from the era that corresponded to his time at TERLS, when he was driving the effort to launch the indigenous RH-75 rocket. In the evening, ambassador to China Subrahmanyam Jaishankar hosted a dinner reception in his honour.

The next day, Dr Kalam met with members of the Chinese People's Institute of Foreign Affairs (CPIFA) over lunch. Vice chairperson of the eleventh NPC (National People's Congress) Standing Committee, Ms Yan Junqi, the chair of the Peking University Council, Mr Zhu Shanlu, and vice-president of CPIFA, Ambassador Lu Shumin, were present. Dr Kalam discussed with his learned counterparts the attributes of the Indian and Chinese civilizations. Specifically, the gathering was concerned with factors that had allowed the greatness of these two civilizations to endure. Notwithstanding that no single ruler had ever commanded the entirety of either of these vast countries until modern times, their resilience was such that they survived numerous invasions and periods of foreign rule. Two important points emerged from this bilateral discussion.

The first of these was the issue of the peoples' traits. If we enumerate the characteristics of Indian and Chinese people, we would likely find common characteristics – simplicity, love of nature, patience, indifference to international affairs, a 'this would not work, I know' attitude, fertility, industry, frugality, love of family life, pacifism, contentment, humour, conservatism and sensuality. The order and intensity of these traits would vary between regions, but these were some vital common traits. They made Indian and Chinese people different from the Mongols and Europeans who, at least for some time, governed their affairs.

The second important point of this discussion was the quality of these two ancient cultures that had convinced many invaders to settle in these countries, rather than return to their erstwhile lands. Conversely, how was it possible for the Indian and Chinese civilizations to survive periodic political disasters? How did they sustain, where other ancient civilizations, such as Rome, were subsumed by their invaders? What made the two great lands so culturally stable?

The consensus was that the factor that had allowed these great cultures to endure was the prominence of the family system. The family system was so well defined and organized in both India and China as to make it impossible for a man to forget his lineage. This form of social immortality – which the Indians and Chinese prized above all earthy possessions – had something of the character of a religion. It was enhanced by the ritual of ancestor worship, and the consciousness of it had penetrated deep into the collective soul of both the Indian and the Chinese people. The invaders were all too anxious to join the local families to claim part of this immortality. Either consciously or unconsciously, they were enamoured of the feeling that when one dies, one does not die, but one's self lives on in the great stream of the family life.

Dr Kalam attended the World Confluence of Humanity, Power and Spirituality in Kolkata on 22 December 2012, organized by the SERI

Foundation. After pondering the discussion at the Beijing Forum, Dr Kalam had asked himself how the evolution of an enlightened society might take place. He said that until now, we have not enjoyed anything approaching an enlightened society. Despite the best efforts of the many religious leaders, scientists, reformers and other inspirational figures, the enlightened society has remained elusive. He proposed some broad conditions under which an enlightened society could thrive:

> I would like to put forward for this important gathering a methodology for evolving a happy, prosperous and peaceful society on our planet. Enlightened society will have three components – education with a value system, religion transformed to spirituality and economic development. With poverty you cannot have peace or spirituality.[2]

Peace itself can be elusive for the best of people. As with all of us, Dr Kalam faced losses that would disturb his equilibrium and lead him to deep spiritual contemplation. Dr Kalam's close friend and colleague since 1982, Gen. R. Swaminathan, passed away on 15 February 2013. Swaminathan was his right-hand man in managing the Defence Research and Development Laboratory when Dr Kalam was the director there, and the DRDO headquarters when he took over as the director general. And he had remained with Dr Kalam throughout. He was with him at Rashtrapati Bhavan, and he lived in the annexe of his post-presidency house in New Delhi till his last day. Swaminathan's passing seemed for a time to weigh down Dr Kalam's irrepressible buoyancy, and he spoke of his profound sadness at Swaminathan's loss on several occasions thereafter. After some time though, he was back to his usual self, and he had put the death of his friend in perspective spiritually:

Arun: Swaminathan suffered for a year with pain. He is now free.

Kalam: He never let his pain interfere with his work.

Arun: Why do good people suffer? Why does God allow them to suffer?

Kalam: Suffering tests the worth and mettle of a person.

Arun: Is it necessary?

Kalam: God has power over all things. The reason why God allows diseases and calamities in a particular situation is beyond our comprehension and for reasons that may not be apparent.

Arun: But suffering is apparent.

Kalam: This life of sixty, seventy ... even a hundred years, is nothing compared to the time of Barzakh. The spirits of genuine believers do not weaken under suffering; nor does suffering frighten them or make them desperate. Swaminathan was a true believer.

Around this time, the nation was reeling under scandal and blatant mismanagement. In the nation's capital, massive street demonstrations against endemic political corruption forewarned of a greater showdown between the people and the political classes. The general elections were a year away when *India Today* organized a conclave on 'Reinventing Democracy'. Dr Kalam was invited to open the discussions with his keynote address on 15 March 2013. Chairman of the India Today Group, Aroon Purie, welcomed him with a terse summation of the failure of the Indian democratic system to deliver good leaders:

> When the youth erupted and defied the barricades and withstood teargas shells in Delhi, no political leader, young or old, had the courage or credibility to face them. The platitudes of politicians, uttered from the comfort zone of power, sounded silly and empty. There seems to be a widening gap between governments and the people.[3]

Dr Kalam opened his speech by quoting British historian Tony Judt from his book *Ill Fares the Land*.

> If you do not talk differently,
> We shall not think differently.

In this book, Tony Judt projected lessons learned from history to forward and challenge readers to debate 'what comes next?' The book made the case for a social democratic society based on social justice within the framework of a capitalist economy. He envisioned prosperous people taking care of the poor sections of society in an institutionalized framework, not as some optional charitable activity. He envisioned high-technology-based enterprises with employees not stripped of their collective bargaining arrangements and working without the fear of 'pink slips'. He envisioned regulation of the economy in the general interest – not by political parties funded by 'big money'. If Dr Kalam had any political vision, it was not far removed from the social democracy of Tony Judt.

He indeed spoke plainly at the conclave. Dr Kalam had never been part of the political establishment; remaining an outsider always allowed him to speak his mind and maintain his integrity. He said that ideally, a leader should spend 30 per cent of his time on politics. But Indian leaders were spending 30 per cent of their time on development and 70 per cent of their time on politics and serving not nation but their vote banks.

Dr Kalam said that he believed it was important to engage young minds with an inspiring vision for thinking and action. 'Many a civilization disappeared in the world because of the absence of a vision,' he said. 'Let us move on with the spirit of "I can do it, we can do it and the nation can do it",' he declared amidst loud applause. When a guest asked how many marks Dr Kalam would give to the Indian democratic system, he said 'five out of ten', and then quipped, 'just pass marks'.

Dr Kalam championed the idea of PURA throughout his presidency. He later made it the theme of his book *Target 3 Billion*[4] that he co-authored with Srijan Pal Singh, a management graduate from the Indian Institute of Management, Ahmedabad. But his efforts were in vain. Except for a few models developed by strong local organizations like Shree Tatyasaheb Kore Warana Sahakari Sakhar Karkhana Limited in Kolhapur, Maharashtra, and Periyar Maniammai University in Thanjavur, Tamil Nadu, the model did not find many takers. Standing before a huge poster on PURA with a picture of Kalam in Kerala in February 2012, the Union rural development minister Jairam Ramesh declared with more than a hint of glee, 'the PURA launched by Kalam has failed'.[5]

Dr Kalam took it all in his stride, and gave little thought to the minister's comments. He was not deterred. This was a man who had known the despair of failure as well as the exultation of success. He had seen one of his cherished rockets crash to pieces of twisted metal into the sea, and yet he had seen many others soar beyond earthly realms. In his youngest years, he had experienced the desolation of a livelihood laid waste by an act of God, with the cyclone that had wrecked his father's boat and uprooted the family's coconut palms. His father's stoic response had been a lifetime template. He had simply uttered a profound universal truth – '*Inna lillahi wa inna ilayhi raji'u*' – 'We are from God and to God we shall return.' Jainulabdeen had then calmly set about rebuilding his boat without complaining about his fate. Among the many lessons imparted to young Azad was one that had helped take him from a fishing village to the highest office in the nation; and that lesson was perseverance.

From all his wisdom of eight decades, Dr Kalam knew that the inspiration that drove one to persevere – 'To strive, to seek to find and not to yield' in Alfred Lord Tennyson's words – came from a wellspring deep within, from the spirit. This was something that must be tapped – in the individual as much as in the nation. He had tapped this source himself, and he saw it as his mission to evoke this in the lives of others, and in the spirit of the nation. And it would be his mission to the last, until his final breath.

His message was nothing if not consistent. He spoke on the occasion of the Prof. P.V. Indiresan Memorial Lecture at the Leadership Conclave 2013, organized by IIT Delhi Alumni Association on 20 April 2013. He counselled that for realizing challenging missions like PURA, what we need is an indomitable spirit. He invoked a message of Maharshi Patanjali 2,500 years ago:

> When you are inspired by some great purpose, some extraordinary project, all your thoughts break their bounds. Your mind transcends limitations, your consciousness expands in every direction, and you find yourself in a new, great and wonderful world. Dormant forces, faculties and talents come alive, and you discover yourself to be a greater person by far than you ever dreamt yourself to be.[6]

Dr Kalam said that he had worked closely with Prof. Indiresan in two important areas – one being the evolution of the technology vision of the *India 2020* document, and the other the pioneering work on sustainable rural development through PURA. He called on IIT Alumni to 'carry forward the vision of Prof. Indiresan to realization by establishing PURAs in India and other developing nations, wherever your business and industrial presence is there as a part of social entrepreneurship'. I saw Dr Kalam's crusade for the PURA idea as a shining example of the virtue of perseverance. And he helped me understand its dynamics. He showed everyone by example that it is not about running a long race – perseverance is actually running many short races, one after the other, never giving up running.

In 2013, Dr Kalam was awarded the Wernher von Braun Memorial Award by the National Space Society (NSS), USA. He received the award on 24 May 2013 at the thirty-second International Space Development Conference (ISDC) at San Diego, California. The theme of the conference was 'Global Collaboration in Twenty-First Century Space'. Dr Kalam turned nostalgic in his acceptance speech and recalled his meeting the legendary rocket guru von Braun.

> On 20 July 1969, the Saturn-V booster injected the lunar module of the Apollo 11 Rocket with two astronauts, Neil Armstrong and Buzz Aldrin, and history was made when Armstrong walked on the moon. For the whole world, von Braun became a hero for making the rocket that took man to the moon. At that time, I was a young fellow. I had just entered into the aeronautical profession, building hovercraft and meteorological rockets. It was a great surprise and fulfilment in my mind to meet my hero, when von Braun visited India at the invitation of Prof. Vikram Sarabhai. I became his host.[7]

Then Dr Kalam rolled out his vision of 'Space Solar Power: Key to a Liveable Planet Earth', which had been germinating in his mind since his visit to the China Academy of Space Technology (CAST) in November of the previous year. Great thoughts are like seeds. Once implanted in the mind, they remain alive and wait for the right time to burst open into a great vision. Dr Kalam learned this by his own experience. All that is needed is perseverance – and above all, purity of mind. If the mind is in the grip of an 'I and me' malaise, the vision cannot thrive. If it is fed by the destructive emotions of attachment and aversion, anger, pride and doubt, the seed of the thought will be poisoned, and the vision would never flourish.

Some of Dr Kalam's visions were doubtless a little beyond their time. But that is the nature of visions. Nonetheless, they were invariably pure; the intent driving him was for the betterment of his people and humanity. He saw the unparalleled potential for this in space. As a young man, he had helped his country reach beyond earthly bounds. Now that this was achieved, he saw that a new paradigm of worldwide cooperation could immeasurably improve the quality of human life. Space endeavours in his early years under Dr Vikram Sarabhai had fostered international collaboration. Similarly, the potential for space to bring mankind together now to solve issues facing the whole of humanity needed a coordinated plan between the world's nations:

> Let us have a World Space Vision 2050 structured to enable mankind to formulate and implement: large scale societal missions (including a Space Solar Power mission) enabled by low-cost access to space; evolution of a comprehensive space security doctrine, policy and programme, and expansion of space exploration and current application missions.
>
> Such a World Space Vision 2050 would enhance the quality of human life, inspire the spirit of international collaborative space exploration, expand the horizons of knowledge and ensure space security for all nations of the world.[8]

Before returning to India, Dr Kalam visited JSS Spiritual Mission in Gaithersburg, Maryland, and Sri Venkateswara temple at Minneapolis created by Madhu Reddy, founder chairman of US Electronics and other Indian community members. Dr Kalam was always enthusiastic about meeting non-resident Indians overseas. He was thrilled to see that not only had they made their mark in other lands, they were living by their own traditions. Families were their sanctuaries and community and temple services their means of connecting with their roots. The Indian diaspora in the United States is seen as an asset to the United States' new economic machine, based on computer science and information technology. The days of brute military force – nations conquering others to control their natural resources – are giving way to a yearning for a new harmonious world, where lives can be better for everyone. It is not a quantum leap – it is a gradual transformation, perhaps part of the evolutionary progression of the human race itself.

6.6

Set the Ball Rolling

> The requirements for our evolution have changed. Survival is no longer sufficient. Our evolution now requires us to develop spiritually – to become emotionally aware and make responsible choices. It requires us to align ourselves with the values of the soul – harmony, cooperation, sharing, and reverence for life.
>
> – Gary Zukav
> American spiritual teacher and author

In the Darbar Hall of Taj Krishna, Hyderabad, on 30 June 2013, renowned scientist Prof. D. Balasubramanian launched our book *Squaring the Circle: Seven Steps to Indian Renaissance* before 200 academicians, journalists, scientists, engineers and medical professionals. The event also celebrated the milestone of the book *Wings of Fire*, which has sold in excess of one million copies all over the world, and been translated into thirteen Indian languages and six foreign languages.

Dr D. Balasubramanian said that it was significant that the book had come out in an atmosphere clouded with negativity. He called Kalam's positivity blended with personal experience, science and faith as the most potent energy in our times. In this book, written in a question-and-answer format, Dr Kalam expresses his concerns on what ails our country at the systemic and the individual levels. Moreover, he suggests ways for transcending these ills through an Indian renaissance.

Explaining that the book had been intended as a guide per se, but is not the answer to all the problems we are currently facing, Dr Kalam said, 'The message is articulated in the book but it is not fully developed, for it is beyond us. I'm setting a ball rolling and I hope you'll all help it move forward.' He was being realistic: he could inspire, ignite minds – he could enlighten the masses of their potential – but they had to follow up his suggestions with actions. His time, we now know, was running out.

The chief minister of Gujarat, Narendra Modi, invited Dr Kalam to address a conclave to discuss 'How government and business can change to provide Indian youth with the opportunities they deserve'. The conclave was hosted by the Citizens for Accountable Governance at Ahmedabad, on 29 June 2013.

I accompanied Dr Kalam on this visit. Dr Kalam gave Narendra Modi a signed copy of *Squaring the Circle*, and said that he was a leader who could accomplish his mission of making India a developed nation by 2020. Dr Kalam enumerated the seven steps he had outlined in his book:

1. Gain understanding of the irrefutable law of cause and effect in all matters. Voting for the wrong leader brings not only misery and gloom but will also alter the destiny of a democratic nation.
2. Face the truth of socio-economic inequality and the history of Partition and undertake reconciliation by developing the minorities, marginalized and poor with a generous mindset and by special effort.
3. Correct our misplaced world views by revamping the education system for the development of a creative mind, a well-integrated self, and the ability to be a useful part of society.
4. Encourage and foster social enterprise to tackle social problems, improve communities and the environment by convergence of technologies at the bottom of the community pyramid.
5. Achieve energy independence by 2030 through nuclear, solar, wind and renewable energy routes. Provide lifeline energy to all our citizens, irrespective of their ability to pay.
6. Indigenize our telecommunication, IT and electronics

manufacturing and proactive security for the nation's interests against cyber and terrorist attacks.

7. Integrate with world economy, following the path of social democracy, and assume leadership of the world in making our planet earth more liveable.

At the conclave in Ahmedabad, Dr Kalam spoke with passion in front of the large gathering of youth leaders from across India. The massive Mahatma Mandir convention hall was reverberating with youthful energy. Dr Kalam told his young audience that poverty and terrorism are the two big enemies of India – the rest in noise.

He said that the Indian psyche is generally savings-oriented, and living within one's means is a part of the national mindset. He explained that the 400-million-strong middle class is a world in itself, with its purchasing power, and all multinational companies would come with their peddling carts to our nation's doorstep. It is there that they belong, Dr Kalam declared. We must guard our doors and never allow them to enter our homes.

Dr Kalam said that there is a famous hadith of Prophet Muhammad: *Salla llahu alayhi wa-alehe wa-sallam* – paradise can only survive under the shade of swords. Unless our country is secure, how would our people give their best and prosper? How can we allow our enemies to walk into our lanes and kill our people? He called for a national campaign to eradicate terrorism:

> I believe that time has come, apart from our multiple agencies forecasting and handling of the terrorist activities, where we need to evolve an aggressive mission called the National Campaign to Eradicate Terrorism (NCET), with a mission-oriented integrated management structure, duly passed as a bill by the parliament.

Dr Kalam was the chief guest at the first convocation of the Indian Institute of Technology at Banaras Hindu University (IIT-BHU). We reached Varanasi on 10 July 2013. The Jeevan Vidya crusader Prof. Rajeev Sangal had taken over as director after the institute was declared an autonomous institution and made as other IITs were, independent of the BHU system. Prof. Rajeev Sangal was very keen to relive the triumphant experience of Dr Kalam attending the first convocation of the International Institute of Information Technology (IIIT), Hyderabad, in 2003. I felt that I had been blessed, being present on both these occasions, separated by more than a decade. As expected, it was a glorious event. Dr Kalam was in his usual fine form, painting his vision with broad brushstrokes and fine touches. His delivery was characteristically warm and inspiring, and I was uplifted at least as much as the students.

Hard work over many years was showing its results. Two events on a single day in August 2013 afforded Dr Kalam the satisfaction of a grandfather seeing his tribe growing.

On 26 August 2013 Dr Kalam inaugurated the International Conference on Computational and Data Intensive Science at NAL, Bangalore, in the presence of his friend Prof. N. Balakrishnan, who was associate director of the Indian Institute of Science at that time. Dr Kalam recalled that Jim Gray of Microsoft fame was lost at sea near San Francisco on 28 January 2007, during a short solo sailing trip to scatter his mother's ashes. In the ensuing search and rescue mission, which was sadly unsuccessful, extensive use was made of GPS data. This foreshadowed the shift to the fourth paradigm of discovery, based on data-intensive science.

Increasingly, scientific breakthroughs will be powered by advanced computing capabilities that help researchers manipulate and explore massive data sets. NAL, Dr Kalam said, was well placed to harness this emerging technology in India. In an age when everything in the world – the energy at home, refrigerators, car components, apparel, medical monitoring devices in the human body and the GPS-assisted movement of people – all become part of the network, India cannot afford to remain a bystander. Now data comes in shapes. You can't visualize them without big data tools like support vector machines. It is time to think in pictures!

At the silver jubilee celebrations on 26 August 2013 of the Research Centre Imarat (RCI), Dr Kalam gave the large gathering of scientists and engineers a golden jubilee mission for the institute. Being the creator of this institution in the 1980s, Dr Kalam was at his natural best. He spoke for more than an hour, with the excitement of a young scientist thrilled with his latest discovery:

> Recently, I was in the Harvard University where Korean American professor of chemistry and of physics, Hongkun Park, showed me his invention of nano needles, which can pierce and deliver content into individual targeted cells. That's how nano-particle science is shaping the biosciences. Then I met the Professor of chemical engineering and physics, Vinothan Manoharan, who showed how the biosciences are in turn shaping the development of new materials. He is using DNA material to design self-assembling particles. When a particular type of DNA is applied on a particle at the atomic level, he is able to generate a predetermined behaviour and automatic assembly from them.
>
> I saw how two different sciences are shaping each other, without any barrier between the technologists. This reciprocating contribution of sciences to one another is going to shape our future and industry needs to be ready for it. Friends, are you ready to bring down the barriers between various technological groups in your institute?

Dr Kalam then suggested a golden jubilee mission for RCI to become the world leader in the convergence of nano-bio-info-eco technologies in avionics, feeding societal spin-offs beyond our comprehension at this time.

Despite a hectic schedule, the years were passing for Dr Kalam, and many of his contemporaries had passed on or were suffering the ravages of the years. From time to time, he would talk to me about his late friend and right-hand man Swaminathan. Perhaps Swaminathan's passing away added urgency to his concern when he heard that his close friend and spiritual mentor Pramukh Swamiji was seriously ill. Pramukh Swamiji was bedridden and had stopped eating. He was now sustained merely by the fluids that were administered him by his worried followers. Dr Kalam promptly decided to visit him.

We travelled to Sarangpur near Rajkot in Gujarat on 11 March 2014. Dr Y.S. Rajan was already there and greeted us. In spite of his condition, Pramukh Swamiji was happy and radiant. He exuded peace and enlightenment. There was not even a flicker of pain or sense of any complaint in him. He did not speak, but looked into Dr Kalam's eyes and held his hand for more than ten minutes. He gave him a rosary and smiled, to the delight of all the sadhus present.

Dr Kalam addressed a gathering of 2,000 sadhus, devotees and students. He recollected his visit to the Akshardham Cultural Complex, New Delhi, on 6 November 2005. On that day, he said he received the answer to the question that had troubled him throughout his life: How could one integrate spirituality and social service? He could never revere religious masters living in seclusion and meditating upon God, without any thought for others. For Dr Kalam, service had been the highest form of worship. He believed any form of worship was incomplete without deeds that benefitted humanity. After meeting Pramukh Swamiji and studying the work done by the BAPS organization under his leadership, Dr Kalam realized that worship and service were indeed indivisible. Those who wished to sincerely serve society must be spiritually pure, and only those who were spiritually pure could sincerely serve society.

Dr Kalam quoted a passage from the book *Satsang*: 'What is left with a person who has given his all? Nothing! But this nothing becomes everything indeed. It becomes an ocean of goodness, of purity and humility, an essence of spirituality that is enough to inspire millions.'[1] He declared that Pramukh Swamiji had now reached the supreme state of personhood, which needs no rank, no recognition; not even veneration. Pramukh Swamiji has become the noble soul. He now lives in this awakened state, not moving anywhere, not saying anything, not doing anything, and yet overseeing all that is being planned, created and managed. His life is an example of selfless service and the creation of excellence. 'In his presence, I have become much more aware of my real self!' Dr Kalam proclaimed. Dr Kalam gave me the task of writing about his spiritual experiences with Pramukh Swamiji, and thus was born the book *Transcendence*.

By this time, the Indian higher education system, comprising over 31,000 institutions, was exhibiting impressive growth. It had become one of the world's largest providers of higher education. On 2 April 2014, Dr Kalam attended the twenty-eighth annual convocation of

T.A. Pai Management Institute, Manipal. The chancellor of Manipal University, Dr Ramdas Pai, received him. The Indian higher education system is plagued by three fundamental challenges of access, equity and quality. The Manipal Group had done commendable work to address these issues.

Dr Kalam, spoke about the importance of being 'good leaders' besides being professional managers. He emphasized that amongst the various resources in the country, ignited minds are the most powerful. He said that there is a global awareness emerging in India, and many world leaders have started valuing India as a leader of South Asian nations. He shared a famous saying of Alexander the Great, who said that he was not afraid of an army of lions led by a sheep, but he was afraid of an army of sheep led by a lion. India needs leaders who develop their teams, rather than glorify their own roles and seek personal aggrandisement, Dr Kalam said.

Dr Kalam referred to the emergence of a new world where education is not marked by boundaries. He envisioned a developed India by 2020, achieved by concrete integrated action plans. He highlighted the importance of achieving energy independence over energy security by the judicious usage of natural resources. In making mention of student activities, he gave accolades to the efforts of the Social Endeavour Group in educating underprivileged children. Dr Kalam exhorted them to work for the betterment of the country through the field of management, in an ethical and responsible manner.

In May 2014, Dr Kalam was invited to the newly established Edinburgh India Institute at the University of Edinburgh in Scotland. The institute was working with the National Institute of Ocean Technology (NIOT), Chennai, the Tata Institute of Fundamental Research, the Delhi University, the Indian Institute of Science and the National Centre for Biological Sciences (NCBS). Internationally acclaimed universities have started coming to India, and are now tapping the immense youthful talent here.

The University of Edinburgh, founded in 1582, played an important role in affording Edinburgh its reputation as a chief intellectual centre during the Age of Enlightenment. Its alumni have included physicist James Clerk Maxwell, naturalist Charles Darwin, philosopher David Hume and inventor Alexander Graham Bell. Vice Chancellor Sir Timothy O'Shea escorted Dr Kalam to various laboratories of the university, and conferred upon Dr Kalam an honorary degree of Doctor of Science. Dr Kalam was aware of the scramble to attract Indian youth to the campuses of all the world's great universities. While he accepted invitations from these universities – to make connections with some of the world's finest minds, to help inspire the youth of the world and to maintain protocol – he was a diehard believer in indigenous education. Dr Kalam never ceased delivering his message that Indian universities can – and indeed they must – rise to the very highest of world standards.

The result of the nation's general elections was declared on 16 May 2014. The incumbent United Progressive Alliance (UPA) was soundly defeated. The BJP had won what would be described – without any sense of hyperbole – a landslide victory. On 26 May 2014, Narendra Modi became the new prime minister of India. He invited heads of state of all the SAARC nations and Mauritius to his swearing-in ceremony.

Leaders from the countries of the region attended this grand event, which was telecast around the country with patriotic pride. President Hamid Karzai of Afghanistan, Prime Minister Tshering Tobgay of Bhutan, President Abdulla Yameen of Maldives, Prime Minister Sushil Koirala of Nepal, Prime Minister Nawaz Sharif of Pakistan and President Rajapaksa of Sri Lanka were all present to witness Modi take his oath of office. Prime Minister Sheikh Hasina of Bangladesh was on a prescheduled visit to Japan; the Speaker of the Bangladesh parliament, Shirin Sharmin Chaudhury, attended in her stead. Prime Minister Navin Ramgoolam of Mauritius also attended the event. Finally, India was behaving like a country of a billion people.

6.7

Made for Life

> History never really says goodbye. History says, "See you later."
>
> – Eduardo Galeano
> Uruguayan journalist

When the Sitaram Jindal Foundation (SJF) approached Dr Kalam for his consent to receive the first SJF Prize of one crore rupees set up as an annual recognition of socially useful work in 2011, he respectfully declined. But when the family argued that his acceptance of the first SJF award would bring glory to the subsequent recipients, Dr Kalam reconsidered. He would only accept the award, he said, on the condition that he would donate the entire sum to organizations of his choice. This was gladly accepted by the foundation, and on the very day he received the one-crore-rupee prize, Dr Kalam made four donations of twenty-five lakh rupees each to charitable organizations he had selected.

The names of the four organizations are not mentioned here, honouring Dr Kalam's wish for keeping his donations anonymous. He believed that publicly acknowledged charitable bequests can be dangerously inebriating for one's ego. Dr Kalam's actions do not find many parallels, and some may not even understand his logic. But what was his logic?

Dr Kalam based his life on righteousness and respect for others, traits that he imbibed from his parents and which were later fostered by his teachers at Schwartz and St Joseph's. He accepted the award out of respect for the great life of Sita Ram Jindal. But he had to give it away to adhere to his own code of conduct. His father had taught him never to accept an untoward gift, and he saw a cash award as just that. He distributed the amount such that a number of organizations would benefit equally, in a manner that would not belittle the SJF award. Moreover, he felt that taking public credit for the bequests he made would simply be another form of untoward benefit.

Dr Kalam was for me as he was for others – a thoughtful, warm and kindly man. When it came to matters of probity, he was insightful and unyielding, even stern – and his conduct was inscrutable. I would always seek Dr Kalam's counsel on such matters, because he possessed a wisdom beyond all measure, yet had such a simple manner of explanation. Our discussions on philosophical concerns would usually take the form of a master–pupil dialogue:

Arun: What is a good life?

Kalam: A good life is an effort to achieve a big, noble aim.

Arun: Including getting rich?

Kalam: Yes. But why you want to get rich is important.

Arun: Okay. But suppose I want to get rich to do good to others, would it make a good aim?

Kalam: It involves consideration of ends and means. Suppose you want a car – the car is your end. You can take a bank loan, or save over years to buy the car, or steal, or accept it as gift from someone – these are your means.

Arun: But suppose I get my car by good means. The car now becomes a means to another end, say, going to work faster. And of course going to work faster is the means to do more work. But that does not happen. The car does not remain a means of transport any more. It becomes a moving corridor that protects the car owner from the miserable humanity around him. How do I keep on minding the goodness of my means?

Kalam: Money is definitely not an end. It is always a means. It derives its value from the end it leads you to.

Arun: Is there any final or ultimate end, an end for which everything else is a means, and an end that is not a means to anything else? Is there is an ultimate end, goal or purpose for human life?

Kalam: What is really good for you is that which meets your natural needs – food, clothing, a house – these are the same for all human beings. Giving away anything more is a plan for living well. Consuming, acquiring and hoarding that which is not needed is a bad plan.

Our sage scientist had quite a penchant for attracting those who lived well by this definition. Dr Kalam had a long-standing friendship with Rev. Fr Thomas Felix, a Catholic priest in Thiruvananthapuram. Fr Thomas Felix had devoted his life for the worthy cause of helping mentally disabled children in India. Fr Felix was the founder of the Central Institute on Mental Retardation (CIMR), a voluntary social service organization. The governing board members of CMIR are selected from the parents of children who are mentally challenged. The aims of this organization are to work for the total development of mentally challenged people by acquiring and disseminating information on methods for their care and education, and to promote awareness of their issues to the public. Dr Kalam participated in the golden jubilee of Father Felix's priestly ordination on 28 May 2014.

Dr Kalam wanted people to offer more than kind words and sentiment to social welfare. He asked the audience, 'What we can offer to Rev. Fr Thomas Felix, such a great soul! Will it be flowers? Shall we pay tribute? I don't think any of this will bring smiles to the face of Fr Felix. But definitely smiles and happiness will come, if today everyone of us takes a single oath. Shall we do it?'

The oath was simple: Today onwards, I will give part of my time, part of my wealth and part of my service, to give value-based quality education to at least one specially abled child in my life.[1]

That day I understood the meaning of a good life. A good life is finding satisfaction in giving a little more than you take. It is not only about money; giving money is relatively simple. It is about giving away your time, giving away your skills, your knowledge – and above all, giving others respect, courage and hope.

Dr Kalam compared life to a vast desert under a blazing sun, a human being just a bird flying over its scorched sands. The bird has two wings upon which it is carried aloft by unseen currents: one wing of gratitude and the other of patience – *shukr* and *sabr*. A good man lives with patience and keeps working without complaining about what he does not have in his life. He lives with gratitude for all that he has already been given – his life, parents and family. Fools without sufficient patience and gratitude to keep themselves airborne, will surely plunge to an unforgiving earth beneath them.

One way that Dr Kalam expressed his gratitude for all that he had been given was through his work with children. He never tired of visiting schools and interacting with them. I see no parallel of Dr Kalam; there is no other person of his eminence, with the full calendar of engagements that he had, who has spent as much time with children. He would quote African American social reformer Frederick Douglass:'It is easier to build strong children than to repair broken men.'

Dr Kalam inaugurated the 150th anniversary of Bishop Cotton Boy's School's founding in Bangalore on 29 June 2014, and the 175th anniversary celebrations of the St Mary's Anglo-Indian Higher Secondary School, Chennai, on 21 August 2014. He had evolved a simple equation of 'Knowledge = Creativity + Righteousness + Courage', and children were grasping it easily and with enthusiasm. Dr Kalam's unaffected manner and sincerity were indeed reaching the hearts of children. By being truly there with them and unmindful of his eminence, he was expressing his love for them. And children appreciated him. Dr Kalam was giving them a taste of what a great life could be. He told me once,'I am sure some of what I tell children they carry home, and may be they are educating their parents.'

In September 2014, Dr Kalam attended the Round Table on Strategies for Drug-resistant and Abro-microbes at the Institute of Microbial Technology (IMTECH), Chandigarh. Dr Girish Sahni, who later became the director general of the Council of Scientific and Industrial Research (CSIR), hosted the meeting. Sitting on the round table were eminent scientists, medical experts, and veterinarians from various organizations, including Dr Kalam's friend Dr G. Padmanabhan. Union minister for science and technology Dr Jitendra Singh was also present.

The problems of virulent viruses and bacteria jumping from animals to human beings – and known bacteria such as tuberculosis becoming resistant to drugs – was discussed at length. Antibiotics have doubtless enabled physicians to treat many of the scourges of humanity, including tuberculosis, pneumonia, meningitis, tetanus, syphilis and gonorrhoea. It emerged at the round table that they have been used much too casually. Antibiotics have been used as a quick fix for simple illnesses like colds, the flu and bronchitis. These are indeed mostly viral infections, and would be managed by the natural immunity of the body in a few days at any rate, without antibiotics.

The use of antibiotics has proliferated to the extent that somewhere in the order of 50 per cent of all antibiotics prescribed for human use are unnecessary. Doctors have given scarce attention to bacteria's natural proclivity to mutate and become drug-resistant in direct proportion to their exposure to antibiotics. And the greed of the poultry and meat industry has compounded the problem. Antibiotics have been mixed with animal feed for more profits, and antibiotics have thus entered human bodies with milk, eggs and meat – by stealth, as it were.

Dr Kalam was not merely conversant with the latest wisdom on how to best deal with the 'superbugs' the medical industry has been unwittingly breeding. He was looking into the future:

> I really believe we've only touched the tip of the iceberg. Right now, we're only looking at a subset of the viruses known to cause disease. We need to figure out what the rest of the iceberg is. As there are wires, transistors, relays, valves, diodes, electronic switches in engineering, so in the biological systems there are genes, proteins, RNAs, promoters,

> inducers, repressors and so on. A good biotech laboratory will be able to engineer a protein that can act as an activator or repressor switch between multiple pathways as is done on a railway junction to direct trains between tracks. India should not miss the boat.[2]

A saint scientist was right in front of my eyes. He was speaking as if channelling a vision of the future from a higher power. Dr Kalam made another prophetic declaration on 22 February 2015 during the chancellor's address at the third convocation of the Indian Institute of Space Science and Technology (IIST), Thiruvananthapuram. He proclaimed, 'Space-based solar power is the key to a livable planet Earth.'

The space-based solar power concept was based on the premise that if large surfaces for collection of solar radiation are placed in an earth orbit, they would receive uninterrupted solar energy directly. There would be no losses of solar radiation due to obstructions such as atmospheric gasses, clouds, dust and other weather events, all of which reduce the efficiency of the collection on the earth's surface. Moreover, a satellite collecting solar energy would receive the sun's energy almost all the time, and not only during the daytime as on earth.

Power could be relatively quickly directed to areas that need it most, without expansive networks of transmission lines. Power would be directed based on demand at particular surface locations based on the base load or peak load power needs. This would not interfere with plant and animal life.

Space-based solar power would require the development of three technology systems: a system to collect solar energy in space; a means of wireless power transmission to earth by microwave or laser, and stations for receiving power on earth. For this titanic effort, all spacefaring nations would need to work together and pool their human and financial resources.

In mid-April 2015, Dr Kalam and I submitted the manuscript for the book *Transcendence: My Spiritual Experiences with Pramukh Swamiji*, and work on the typesetting and printing was quickly under way. Dr Kalam monitored the progress almost on a daily basis and as soon as the book came in his hands on 15 June 2015, he called

Sadhu Brahmaviharidas to organize his meeting with Pramukh Swamiji.

We travelled to Ahmedabad on 19 June 2015. That night, almost at 1.30 a.m. he called for the first copy of the book and began to sign it for Pramukh Swamiji. 'How should I address him?' he asked.

'You can write, "To my dear friend",' I said.

'What a funny guy you are; he is not my friend; he is my teacher, my ultimate spiritual teacher, indeed,' Dr Kalam said.

Sheridon suggested, 'Then write, "My spiritual teacher".'

Dr Kalam retorted, 'Why just "My" spiritual teacher? Who am I? He is the great spiritual teacher of everyone, the whole world. I am a nobody.'

Hence, he removed 'My' and personally chose to write on the book: 'Maha Pramukh Swamiji, Revered spiritual teacher. My respects.'

He firmly refused to use a helicopter to go to Sarangpur from Ahmedabad and decided to travel by road. When Sadhu Brahmaviharidas once again requested, keeping in mind the monsoon rains, rough roads, long journey and his age, Dr Kalam reasoned, 'This is a pilgrimage and a pilgrimage is best done on foot; if I had it my way, I would walk to Sarangpur … at least I have a car!'

On 20 June 2015, Dr Kalam presented the autographed copy to Pramukh Swamiji.

Dr Kalam said, 'This has been a very dear project for many years. The day Akshardham was inaugurated in Delhi, I made a promise to Pramukh Swamiji that I would write a book on his great spiritual life. Today I have fulfilled my promise.' While handing over the book to Pramukh Swamiji, Dr Kalam said, 'You are a great teacher, a great spiritual teacher. I've learnt a great lesson from you: how to remove "I" and "Me" (I-ness and My-ness).'

Dr Kalam read some passages from the book before Swamiji and asked him to bless all those who had helped him in making the book possible.

After the meeting, Dr Kalam was welcomed in an assembly of Swaminarayan sadhus and 3,000 youths. First, he described his fulfilling meeting with Pramukh Swami Maharaj and then I was surprised that he chose the occasion to narrate the story of his own life, something he had not done before.

'When I gave the book, Pramukh Swamiji smiled. That smile, what does it mean? Everybody smiles, but when Pramukh Swamiji smiles, it means something. I was in the company of Pramukh Swamiji for fifty minutes. At the end, I understood a great message, something I had read about and often said.'

> Where there is righteousness in the heart, there will be beauty in the character.
> Where there is beauty in the character, there will be harmony in the home.
> Where there is harmony in the home, there will be order in the nations.
> When there is order in the nations, there will peace in the world.[3]

'By meeting Pramukh Swamiji, I saw righteousness in his heart and peace in the world. That is what I saw today and felt bliss.'

He continued:

> I was born in the island of Rameswaram in the vicinity of great Shiva temple. I recall, as a ten-year-old boy, I was seeing three personalities meet from time to time in our home: Pakshi Lakshmana Shastrigal, the Vedic scholar and head priest of the famous Rameswaram temple; Rev. Father Bodal, who built the first church in Rameswaram Island, and my father, who was an imam in the mosque. These three personalities would sit in our courtyard, each with a glass of buttermilk or a cup of tea, and would discuss and find solutions to the various problems facing the community.
>
> I have been blessed with some great teachers, who shaped me at different stages of my life starting with my father, Jainulabdeen. My father taught me to view one's role in life as that of an instrument or vessel, through which one takes with one hand and gives with the other. 'There is only one light, you and I are holes on the lampshade,' he would say. My father lived a simple life but never lost sight of the underlying divinity. Throughout my life, I tried to emulate my father in this regard.
>
> As a young engineer, I worked with Dr Brahm Prakash. He taught me how tolerance of others' views and opinions is essential in building teams and accomplishing tasks that are beyond the individuals' capacities. He taught me that life is a precious gift, but it

comes with responsibility. With this gift, we are expected to use our talents to make the world a better place, to live an ethical and well-balanced life, and to prepare for the spiritual life, which is eternal.

As a project director, I worked with Professor Satish Dhawan, who taught me that a good leader takes the responsibility for the failures of his team, but gives the credit of his success to his team. When I asked him the secret of his brilliance, he told me: 'Academic brilliance is no different than the brilliance of a mirror. Once dust is removed, the mirror shines and the reflection is clear. We can remove impurities by living pure and ethical lives and serving humanity, and God will shine through us.'

Later, I met Jain Muni Acharya Mahapragya, who made me realize the affirmation of a divine life upon earth and an immortal sense in mortal existence. He taught me that our consciousness is the birthplace of our ethics. Together we wrote a book *Family and the Nation* and highlighted two steps to the process of listening to our conscience to become self-aware so that we can connect to our consciences, and to act on what our consciences say.

It was an important spiritual day of my life when I first met Pramukh Swamiji. After our first meeting and over the next fourteen years, we maintained a close spiritual connection. Last year, when I was here in Sarangpur on 11 March 2014 to see Pramukh Swamiji, I had a deep spiritual experience. Swamiji held my hand for ten minutes. No words were spoken. We looked into each other's eyes in a profound communication of consciousness. In these moments, a world vision based on Mother Earth was intuitively communicated to me by spiritual connectivity with a message 'Unity – Unity – and Unity of Minds'.

In a revelatory flash, I realized that the struggle between happiness and unhappiness that had so far been the story of human existence and the struggle between peace and war that had been the history of the human race must change. In the silence of his grip on my hand, I heard: 'Kalam, go and tell everyone that the power that would lead us to eternal victory amid these struggles is the power of good within us. Communicate to humankind the vision of a harmonious world. This vision would be greater than any other goal ever aspired to by humanity.'

> In conclusion friends, I would like to ask you, what would you like to do to make this planet Earth liveable? You have to evolve yourself and shape your life. You should write it on a page. That page may be a very important page in the book of human history. And you will be remembered for creating that one page in the history of the nation – whether that page is the page of invention, the page of innovation or the page of discovery or the page of creating societal change or a page of removing the poverty or the page of fighting injustice or planning and executing the mission of networking rivers and the page of evolving a clean environment with solar energy for generating a liveable planet Earth.

On our way back from Sarangpur, I asked, 'Sir, now that this project is successfully completed, what is the next writing work I should do?' Dr Kalam said, 'I always talked about elevating religion to spirituality but I never had a clear picture in my mind and that is why it has not happened. After studying the mission of Pramukh Swamiji and seeing its impact on his devotees, all blessed with peace and prosperity, I realized that the Ekantik dharma of Swaminarayan gurus is that model of elevating religion to spirituality that was eluding me. So, you should meet all Swaminarayan Sadgurus, sit at their feet and capture fully the essence of Ekantik dharma and present it to the youth in a language that they can understand.'

'Sir, will you be the co-author?'

He did not answer immediately and kept looking at me. It was a strange pause, and I felt uneasy. He said, 'I do not know when Pramukh Swamiji and I will meet again. We have established a divine bonding, which is forever. He has indeed transformed me. He is the ultimate stage of the spiritual ascent in my life. Pramukh Swamiji has put me in a God-synchronous orbit. No manoeuvres are required any more, as I am placed in my final position in eternity.'

He was recalling the words he had written in *Transcendence*, and their tone and finality scared me. 'No more books with me, buddy, be on your own now. Become a great author. Today everyone knows you as my co-author. A day will come when while reading your books, people will say, "Kalam was his co-author."'

This was my last meeting with Dr Kalam. We spoke, though, almost daily. On 26 July 2015, he called me in the afternoon. I was sitting with my family at my son Aseem's house in Bangalore. 'I am going with Srijan to Shillong tomorrow. I am speaking on the Liveable Planet Earth. Anything you want me to add?' he asked.

'Sir, you introduced this idea in Beijing in 2012, the world needs to act on it, nothing needs to be added for the speech.'

'Funny guy! Each one has to play a role. Things will happen.'

Srijan recalled the next day, 27 July 2015, as follows.

> Our day, 27 July, began at twelve noon, when we took our seats in the flight to Guwahati. Dr Kalam was 1'A' and I was 1'C'. He was wearing a dark colour 'Kalam suit' … Long, two and a half hours of flying in the monsoon weather. That was followed by another two-and-a-half hours of driving to IIM Shillong … after this, we went to the lecture hall. He did not want to be late for the lecture. 'Students should never be made to wait.'[4]

A thunderous applause from hundreds of students welcomed Dr Kalam. He stood before a packed auditorium.

'The topic I have selected is: "Creating a Liveable Planet Earth". Dear friends …

6.8

Aalam-e-Barzakh

> Ancient Egyptians believed that upon death they would be asked two questions and their answers would determine whether they could continue their journey in the afterlife. The first question was, "Did you bring joy?" The second was, "Did you find joy?"
>
> – Leo Buscaglia
> American author and speaker

Before a stunned gathering of 500 students and teachers, Dr Kalam staggered and fell backwards, crumpling to the floor of the stage. The hall was still with an uncertain silence. His final moments with us did not look dramatic; it seemed to many that he had fainted. One moment there was vintage Dr A.P.J. Abdul Kalam – resplendent in his tailored 'Kalam suit', charismatic and engaging, his quiet measured tones entrancing the audience – and the next moment he was no more. India's most beloved scientist, politician, sage and visionary – the nation's inspiring bachelor uncle – had departed. And he had gone in the midst of fulfilling his quest to enliven India's youth with a passion for learning, for striving. His work was now done. It was 6.30 p.m. on 27 July 2015.

There was nothing anyone could do. Numbed by denial, his aides summoned an ambulance, and he was taken to the Bethany Hospital. He was frantically rushed into the ICU, where a team of doctors made a last, futile bid to bring him back to life. The news flashed on television at around 8 p.m., and a shocked nation paused to assimilate, reflect – and grieve. Tributes of flowers and candles appeared below billboard-sized portraits; mourners took to the streets. The Indian people had lost a family member, and they would have to observe their own rites.

The Union cabinet met and declared a seven-day period of national mourning. Prime Minister Narendra Modi said,

> India mourns the loss of a great scientist, a wonderful President and above all, an inspiring individual. My mind is filled with so many memories, so many interactions with him. I always marvelled at his intellect; I learnt so much from him. He enjoyed being with people; people and youngsters adored him. He loved students and spent his final moments among them.[1]

The Indian Air Force flew the mortal remains of Dr Kalam, wrapped in the Indian tricolour, to New Delhi. Dr Kalam was not a man for pageantry, but the ardent patriot that he was, he would surely have appreciated the national flag as his shroud. Prime Minister Modi received the mortal remains at the airport. Dr Kalam's body was kept in state at his residence, where thousands of people came to pay their last respects: politicians across the spectrum, officials, friends and ordinary citizens. There were queues till past midnight. In the early hours of 28 July 2015, his grand-niece sat by the coffin and recited verses from the Holy Quran.

> *Kullu nafsin tha-iqatu almawti wa-innama tuwaffawna ojoorakum yawma alqiyamati faman zuhziha AAani alnnari waodkhila aljannata faqad faza wama alhayatu alddunya illa mataAAu alghuroori*

> Every human being is bound to taste death: but only on the Day of Resurrection will you be requited in full [for whatever you have done] – whereupon he that shall be drawn away from the fire and brought into paradise will indeed have gained a triumph: for the life of this world is nothing but an enjoyment of self-delusion.[2]

Someone bravely asked Dr B. Soma Raju if Dr Kalam was suffering from any unattended illness. Dr Soma Raju gave him a cold stare and said, 'Illness is not a precondition for death, which is as natural an event as birth. Everyone who is born has to die one day. Actually, Dr Kalam died a great death. Doing what he loved most, in full view of people, without suffering for a moment. Without inconveniencing anyone. His death was as open and pure as was his life.'

Dr Kalam was laid to rest on 30 July 2015 at 11.30 a.m. with military honours. Prime Minister Narendra Modi gave Dr Kalam the last salute. Several Union ministers, governors, chief ministers, the chiefs of the army, navy and the air force – and predictably, hundreds of thousands of common people – gathered at the Pei Karumbu Ground at Rameswaram Island to bid farewell to this great son of India. It was indeed a sea of humanity. The sight of people from all walks of life – cutting across caste, creed and religion – bidding Dr Kalam a tearful goodbye in a peaceful and restrained manner would be the envy of the mightiest of this world.

When I was crossing the Pamban bridge on my return from the burial, the vast expanse of sea stared at me. My eyes welled up at the reality of a boy born here on the island; I was leaving him behind, finally returned to its sands. The words of Sufi Saint Baba Farid echoed in my heart:

> Says Farid, you must fathom the ocean; it contains all you need and desire.
> Why soil your hands searching the little ponds?
> Says Farid, the Creator is in the creation and the creation in the Creator.
> Whom shall we blame when He is everywhere?

The story of the man Kalam ends here, but the story of the soul Kalam will continue. Different religions offer different descriptions of the afterlife. There are two broad belief systems. One is that after death, the soul reincarnates with a new body and sustains this through an endless cycle, until it attains the purity of merging with the Absolute. The other is that the soul lives in the grave and waits for the resurrection on the Day of Judgement by the Almighty. The evil are destroyed in hellfire and the good are admitted into paradise. The existence of the soul and the afterlife, in any event, is accepted in both belief systems.

The period from the moment of burial to the resurrection on the Day of Judgement is called Barzakh. The existential realm of spirits is called Aalam-e-Barzakh. This unseen realm is far larger than the seen world of ours, along with its vast lands and skies. Compared with the realm of Barzakh, this world is like a tiny plant in an infinitely expansive forest. When one dies, he becomes free unto this vast world of the spirits.

The soul body in Barzakh has the same attachment with this world as the body has with a mother's womb. We are created in the womb, complete and perfect – but once we are born out of it, we cannot go back there and live as we had been created. So it is the case with a person buried in the grave; there is no return to this world for repentance or correction. One must become reconciled with the consequences of one's deeds.

The physical body decomposes in due course and turns into dust, yet the soul body remains alive. The soul body is finer than air. For it, there are no barriers that our physical bodies face in this material world. The soul body can see anything and everything from everywhere. Of course, the soul body remains in this very world and does not go away and out of it, but now it has no limitations like time and space. Just as the sun that remains in the sky covers the whole earth with its rays, the soul body remains in the grave, but it can be present anywhere.

What can millions of Dr Kalam's admirers, followers and friends do to reflect the light of his soul body into their inner world and upon the people around them? In raising this question, I am also questioning my own self. The answer lies in the understanding of Dr Kalam's legacy. What is the sum and substance of the life of A.P.J. Abdul Kalam? Reflecting on his life, from his ultimate call for a more liveable planet Earth and enlightened citizenry back to his earliest years, we can perceive the unmistakeable workings of three modes of living derived from three divine foundations.

The three divine foundations of Dr Kalam's life were imagination, piousness and faith in God. From these emerged righteousness, integrity and courage. These three modes of living or qualities drove his conviction for making India a developed country by 2020. They later ignited his desire for evolving a global movement to make our planet more liveable, using technologies to mitigate the effects of climate change, grow more food and enjoy a clean environment. Before concluding this book, some mention of the manner in which these three foundations and three modes of living were manifest in Dr Kalam is appropriate.

Imagination, piousness and faith in God were inculcated in Dr Kalam early in his life by his father. His father taught him that imagination is the facility that differentiates human beings from other animals in the world. Imagination is indeed a faculty of the soul. It is the imperative duty of parents and early teachers to ensure that children use their imaginations. Dr Kalam would devote much time in asking children what they want to become in their later lives. He would say that if a child does not know the answer to this question, it is a serious issue.

Dr Kalam's father told him that according to Imam Nawawi's Hadith Qudsi, Allah declared, 'Neither My Earth nor My Heavens can contain Me, but the heart of a Believing Servant can.'[3] Why did Allah say this? Allah said this because He granted human beings the power of imagination. The reality of the true nature of man's heavenly origins is his imagination, which has no limits. That an unlimited capacity to imagine is bestowed by Allah is indeed an honour for us. Through imagination, man is gifted with an understanding that is profound – far above the rest of creation.

For this reason, Dr Kalam conveyed the importance of imagination to millions of children in his countless visits to schools. He developed an algorithm of applying imagination in real life. He said, 'Dream, dream, dream; dreams lead to thoughts; thoughts lead to action; action brings change.' The dream Dr Kalam was referring to must not be confounded with fantasy. His idea of dreaming was an exercise of thought firmly grounded by nature. Dr Kalam's call to children about dreaming was meant to connote that which is normally inaccessible to sense perception and cannot be perceived without imagination.

The second divine foundation for Dr Kalam was piousness. He asked me while we were taking tea together on the lawns of Rashtrapati Bhavan, 'Tell me, buddy, would you pour the tea into a dirty cup?'

I said, 'How could anyone do that? The cup has to be cleaned first, and only then tea can be poured into it. Even if the tea is poured in an unclean cup, it can't be consumed. It must be thrown away.'

Dr Kalam then said, 'Fantastic. Similarly, Allah does not pour heavenly grants of pure illuminated knowledge into the hearts of dirty ones; only those with pure and clean hearts will receive heavenly grants. Allah looks into the hearts of man and He chooses who amongst them will be recipients of divine honour and grants.'

Dr Kalam wondered, 'It is such a simple fact – how could anyone ignore it? I learned very early in life that those who seek knowledge from the divine must know that it is only poured into pure hearts.'

The third divine foundation in Dr Kalam's life was faith in God. Allah had given man the highest station and rank of all of creation and the capacity to bear witness to His oneness in all creatures. But despite his high rank and station, man always remained weak. Dr Kalam shared with me an insight from his childhood. Dr Kalam's father once told him, 'See yourself always as a zero, and Allah as the one. Now if the zero is placed on the left of the one, it remains as one. This is the original position of man – a zero. But if Allah wants to bestow upon a person any grant, He moves this zero to the right of the one, and you become ten; you now have value!'

Dr Kalam had never forgotten this. He understood that it is by God's grace that we are given everything; and conversely, without God, we are nothing. His faith in God was immovable. Every day when he awoke, he remembered it was God that made him capable of what he was doing, seeing, understanding and knowing. Throughout his life, without ever straying from this morning reflection, Dr Kalam obeyed, respected, submitted to and worshipped Allah.

In 2002, I visited China in connection with the translation of *Wings of Fire* into Mandarin. For President Kalam, the publishers sent back with me a selection of books from the ancient Chinese philosopher Confucius. The principles of 'Li' and 'Yi', explained by Confucius in his book *Analects,* captivated him.

'Li' is human-heartedness, empathy, or humaneness, and 'Yi' is righteousness. Confucius defined 'Li' as the ability to empathize with the discomfort and pain of others around you. On the other hand, righteousness is the ability to behave in accordance with the demands of a given social situation. In the interest of collective and societal well-being, the righteous person is the one who is cognizant of 'Yi' – what ought to be done. But 'Yi' is thus placed frequently in opposition to 'Li', meaning the benefit of those who are family members, relatives and other known people. Confucius stated that the righteous and thus superior person understands 'Yi', but the petty-minded only understand 'Li'. Confucius taught that humans are fundamentally good, but somewhat prone to stray. The cultivation of virtue thus demands self-discipline and a strong emphasis on education.

Dr Kalam derived his idea of integrity from the Bible, and was particularly influenced by its teachings when he was studying at Schwartz. Corruption has become a major issue in India; it is seen quite regularly in the lives of public officials, business people and even in the lives of ordinary people. Dr Kalam saw corruption as a problem of people behaving differently in their homes to the way they behave in public. He took integrity in the literal sense of the word 'integer' and understood it as the wholeness of a person. Just as a whole number, a person of integrity must live not divided, not a different person in different circumstances. A person of integrity must be the same person in private that he is in public. A young Kalam saw integrity appearing so regularly in the Bible. God instructed Solomon to walk with 'integrity of heart and uprightness' as his father did.[4] David said, 'I know, my God, that you test the heart and are pleased with integrity.'[5] And 'David shepherded them with integrity of heart, with skilful hands.'[6]

Dr Kalam developed a conviction in his life that one who walks in integrity walks securely. He believed that wrong things, however cleverly done, would always be found out. A person of integrity would not only have a good reputation, but also sleep in peace and without fear. 'Integrity provides a safe path through life. Falsehood and the treacherous ways are like a self-destruct system in a missile. God will use them if He finds that one is straying from the designated trajectory,' Dr Kalam told me.

Dr Kalam publically differed with the anti-corruption movement launched by Anna Hazare. While he understood Anna Hazare's intent, he felt that no law would ever halt corruption. Corruption starts in families. It is indeed the manifestation of a character flaw. There has been an increasing laxity of moral laws that have previously served Indian society well. Of late, people have been fashioning their own moral codes. There is no moral consensus in this country as there was in earlier years, when our institutions commanded public respect. Dr Kalam wrote *Family and Nation*[7] with Acharya Mahapragya, and in its pages presented his thoughts on this in no uncertain terms.

Dr Kalam was very fond of the character of Nachiketa, as told in the *Katha Upanishad*. During his visit to Swaminarayn Akshardham in Gandhinagar, he was enchanted by the Sat-Chit-Anand Water Show which reveals India's ancient secret through the story of Nachiketa and said, 'Thousands of Nachiketas will be created in India due to this water show.' He saw in Nachiketa the embodiment of courage and confidence. He questioned Yama, the mighty god of Death and asked what comes after death. Dr Kalam said that Yama's answer to Nachiketa indeed constitutes India's eternal truth, one which it alone holds today in the world.'Only the body dies, O Nachiketa, the soul is immortal and is reborn life after life, till one reaches perfection.'

This idea of perfection, Dr Kalam discovered in his ultimate spiritual teacher Pramukh Swamiji, in whom, he often said, he experienced all the great values he had read, dreamt and seen in the great lives of Socrates, Lincoln, Abdul Qadir, Galileo, Einstein, Thiruvalluvar, Gandhi. This he clearly and concisely expressed in his last book *Transcendence* as his final word to the world.

So, without the foundation of imagination, piousness and faith in God, a life lived is indeed a life wasted. It is from these three divine foundations that one later derives the three modes of living of righteousness, integrity and courage. These cannot be garnered by a mere intellectual understanding. Righteousness, integrity and courage emanate only from the divine endowments of imagination, personal discipline of piousness, and an unwavering faith in God in all situations and circumstances. Just as these three principles shaped

Dr Kalam's life and drove his quests for developing India and making our planet more liveable, they would bring enduring happiness and prosperity to our own lives. This is the legacy of Dr Kalam.

Once I asked Dr Kalam how he looked back at his life. He said, 'As a young person I always obeyed the orders I received from my conscience. My heart was always attached to my parents, to my sister Zohara and my brother Maracayer and other people in the family, to my teachers and those who helped me when I needed them. I considered all people who crossed my path, for good or bad, with equal respect, for it was God's will that they were nice or harsh to me. I was afraid of any intoxication and temptations. I gave away most of my earnings to charity and never allowed it to be known to anyone. I was equitable when leadership positions were given to me. As a policy, I loved to be alone while remembering Allah in situations when tears must wash my soul of anguish and torment.'

I have been blessed to live a full thirty three years of my life in the shadow of the giant that Dr Kalam indeed was. Through various stages of our association, first as his subordinate scientist at the Defence Research and Development Laboratory, then as a foot soldier in his crusade for developing civilian spin-offs of defence technologies in health care, then as his biographer, then as a member of his presidential team – and finally a seeker following his spiritual path – I found in Dr Kalam a true rishi of modern India. I saw Rishi Agastya in his birth in Rameswaram, Rishi Vishwamitra in his leadership of the country's missile development and Rishi Kapila in his grasp of eternal spiritual truths.

The sage scientist Kalam lived the life of a pious Muslim, respectful of all other religions and deeply spiritual in his world view. He did not wear his religion on his coat lapel, but lived its highest ideals throughout his life. While he was most guarded defending his core religious values, he was also open to the good coming from other religions. He could see the oneness of God in its truest sense, and saw service to mankind as the most fundamental religious practice. He understood peace as the ultimate purpose and enterprise of all human endeavours.

In a sense, he is much more powerful and nearer than he had ever been to us. He envisioned a developed India and a more liveable earth as the twenty-first century progresses, and predicted that this would happen. But he could only set a vision, urge us on, inspire us and provide direction. We must 'keep the ball rolling', as he would often remind me.

Love is never extinguished by death. The reverence for Dr Kalam would surely continue, and his adulation by the Indian people would find a different expression now. Just as there is an aura around a light, there is an unseen aura of divinity surrounding the graves of pious people, such as saints. Doubtless, people will thus be drawn to the grave of Dr A.P.J. Abdul Kalam from afar, to be touched by the goodness of his spirit. Greater good, however, would come by living with his ideals and pursuing his visions. Our veneration is perhaps best done in emulation rather than obeisance.

In A.P.J. Abdul Kalam, we have known a true paragon of enlightened humanity – a rare soul who could accept life's realities calmly yet never cease pursuing the greatness of the spirit beyond. As much a modern sage as an eminent scientist and leader, Dr Kalam tells us that we must live by imagination to strive beyond knowing, to aspire beyond understanding. We should remember his profound wisdom and learning, and that this would never extinguish his childlike wonder of the universe and joy in the happiness of others. In following his example and heeding his words, we may come to live with principle as he lived, act with faith as he acted and pursue our dreams as he exhorted us.

Notes

PART ONE: SIMULATION

1.1 The Paradise of Hope

1. Quran 42:30 Ash Shura; Translation Yusuf Ali.
2. A.P.J. Abdul Kalam with Arun Tiwari, *Wings of Fire*, University Press, 1999.

1.2 The Beginning

1. A.P.J. Abdul Kalam with Arun Tiwari, *Wings of Fire*, University Press, 1999.
2. Napoleon Hill, *The Law of Success*, Embassy Books, 2010.
3. A.P.J. Abdul Kalam and Arun Tiwari, *You Are Born to Blossom*, Ocean Books, 2005.

1.3 Disillusioned Learner

1. A.P.J. Abdul Kalam with Arun Tiwari, *Wings of Fire*, University Press, 1999.
2. http://www.abdulkalam.com/kalam/jsp/display_searchcontent.jsp
3. http://www.abdulkalam.com/kalam/jsp/display_searchcontent.jsp
4. K.V.A. Pandalai @http://www.newindiadigest.com/kalam.htm

1.4 Bootstrapping

1. A.P.J. Abdul Kalam with Arun Tiwari, *Wings of Fire*, University Press, 1999.
2. A.P.J. Abdul Kalam, Special Address at MIT Alumni Association, Chennai, 11August 2012.
3. A.P.J. Abdul Kalam with Arun Tiwari, *Wings of Fire*.

1.5 Cog in the Wheel

1. A.P.J. Abdul Kalam with Arun Tiwari, *Wings of Fire*, University Press, 1999.
2. Ibid.

1.6 Noah's Ark

1. A.P.J. Abdul Kalam with Arun Tiwari, *Wings of Fire*,, University Press, 1999, p. 27.
2. Jawaharlal Nehru, Rajya Sabha, 1963 @ http://www.rediff.com/news/2002/dec/18chin.htm
3. https://history.state.gov/milestones/1961-1968/cuban-missile-crisis
4. A.P.J. Abdul Kalam with Arun Tiwari, *Wings of Fire*.
5. Ibid., p. 29.

1.7 No Free Lunch

1. A.P.J. Abdul Kalam with Arun Tiwari, *Wings of Fire*, University Press, 1999, p. 31.
2. A.P.J. Abdul Kalam,Address at the youth meet at Swaminarayan Sanstha (BAPS), Sarangpur, Gujarat, 20 June 2015.
3. R. Aravamudan @http://www.rediff.com/news/2002/jul/18spec.htm
4. A.P.J. Abdul Kalam with Arun Tiwari, *Wings of Fire*, p. 47.
5. Ibid., p. 178.

1.8 Unreasonable Men

1. A.P.J. Abdul Kalam with Arun Tiwari, *Wings of Fire*, University Press, 1999, p. 49.
2. Ibid., p. 54.

PART TWO: CREATION

2.1 Indra's Net

1. President Kalam's address at the Multimedia Teleconference to the Centre of Aerospace Strategic Studies (CESA) and the National Centre for Space Studies (CNES), France, on 'Space – a conceptual challenge to the Defence'; http://pib.nic.in/newsite/erelcontent.aspx?relid=28466
2. A.P.J. Abdul Kalam with Arun Tiwari, *Wings of Fire*, University Press, 1999, p. 64.
3. B. Indira Devi, owner of Indira Lodge @ http://indianexpress.com/

article/india/india-others/apj-abdul-kalam-led-a-reclusive-life-in-thiruvananthapuram-tenant/
4. A.P.J. Abdul Kalam with Arun Tiwari, *Wings of Fire*, University Press, 1999, p. 86.

2.2 Vasudhaiva Kutumbakam

1. A.P.J. Abdul Kalam with Arun Tiwari, *Wings of Fire*, University Press, 1999, p. 88.
2. A.P.J. Abdul Kalam and Arun Tiwari, *Squaring the Circle*, University Press, 2013, p. 196.
3. A.P.J. Abdul Kalam with Arun Tiwari, *Wings of Fire*, University Press, 1999, p. 93.
4. Ibid., p. 104.

2.3 Smiling Buddha

1. A.P.J. Abdul Kalam with Arun Tiwari, *Wings of Fire*, University Press, 1999, p. 113.
2. Ibid., p. 116.
3. Ibid., p. 122.

2.4 Strength Respects Strength

1. A.P.J. Abdul Kalam with Arun Tiwari, *Wings of Fire*, University Press, 1999, p. 124.
2. http://www.vijaybhatkar.org/index.php?option=com_content&view=article&id=117&Itemid=59

2.5 Crystal Cathedral

1. A.P.J. Abdul Kalam with Arun Tiwari, *Wings of Fire*, University Press, 1999, p. 125.
2. Ibid., p. 134.
3. Ibid., p. 138.

2.6 Chariot of Fire

1. A.P.J. Abdul Kalam with Arun Tiwari, *Wings of Fire*, University Press, 1999, p. 150.
2. Ibid., p. 152.
3. A.P.J. Abdul Kalam, *Ignited Minds*, Penguin Books, 2002.
4. A.P.J. Abdul Kalam with Arun Tiwari, *Wings of Fire*, p. 162.

5. Amartya Sen, *The Argumentative India,* 1St ed., Penguin, London, 2006.
6. A.P.J. Abdul Kalam with Arun Tiwari, *Wings of Fire,* p. 164.

2.7 Prophet of Self-reliance

1. The Care Hospitals organization, with hospitals across twelve cities of India, is valued at 300 million dollars at the time of writing of this book in 2015.
2. Alexis Careel, *Man the Unknown,* Wilco Publishing House, 2010.
3. The Department of Health and Family Welfare has released a draft amendment which proposes complete overhaul of the existing law through the Drugs and Cosmetics (Amendment) Bill, 2015.
4. It took twenty-three years to happen when Rs 100 crore was allocated in 2015–16 Union budget.

2.8 The Razor's Edge

1. A. Sivathanu Pillai, *The Path Unexplored,* Pentagon Press, 2014.
2. ADA is the nodal agency for the design and development of Light Combat Aircraft (LCA) partnered by HAL, DRDO and CSIR Laboratories, public and private sector industries and academic institutions.
3. A.P.J. Abdul Kalam with Y.S. Rajan, *India 2020: A Vision for the New Millennium,* Penguin India, New Delhi, 1997.

PART THREE: REALIZATION

3.1 Major General Prithviraj

1. A.P.J. Abdul Kalam and Arun Tiwari, *Squaring the Circle,* University Press, 2013, p. 208.
2. At the time of writing of this book (2015), *Wings of Fire* has sold 1.5 million copies and been translated into fourteen Indian and six world languages, namely, Russian, French, Chinese, Korean, Thai and Arabic.
3. A.P.J. Abdul Kalam and Arun Tiwari, *Squaring the Circle,* p. 225.

3.2 Aarif

1. A.P.J. Abdul Kalam, Address during the Silver Jubilee Celebrations of TIFAC, New Delhi, 10 February 2012.
2. A.P.J. Abdul Kalam, *Ignited Minds,* Penguin Books, 2002, p. 124.

3. A.P.J. Abdul Kalam, *Ignited Minds*, p. 72.
4. Ibid., p. 26.
5. *The Hindu*, 22 August 2006.
6. A.P.J. Abdul Kalam, *Ignited Minds*, Penguin Books, 2002, p. 28.
7. Ibid., p. 30.

3.3 Who Is Our Enemy?

1. Kota Harinarayana@ http://www.thehindubusinessline.com/2001/01/13/stories/041367ju.htm
2. P.V. Inderesan @www.thehindu.com/todays-paper/tp-national/tp-andhrapradesh/pura-is-the-answer-to-rural-ills-expert/article1560466.ece
3. A.P.J. Abdul Kalam, *Turning Points*, HarperCollins India, 2012.
4. Reminiscences of Samaresh Singh@ http://www.dailyo.in/politics/rip-apj-abdul-kalam-missile-man-nasa-isro-president-bokaro/story/1/5276.html
5. Roddam Narasimha @ http://www.thequint.com/opinion/2015/07/29/kalam-broke-up-nations-development-to-a-series-of-doable-projects
6. Krisnha Prasad@http://mcomments.outlookindia.com/story.aspx?sid=4&aid=216160
7. A.P.J. Abdul Kalam and Arun Tiwari, *Squaring the Circle*, University Press, 2013.
8. Thomas Moore, *Care of the Soul*, HarperCollins, 1992.

3.4 Kingdom of God

1. Dr Srinivas Bhogle @ https://bademian.wordpress.com/2015/08/15/kalam-as-i-saw-him/
2. Prof. A. Kalanidhi @ http://www.rediff.com/news/2002/jul/03spec1.htm
3. T. Nagarajan @ http://www.newindianexpress.com/cities/chennai/Abdul-Kalams-Room-at-Anna-University-Turns-Into-a-Memorial/2015/08/01/article2951415.ece
4. A.P.J. Abdul Kalam, *Ignited Minds*, Penguin Books, 2002, p. 80.
5. Ibid., p. 81.
6. Bhavdeep Kang@http://mcomments.outlookindia.com/story.aspx?sid =4&aid=216161
7. Prabhu Chawla with Rajeev Deshpande @ http://indiatoday.intoday.

in/story/surprise-choice-missile-man-apj-abdul-kalam-set-to-become-12th-president-of-india/1/219480.html
8. B.R. Srikanth @http://mcomments.outlookindia.com/story.aspx?sid=4&aid=216158
9. Josy Joseph @http://www.rediff.com/news/2002/jun/19josy.htm
10. Saeed Naqvi, *The Indian Express*, 21 June 2002.
11. http://www.tribuneindia.com/2002/20020719/main1.htm
12. A.P.J.M. Maracayer @ http://www.rediff.com/news/2002/jul/24spec1.htm

3.5 Angel and Marshal

1. http://www.thehindu.com/2002/08/10/stories/2002081004560100.htm
2. A.P.J. Abdul Kalam, *Turning Points*, HarperCollins, 2012.
3. A.P.J. Abdul Kalam with Arun Tiwari, *Transcendence*, HarperCollins, 2015, p. 11.
4. A.P.J. Abdul Kalam and Arun Tiwari, *Guiding Souls*, Ocean Books, 2005.
5. http://timesofindia.indiatimes.com/india/Bhopal-gas-victims-plea-to-Kalam/articleshow/20901951.cms
6. http://www.thehindu.com/2002/09/06/stories/2002090604631200.htm
7. A.P.J. Abdul Kalam with Arun Tiwari, *Transcendence*, HarperCollins, 2015, p. 15.

3.6 Thinking Is Growth

1. SekharDatta@http://www.telegraphindia.com/1150729/jsp/northeast/story_34173.jsp#.VdHNhsaqqko
2. http://www.telegraphindia.com/1100728/jsp/northeast/story_12736602.jsp
3. A.P.J. Abdul Kalam @ http://www.abdulkalam.nic.in/abdulkalam/sllatest1.jsp?id=12
4. Dr S.C. Jamir @ http://www.dailypioneer.com/state-editions/bhubaneswar/take-me-to-the-most-backward-village-in-your-state.html
5. A.P.J. Abdul Kalam @ http://www.abdulkalam.nic.in/abdulkalam/sllatest1.jsp?id=16

6. A.P.J. Abdul Kalam @ http://www.abdulkalam.nic.in/abdulkalam/sllatest1.jsp?id=20
7. Ibid.

3.7 Birth of a Humanist

1. A.P.J. Abdul Kalam @ http://www.abdulkalam.nic.in/abdulkalam/sllatest1.jsp?id=25
2. Dr Kalam inspired four young engineers – Vikram Mordani, Naresh Alreja, S.G. Prasad and Aseem Tiwari – to digitize the obsolete Cath. Labs. The project was successfully completed. A Cath Lab stands for catheterization laboratory, a diagnostic imaging equipment used to visualize the arteries and chambers of the heart.
3. A.P.J. Abdul Kalam @ http://www.abdulkalam.nic.in/abdulkalam/sllatest1.jsp?id=27
4. http://www.icrisat.org/what-we-do/satrends/dec2002.htm
5. A.P.J. Abdul Kalam @http://www.abdulkalam.nic.in/abdulkalam/sllatest1.jsp?id=36
6. A.P.J. Abdul Kalam @ http://www.abdulkalam.nic.in/abdulkalam/sllatest1.jsp?id=30
7. A.P.J. Abdul Kalam @ http://www.abdulkalam.nic.in/abdulkalam/sllatest1.jsp?id=33
8. A.P.J. Abdul Kalam @http://www.abdulkalam.nic.in/abdulkalam/sllatest1.jsp?id=35

3.8 Gem in the Lotus

1. A.P.J. Abdul Kalam @http://www.abdulkalam.nic.in/abdulkalam/sllatest1.jsp?id=48
2. A.P.J. Abdul Kalam @ http://www.abdulkalam.nic.in/abdulkalam/sllatest1.jsp?id=50
3. The resolution GA/RES/53/22, proposed by the Islamic Republic of Iran and supported by a large number of countries, invites'Governments, the United Nations system, including the United Nations Educational, Scientific and Cultural Organization.
4. A.P.J. Abdul Kalam @ http://www.abdulkalam.com/kalam/jsp/display_hints.jsp?menuid=38&menuname=Myper cent20Presidentialper cent20Address&starts=0&ends=0
5. http://http://www.telegraphindia.com/1030126/asp/nation/story_1609746.asp

6. https://www.wilsoncenter.org/sites/default/files/asia_rpt_120rev_0.pdf

PART FOUR: EXPANSION

4.1 Tamaso Ma Jyotirgamaya

1. A.P.J. Abdul Kalam with Arun Tiwari, *Wings of Fire*, University Press, 1999, p. 175.
2. http://www.thehindu.com/2003/02/22/stories/2003022205980400.htm

4.2 Anjuman

1. A.P.J. Abdul Kalam @ http://www.abdulkalam.nic.in/abdulkalam/sllatest1.jsp?id=85
2. A.P.J. Abdul Kalam @ http://www.abdulkalam.nic.in/abdulkalam/sllatest1.jsp?id=91
3. Shaikh Muhammad Ibn Yahya Al-Tadifi and Shaikh Muhammad ibn Yahya At-Tadifi, translated by Muhtar Holland, *'Necklaces of Gems (Qada'id Al-jawahir): A Biography of Shaikh 'Abd Al-Qadir Al-Jilani,'* Al-Baz Publishing, 1995.
4. A.P.J. Abdul Kalam @http://www.abdulkalam.nic.in/abdulkalam/sllatest1.jsp?id=96
5. timesofindia.indiatimes.com/india/Kalams-moment-of-disappointment-in-Gaya/articleshow/48252273.cms
6. http://www.thehindu.com/2003/08/20/stories/2003082007650400.htm

4.3 Samagam

1. A.P.J. Abdul Kalam with Arun Tiwari, *You Are Born to Blossom*, Ocean Books, 2005.

4.4 The World Machine

1. http://www.khaleejtimes.com/article/20031021/ARTICLE/310219957/1002
2. http://www.larouchepub.com/eiw/public/2003/eirv30n49-20031219/eirv30n49-20031219_012-india_sudan_strategic_energy_coo.pdf

3. A.P.J. Abdul Kalam @ http://www.abdulkalam.nic.in/abdulkalam/sllatest1.jsp?id=369
4. A.P.J. Abdul Kalam @ http://www.abdulkalam.nic.in/abdulkalam/sllatest1.jsp?id=371
5. Islamic name of Jeremiah, also called 'the weeping prophet'. He was one of the major prophets of the Hebrew Bible.
6. A.P.J. Abdul Kalam @ http://www.abdulkalam.nic.in/abdulkalam/sllatest1.jsp?id=191
7. A.P.J. Abdul Kalam @http://www.abdulkalam.nic.in/abdulkalam/sllatest1.jsp?id=203

4.5 The Deserted Village

1. Zia Haq @ http://www.hindustantimes.com/india-news/real-india-lives-in-villages/article1-278701.aspx
2. A.P.J. Abdul Kalam @ http://www.abdulkalam.nic.in/abdulkalam/sllatest1.jsp?id=234
3. Ibid.
4. A.P.J.Abdul Kalam @ http://www.abdulkalam.nic.in/abdulkalam/sllatest1.jsp?id=233
5. A.P.J. Abdul Kalam with Arun Tiwari, *Transcendence*, HarperCollins, Noida, India, 2015, p. 19.
6. Ibid.
7. A.P.J. Abdul Kalam @http://www.abdulkalam.nic.in/abdulkalam/sllatest1.jsp?id=222
8. At the time of writing this book in August 2015 the link is under construction.
9. A.P.J. Abdul Kalam @ http://www.abdulkalam.nic.in/abdulkalam/sllatest1.jsp?id=277
10. A.P.J. Abdul Kalam and Arun Tiwari, *Squaring the Circle*, University Press, 2013, p. 244.

4.6 Nation Builders

1. A.P.J. Abdul Kalam @ http://www.abdulkalam.nic.in/abdulkalam/sllatest1.jsp?id=295
2. A.P.J. Abdul Kalam @ http://www.abdulkalam.nic.in/abdulkalam/sllatest1.jsp?id=298
3. A.P.J. Abdul Kalam @ http://www.abdulkalam.nic.in/abdulkalam/sllatest1.jsp?id=300

4.7 We the People

1. A.P.J. Abdul Kalam @ http://www.abdulkalam.nic.in/abdulkalam/sllatest1.jsp?id=297
2. http://www.rediff.com/election/2004/may/10prez.htm
3. http://m.rediff.com/election/2004/may/11kalam.htm
4. Guruprasad @ http://guruprasad.net/posts/the-untold-story-of-how-bjp-lost-2004-elections/
5. A.P.J. Abdul Kalam @ http://www.abdulkalam.nic.in/abdulkalam/sllatest1.jsp?id=308
6. A.P.J. Abdul Kalam, *Turning Points*, HarperCollins India, Noida, India, 2012, p. 135.
7. http://www.thehindu.com/2004/07/24/stories/2004072403710500.htm
8. A.P.J. Abdul Kalam @ http://www.abdulkalam.nic.in/abdulkalam/sllatest1.jsp?id=331
9. A.P.J. Abdul Kalam @ http://www.abdulkalam.nic.in/abdulkalam/sllatest1.jsp?id=333
10. A.P.J. Abdul Kalam and Arun Tiwari, *Squaring the Circle*, University Press, 2013, pp. 43–44.

4.8 Creative Leaders

1. A.P.J. Abdul Kalam @ http://www.abdulkalam.nic.in/abdulkalam/sllatest1.jsp?id=395
2. A.P.J. Abdul Kalam @ http://www.abdulkalam.nic.in/abdulkalam/sllatest1.jsp?id=424
3. A.P.J. Abdul Kalam @ http://www.abdulkalam.nic.in/abdulkalam/sllatest1.jsp?id=443
4. A.P.J. Abdul Kalam and Arun Tiwari, *Squaring the Circle*, University Press, 2013, p. 134–135.
5. A.P.J. Abdul Kalam @ http://www.abdulkalam.nic.in/abdulkalam/sllatest1.jsp?id=462
6. http://www.rediff.com/news/2005/jan/25prez.htm
7. A.P.J. Abdul Kalam @ http://www.abdulkalam.nic.in/abdulkalam/sllatest1.jsp?id=480
8. A.P.J. Abdul Kalam @ http://www.abdulkalam.nic.in/abdulkalam/sllatest1.jsp?id=478
9. A.P.J. Abdul Kalam @ http://www.abdulkalam.nic.in/abdulkalam/sllatest1.jsp?id=488

10. A.P.J. Abdul Kalam @ http://www.abdulkalam.nic.in/abdulkalam/sllatest1.jsp?id=495
11. Ibid.

PART FIVE: DISPERSION

5.1 Determination Is Power

1. P.M. Nair, *The Kalam Effect*, HarperCollins, 2008, pp. 72–73.
2. A.P.J. Abdul Kalam and Arun Tiwari, *Squaring the Circle*, University Press, 2013, p. 197.
3. A.P.J. Abdul Kalam, *Turning Points*, HarperCollins India, 2012, p. x.
4. A.P.J. Abdul Kalam and Arun Tiwari, *Squaring the Circle*, p. 4.
5. Ibid., p. 5.

5.2 Lend Me Your Ears

1. A.P.J. Abdul Kalam @ http://www.abdulkalam.nic.in/abdulkalam/sllatest1.jsp?id=530
2. A.P.J. Abdul Kalam @ http://www.abdulkalam.nic.in/abdulkalam/sllatest1.jsp?id=540
3. A.P.J. Abdul Kalam @ http://www.abdulkalam.nic.in/abdulkalam/sllatest1.jsp?id=595
4. The Bible, Psalm 23: 1–4.

5.3 Instruments of God

1. A.P.J. Abdul Kalam with Arun Tiwari, *Transcendence*, HarperCollins, Noida, India, 2015, p. 29.
2. A.P.J. Abdul Kalam @ http://www.abdulkalam.nic.in/abdulkalam/sllatest1.jsp?id=652
3. A.P.J. Abdul Kalam @ http://www.abdulkalam.nic.in/abdulkalam/sllatest1.jsp?id=685

5.4 A Man's Compass

1. http://www.thehindu.com/todays-paper/supreme-court-indicts-governor-buta-singh/article3244593.ece
2. http://www.outlookindia.com/article/one-billion-people-one-vision/229954
3. http://www3.ntu.edu.sg/corpcomms2/Documents/2006/Feb/

TODAY-03.02.06-8 per cent20President per cent20Kalam per cent20Visit.pdf
4. http://enewsletter.ntu.edu.sg/ClassACTStaging/Sep08/campusnews/3.asp
5. Kalam salaams Filipino nursing @ http://archive.deccanherald.com/Deccanherald/feb42006/national18620200623.asp
6. http://specials.rediff.com/news/2006/feb/07sld6.htm
7. http://www.rediff.com/news/2006/feb/09kalam.htm
8. A.P.J. Abdul Kalam @ http://www.abdulkalam.nic.in/abdulkalam/sllatest1.jsp?id=743

5.5 I Will Fly

1. A.P.J. Abdul Kalam with Arun Tiwari, *Transcendence*, HarperCollins, Noida, India, 2015, p. 35.
2. http://www.rediff.com/news/special/kalam-on-wings-of-fire/20150728.htm
3. P.M. Nair, *The Kalam Effect*, HarperCollins, Noida, India, 2008, p. 113.
4. A.P.J. Abdul Kalam with Arun Tiwari, *Transcendence*, p. 36.
5. Ibid., p. 37.
6. A.P.J. Abdul Kalam @ http://www.abdulkalam.nic.in/abdulkalam/sllatest1.jsp?id=879

5.6 What Can I Give?

1. http://www.dnaindia.com/india/report-full-text-republic-day-speech-of-dr-apj-abdul-kalam-1956602
2. http://www.rediff.com/news/2007/jan/31look1.htm
3. A.P.J.Abdul Kalam@http://www.abdulkalam.nic.in/abdulkalam/sllatest1.jsp?id=958
4. A.P.J.Abdul Kalam@http://www.abdulkalam.nic.in/abdulkalam/sllatest1.jsp?id=959
5. A.P.J. Abdul Kalam @http://www.abdulkalam.nic.in/abdulkalam/sllatest1.jsp?id=975
6. The Military Cross (MC) is a military decoration awarded to officers of the British armed forces in recognition of 'an act or acts of exemplary gallantry during active operations against the enemy'.
7. A.P.J. Abdul Kalam @ http://www.abdulkalam.nic.in/abdulkalam/sllatest1.jsp?id=980

8. The Sangam period is the period in the history of ancient southern India spanning from the third century BC to the fourth century AD.
9. http://www.pib.nic.in/newsite/erelease.aspx?relid=27125
10. http://www.thehindu.com/todays-paper/kalams-address-extraordinary/article1833704.ece

5.7 Awakening

1. Translation by Rudyard Kipling.
2. Hellenic is a synonym for Greek.
3. A.P.J. Abdul Kalam, Arun Tiwari, *Squaring the Circle*, University Press, 2013, p. vi.
4. A.P.J. Abdul Kalam @ http://www.abdulkalam.nic.in/abdulkalam/sllatest1.jsp?id=1037
5. http://www.rediff.com/news/2007/jun/23prezpoll3.htm

5.8 One Man's Bible

1. A.P.J. Abdul Kalam, *Turning Points*, HarperCollins India, 2012, Noida, India, pp. 150–51.
2. http://www.andhranews.net/India/2007/July/23-President-Kalam-farewell-9039.asp
3. A.P.J. Abdul Kalam @ http://www.abdulkalam.nic.in/abdulkalam/sllatest1.jsp?id=1071
4. Gao Xingjian, *One Man's Bible*, Harper, 2002.
5. http://www.tribuneindia.com/2007/20070724/edit.htm#5

PART SIX: EMANCIPATION

6.1 Where Eagles Soar

1. http://aviationweek.typepad.com/space/2007/03/human_space_exp.html
2. http://www.abdulkalam.com/kalam/theme/jsp/guest/content-display-more.jsp
3. Ibid.
4. https://www.cmu.edu/news/archive/2007/October/oct26_kalam.shtml
5. http://www.abdulkalam.com/kalam/theme/jsp/guest/content-display-more.jsp

6. http://news.rice.edu/2007/10/19/kalam-lecture-delivers-bold-vision-for-space-science-technology/
7. B.S. Prakash @ http://www.rediff.com/news/2007/nov/01bsp.htm
8. http://www.nriinternet.com/NRI_Awards/UK/A_Z/K/King_Charles_Award/APJ_Abdul_Kalam.htm

6.2 Into the Uncharted

1. http://www.abdulkalam.com/kalam/theme/jsp/guest/content-display.jsp
2. Ibid.
3. Ibid.
4. http://knowledge.wharton.upenn.edu/article/former-president-apj-abdul-kalam-a-leader-should-know-how-to-manage-failure/
5. http://philanthropynewsdigest.org/news/india-studies-endowment-fund-established-at-university-of-kentucky
6. http://www.abdulkalam.com/kalam/theme/jsp/guest/content-display.jsp

6.3 Transformers

1. Sam Pitroda, '*Exploding Freedom: Roots in Technology*', Allied Publishers Ltd, 1993, p. x.
2. Nelson Mandela, *Long Walk to Freedom*, Macdonald Purnell, 1995.
3. http://www.oneindia.com/india/apj-abdul-kalam-endorsed-nuclear-deal-manmohan-singh-1821805.html
4. http://in.rbth.com/articles/2011/11/10/former_indian_president_kalam_bats_for_kudankulam_protestors_defiant_13224
5. http://www.newindianexpress.com/cities/chennai/Missile-Mans-Brave-K-ampaign-for-Plant/2015/07/29/article2945886.ece
6. http://www.malaysia-today.net/malaysian-leaders-must-learn-from-abdul-kalam/
7. http://www.abdulkalam.com/kalam/theme/jsp/guest/content-display.jsp
8. http://panos.org.uk/features/what-the-president-told-bill-gates/

6.4 Prove All Things

1. The Bible, I Thessalonians 5: 20–21.
2. http://southasiainstitute.harvard.edu/2015/07/the-passing-of-an-idealist/#more-19443

3. http://www.abdulkalam.com/kalam/theme/jsp/guest/content-display.jsp
4. Ibid.

6.5 Liveable Planet Earth

1. http://www.abdulkalam.com/kalam/theme/jsp/guest/content-display.jsp
2. Ibid.
3. conclave.intoday.in/article/india-today-conclave-2013-reinventing-democracy-the-youth-experiment-apj-abdul-kalam/3579/39.html
4. A.P.J. Abdul Kalam with Srijan Pal Singh, *Target 3 Billion*, Penguin Books, New Delhi, 2011.
5. http://www.dnaindia.com/india/report-jairam-ramesh-criticises-apj-abdul-kalams-pura-launches-his-own-version-1654306
6. *Patanjali Yoga Sutra*, Samadhi pada, Verse 51.
7. http://www.abdulkalam.com/kalam/theme/jsp/guest/content-display.jsp
8. http://www.abdulkalam.com/kalam/theme/jsp/guest/content-display.jsp

6.6 Set the Ball Rolling

1. BAPS, *Satsang: Moments with Pramukh Swami Maharaj*, Swaminarayan Aksharpith, Ahmedabad, 1995.

6.7 Made for Life

1. http://www.abdulkalam.com/kalam/theme/jsp/guest/content-display-more.jsp
2. Ibid.
3. http://www.solitaryroad.com/pra305.html. This was a verse by Confucius that Dr Kalam often invoked during his days as president.
4. https://www.facebook.com/SrijanPalSingh/posts/1036964249687030

6.8 Aalam-e-Barzakh

1. http://www.narendramodi.in/pm-condoles-the-passing-away-of-former-president-of-india-dr-apj-abdul-kalam-210286
2. Surat'Āli `Imrān; Verse 3: 185; Translation: Muhammad Asad.
3. http://www.livingislam.org/d/khyl_e.html#fnref:22

4. The Bible, 1 Kings 9:4.
5. The Bible, 1 Chronicles 29:17.
6. The Bible, Psalm 78:70–72.
7. A.P.J. Abdul Kalam and Acharya Mahapragya, *The Family and Nation*, HarperCollins Publishers, Noida, India, 2012.

Acknowledgements

This book is my tribute to Dr A.P.J. Abdul Kalam, in whose benevolent shadow I spent more than thirty-three years of my life. I felt duty-bound to present for posterity what I know of the great man who dreamed of a developed India and a more liveable planet and tirelessly campaigned for these ideas amongst the youth till literally his last moment.

Dr Kalam bestowed upon me the highest honour of my life by visiting my mother's home at Meerut to tell her that '(her) son is a good guy'. I place this book at the feet of my mother Smt. Upasana Tiwari and A.P.J.M. Maracayer, Dr Kalam's elder brother, in anticipation that the soul body of Dr Kalam will be pleased with my effort.

This book would not have been possible without the painstaking work of V. Ponraj, my former colleague at DRDO and the constant companion of Dr Kalam since 2002. Ponraj single-handedly archived all his lectures and I do not have enough words to describe his devotion for Dr Kalam and his contribution in his service.

At DRDL, I worked under four of Dr Kalam's friends and contemporaries: Lt General Dr V.J. Sundaram, K. Rama Rao, Dr R.N. Agarwal and the late Maj. Gen. R. Swaminathan. These senior scientists and military officers have been most kind and caring to me. My association with Dr Kalam would not have been possible without their holding my hand during my baby steps in the missile programme. Dr Kalam spotted me because I was sitting on their towering shoulders.

I gratefully recall the time I spent with Dr Y.S. Rajan, Dr A.

Sivathanu Pillai, Dr Kota Harinaryana, D. Narayanamoorthi and Prof. N. Balakrishnan. I also gratefully recall their support. They came into my life through Dr Kalam and blessed me with their kindness and immense knowledge. I offer my sincere thanks to these great souls.

Dr B. Soma Raju and Dr Kalam formed the two poles of my professional world. I resigned my secure government job in 1996 to develop spin-offs of defence technology in a civilian set-up. It was against conventional wisdom, but Dr Soma Raju never let me down. And when we received Dr Kalam's mortal remains at his residence together, it was a conviction truthfully exercised and a trust faithfully lived. Thank you, Dr B. Soma Raju.

Dr Kalam introduced me to Sadhu Brahmaviharidas Swamiji to take his guidance in writing the book *Transcendence*. This association turned out to be my portal to the higher unseen world. I have been transformed as a human being, and my heart has been filled with peace that was never there before. In the Indian tradition we don't thank gurus, we bow before them. So I bow in reverence before Sadhu Brahmaviharidas Swamiji.

P.T. Rajasekharan had been working with Dr Kalam on the *Nobel Prize All* project, and it had been a wonderful association. He helped me with his immense knowledge and experience in raising my work to an international level. Thank you, Mr Rajasekharan, for holding my hand.

During the writing of *Transcendence* I worked with Mr Carl Harte and experienced a powerful spiritual connection. This connection worked wonderfully in the writing of this book. We have not met in person yet, but our collaboration is testimony to the power of the unseen and the physical impact of the spiritual force. But for his editorial efforts, the book would not have seen the light of day as fast as it has.

I thank H. Sheridon, R.K. Prasad and Dhan Shyam Sharma in Delhi and S.G. Prasad and S.A. Taimiya in Hyderabad, for always being with me whenever I needed them, without my asking.

I thank P.M. Sukumar, former CEO, HarperCollins Publishers, who motivated me to write this book, V.K. Karthika, publisher and chief editor, HarperCollins, and Shantanu Ray Chaudhuri, editor of this book, who made the book possible.

Finally, I thank my wife Anjana, sons Aseem and Amol and their families for their support. Each one of us has been blessed by Dr Kalam, including my grandson Agastya, whom Dr Kalam taught 'A' for Apple and 'O' for Orange, showing him the fruits at Raj Bhavan in Hyderabad on 11 January 2014.

And dear reader, I don't know you yet, but whenever this book reaches you, please accept my most sincere thanks for believing in the goodness of Dr Kalam and sparing time to read his story.

Shakespeare was only partly right when he wrote 'Life's but a walking shadow …' May I rewrite his lines thus:

> Life's but a walking shadow, there comes a player,
> That inspires and performs his hour upon the stage,
> And then is remembered forever. It is a tale
> Told time and again, full of conviction and faith,
> Signifying human existence on this planet.

Dr A.P.J. Abdul Kalam was one such player … and I sat in the audience. Jai Ho!

5 September 2015 — Arun Tiwari
Hyderabad

Index